JOHN MILTON'S
PARADISE LOST

In Plain
English

JOHN MILTON'S
PARADISE LOST

In Plain
English

A Simple, Line by Line Paraphrase
of the Complicated Masterpiece

Joseph Lanzara

New Arts Library

ISBN 978-0-9639621-5-7
Library of Congress Control Number: 2008933258

Published by New Arts Library
P.O. Box 319, Belleville, New Jersey 07109

Student discounts available at www.paradiselost.org

Printed in the United States of America

Contents

IN PLAIN ENGLISH

Book I

PARADISE LOST

1.   Of Mans First Disobedience, and the Fruit
Of that Forbidden Tree, whose mortal tast
Brought Death into the World, and all our woe,
With loss of Eden, till one greater Man
Restore us, and regain the blissful Seat,

6. Sing Heav'nly Muse, that on the secret top
Of Oreb, or of Sinai, didst inspire
That Shepherd, who first taught the chosen Seed,
In the Beginning how the Heav'ns and Earth
Rose out of Chaos: Or if Sion Hill
Delight thee more, and Siloa's Brook that flow'd

12. Fast by the Oracle of God; I thence
Invoke thy aid to my adventrous Song,
That with no middle flight intends to soar
Above th' Aonian Mount, while it pursues
Things unattempted yet in Prose or Rhime.

17. And chiefly Thou O Spirit, that dost prefer
Before all Temples th' upright heart and pure,

19. Instruct me, for Thou know'st; Thou from the first
Wast present, and with mighty wings outspread
Dove-like satst brooding on the vast Abyss
And mad'st it pregnant: What in me is dark

23. Illumin, what is low raise and support;
That to the highth of this great Argument
I may assert Eternal Providence,
And justifie the wayes of God to men.

27.   Say first, for Heav'n hides nothing from thy view
Nor the deep Tract of Hell, say first what cause
Mov'd our Grand Parents in that happy State,
Favour'd of Heav'n so highly, to fall off
From thir Creator, and transgress his Will
For one restraint, Lords of the World besides?

33. Who first seduc'd them to that foul revolt?
Th' infernal Serpent; he it was, whose guile
Stird up with Envy and Revenge, deceiv'd
The Mother of Mankind, what time his Pride *MOTIF*

37. Had cast him out from Heav'n, with all his Host
Of Rebel Angels, by whose aid aspiring
To set himself in Glory above his Peers,
He trusted to have equal'd the most High,
If he oppos'd; and with ambitious aim
Against the Throne and Monarchy of God

Chapter 1

IN PLAIN ENGLISH

1.   Tell me about man's first sin, when he tasted the forbidden fruit and caused all our troubles, until Jesus came and saved us.

6. Inspire me with this knowledge. You are the heavenly spirit who inspired Moses in his teachings.

12. I'm asking for your help because I want to write a great work different from any that has ever been written before.

17. I want you to teach me, Holy Spirit, because you value goodness more than fancy churches.

19. You know everything. You were there at the beginning. You sat like a dove with your wings spread over the dark emptiness and made it come to life.

23. Enlighten me where I am ignorant and strengthen my abilities so that I can correctly explain God's great purpose to men.

27.   You know everything about Heaven and Hell, so tell me, what was it that made Adam and Eve go against God's orders? They seemed so happy. He had given them the whole world, except for one little thing.

33. Who made them do this awful thing? It was the snake, wasn't it. His envy and thirst for revenge made him go trick Eve the way he did.

37. His pride had gotten him thrown out of Heaven with all his followers. They supported him in his ambition to glorify himself—even to the point of waging war against God.

Rais'd impious War in Heav'n and Battel proud
44. With vain attempt. Him the Almighty Power
Hurld headlong flaming from th' Ethereal Skie
With hideous ruine and combustion down
To bottomless perdition, there to dwell
In Adamantine Chains and penal Fire,
Who durst defie th' Omnipotent to Arms.
50. Nine times the Space that measures Day and Night
To mortal men, he with his horrid crew
Lay vanquisht, rowling in the fiery Gulfe
Confounded though immortal: But his doom
54. Reserv'd him to more wrath; for now the thought
Both of lost happiness and lasting pain
56. Torments him; round he throws his baleful eyes
That witness'd huge affliction and dismay
Mixt with obdurate pride and stedfast hate:
59. At once as far as Angels kenn he views
60. The dismal Situation waste and wilde,
A Dungeon horrible, on all sides round
As one great Furnace flam'd, yet from those flames
No light, but rather darkness visible
Serv'd onely to discover sights of woe,
Regions of sorrow, doleful shades, where peace
And rest can never dwell, hope never comes
That comes to all; but torture without end
Still urges, and a fiery Deluge, fed
With ever-burning Sulphur unconsum'd:
70. Such place Eternal Justice had prepar'd
For those rebellious, here thir Prison ordain'd
In utter darkness, and thir portion set
73. As far remov'd from God and light of Heav'n
As from the Center thrice to th' utmost Pole.
O how unlike the place from whence they fell!
76. There the companions of his fall, o'rewhelm'd
With Floods and Whirlwinds of tempestuous fire,
He soon discerns, and weltring by his side
One next himself in power, and next in crime
80. Long after known in Palestine, and nam'd
81. Beelzebub. To whom th' Arch-Enemy,
And thence in Heav'n call'd Satan, with bold words
Breaking the horrid silence thus began.
84.   If thou beest he; But O how fall'n! how chang'd
From him, who in the happy Realms of Light
Cloth'd with transcendent brightness didst out-shine
87. Myriads though bright: If he Whom mutual league,
United thoughts and counsels, equal hope
And hazard in the Glorious Enterprize,
Joynd with me once, now misery hath joynd
In equal ruin: into what Pit thou seest

44. But he was doomed to fail. After a terrible war, God threw him into Hell for daring to fight him.

50. For nine days he and his evil followers were lying helpless in the fires of Hell.

54. But soon he grew angry, thinking about all the lost pleasures and the unending pain.
56. He looked around and saw a lot of suffering. But he only felt stubborn pride and hatefulness.

59. As far as he could see there were flames, but they burned dark instead of bright, and they only revealed sorrow and hopelessness.
60. These fires would never go out and the torture would never end.

70. This is the place Justice made for those who rebel against God.

73. It was as far from Heaven and Heaven's light and as different from Heaven as it could be.

76. This is where he saw all his defeated followers. And there, wallowing in the flames right next to him, was his top assistant.

80. Later we would know him as Beelzebub.
81. His leader, who they called Satan, finally spoke:

84.   "*Is this really you? If you are who I think you are, how you've changed! Your brightness that outshined everyone is gone.*
87. *If you're the one who joined me in planning and undertaking our grand mission—it looks like now we are joined again, but in misery.*

92. From what highth fall'n, so much the stronger prov'd
    He with his Thunder: and till then who knew
94. The force of those dire Arms? yet not for those,
    Nor what the Potent Victor in his rage
    Can else inflict, do I repent or change,
97. Though chang'd in outward lustre; that fixt mind
    And high disdain, from sence of injur'd merit,
    That with the mightiest rais'd me to contend,
100. And to the fierce contention brought along
    Innumerable force of Spirits arm'd
    That durst dislike his reign, and me preferring,
    His utmost power with adverse power oppos'd
    In dubious Battel on the Plains of Heav'n,
105. And shook his throne. What though the field be lost?
    All is not lost; the unconquerable Will,
    And study of revenge, immortal hate,
    And courage never to submit or yield:
109. And what is else not to be overcome?
    That Glory never shall his wrath or might
111. Extort from me. To bow and sue for grace
    With suppliant knee, and deifie his power,
    Who from the terrour of this Arm so late
    Doubted his Empire, that were low indeed,
115. That were an ignominy and shame beneath
    This downfall; since by Fate the strength of Gods
117. And this Empyreal substance cannot fail,
    Since through experience of this great event
    In Arms not worse, in foresight much advanc't,
120. We may with more successful hope resolve
    To wage by force or guile eternal Warr
    Irreconcileable, to our grand Foe,
    Who now triumphs, and in th' excess of joy
    Sole reigning holds the Tyranny of Heav'n.
125. So spake th' Apostate Angel, though in pain,
    Vaunting aloud, but rackt with deep despare:
127. And him thus answer'd soon his bold Compeer.
    O Prince, O Chief of many Throned Powers,
    That led th' imbattelld Seraphim to Warr
    Under thy conduct, and in dreadful deeds
    Fearless, endanger'd Heav'ns perpetual King;
132. And put to proof his high Supremacy,
    Whether upheld by strength, or Chance, or Fate,
134. Too well I see and rue the dire event,
    That with sad overthrow and foul defeat
    Hath lost us Heav'n, and all this mighty Host
    In horrible destruction laid thus low,
138. As far as Gods and Heav'nly Essences
    Can perish: for the mind and spirit remains
    Invincible, and vigour soon returns,

92. *Look at how far we fell! It turns out he was much stronger than us after all, but how could we know that?*

94. *But I don't care what he did to us, or may still do, I'm not sorry. And I'm not going to change.*

97. *My appearance may have changed, but the indignity I suffered that caused me to fight him hasn't changed.*

100. *And what made the multitudes agree with me and join me in battling him and shaking up his kingdom—that hasn't changed.*

105. *So what if we lost some ground? He'll never be able to take away my free will, my revenge, my hate, or my courage never to give up.*

109. *And if I still have all that, what did he win?*

111. *Am I supposed to kneel and beg for mercy from him who I just gave some serious worry about the safety of his empire?*

115. *That would be worse shame than the defeat we just had.*

117. *We can't die, and we can't be physically hurt, but we have learned a lot from this experience.*

120. *Whether we do it by outright battle or some more devious way, we can fight our enemy forever—that tyrant in Heaven who sits there now, gloating over his victory."*

125. Satan said these words forcefully though he was in pain and despair.

127. Beelzebub responded, "*Oh Prince, you bravely led the rebelling angels against Heaven's king.*

132. *But he defeated us, whether by his greater strength or just good luck, I don't know.*

134. *Now, too late, I see only too well the sad outcome of our plan— the loss of Heaven, and all our comrades left in such sad shape.*

138. *But we are like gods and can't die. Our minds and spirits are indestructible, and soon our strength will return, although our glory and joy are gone forever.*

Though all our Glory extinct, and happy state
Here swallow'd up in endless misery.

143. But what if he our Conquerour, (whom I now
Of force believe Almighty, since no less
Then such could hav orepow'rd such force as ours)

146. Have left us this our spirit and strength intire
Strongly to suffer and support our pains,
That we may so suffice his vengeful ire,

149. Or do him mightier service as his thralls
By right of Warr, what e're his business be
Here in the heart of Hell to work in Fire,
Or do his Errands in the gloomy Deep;

153. What can it then avail though yet we feel
Strength undiminisht, or eternal being
To undergo eternal punishment?

156. Whereto with speedy words th' Arch-fiend reply'd.
Fall'n Cherube, to be weak is miserable
Doing or Suffering: but of this be sure,
To do ought good never will be our task,
But ever to do ill our sole delight,
As being the contrary to his high will

162. Whom we resist. If then his Providence
Out of our evil seek to bring forth good,
Our labour must be to pervert that end,
And out of good still to find means of evil;

166. Which oft times may succeed, so as perhaps
Shall grieve him, if I fail not, and disturb
His inmost counsels from thir destind aim.

169. But see the angry Victor hath recall'd
His Ministers of vengeance and pursuit
Back to the Gates of Heav'n: The Sulphurous Hail
Shot after us in storm, oreblown hath laid
The fiery Surge, that from the Precipice
Of Heav'n receiv'd us falling, and the Thunder,
Wing'd with red Lightning and impetuous rage,
Perhaps hath spent his shafts, and ceases now
To bellow through the vast and boundless Deep.

178. Let us not slip th' occasion, whether scorn,
Or satiate fury yield it from our Foe.

180. Seest thou yon dreary Plain, forlorn and wilde,
The seat of desolation, voyd of light,
Save what the glimmering of these livid flames

183. Casts pale and dreadful? Thither let us tend
From off the tossing of these fiery waves,
There rest, if any rest can harbour there,

186. And reassembling our afflicted Powers,
Consult how we may henceforth most offend
Our Enemy, our own loss how repair,
How overcome this dire Calamity,

143. *Now I think our Conqueror must really be almighty. How else could he defeat an army like ours?*

146. *But what if he left us alive just to make us suffer?*

149. *Or maybe he wants to make us his slaves to do whatever strange things he thinks up for us to do in this dark pit.*

153. *What good is it if we remain alive and healthy forever if it's only so we can suffer forever?"*

156.   Satan answered quickly, *"I know it stinks to be under his power, but I'll tell you one thing—we will never do good deeds again. We'll get all our pleasure from doing evil, because it's the opposite of what he wants.*

162. *And if he tries to turn our evil actions into something good, we'll find another way to turn them into evil again.*

166. *And sometimes we'll succeed, and disrupt his plans and cause him a lot of grief.*

169. *But look around—the enemy forces have gone back to Heaven, and the storm that surrounded us is calm now.*

178. *Maybe his anger has been satisfied, or maybe he's turning his back on us in contempt—either way, let's take advantage of the opportunity.*

180. *See that dark barren plain over there?*

183. *Let's get out of these flames and go rest there—if we can get any rest in this miserable place.*

186. *Let's gather everybody there and decide how we can recover from this disaster and make more trouble for the enemy."*

What reinforcement we may gain from Hope,
If not what resolution from despare.

192.   Thus Satan talking to his neerest Mate
With Head up-lift above the wave, and Eyes

194.   That sparkling blaz'd, his other Parts besides
Prone on the Flood, extended long and large
Lay floating many a rood, in bulk as huge
As whom the Fables name of monstrous size,
Titanian, or Earth-born, that warr'd on Jove,
Briareos or Typhon, whom the Den
By ancient Tarsus held, or that Sea-beast
Leviathan, which God of all his works
Created hugest that swim th' Ocean stream:
Him haply slumbring on the Norway foam
The Pilot of some small night-founder'd Skiff,
Deeming some Island, oft, as Sea-men tell,
With fixed Anchor in his skaly rind
Moors by his side under the Lee, while Night
Invests the Sea, and wished Morn delayes:
So stretcht out huge in length the Arch-fiend lay

210.   Chain'd on the burning Lake, nor ever thence
Had ris'n or heav'd his head, but that the will
And high permission of all-ruling Heaven
Left him at large to his own dark designs,

214.   That with reiterated crimes he might
Heap on himself damnation, while he sought
Evil to others, and enrag'd might see

217.   How all his malice serv'd but to bring forth
Infinite goodness, grace and mercy shewn
On Man by him seduc't, but on himself
Treble confusion, wrath and vengeance pour'd.

221.   Forthwith upright he rears from off the Pool
His mighty Stature; on each hand the flames
Driv'n backward slope thir pointing spires, and rowld
In billows, leave i'th' midst a horrid Vale.

225.   Then with expanded wings he stears his flight
Aloft, incumbent on the dusky Air
That felt unusual weight, till on dry Land
He lights, if it were Land that ever burn'd
With solid, as the Lake with liquid fire;

230.   And such appear'd in hue, as when the force
Of subterranean wind transports a Hill
Torn from Pelorus, or the shatter'd side
Of thundring Ætna, whose combustible
And fewel'd entrals thence conceiving Fire,
Sublim'd with Mineral fury, aid the Winds,
And leave a singed bottom all involv'd

237.   With stench and smoak: Such resting found the sole

238.   Of unblest feet. Him followed his next Mate,

192.   As Satan spoke to his companion only his head and blazing eyes were up above the flames.

194.   The rest of his body was stretched out on the lake of fire like a big whale—the kind that sailors, they say, sometimes mistake for an island and spend the night anchored by its side.

210.   And he might never have got out of that lake, or even lifted his head, if God didn't decide to allow it.

214.   God left him free to commit his many crimes and pile more damnation on himself while he tried to harm others.

217.   But he would find that the result would be God's goodness, grace, and mercy given to man, while he suffered God's punishment over and over.

221.   So Satan got up, and the flames rolled back leaving a big open space where he had been lying.

225.   Then he spread his wings and flew up into the polluted air and landed on dry land—if you could call it land, since it was as hot as fire.

230.   The smoke and the stink and the color of the hill was like an erupted volcano.

237.   This land was meant for people who were not blessed.

238.   Beelzebub followed Satan. They were both proud to have gotten out of the lake by their own power, or so they believed.

Both glorying to have scap't the Stygian flood
As Gods, and by thir own recover'd strength,
Not by the sufferance of supernal Power.

242.   Is this the Region, this the Soil, the Clime,
Said then the lost Arch-Angel, this the seat
That we must change for Heav'n, this mournful gloom

245. For that celestial light? Be it so, since he
Who now is Sovran can dispose and bid
What shall be right: fardest from him is best

248. Whom reason hath equald, force hath made supream

249. Above his equals. Farewel happy Fields
Where Joy for ever dwells: Hail horrours, hail
Infernal world, and thou profoundest Hell

252. Receive thy new Possessor: One who brings
A mind not to be chang'd by Place or Time.

254. The mind is its own place, and in it self
Can make a Heav'n of Hell, a Hell of Heav'n.

256. What matter where, if I be still the same,

257. And what I should be, all but less then he

258. Whom Thunder hath made greater? Here at least
We shall be free; th' Almighty hath not built

260. Here for his envy, will not drive us hence:

261. Here we may reign secure, and in my choyce
To reign is worth ambition though in Hell:

263. Better to reign in Hell, then serve in Heav'n.

264. But wherefore let we then our faithful friends,
Th' associates and copartners of our loss
Lye thus astonisht on th' oblivious Pool,

267. And call them not to share with us their part
In this unhappy Mansion, or once more
With rallied Arms to try what may be yet
Regaind in Heav'n, or what more lost in Hell?

271.   So Satan spake, and him Beelzebub
Thus answer'd. Leader of those Armies bright,
Which but th' Onmipotent none could have foyld,

274. If once they hear that voyce, thir liveliest pledge
Of hope in fears and dangers, heard so oft
In worst extreams, and on the perilous edge
Of battel when it rag'd, in all assaults
Thir surest signal, they will soon resume
New courage and revive, though now they lye

280. Groveling and prostrate on yon Lake of Fire,
As we erewhile, astounded and amaz'd,
No wonder, fall'n such a pernicious highth.

283.   He scarce had ceas't when the superiour Fiend

284. Was moving toward the shoar; his ponderous shield
Ethereal temper, massy, large and round,
Behind him cast; the broad circumference
Hung on his shoulders like the Moon, whose Orb

242.   *"So this is what we get in exchange for Heaven,"* said
Satan, *"this gloom in place of Heaven's light?*

245.   *Fine! Since he gets to keep his dictatorship up there, the farther
we are from him the better.*

248.   *We had equal rights, but the power of his force was stronger,
so he gets to be king.*

249.   *So goodbye to happy Heaven and hello horrors of Hell!*

252.   *Welcome your new master—one who brings a mind that does
not change by place or time.*

254.   *The attitude you have can make Heaven feel like Hell or Hell
feel like Heaven.*

256.   *What does it matter where I am if I'm still the same?*

257.   *I'm as great as he is in every way except for his power of
force.*

258.   *Here at least we'll be free. God didn't build this place for any
other use.*

260.   *He won't drive us out of here. Here we can safely rule.*

261.   *And for me, to be a ruler is a worthwhile ambition, even if
you're in Hell.*

263.   *I'd rather be a king in Hell than a slave in Heaven.*

264.   *But let's not leave our friends lying in that lake of fire.*

267.   *We may as well let them join us in our misery and regroup to
see what we can salvage from our fall from Heaven, or what
more bad news waits for us in Hell."*

271.   Beelzebub answered, *"Sir, nothing less than the Almighty
could have beaten this army.*

274.   *If they hear your voice, the voice that reassured them in the
worst moments of battle, it will revive their strength and
courage.*

280.   *It's no wonder they're all still lying around groveling and con-
fused, like we were after falling so far."*

283.   He wasn't even finished speaking when Satan was already
going toward the shore.

284.   Hanging on his shoulders was a big round shield that looked like
the moon.

Through Optic Glass the Tuscan Artist views
At Ev'ning from the top of Fesole,
Or in Valdarno, to descry new Lands,
Rivers or Mountains in her spotty Globe.

292. His Spear, to equal which the tallest Pine
Hewn on Norwegian hills, to be the Mast
Of some great Ammiral, were but a wand,
He walkt with to support uneasie steps

296. Over the burning Marle, not like those steps

297. On Heavens Azure, and the torrid Clime
Smote on him sore besides, vaulted with Fire;

299. Nathless he so endur'd, till on the Beach

300. Of that inflamed Sea, he stood and call'd

301. His Legions, Angel Forms, who lay intrans't
Thick as Autumnal Leaves that strow the Brooks
In Vallombrosa, where th' Etrurian shades
High overarch't imbowr; or scatterd sedge
Afloat, when with fierce Winds Orion arm'd
Hath vext the Red-Sea Coast, whose waves orethrew
Busiris and his Memphian Chivalry,
While with perfidious hatred they pursu'd
The Sojourners of Goshen, who beheld
From the safe shore thir floating Carkases

311. And broken Chariot Wheels, so thick bestrown
Abject and lost lay these, covering the Flood,
Under amazement of thir hideous change.

314. He call'd so loud, that all the hollow Deep

315. Of Hell resounded. Princes, Potentates,
Warriers, the Flowr of Heav'n, once yours, now lost,
If such astonishment as this can sieze

318. Eternal spirits; or have ye chos'n this place
After the toyl of Battel to repose
Your wearied vertue, for the ease you find
To slumber here, as in the Vales of Heav'n?

322. Or in this abject posture have ye sworn

323. To adore the Conquerour? who now beholds
Cherube and Seraph rowling in the Flood
With scatter'd Arms and Ensigns, till anon
His swift pursuers from Heav'n Gates discern
Th' advantage, and descending tread us down
Thus drooping, or with linked Thunderbolts
Transfix us to the bottom of this Gulfe

330. Awake, arise, or be for ever fall'n.

331.   They heard, and were abasht, and up they sprung
Upon the wing, as when men wont to watch
On duty, sleeping found by whom they dread,
Rouse and bestir themselves ere well awake.

335. Nor did they not perceave the evil plight
In which they were, or the fierce pains not feel;

292. He used his long spear that was bigger than the mast of a big ship to balance himself as he walked on the hot ground.

296. It was so different from Heaven's soft ground.
297. The hot air burned him as he walked.

299. He stood on the beach facing the burning sea.
300. He called to his legions.
301. The fallen angels were spread around like autumn leaves on a shady brook, or like seaweed floating near the corpses and broken chariot wheels of Pharaoh's army when they were chasing the Jews across the parted sea and it closed over them and drowned them.

311. The angels were just laying there in state of shock. Their bodies covered the whole lake.

314. Satan's loud voice echoed all around.
315. *"Princes and warriors, you were once the rulers of Heaven— not the kind one expects to find in this confused state.*

318. *Or is this the place you choose to rest after battle. Maybe you find it as restful here as in the fields of Heaven.*

322. *Or maybe you just want to kneel and grovel before your conqueror.*
323. *And then, seeing you helpless and unarmed, he can take advantage of the situation and send his forces after us again to trample us down some more, or permanently tie us to the bottom of Hell with a chain of thunderbolts.*

330. *Wake up and pull yourselves together!"*
331.   His words shamed them. They were like watchmen caught sleeping at their post.
335. They quickly rose up and flew out of the lake, although they were in pain. They spread out like the swarm of locusts that plagued Egypt.

NINE PLAGUES THAT
DESTROYED

Yet to thir Generals Voyce they soon obeyd
Innumerable. As when the potent Rod
Of Amrams Son in Egypts evill day
Wav'd round the Coast, up call'd a pitchy cloud
Of Locusts, warping on the Eastern Wind,
That ore the Realm of impious Pharaoh hung
Like Night, and darken'd all the Land of Nile:
344. So numberless were those bad angels seen
Hovering on wing under the Cope of Hell
'Twixt upper, nether, and surrounding Fires;
347. Till, as a signal giv'n, th' uplifted Spear
Of thir great Sultan waving to direct
Thir course, in even ballance down they light
350. On the firm brimstone, and fill all the Plain;
351. A multitude, like which the populous North
Pour'd never from her frozen loyns, to pass
Rhene or the Danaw, when her barbarous Sons
Came like a Deluge on the South, and spread
Beneath Gibralter to the Lybian sands.
356. Forthwith from every Squadron and each Band
The Heads and Leaders thither hast where stood
358. Thir great Commander; Godlike shapes and forms
Excelling human, Princely Dignities,
And Powers that earst in Heaven sat on Thrones;
361. Though of thir Names in heav'nly Records now
Be no memorial blotted out and ras'd
By thir Rebellion, from the Books of Life.
364. Nor had they yet among the Sons of Eve
Got them new Names, till wandring ore the Earth,
Through Gods high sufferance for the tryal of man,
367. By falsities and lyes the greatest part
Of Mankind they corrupted to forsake
God thir Creator, and th' invisible
Glory of him that made them, to transform
Oft to the Image of a Brute, adorn'd
With gay Religions full of Pomp and Gold,
And Devils to adore for Deities:
Then were they known to men by various Names,
And various Idols through the Heathen World.
376. Say, Muse, thir Names then known, who first, who last,
Rous'd from the slumber, on that fiery Couch,
378. At thir great Emperors call, as next in worth
Came singly where he stood on the bare strand,
While the promiscuous croud stood yet aloof?
381. The chief were those who from the Pit of Hell
Roaming to seek thir prey on earth, durst fix
383. Thir Seats long after next the Seat of God,
Thir Altars by his Altar, Gods ador'd
Among the Nations round, and durst abide

344. Great masses of fallen angels were flying around under Hell's ceiling.

347. Satan raised his spear and directed them to land.

350. They landed and filled the whole plain.
351. They looked like mobs of barbarians about to invade Rome.

356. The leaders from each band came forward to where Satan was.
358. They were superhuman beings, former kings of Heaven.

361. But now all record of their ever having existed in Heaven has been erased because of their rebellion.

364. Later, God would allow them to come to Earth to test mankind. Then they would get new names.

367. They would corrupt most of mankind with their lies. Men would come to worship idols and devils.

376. Heavenly spirit, what were the names of those devils that came out of the lake of fire?
378. One by one they came forward from the mixed crowd to answer Satan's call.

381. Chief among them were those who would later wander through all the nations of Earth and become adored as gods.
383. They would defy God and place their cursed shrines in his holy churches.

Jehovah thundring out of Sion, thron'd
Between the Cherubim; yea, often plac'd
Within his Sanctuary it self thir Shrines,
Abominations; and with cursed things
His holy Rites, and solemn Feasts profan'd,
And with thir darkness durst affront his light.

392. First Moloch, horrid King besmear'd with blood
Of human sacrifice, and parents tears,
Though for the noyse of Drums and Timbrels loud
Thir childrens cries unheard, that past through fire
To his grim Idol. Him the Ammonite

397. Worshipt in Rabba and her watry Plain,
In Argob and in Basan, to the stream
Of utmost Arnon. Nor content with such
Audacious neighbourhood, the wisest heart
Of Solomon he led by fraud to build
His Temple right against the Temple of God
On that opprobrious Hill, and made his Grove
The pleasant Vally of Hinnom, Tophet thence
And black Gehenna call'd, the Type of Hell.

406. Next Chemos, th' obscene dread of Moabs Sons,
From Aroar to Nebo, and the wild
Of Southmost Abarim; in Hesebon
And Horonaim, Seons Realm, beyond
The flowry Dale of Sibma clad with Vines,
And Eleale to th' Asphaltick Pool.

412. Peor his other Name, when he entic'd
Israel in Sittim on thir march from Nile
To do him wanton rites, which cost them woe.
Yet thence his lustful Orgies he enlarg'd
Even to that Hill of scandal, by the Grove
Of Moloch homicide, lust hard by hate;
Till good Josiah drove them thence to Hell.

419. With these came they, who from the bordring flood
Of old Euphrates to the Brook that parts
Egypt from Syrian ground, had general Names
Of Baalim and Ashtaroth, those male,

423. These Feminine. For Spirits when they please
Can either Sex assume, or both; so soft
And uncompounded is thir Essence pure,
Not ti'd or manacl'd with joynt or limb,
Nor founded on the brittle strength of bones,
Like cumbrous flesh; but in what shape they choose
Dilated or condens't, bright or obscure,
Can execute thir aerie purposes,
And works of love or enmity fulfill.

432. For those the Race of Israel oft forsook
Thir living strength, and unfrequented left
His righteous Altar, bowing lowly down

392. First came Moloch. Children would be burned alive in sacrifice to his idol.

397. He would be worshiped in Jordan and would make Solomon build a temple against God.

406. Next came Chemosh, who would be worshiped by the Moabites.

412. When the Jews escaped bondage in Egypt, they defied Moses by worshiping Chemosh, also called Peor. He lead them in sinful sex orgies. They were severely punished by God.

419. Then some came who would change their sex back and forth from male to female.

423. All spirits can change shape or sex as they choose, for whatever reason, loving or hateful.

432. These devils would lead people to worship beasts as gods and die violent deaths.

To bestial Gods; for which thir heads as low
Bow'd down in Battel, sunk before the Spear
Of despicable foes. With these in troop

438. Came Astoreth, whom the Phoenicians call'd
Astarte, Queen of Heav'n, with crescent Horns;
To whose bright Image nightly by the Moon
Sidonian Virgins paid thir Vows and Songs,
In Sion also not unsung, where stood
Her Temple on th' offensive Mountain, built
By that uxorious King, whose heart though large,
Beguil'd by fair Idolatresses, fell

446. To Idols foul. Thammuz came next behind,
Whose annual wound in Lebanon allur'd
The Syrian Damsels to lament his fate
In amorous dittyes all a Summers day,
While smooth Adonis from his native Rock
Ran purple to the Sea, suppos'd with blood

452. Of Thammuz yearly wounded: the Love-tale
Infected Sions daughters with like heat,
Whose wanton passions in the sacred Porch
Ezekiel saw, when by the Vision led
His eye survay'd the dark Idolatries

457. Of alienated Judah. Next came one
Who mourn'd in earnest, when the Captive Ark
Maim'd his brute Image, head and hands lopt off
In his own Temple, on the grunsel edge,
Where he fell flat, and sham'd his Worshipers:
Dagon his Name, Sea Monster, upward Man
And downward Fish: yet had his Temple high
Rear'd in Azotus, dreaded through the Coast
Of Palestine, in Gath and Ascalon
And Accaron and Gaza's frontier bounds.

467. Him follow'd Rimmon, whose delightful Seat
Was fair Damascus, on the fertil Banks
Of Abbana and Pharphar, lucid streams.
He also against the house of God was bold:
A Leper once he lost and gain'd a King,
Ahaz his sottish Conquerour, whom he drew
Gods Altar to disparage and displace
For one of Syrian mode, whereon to burn
His odious off'rings, and adore the Gods

476. Whom he had vanquisht. After these appear'd
A crew who under Names of old Renown,
Osiris, Isis, Orus and their Train
With monstrous shapes and sorceries abus'd
Fanatic Egypt and her Priests, to seek
Thir wandring Gods disguis'd in brutish forms

482. Rather then human. Nor did Israel scape
Th' infection when thir borrow'd Gold compos'd

438. Then came Astoreth, who was worshiped in Solomon's evil temple as the queen of Heaven.

446. Next was Adonis. Syrian women sang sad love songs about how he would bleed a river of blood every year.

452. That would make all the Jewish women become sexually aroused.

457. Then there was the sea-monster, Dagon, who was upper part man and lower part fish. When the Philistines put the Ark of the Lord in the temple of Dagon, the next morning they found the idol's head and hands cut off.

467. Rimmon would be rejected by a poor leper, but a stupid king would build an alter to him.

476. After these came the future gods of Egypt: Osiris, Isis, and their group, who took the shape of beasts.

482. Even Israel would be invaded by these devils, as when they worshiped a golden calf in place of God.

The Calf in Oreb: and the Rebel King
Doubl'd that sin in Bethel and in Dan,
Lik'ning his Maker to the Grazed Ox,
487. Jehovah, who in one Night when he pass'd
From Egypt marching, equal'd with one stroke
Both her first born and all her bleating Gods.
490. Belial came last, then whom a Spirit more lewd
Fell not from Heaven, or more gross to love
492. Vice for it self: To him no Temple stood
Or Altar smoak'd; yet who more oft then hee
In Temples and at Altars, when the Priest
Turns Atheist, as did Ely's Sons, who fill'd
With lust and violence the house of God.
497. In Courts and Palaces he also Reigns
And in luxurious Cities, where the noyse
Of riot ascends above thir loftiest Towrs,
500. And injury and outrage: And when Night
Darkens the Streets, then wander forth the Sons
Of Belial, flown with insolence and wine.
503. Witness the Streets of Sodom, and that night
In Gibeah, when the hospitable door
Expos'd a Matron to avoid worse rape.
506. These were the prime in order and in might;
The rest were long to tell, though far renown'd,
508. Th' Ionian Gods, of Javans Issue held
Gods, yet confest later then Heav'n and Earth
Thir boasted Parents; Titan Heav'ns first born
With his enormous brood, and birthright seis'd
By younger Saturn, he from mightier Jove
His own and Rhea's Son like measure found;
So Jove usurping reign'd: these first in Creet
And Ida known, thence on the Snowy top
Of cold Olympus rul'd the middle Air
Thir highest Heav'n; or on the Delphian Cliff,
Or in Dodona, and through all the bounds
519. Of Doric Land; or who with Saturn old
Fled over Adria to th' Hesperian Fields,
And ore the Celtic roam'd the utmost Isles.
522. All these and more came flocking; but with looks
Down cast and damp, yet such wherein appear'd
Obscure some glimps of joy, to have found thir chief
Not in despair, to have found themselves not lost
In loss it self; which on his count'nance cast
Like doubtful hue: but he his wonted pride
528. Soon recollecting, with high words, that bore
Semblance of worth, not substance, gently rais'd
Thir fainting courage, and dispel'd thir fears.
531. Then strait commands that at the warlike sound
Of Trumpets loud and Clarions be upreard

487. Only the faithful were spared God's anger when he killed all the firstborn children on Passover.

490. Belial came last, the lowest spirit of all. He loved sin for its own sake.

492. No temples would be built for him, but he would corrupt priests and bring sex and violence into churches.

497. He would influence kings and rich men.

500. He would send drunkards into the streets at night to cause trouble.

503. You remember how in Sodom one man offered his daughters to the drunkards so they wouldn't rape men.

506. These were the main ones, but there were many more, too many to tell.

508. There was Titan and Saturn and Zeus and all the ones that would become the Greek gods of Mt. Olympus.

519. They would spread through Italy and even Great Britain.

522. All these and more came forward. They were sad but their leader's show of confidence encouraged them.

528. Satan would restore their courage with words that sounded inspiring but had not much truth.

531. He ordered them to blow their trumpets and raise his banner.

533. His mighty Standard; that proud honour claim'd
Azazel as his right, a Cherube tall:
Who forthwith from the glittering Staff unfurld
Th' Imperial Ensign, which full high advanc't
Shon like a Meteor streaming to the Wind
538. With Gemms and Golden lustre rich imblaz'd,
Seraphic arms and Trophies: all the while
540. Sonorous mettal blowing Martial sounds:
At which the universal Host upsent
A shout that tore Hells Concave, and beyond
Frighted the Reign of Chaos and old Night.
All in a moment through the gloom were seen
545. Ten thousand Banners rise into the Air
With Orient Colours waving: with them rose
A Forest huge of Spears: and thronging Helms
Appear'd, and serried shields in thick array
Of depth immeasurable: Anon they move
550. In perfect Phalanx to the Dorian mood
Of Flutes and soft Recorders; such as rais'd
To hight of noblest temper Hero's old
Arming to Battel, and in stead of rage
Deliberate valour breath'd, firm and unmov'd
With dread of death to flight or foul retreat
Nor wanting power to mitigate and swage
With solemn touches, troubl'd thoughts, and chase
Anguish and doubt and fear and sorrow and pain
From mortal or immortal minds. Thus they
560. Breathing united force with fixed thought
Mov'd on in silence to soft Pipes that charm'd
Thir painful steps o're the burnt soyle; and now
563. Advanc't in view, they stand, a horrid Front
Of dreadful length and dazling Arms, in guise
Of Warriers old with order'd Spear and Shield,
Awaiting what command thir mighty Chief
567. Had to impose: He through the armed Files
Darts his experienc't eye, and soon traverse
The whole Battalion views, thir order due,
Thir visages and stature as of Gods,
Thir number last he summs. And now his heart
Distends with pride, and hardning in his strength
Glories: For never since created man,
Met such imbodied force, as nam'd with these
Could merit more then that small infantry
Warr'd on by Cranes: though all the Giant brood
Of Phlegra with th' Heroic Race were joyn'd
That fought at Theb's and Ilium, on each side
Mixt with auxiliar Gods; and what resounds
In Fable or Romance of Uthers Son
Begirt with British and Armoric Knights;

533. The tall Cherub, Azazel, unrolled Satan's bright emblem in the wind.

538. It was decorated with gold and jewels.

540. Trumpets sounded and the angels gave a loud shout that could be heard even in the darkness beyond Hell.

545. They raised thousands of banners and spears and helmets and shields

550. They moved forward in order, to the sound of flutes—not as heroes ready for battle, but to try to relieve their doubts and fears.

560. United, they walked across the hot ground in silence, listening to the soft music.

563. Finally they stood before their chief, and waited for him to speak. They were in a very long row. In their battle gear they looked like the ancient warriors we see in history books.

567. Satan looked them over. He was impressed. He knew that never again would such a great army as this come together—not the Trojans or King Arthur's Knights or any of the conquering warriors of mankind.

And all who since, Baptiz'd or Infidel
Jousted in Aspramont or Montalban,
Damasco, or Marocco, or Trebisond,
Or whom Biserta sent from Afric shore
When Charlemain with all his Peerage fell

587. By Fontarabbia. Thus far these beyond
Compare of mortal prowess, yet observ'd

589. Thir dread commander: he above the rest
In shape and gesture proudly eminent

591. Stood like a Towr; his form had yet not lost
All her Original brightness, nor appear'd
Less then Arch Angel ruind, and th' excess
Of Glory obscur'd: As when the Sun new ris'n
Looks through the Horizontal misty Air
Shorn of his Beams, or from behind the Moon
In dim Eclips disastrous twilight sheds
On half the Nations, and with fear of change
Perplexes Monarchs. Dark'n'd so, yet shon

600. Above them all th' Arch Angel: but his face
Deep scars of Thunder had intrencht, and care
Sat on his faded cheek, but under Browes
Of dauntless courage, and considerate Pride
Waiting revenge: cruel his eye, but cast

605. Signs of remorse and passion to behold
The fellows of his crime, the followers rather
(Far other once beheld in bliss) condemn'd
For ever now to have thir lot in pain,
Millions of Spirits for his fault amerc't
Of Heav'n, and from Eternal Splendors flung

611. For his revolt, yet faithfull how they stood,

612. Thir Glory witherd. As when Heavens Fire
Hath scath'd the Forrest Oaks, or Mountain Pines,
With singed top thir stately growth though bare

615. Stands on the blasted Heath. He now prepar'd
To speak; whereat thir doubl'd Ranks they bend
From wing to wing, and half enclose him round
With all his Peers: attention held them mute.

619. Thrice he assayd, and thrice in spight of scorn,
Tears such as Angels weep, burst forth: at last

621. Words interwove with sighs found out thir way.

622.   O Myriads of immortal Spirits, O Powers
Matchless, but with th' Almighty, and that strife
Was not inglorious, though th' event was dire,
As this place testifies, and this dire change

626. Hateful to utter: but what power of mind
Foreseeing or presaging, from the Depth
Of knowledge past or present, could have fear'd,
How such united force of Gods, how such
As stood like these, could ever know repulse?

587. Satan felt that his followers couldn't be compared to anybody else.
589. He stood there like a tower above the rest.

591. He still looked like an archangel, but he wasn't as bright anymore. It was like when the sun shines through a mist.

600. His face showed signs of stress, but there was revenge in his eyes.

605. He was sad to see all his followers—millions—doomed to suffer pain forever because of him.

611. He was touched that they were still faithful to him.
612. Their glory was faded. They were like a forest after a fire.

615. As he got ready to speak, the crowd moved closer and circled him.

619. He started to speak three times, but he was too choked up with emotion. He cried a little and was annoyed with himself for it.
621. Finally, sighing, he began.
622.   *"Oh, immortal spirits! Only the Almighty could have matched your power. Your fight was not without glory, even if the result was bad.*
626. *Who would've guessed that a force like ours could ever be defeated?*

631. For who can yet beleeve, though after loss,
     That all these puissant Legions, whose exile
     Hath emptied Heav'n, shall fail to re-ascend
     Self-rais'd, and repossess thir native seat?
     For mee be witness all the Host of Heav'n,
     If counsels different, or danger shun'd
637. By me, have lost our hopes. But he who reigns
     Monarch in Heav'n, till then as one secure
     Sat on his Throne, upheld by old repute,
     Consent or custome, and his Regal State
     Put forth at full, but still his strength conceal'd,
642. Which tempted our attempt, and wrought our fall.
643. Henceforth his might we know, and know our own
     So as not either to provoke, or dread
     New warr, provok't; our better part remains
     To work in close design, by fraud or guile
     What force effected not: that he no less
648. At length from us may find, who overcomes
     By force, hath overcome but half his foe.
650. Space may produce new Worlds; whereof so rife
     There went a fame in Heav'n that he ere long
     Intended to create, and therein plant
     A generation, whom his choice regard
     Should favour equal to the Sons of Heaven:
655. Thither, if but to pry, shall be perhaps
     Our first eruption, thither or elsewhere:
     For this Infernal Pit shall never hold
     Cælestial Spirits in Bondage, nor th' Abyss
659. Long under darkness cover. But these thoughts
660. Full Counsel must mature: Peace is despaird,
     For who can think Submission? Warr then, Warr
     Open or understood must be resolv'd.
663.   He spake: and to confirm his words, out-flew
     Millions of flaming swords, drawn from the thighs
     Of mighty Cherubim; the sudden blaze
     Far round illumin'd hell: highly they rag'd
667. Against the Highest, and fierce with grasped arms
     Clash'd on thir sounding Shields the din of war,
     Hurling defiance toward the vault of Heav'n.
670.   There stood a Hill not far whose griesly top
     Belch'd fire and rowling smoak; the rest entire
     Shon with a glossie scurff, undoubted sign
     That in his womb was hid metallic Ore,
674. The work of Sulphur. Thither wing'd with speed
     A numerous Brigad hasten'd. As when Bands
     Of Pioners with Spade and Pickax arm'd
     Forerun the Royal Camp, to trench a Field,
     Or cast a Rampart. Mammon led them on,
679. Mammon, the least erected Spirit that fell

631. *Even now I can't believe that we couldn't win back our native land if we tried.*

637. *No one questioned God's rule. He reigned a long time and always kept secret how powerful he really was.*

642. *He tricked us into attempting to fight him.*
643. *Now we know his strength compared to our own. It's best now to work against him by cunning and trickery.*

648. *Let him find out that winning by force is only half a victory.*

650. *We may find new worlds to conquer. There was a prophecy that he would create one and place creatures there that he would value as highly as the angels.*

655. *Maybe we'll go explore our possibilities there—if not there, then someplace else. This damned place will never hold us prisoners for long.*

659. *But these are things we must carefully discuss.*
660. *We'll never be at peace here. And submitting to his will is out of the question. So it's war—but we must decide exactly what kind of war."*

663.   The angels drew their swords and waved them high to show their approval of what Satan said. Hell lit up with the reflected light from the many swords.

667. Then they banged their swords against their shields to show defiance against God.

670.   Nearby was a volcano that shot forth eruptions and had a shiny hillside. This was a sign that it contained metallic ores beneath.

674. Like a band of pioneers setting up camp, a group of angels flew to the hill, led by Mammon.

679. He was one of the lowest angels. Even in Heaven he was more impressed by the gold in Heaven's pavement than by the glory of God.

From heav'n, for ev'n in heav'n his looks and thoughts
Were always downward bent, admiring more
The riches of Heav'ns pavement, trod'n Gold,
Then aught divine or holy else enjoy'd
684. In vision beatific: by him first
Men also, and by his suggestion taught,
Ransack'd the Center, and with impious hands
Rifl'd the bowels of thir mother Earth
688. For Treasures better hid. Soon had his crew
Op'nd into the Hill a spacious wound
690. And dig'd out ribs of Gold. Let none admire
That riches grow in Hell; that soyle may best
692. Deserve the precious bane. And here let those
Who boast in mortal things, and wond'ring tell
Of Babel, and the works of Memphian Kings
Learn how thir greatest Monuments of Fame,
And Strength and Art are easily out-done
697. By Spirits reprobate, and in an hour
What in an age they with incessant toyle
And hands innumerable scarce perform.
700. Nigh on the Plain in many cells prepar'd,
That underneath had veins of liquid fire
702. Sluc'd from the Lake, a second multitude
With wondrous Art found out the massie Ore,
Severing each kind, and scum'd the Bullion dross:
705. A third as soon had form'd within the ground
A various mould, and from the boyling cells
By strange conveyance fill'd each hollow nook,
708. As in an Organ from one blast of wind
To many a row of Pipes the sound-board breaths.
710. Anon out of the earth a Fabrick huge
Rose like an Exhalation, with the sound
Of Dulcet Symphonies and voices sweet,
713. Built like a Temple, where Pilasters round
Were set, and Doric pillars overlaid
With Golden Architrave; nor did there want
Cornice or Freeze, with bossy Sculptures grav'n,
The Roof was fretted Gold. Not Babilon,
718. Nor great Alcairo such magnificence
Equal'd in all thir glories, to inshrine
Belus or Serapis thir Gods, or seat
Thir Kings, when Ægypt with Assyria strove
722. In wealth and luxurie. Th' ascending pile
Stood fixt her stately highth, and strait the dores
Op'ning thir brazen foulds discover wide
725. Within, her ample spaces, o're the smooth
And level pavement: from the arched roof
Pendant by suttle Magic many a row
Of Starry Lamps and blazing Cressets fed

684. He would teach men to dig up the earth searching for treasures they'd be better off without.

688. Soon his crew had made a large excavation and were extracting gold.

690. Don't be surprised that gold is found in Hell. Where better could it belong, since it causes so much trouble?

692. And anyone who is impressed by the great things men build, like the Tower of Babel or the pyramids of Egypt, should see what angels can do—even bad ones.

697. They can do in an hour what would take many men a lifetime to accomplish.

700. On the nearby plain they made containers and channeled molten metal into them.

702. A second crew skimmed off the waste and skillfully separated the different kinds of materials.

705. A third team poured it, boiling, into various molds they had formed in the ground.

708. The process was like an organ that sends wind to many different pipes to make different sounds.

710. Soon a huge structure rose, like a beautiful symphony coming up out of the land.

713. It was built like a Greek temple, with columns all around. Above were sculptured ornaments and the roof was made of elaborate gold carvings.

718. The wonders built by Babylon or Egypt to glorify their gods and kings could not equal this magnificence.

722. When it was complete, the brass doors opened wide.

725. Inside was a wide open space. From the arched ceiling hung many rows of iron oil lamps that burned as bright as daylight.

ORGANS / INSTRUMENTS

With Naphtha and Asphaltus yeilded light
730. As from a sky. The hasty multitude
Admiring enter'd, and the work some praise
732. And some the Architect: his hand was known
In Heav'n by many a Towred structure high,
Where Scepter'd Angels held thir residence,
And sat as Princes, whom the supreme King
Exalted to such power, and gave to rule,
Each in his Hierarchie, the Orders bright.
738. Nor was his name unheard or unador'd
In ancient Greece; and in Ausonian land
Men call'd him Mulciber; and how he fell
741. From Heav'n, they fabl'd, thrown by angry Jove
Sheer o're the Chrystal Battlements: from Morn
To Noon he fell, from Noon to dewy Eve,
A Summers day; and with the setting Sun
Dropt from the Zenith like a falling Star,
746. On Lemnos th' Ægean Ile: thus they relate,
Erring; for he with this rebellious rout
748. Fell long before; nor aught avail'd him now
To have built in Heav'n high Towrs; nor did he scape
By all his Engins, but was headlong sent
With his industrious crew to build in hell.
752. Mean while the winged Haralds by command
Of Sovran power, with awful Ceremony
And Trumpets sound throughout the Host proclaim
A solemn Councel forthwith to be held
756. At Pandæmonium, the high Capital
Of Satan and his Peers: thir summons call'd
From every Band and squared Regiment
759. By place or choice the worthiest; they anon
With hunderds and with thousands trooping came
761. Attended: all access was throng'd, the Gates
And Porches wide, but chief the spacious Hall
(Though like a cover'd field, where Champions bold
Wont ride in arm'd, and at the Soldans chair
Defi'd the best of Paynim chivalry
To mortal combat or carreer with Lance)
767. Thick swarm'd, both on the ground and in the air,
Brusht with the hiss of russling wings. As Bees
In spring time, when the Sun with Taurus rides,
Pour forth thir populous youth about the Hive
In clusters; they among fresh dews and flowers
Flie to and fro, or on the smoothed Plank,
The suburb of thir Straw-built Cittadel,
New rub'd with Baum, expatiate and confer
775. Thir State affairs. So thick the aerie crowd
Swarm'd and were straitn'd; till the Signal giv'n.
Behold a wonder! they but now who seemd

730. The angels couldn't wait to go see the inside. They admired it all and praised the architect.

732. His work was well known in Heaven. He designed the homes of high ranking angels.

738. He would later be known in Greece and Italy by the name Vulcan.

741. They would tell how his angry father, Zeus, threw him out of Olympus down onto the island of Lemnos in the Aegean Sea.

746. But they were wrong. He fell long before that.

748. The high towers he built in Heaven were no help to him now.

752. The herald angels flew out and blew their trumpets to announce that a high council meeting was to be held.

756. The place was called Pandemonium, Satan's palace.

759. All the highest ranking angels came by the thousands.

761. They mobbed the entrance and everybody went inside till the whole hall was crowded, even though it was as big as the arenas where grand tournaments are held for kings.

767. The place swarmed like a beehive, with angels filling all the air as well as the ground.

775. A signal was given, and magically all the giant angels were shrunk to the size of dwarfs or elves. From being tightly packed they were now able to move around in spacious comfort, though there were just as many as before.

In bigness to surpass Earths Giant Sons
Now less then smallest Dwarfs, in narrow room
Throng numberless, like that Pigmean Race
Beyond the Indian Mount, or Faerie Elves,
Whose midnight Revels, by a Forrest side
Or Fountain some belated Peasant sees,
Or dreams he sees, while over-head the Moon
Sits Arbitress, and neerer to the Earth
Wheels her pale course, they on thir mirth and dance
Intent, with jocond Music charm his ear;
At once with joy and fear his heart rebounds.
Thus incorporeal Spirits to smallest forms
Reduc'd thir shapes immense, and were at large,
Though without number still amidst the Hall
792.   Of that infernal Court. But far within
And in thir own dimensions like themselves
The great Seraphic Lords and Cherubim
In close recess and secret conclave sat
A thousand Demy-Gods on golden seats,
797.   Frequent and full. After short silence then
And summons read, the great consult began

.

792. Deep inside the palace a thousand of the highest angels were still in their normal size. They gathered on golden seats, behind closed doors

797. After some formalities, the great consultation began.

Book II

PARADISE LOST

1. High on a Throne of Royal State, which far
    Outshon the wealth of Ormus and of Ind,
    Or where the gorgeous East with richest hand
    Showrs on her Kings Barbaric Pearl and Gold,
5. Satan exalted sat, by merit rais'd
    To that bad eminence; and from despair
7. Thus high uplifted beyond hope, aspires
8. Beyond thus high, insatiate to pursue
    Vain Warr with Heav'n, and by success untaught
10. His proud imaginations thus displaid
11. Powers and Dominions, Deities of Heav'n,
    For since no deep within her gulf can hold
    Immortal vigor, though opprest and fall'n,
14. I give not Heav'n for lost. From this descent
15. Celestial vertues rising, will appear
    More glorious and more dread then from no fall,
    And trust themselves to fear no second fate:
18. Mee though just right, and the fixt Laws of Heav'n
    Did first create your Leader, next free choice,
    With what besides, in Counsel or in Fight,
    Hath bin achievd of merit, yet this loss
22. Thus farr at least recover'd, hath much more
    Establisht in a safe unenvied Throne
24. Yielded with full consent. The happier state
    In Heav'n, which follows dignity, might draw
    Envy from each inferior; but who here
    Will envy whom the highest place exposes
    Formost to stand against the Thunderers aim
    Your bulwark, and condemns to greatest share
30. Of endless pain? where there is then no good
    For which to strive, no strife can grow up there
    From Faction; for none sure will claim in Hell
    Precedence, none, whose portion is so small
    Of present pain, that with ambitious mind
35. Will covet more. With this advantage then
    To union, and firm Faith, and firm accord,
    More then can be in Heav'n, we now return
    To claim our just inheritance of old,
39. Surer to prosper then prosperity
40. Could have assur'd us; and by what best way,
    Whether of open Warr or covert guile,
    We now debate; who can advise, may speak.

Chapter 2

IN PLAIN ENGLISH

1.   Satan sat on his throne. It was fancier than the richest kings of Persia or India had.

5. He had become the king of evil.
7. It was more than he hoped for, and now he was greedy for more.
8. Instead of learning from his defeat, he just wanted to fight God some more.
10. So he began to tell his dream to the assembly.
11.   *"Gods of Heaven!—I still call you that because no place, however deep and dark, can weaken immortal power.*
14. *I'm not giving up on Heaven.*
15. *We will rise up more glorious and more feared than if we never fell, and not be afraid that we might lose again.*
18. *Heaven's law made me your leader. The rights of justice gave us free will. And our achievements gave us honor and glory.*

22. *Now we have it all back again, and in a much safer place. He willingly gave us this kingdom. Nobody would want to take it away from us.*
24. *The powers that rule in the comfort of Heaven might be envied, but who's going to envy whoever rules in Hell and is in constant pain and under constant threat of attack from above?*
30. *Where there's nothing to steal, there are no thieves. Nobody wants to gain worse pain for himself than he already has.*

35. *That makes us more firmly united. Now we can fight for what is rightly ours.*

39. *We have a better chance of succeeding now than when we were in the comforts of Heaven.*
40. *Now it's just a matter of deciding how to go about it. Who wants to speak?"*

43.   He ceas'd, and next him Moloc, Scepter'd King
Stood up, the strongest and the fiercest Spirit
That fought in Heav'n; now fiercer by despair:

46. His trust was with th' Eternal to be deem'd
Equal in strength, and rather then be less

48. Care'd not to be at all; with that care lost
Went all his fear: of God, or Hell, or worse
He reck'd not, and these words thereafter spake.

51.   My sentence is for open Warr: Of Wiles,

52. More unexpert, I boast not: them let those

53. Contrive who need, or when they need, not now.

54. For while they sit contriving, shall the rest,
Millions that stand in Arms, and longing wait
The Signal to ascend, sit lingring here
Heav'ns fugitives, and for thir dwelling place
Accept this dark opprobrious Den of shame,
The Prison of his Tyranny who Reigns

60. By our delay? no, let us rather choose
Arm'd with Hell flames and fury all at once
O're Heav'ns high Towrs to force resistless way,
Turning our Tortures into horrid Arms
Against the Torturer; when to meet the noise
Of his Almighty Engin he shall hear
Infernal Thunder, and for Lightning see
Black fire and horror shot with equal rage

68. Among his Angels; and his Throne it self
Mixt with Tartarean Sulphur, and strange fire,
His own invented Torments. But perhaps

71. The way seems difficult and steep to scale
With upright wing against a higher foe.
Let such bethink them, if the sleepy drench
Of that forgetful Lake benumm not still,
That in our proper motion we ascend
Up to our native seat: descent and fall
To us is adverse. Who but felt of late
When the fierce Foe hung on our brok'n Rear
Insulting, and pursu'd us through the Deep,
With what compulsion and laborious flight
We sunk thus low? Th' ascent is easie then;

82. Th' event is fear'd; should we again provoke
Our stronger, some worse way his wrath may find
To our destruction: if there be in Hell

85. Fear to be worse destroy'd: what can be worse
Then to dwell here, driv'n out from bliss, condemn'd
In this abhorred deep to utter woe;
Where pain of unextinguishable fire
Must exercise us without hope of end
The Vassals of his anger, when the Scourge
Inexorably, and the torturing hour

43.   Moloch stood up. He was the strongest and fiercest angel in the war.

46. He wanted to be as strong as God, otherwise to him life wasn't worth living.

48. He was willing to risk everything.

51.   *"I vote for war,"* he said.

52. *"I don't know anything about trickery.*

53. *Those of you who want to sit around conspiring, do it on your own time!*

54. *What do you expect the rest of us to do—sit around and wait in this hell-hole while our warden sits above on his comfortable throne?*

60. *No! Let's take these damned hell-flames and attack his angels with them.*

68. *He invented these tortures. Let's return them to him and dump sulfur and black fire on his throne.*

71. *It won't be as hard as you think. Being chased downward and falling like we did is unnatural to us. But we can fly upward more easily, and take them by surprise.*

82. *Are you afraid to make him mad again? What more can he do to us?*

85. *What's worse than this?—where fire tortures us without end, and we're slaves at his mercy to punish whenever and in whatever way he wants.*

92.   Calls us to Penance? More destroy'd then thus
      We should be quite abolisht and expire.
      What fear we then? what doubt we to incense
      His utmost ire? which to the highth enrag'd,
      Will either quite consume us, and reduce
      To nothing this essential, happier farr
      Then miserable to have eternal being:

99.   Or if our substance be indeed Divine,
      And cannot cease to be, we are at worst
      On this side nothing; and by proof we feel
      Our power sufficient to disturb his Heav'n,
      And with perpetual inrodes to Allarme,
      Though inaccessible, his fatal Throne:

105. Which if not Victory is yet Revenge.

106. He ended frowning, and his look denounc'd
      Desperate revenge, and Battel dangerous

108. To less then Gods. On th' other side up rose
      Belial, in act more graceful and humane;
      A fairer person lost not Heav'n; he seemd
      For dignity compos'd and high exploit:
      But all was false and hollow; though his Tongue
      Dropt Manna, and could make the worse appear
      The better reason, to perplex and dash
      Maturest Counsels: for his thoughts were low;
      To vice industrious, but to Nobler deeds
      Timorous and slothful: yet he pleas'd the ear,
      And with perswasive accent thus began.

119. I should be much for open Warr, O Peers,
      As not behind in hate; if what was urg'd
      Main reason to persuade immediate Warr,
      Did not disswade me most, and seem to cast
      Ominous conjecture on the whole success:
      When he who most excels in fact of Arms,
      In what he counsels and in what excels
      Mistrustful, grounds his courage on despair
      And utter dissolution, as the scope
      Of all his aim, after some dire revenge.

129. First, what Revenge? the Towrs of Heav'n are fill'd
      With Armed watch, that render all access
      Impregnable; oft on the bordering Deep
      Encamp thir Legions, or with obscure wing
      Scout farr and wide into the Realm of night,

134. Scorning surprize. Or could we break our way
      By force, and at our heels all Hell should rise
      With blackest Insurrection, to confound
      Heav'ns purest Light, yet our great Enemy
      All incorruptible would on his Throne
      Sit unpolluted, and th' Ethereal mould
      Incapable of stain would soon expel

92. *How much worse could things get? If he decides to kill us, let him. At least we'll be out of here.*

99. *And if we really are immortal and can't die, then we can make his life miserable with repeated attacks forever.*

105. *If not victory, at least we can get our revenge."*
106. On Moloch's face was a look of contempt for anyone who was afraid to undertake what he suggested.

108. Next to stand and speak was Belial. He was handsome. His voice was sweet. But he was a con artist. Beneath his dignified appearance he was lazy and immoral.

119. *"I would go along with the idea of more war," he said, "except that our most expert warrior bases everything on despair and a hope for death—all to accomplish some kind of revenge.*

129. *How could we succeed? Heaven is surrounded with armed guards. And scouts patrol all the dark outer spaces.*

134. *Are we supposed to bring Hell's fire with us to fight God's forces while he sits safe and untouchable? He would soon throw us all back into Hell again.*

Her mischief, and purge off the baser fire
142. Victorious. Thus repuls'd, our final hope
Is flat despair; we must exasperate
Th' Almighty Victor to spend all his rage,
And that must end us, that must be our cure,
146. To be no more; sad cure; for who would loose,
Though full of pain, this intellectual being,
Those thoughts that wander through Eternity,
To perish rather, swallowd up and lost
In the wide womb of uncreated night,
151. Devoid of sense and motion? and who knows,
Let this be good, whether our angry Foe
Can give it, or will ever? how he can
Is doubtful; that he never will is sure.
155. Will he, so wise, let loose at once his ire,
Belike through impotence, or unaware,
To give his Enemies thir wish, and end
Them in his anger, whom his anger saves
To punish endless? wherefore cease we then?
Say they who counsel Warr, we are decreed,
Reserv'd and destin'd to Eternal woe;
162. Whatever doing, what can we suffer more,
163. What can we suffer worse? is this then worst,
Thus sitting, thus consulting, thus in Arms?
165. What when we fled amain, pursu'd and strook
With Heav'ns afflicting Thunder, and besought
The Deep to shelter us? this Hell then seem'd
168. A refuge from those wounds: or when we lay
Chain'd on the burning Lake? that sure was worse.
170. What if the breath that kindl'd those grim fires
Awak'd should blow them into sevenfold rage
And plunge us in the flames? or from above
Should intermitted vengeance arm again
174. His red right hand to plague us? what if all
Her stores were open'd, and this Firmament
Of Hell should spout her Cataracts of Fire,
Impendent horrors, threatning hideous fall
One day upon our heads; while we perhaps
Designing or exhorting glorious warr,
Caught in a fierie Tempest shall be hurl'd
Each on his rock transfixt, the sport and prey
Of racking whirlwinds, or for ever sunk
Under yon boyling Ocean, wrapt in Chains;
There to converse with everlasting groans,
Unrespited, unpitied, unrepreevd,
186. Ages of hopeless end; this would be worse.
187. Warr therefore, open or conceal'd, alike
188. My voice disswades; for what can force or guile
With him, or who deceive his mind, whose eye

142. *Are we supposed to make God mad enough to kill us? Is that our last hope?*

146. *I don't think so. Who wants to lose their life, their mind, or their power.*

151. *Even if that's really what we want, God may not even be able to kill us. Anyway he wouldn't if he could.*

155. *He's too smart to give us what we want. He wants to keep us alive to punish forever.*

162. *I hear that whatever we do we can't make matters worse. Really? Is this the worst possible condition?*
163. *Is this the worst thing—to sit in comfort, discussing?—to still have all our weapons?*
165. *Remember when we were bombarded with Heavens warfare. This Hell seemed a safe refuge.*
168. *How about wallowing in that lake of fire. Wasn't that worse?*
170. *What if those flames explode and cover us all here?*

174. *What if while we sit planning war, God raises storms that toss us back into the boiling lake, each one chained to a rock there forever?*

186. *Wouldn't that be worse?*
187. *So I'm against war, whether by violence or trickery.*
188. *How can we deceive God? He sees everything.*

        Views all things at one view? he from heav'ns highth

191. All these our motions vain, sees and derides;

192. Not more Almighty to resist our might
        Then wise to frustrate all our plots and wiles.

194. Shall we then live thus vile, the race of Heav'n
        Thus trampl'd, thus expell'd to suffer here

196. Chains and these Torments? better these then worse

197. By my advice; since fate inevitable
        Subdues us, and Omnipotent Decree

199. The Victors will. To suffer, as to doe,
        Our strength is equal, nor the Law unjust

201. That so ordains: this was at first resolv'd,
        If we were wise, against so great a foe
        Contending, and so doubtful what might fall.

204. I laugh, when those who at the Spear are bold
        And vent'rous, if that fail them, shrink and fear
        What yet they know must follow, to endure
        Exile, or ignominy, or bonds, or pain,

208. The sentence of thir Conquerour: This is now
        Our doom; which if we can sustain and bear,

210. Our Supream Foe in time may much remit
        His anger, and perhaps thus farr remov'd
        Not mind us not offending, satisfi'd
        With what is punish't; whence these raging fires
        Will slack'n, if his breath stir not thir flames.
        Our purer essence then will overcome
        Thir noxious vapour, or enur'd not feel,
        Or chang'd at length, and to the place conformd
        In temper and in nature, will receive
        Familiar the fierce heat, and void of pain;
        This horror will grow milde, this darkness light,

221. Besides what hope the never-ending flight
        Of future dayes may bring, what chance, what change
        Worth waiting, since our present lot appeers
        For happy though but ill, for ill not worst,
        If we procure not to our selves more woe.

226.   Thus Belial with words cloath'd in reasons garb
        Counsell'd ignoble ease, and peaceful sloath,

228. Not peace: and after him thus Mammon spake.

229.   Either to disinthrone the King of Heav'n
        We warr, if Warr be best, or to regain
        Our own right lost: him to unthrone we then
        May hope when everlasting Fate shall yeild
        To fickle Chance, and Chaos judge the strife:

234. The former vain to hope argues as vain
        The latter: for what place can be for us
        Within Heav'ns bound, unless Heav'ns Lord supream
        We overpower? Suppose he should relent

191. *He's laughing at our plans.*
192. *He's not only stronger than us, but he can get inside our heads.*
194. *So should we just accept whatever tortures this place has to give?*
196. *Better these than worse things.*
197. *We can't undo this outcome.*

199. *You would think that if we're strong enough to fight we should be strong enough to take the consequences.*
201. *We should've known this might be the outcome.*

204. *Funny how those who are so brave to go out and fight act so surprised to find they might actually have to suffer the consequences if they lose.*
208. *We lost. So here we are. If we just shut up and take it, God may leave us alone.*
210. *In time he may forget about us. These fires may weaken, or our bodies may become accustomed and not mind them so much.*

221. *You never know what the future might bring. Let's wait and see, and not make matters worse."*

226. So Belial finished his 'do nothing' speech.

228. Then Mammon spoke:
229. *"The chances are slim that we could win if we returned to war.*

234. *But if we want to regain our lost place that's what we would have to do.*

238. And publish Grace to all, on promise made
Of new Subjection; with what eyes could we
Stand in his presence humble, and receive
Strict Laws impos'd, to celebrate his Throne
With warbl'd Hymns, and to his Godhead sing
Forc't Halleluiah's; while he Lordly sits
Our envied Sovran, and his Altar breathes
Ambrosial Odours and Ambrosial Flowers,
Our servile offerings. This must be our task
In Heav'n, this our delight; how wearisom
248. Eternity so spent in worship paid
249. To whom we hate. Let us not then pursue
By force impossible, by leave obtain'd
Unacceptable, though in Heav'n, our state
252. Of splendid vassalage, but rather seek
Our own good from our selves, and from our own
Live to our selves, though in this vast recess,
255. Free, and to none accountable, preferring
Hard liberty before the easie yoke
257. Of servile Pomp. Our greatness will appeer
Then most conspicuous, when great things of small,
Useful of hurtful, prosperous of adverse
We can create, and in what place so e're
Thrive under evil, and work ease out of pain
262. Through labour and indurance. This deep world
Of darkness do we dread? How oft amidst
Thick clouds and dark doth Heav'ns all-ruling Sire
Choose to reside, his Glory unobscur'd,
And with the Majesty of darkness round
Covers his Throne; from whence deep thunders roar
Must'ring thir rage, and Heav'n resembles Hell?
269. As he our darkness, cannot we his Light
270. Imitate when we please? This Desart soile
Wants not her hidden lustre, Gemms and Gold;
Nor want we skill or Art, from whence to raise
Magnificence; and what can Heav'n shew more?
274. Our torments also may in length of time
Become our Elements, these piercing Fires
As soft as now severe, our temper chang'd
Into their temper; which must needs remove
278. The sensible of pain. All things invite
To peaceful Counsels, and the settl'd State
Of order, how in safety best we may
Compose our present evils, with regard
Of what we are and were, dismissing quite
All thoughts of warr: ye have what I advise.
284.   He scarce had finisht, when such murmur filld
Th' Assembly, as when hollow Rocks retain

238. *Let's say he forgives us all if we promise to worship him. Are you ready to follow his laws, sing his praises, bring him flowers?*

248. *It would make us sick to spend eternity worshiping the one we hate.*

249. *Let's forget about waging a war we can't win, or returning to Heaven in miserable slavery.*

252. *Let's make the best of what we have here where we don't owe anybody anything.*

255. *Better to be free in a hard place than slaves in a palace.*

257. *It will be more impressive if we make great achievements under these poor conditions.*

262. *What's so terrible about living in darkness? Doesn't God sometimes draw dark clouds around himself when he's in the mood?*

269. *Just as he creates darkness out of light, we can create light out of darkness.*

270. *We found riches under this ground, and we have the skill to build great things. What more does Heaven have to offer?*

274. *In time, these fires may soften and our bodies may become accustomed to them.*

278. *All things considered, it's best we maintain peace and order and find ways to improve our surroundings, and forget about war."*

284.   There was loud murmuring throughout the hall when he finished.

286. The sound of blustring winds, which all night long
Had rous'd the Sea, now with hoarse cadence lull
Sea-faring men orewatcht, whose Bark by chance
Or Pinnace anchors in a craggy Bay
290. After the Tempest: Such applause was heard
As Mammon ended, and his Sentence pleas'd,
292. Advising peace: for such another Field
They dreaded worse then Hell: so much the fear
Of Thunder and the Sword of Michael
295. Wrought still within them; and no less desire
To found this nether Empire, which might rise
By pollicy, and long process of time,
In emulation opposite to Heav'n.
299. Which when Beelzebub perceiv'd, then whom,
Satan except, none higher sat, with grave
Aspect he rose, and in his rising seem'd
302. A Pillar of State; deep on his Front engraven
Deliberation sat and public care;
And Princely counsel in his face yet shon,
Majestic though in ruin: sage he stood
With Atlantean shoulders fit to bear
307. The weight of mightiest Monarchies; his look
Drew audience and attention still as Night
Or Summers Noon-tide air, while thus he spake.
310.   Thrones and Imperial Powers, off-spring of heav'n
Ethereal Vertues; or these Titles now
Must we renounce, and changing stile be call'd
313. Princes of Hell? for so the popular vote
Inclines, here to continue, and build up here
A growing Empire; doubtless; while we dream,
316. And know not that the King of Heav'n hath doom'd
This place our dungeon, not our safe retreat
Beyond his Potent arm, to live exempt
From Heav'ns high jurisdiction, in new League
Banded against his Throne, but to remaine
In strictest bondage, though thus far remov'd,
Under th' inevitable curb, reserv'd
323. His captive multitude: For he, be sure
In heighth or depth, still first and last will Reign
Sole King, and of his Kingdom loose no part
By our revolt, but over Hell extend
His Empire, and with Iron Scepter rule
Us here, as with his Golden those in Heav'n.
329. What sit we then projecting peace and Warr?
Warr hath determin'd us, and foild with loss
331. Irreparable; tearms of peace yet none
Voutsaft or sought; for what peace will be giv'n
To us enslav'd, but custody severe,
And stripes, and arbitrary punishment

286. It was like the sound sailors might hear after a storm, as winds echo through the rocks.

290. You could tell they were pleased by his speech.

292. They dreaded the thought of returning to war.

295. Also, they liked the idea of building a new empire that might someday match Heaven.

299. Beelzebub, who was next in rank to Satan, stood up.

302. He had a concerned look on his face. He looked majestic, but a little weather-beaten. He had shoulders like Atlas.

307. The crowd became silent.

310.   *"Imperial Powers,"* he said, *"Sons of Heaven—or should we rename ourselves Princes of Hell?*

313. *That seems to be what you all want—to build some dream empire, joined in some new anti-God brotherhood, safely out of God's reach.*

316. *Don't you know that you are captives in his dungeon, not in some safe retreat.*

323. *He's not going to give up any part of his kingdom, or any of the power he has over us.*

329. *What are we doing sitting here debating war and peace? We already fought the war and lost.*

331. *There are no terms of peace. We are enslaved and subject to his punishment.*

Inflicted? and what peace can we return,
336. But to our power hostility and hate,
Untam'd reluctance, and revenge though slow,
338. Yet ever plotting how the Conqueror least
May reap his conquest, and may least rejoyce
In doing what we most in suffering feel?
341. Nor will occasion want, nor shall we need
With dangerous expedition to invade
Heav'n, whose high walls fear no assault or Siege,
Or ambush from the Deep. What if we find
Some easier enterprize? There is a place
346. (If ancient and prophetic fame in Heav'n
Err not) another World, the happy seat
Of some new Race call'd Man, about this time
349. To be created like to us, though less
In power and excellence, but favour'd more
Of him who rules above; so was his will
Pronounc'd among the Gods, and by an Oath,
That shook Heav'ns whol circumference, confirm'd.
354. Thither let us bend all our thoughts, to learn
What creatures there inhabit, of what mould,
Or substance, how endu'd, and what thir Power,
And where thir weakness, how attempted best,
358. By force or suttlety: Though Heav'n be shut,
And Heav'ns high Arbitrator sit secure
In his own strength, this place may lye expos'd
The utmost border of his Kingdom, left
362. To their defence who hold it: here perhaps
Som advantagious act may be achiev'd
By sudden onset, either with Hell fire
To waste his whole Creation, or possess
All as our own, and drive as we were driven,
The punie habitants, or if not drive,
368. Seduce them to our Party, that thir God
May prove thir foe, and with repenting hand
Abolish his own works. This would surpass
Common revenge, and interrupt his joy
In our Confusion, and our Joy upraise
373. In his disturbance; when his darling Sons
Hurl'd headlong to partake with us, shall curse
Thir frail Original, and faded bliss,
376. Faded so soon. Advise if this be worth
Attempting, or to sit in darkness here
Hatching vain Empires. Thus Beelzebub
379. Pleaded his devilish Counsel, first devis'd
By Satan, and in part propos'd: for whence,
But from the Author of all ill could Spring
So deep a malice, to confound the race
Of mankind in one root, and Earth with Hell

336. *In return all we can give him is our hate, and maybe soon, our revenge.*

338. *We will never stop planning ways to lessen his victory.*

341. *We don't have to try the impossible—to invade Heaven again. There may be easier ways.*

346. *If the prophecy in Heaven was true, there's another world and a creature called man that was to be created about this time.*

349. *He would be like us, but less powerful. But God would love him more than the angels. That's what he told us.*

354. *Let's find out more about these creatures and their weaknesses.*

358. *Heaven and God may be out of our reach, but this place may not have any defense.*

362. *Maybe we'll destroy it all with hellfire, or maybe take it over and drive out it's weak inhabitants. Or maybe even win them over to our side.*

368. *Then God may decide to destroy his own creation in anger. That would be great revenge.*

373. *Imagine his darlings thrown into this pit with us, cursing him.*

376. *What about it? Isn't that better than sitting around here in the dark, thinking up pipe dreams?"*

379. Of course this idea had already been thought up by Satan. Who else but the master of evil could come up with such a nasty plan—to turn Earth into Hell, just to spite God?

To mingle and involve, done all to spite
385. The great Creatour? But thir spite still serves
386. His glory to augment. The bold design
Pleas'd highly those infernal States, and joy
Sparkl'd in all thir eyes; with full assent
They vote: whereat his speech he thus renews.
390.   Well have ye judg'd, well ended long debate,
Synod of Gods, and like to what ye are,
Great things resolv'd; which from the lowest deep
Will once more lift us up, in spight of Fate,
Neerer our ancient Seat; perhaps in view
Of those bright confines, whence with neighbouring Arms
396. And opportune excursion we may chance
Re-enter Heav'n; or else in some milde Zone
Dwell not unvisited of Heav'ns fair Light
Secure, and at the brightning Orient beam
Purge off this gloom; the soft delicious Air,
To heal the scarr of these corrosive Fires
402. Shall breath her balme. But first whom shall we send
In search of this new world, whom shall we find
Sufficient? who shall tempt with wandring feet
The dark unbottom'd infinite Abyss
And through the palpable obscure find out
His uncouth way, or spread his aerie flight
Upborn with indefatigable wings
Over the vast abrupt, ere he arrive
The happy Ile; what strength, what art can then
Suffice, or what evasion bear him safe
Through the strict Senteries and Stations thick
Of Angels watching round? Here he had need
414. All circumspection, and we now no less
Choice in our suffrage; for on whom we send,
The weight of all and our last hope relies.
417.   This said, he sat; and expectation held
His look suspence, awaiting who appeer'd
To second, or oppose, or undertake
The perilous attempt; but all sat mute,
Pondering the danger with deep thoughts; and each
422. In others count'nance read his own dismay
Astonisht: none among the choice and prime
Of those Heav'n-warring Champions could be found
So hardie as to proffer or accept
426. Alone the dreadful voyage; till at last
Satan, whom now transcendent glory rais'd
Above his fellows, with Monarchal pride
Conscious of highest worth, unmov'd thus spake.
   O Progeny of Heav'n, Empyreal Thrones,
With reason hath deep silence and demurr
Seis'd us, though undismaid: long is the way

385. But he didn't know the result would ultimately mean greater glory for God.
386. The council loved the idea and voted their approval.

390. Beelzebub said, "*Good. We have made a great decision here today. It will improve our situation.*

396. *It may even result in eventually regaining Heaven, or maybe relocating to some nice place nearby that gets some of Heaven's light.*

402. *But first let's decide who we want to send in search of this new world. Who can handle this journey through black chaos, and get past any angels on guard.*

414. *We need to choose carefully. He will hold our last hope in his hands."*

417. He sat down and waited, but everyone was silent.

422. They all stared at each other dumbly, but not one of those great warriors of Heaven stepped forward.

426. At last Satan proudly rose and said, "*You're all silent, and with good reason. It's a long, hard way out of Hell.*

And hard, that out of Hell leads up to light;
434. Our prison strong, this huge convex of Fire,
Outrageous to devour, immures us round
Ninefold, and gates of burning Adamant
Barr'd over us prohibit all egress.
These past, if any pass, the void profound
Of unessential Night receives him next
Wide gaping, and with utter loss of being
Threatens him, plung'd in that abortive gulf.
442. If thence he scape into whatever world,
Or unknown Region, what remains him less
Then unknown dangers and as hard escape.
445. But I should ill become this Throne, O Peers,
And this Imperial Sov'ranty, adorn'd
With splendor, arm'd with power, if aught propos'd
And judg'd of public moment, in the shape
Of difficulty or danger could deterr
450. Mee from attempting. Wherefore do I assume
These Royalties, and not refuse to Reign,
Refusing to accept as great a share
Of hazard as of honour, due alike
To him who Reigns, and so much to him due
Of hazard more, as he above the rest
456. High honourd sits? Go therefore mighty Powers,
Terror of Heav'n, though fall'n; intend at home,
While here shall be our home, what best may ease
The present misery, and render Hell
More tollerable; if there be cure or charm
To respite or deceive, or slack the pain
462. Of this ill Mansion: intermit no watch
Against a wakeful Foe, while I abroad
Through all the Coasts of dark destruction seek
465. Deliverance for us all: this enterprize
466. None shall partake with me. Thus saying rose
The Monarch, and prevented all reply,
Prudent, least from his resolution rais'd
Others among the chief might offer now
(Certain to be refus'd) what erst they fear'd;
And so refus'd might in opinion stand
His Rivals, winning cheap the high repute
473. Which he through hazard huge must earn. But they
Dreaded not more th' adventure then his voice
475. Forbidding; and at once with him they rose;
Thir rising all at once was as the sound
477. Of Thunder heard remote. Towards him they bend
With awful reverence prone; and as a God
Extoll him equal to the highest in Heav'n:
480. Nor fail'd they to express how much they prais'd,
That for the general safety he despis'd

434. *Our prison is strong. You have to get past the strong gates that lock us in. Then you go out into the void that threatens to make you disappear in its blackness.*

442. *If you make it through to the unknown world, you face more unknown dangers and difficult escapes.*

445. *I wouldn't be worthy of this throne, my friends, if I shirked my duty to do what you judged necessary.*

450. *So I'll go. What right would I have to assume the glory of this throne but not the dangers?*

456. *While I head out, you all go and explore this place and see what ways you can find to improve our bleak environment.*

462. *Don't let down your guard. Keep watch against further attack.*

465. *I'll make this journey alone."*
466. He said this so no one could try to look brave by offering to join him, knowing he wouldn't let them.

473. They got the message and kept quiet.

475. Everybody got up, making a sound like distant thunder.

477. They bowed to him as their god.

480. They praised him for risking his safety for the good of the rest.

482. His own: for neither do the Spirits damn'd
Loose all thir vertue; least bad men should boast
Thir specious deeds on earth, which glory excites,
Or clos ambition varnisht o're with zeal.

486. Thus they thir doubtful consultations dark
Ended rejoycing in thir matchless Chief:

488. As when from mountain tops the dusky clouds
Ascending, while the North wind sleeps, O'respread
Heav'ns chearful face, the lowring Element
Scowls ore the dark'nd lantskip Snow, or showre;
If chance the radiant Sun with farewell sweet
Extend his ev'ning beam, the fields revive,
The birds thir notes renew, and bleating herds
Attest thir joy, that hill and valley rings.

496. O shame to men! Devil with Devil damn'd
Firm concord holds, men onely disagree
Of Creatures rational, though under hope
Of heavenly Grace; and God proclaiming peace,
Yet live in hatred, enmity, and strife
Among themselves, and levie cruel warres,
Wasting the Earth, each other to destroy:

503. As if (which might induce us to accord)
Man had not hellish foes anow besides,
That day and night for his destruction waite.

506.   The Stygian Counsel thus dissolv'd; and forth
In order came the grand infernal Peers:

508. Midst came thir mighty Paramount, and seemd
Alone th' Antagonist of Heav'n, nor less
Than Hells dread Emperour with pomp Supream,
And God-like imitated State; him round
A Globe of fierie Seraphim inclos'd
With bright imblazonrie, and horrent Arms.

514. Then of thir Session ended they bid cry
With Trumpets regal sound the great result:
Toward the four winds four speedy Cherubim
Put to thir mouths the sounding Alchymie
By Haralds voice explain'd: the hollow Abyss

519. Heard farr and wide, and all the host of Hell
With deafning shout, return'd them loud acclaim.

521. Thence more at ease thir minds and somwhat rais'd

522. By false presumptuous hope, the ranged powers
Disband, and wandring, each his several way
Pursues, as inclination or sad choice
Leads him perplext, where he may likeliest find
Truce to his restless thoughts, and entertain
The irksom hours, till his great Chief return.

528.   Part on the Plain, or in the Air sublime
Upon the wing, or in swift Race contend,
As at th' Olympian Games or Pythian fields;

482. It seems even bad spirits have some admirable qualities, unlike bad humans.

486. They ended their evil meeting, cheered up by their admiration for their king.

488. It felt like the sun coming out after a rainy day.

496. Isn't it shameful to think how devils can be so agreeable among themselves, while humans live in hatred, waging terrible wars against each other!

503. As if we didn't have enough enemies from Hell trying to destroy us.

506.   The leaders came out of the palace in order.

508. Satan was surrounded with attendants with arms and banners, like a god.

514. Cherubs flew out blowing their trumpets. The sounds turned into voices which gave news about the meeting's results.

519. Everyone cheered.

521. Their hopes were raised.

522. So they went wandering around, looking for ways to amuse themselves while waiting for Satan's return.

528.   Some of them had chariot races and played Olympic games.

Part curb thir fierie Steeds, or shun the Goal
With rapid wheels, or fronted Brigads form.
As when to warn proud Cities warr appears
Wag'd in the troubl'd Skie, and Armies rush
To Battel in the Clouds, before each Van
Prick forth the Aerie Knights, and couch thir Spears
Till thickest Legions close; with feats of Arms
From either end of Heav'n the welkin burns.

539. Others with vast Typhœan rage more fell
Rend up both Rocks and Hills, and ride the Air
In whirlwind; Hell scarce holds the wilde uproar.
As when Alcides from Oechalia Crown'd
With conquest, felt th' envenom'd robe, and tore
Through pain up by the roots Thessalian Pines,
And Lichas from the top of Oeta threw

546. Into th' Euboic Sea. Others more milde,
Retreated in a silent valley, sing
With notes Angelical to many a Harp
Thir own Heroic deeds and hapless fall
By doom of Battel; and complain that Fate
Free Vertue should enthrall to Force or Chance.

552. Thir Song was partial, but the harmony
(What could it less when Spirits immortal sing?)
Suspended Hell, and took with ravishment

555. The thronging audience. In discourse more sweet
(For Eloquence the Soul, Song charms the Sense,)
Others apart sat on a Hill retir'd,
In thoughts more elevate, and reason'd high
Of Providence, Foreknowledge, Will and Fate,
Fixt Fate, free will, foreknowledg absolute,

561. And found no end, in wandring mazes lost.
Of good and evil much they argu'd then,
Of happiness and final misery,
Passion and Apathie, and glory and shame,
Vain wisdom all, and false Philosophie:
Yet with a pleasing sorcerie could charm
Pain for a while or anguish, and excite
Fallacious hope, or arm th' obdured brest
With stubborn patience as with triple steel.

570. Another part in Squadrons and gross Bands,
On bold adventure to discover wide
That dismal world, if any Clime perhaps
Might yield them easier habitation, bend

574. Four ways thir flying March, along the Banks
Of four infernal Rivers that disgorge
Into the burning Lake thir baleful streams;

577. Abhorred Styx the flood of deadly hate,
Sad Acheron of sorrow, black and deep;
Cocytus, nam'd of lamentation loud

539. Others let off steam by tearing up the rocks and hills.

546. Some of the gentler angels went off to a quiet spot and made up songs about their tragedy.

552. Their lyrics were inaccurate, but the music was as sweet as you would expect from angels.

555. Another group had discussions about things like free will and fate, and good and evil.

561. Their reasoning was all mixed up, but they enjoyed talking anyway.

570. Some others went exploring around Hell, to see if they could find any better conditions.

574. They separated into four bands and followed four rivers that fed the lake of fire.

577. Styx was the river of hate, Acheron the river of sadness, Cocytus of loud crying, and Phlegethon of anger.

Heard on the ruful stream; fierce Phlegeton
Whose waves of torrent fire inflame with rage.

582. Farr off from these a slow and silent stream,
Lethe the River of Oblivion roules
Her watrie Labyrinth, whereof who drinks,
Forthwith his former state and being forgets,
Forgets both joy and grief, pleasure and pain.

587. Beyond this flood a frozen Continent
Lies dark and wilde, beat with perpetual storms
Of Whirlwind and dire Hail, which on firm land
Thaws not, but gathers heap, and ruin seems
Of ancient pile; all else deep snow and ice,
A gulf profound as that Serbonian Bog
Betwixt Damiata and Mount Casius old,
Where Armies whole have sunk: the parching Air
Burns frore, and cold performs th' effect of Fire.

596. Thither by harpy-footed Furies hail'd,
At certain revolutions all the damn'd
Are brought: and feel by turns the bitter change
Of fierce extreams, extreams by change more fierce,
From Beds of raging Fire to starve in Ice
Thir soft Ethereal warmth, and there to pine

602. Immovable, infixt, and frozen round,
Periods of time, thence hurried back to fire.

604. They ferry over this Lethean Sound
Both to and fro, thir sorrow to augment,
And wish and struggle, as they pass, to reach
The tempting stream, with one small drop to loose
In sweet forgetfulness all pain and woe,
All in one moment, and so neer the brink;

610. But fate withstands, and to oppose th' attempt
Medusa with Gorgonian terror guards
The Ford, and of it self the water flies
All taste of living wight, as once it fled

614. The lip of Tantalus. Thus roving on
In confus'd march forlorn, th' adventrous Bands
With shuddring horror pale, and eyes agast
View'd first thir lamentable lot, and found
No rest: through many a dark and drearie Vaile
They pass'd, and many a Region dolorous,
O'er many a Frozen, many a fierie Alpe,

621. Rocks, Caves, Lakes, Fens, Bogs, Dens, and shades of death,

622. A Universe of death, which God by curse
Created evil, for evil only good,

624. Where all life dies, death lives, and Nature breeds,
Perverse, all monstrous, all prodigious things,
Abominable, inutterable, and worse
Then Fables yet have feign'd, or fear conceiv'd,
Gorgons and Hydra's, and Chimera's dire.

582. And beyond these was a slow, silent stream, Lethe. If you drank its water you would forget everything.

587. Beyond that there was all ice and snowstorms and piles of snow that looked like ancient ruins, deep enough to sink a whole army.

596. When the damned go to Hell, some of them will be brought here sometimes, from fire to ice, to feel the pain and shock of the opposite extremes.

602. They'll be frozen into the ice for a while, then brought back into fire.
604. As they're brought back and forth over the river Lethe, they'll try to drink from it to forget their sorrow.

610. But monsters guard the river, and the water sinks away whenever they try to drink it.

614. So the angels wandered through Hell and were horrified at these things.

621. They passed frozen mountains, volcanoes, dark caves, swamps and lakes—a universe of death.
622. God created all this evil just for them.

624. Here life dies, death lives, and nature creates unbelievable monsters.

629.   Mean while the Adversary of God and Man,
        Satan with thoughts inflam'd of highest design,
        Puts on swift wings, and towards the Gates of Hell
632.   Explores his solitary flight; som times
        He scours the right hand coast, som times the left,
        Now shaves with level wing the Deep, then soares
        Up to the fiery Concave touring high.
636.   As when farr off at Sea a Fleet descri'd
        Hangs in the Clouds, by Æquinoctial Winds
        Close sailing from Bengala, or the Iles
        Of Ternate and Tidore, whence Merchants bring
        Thir spicie Drugs: they on the Trading Flood
        Through the wide Ethiopian to the Cape
        Ply stemming nightly toward the Pole. So seem'd
643.   Farr off the flying Fiend: at last appeer
        Hell bounds high reaching to the horrid Roof,
645.   And thrice threefold the Gates; three folds were Brass,
        Three Iron, three of Adamantine Rock,
647.   Impenetrable, impal'd with circling fire,
648.   Yet unconsum'd. Before the Gates there sat
        On either side a formidable shape;
650.   The one seem'd Woman to the waste, and fair,
        But ended foul in many a scaly fould
        Voluminous and vast, a Serpent arm'd
        With mortal sting: about her middle round
654.   A cry of Hell Hounds never ceasing bark'd
        With wide Cerberian mouths full loud, and rung
656.   A hideous Peal: yet, when they list, would creep,
        If aught disturb'd thir noyse, into her woomb,
        And kennel there, yet there still bark'd and howl'd
659.   Within unseen. Farr less abhorrd than these
        Vex'd Scylla bathing in the Sea that parts
        Calabria from the hoarse Trinacrian shore:
        Nor uglier follow the Night-Hag, when call'd
        In secret, riding through the Air she comes
        Lur'd with the smell of infant blood, to dance
        With Lapland Witches, while the labouring Moon
666.   Eclipses at thir charms. The other shape,
        If shape it might be call'd that shape had none
        Distinguishable in member, joynt, or limb,
669.   Or substance might be call'd that shadow seem'd,
        For each seem'd either; black it stood as Night,
671.   Fierce as ten Furies, terrible as Hell,
672.   And shook a dreadful Dart; what seem'd his head
        The likeness of a Kingly Crown had on.
674.   Satan was now at hand, and from his seat
        The Monster moving onward came as fast
        With horrid strides, Hell trembled as he strode.
677.   Th' undaunted Fiend what this might be admir'd,

629.   Meanwhile Satan flew to the gates of Hell alone.

632.   He flew high and low and back and forth from the right to the left hand edges of Hell.

636.   In the distance he looked something like the ships that sail back and forth in the night through storms around the Cape of Good Hope to the Indian Ocean carrying spices.

643.   At last he came to the gates at the end of Hell.

645.   They reached up to the roof and were made of six layers— three of brass, three of iron, and three of rock.
647.   Flames circled around them but didn't burn them.
648.   Two scary figures sat in front of the gates, one on each side.
650.   One was a beautiful woman above the waist and a big snake from the waist down.

654.   Loud barking dogs circled her.

656.   If anything disturbed them they would crawl inside her uterus and continue barking there.

659.   They were more hideous than any witch's dogs.

666.   The other creature had no shape.

669.   It was like a shadow.

671.   It was very fierce and carried a dart.
672.   A crown was on what might have been his head.

674.   When Satan got close, the creature got up and quickly came to meet him. His steps shook the ground.
677.   Satan was impressed, but he wasn't afraid of anybody except God and his Son.

Admir'd, not fear'd; God and his Son except,
Created thing naught valu'd he nor shun'd
And with disdainful look thus first began.

681.   Whence and what art thou, execrable shape,
That dar'st, though grim and terrible, advance
Thy miscreated Front athwart my way

684. To yonder Gates? through them I mean to pass,
That be assured, without leave askt of thee:
Retire, or taste thy folly, and learn by proof,
Hell-born, not to contend with Spirits of Heav'n.
    To whom the Goblin full of wrauth reply'd,

689. Art thou that Traitor Angel, art thou hee,
Who first broke peace in Heav'n and Faith, till then
Unbrok'n, and in proud rebellious Arms
Drew after him the third part of Heav'ns Sons

693. Conjur'd against the highest, for which both Thou
And they outcast from God, are here condemn'd
To waste Eternal dayes in woe and pain?

696. And reck'n'st thou thy self with Spirits of Heav'n,

697. Hell-doom'd, and breath'st defiance here and scorn
Where I reign King, and to enrage thee more,

699. Thy King and Lord? Back to thy punishment,
False fugitive, and to thy speed add wings,
Least with a whip of Scorpions I pursue
Thy lingring, or with one stroke of this Dart
Strange horror seise thee, and pangs unfelt before.

704.   So spake the grieslie terror, and in shape,
So speaking and so threatning, grew tenfold

706. More dreadful and deform: on th' other side
Incenst with indignation Satan stood
Unterrifi'd, and like a Comet burn'd,
That fires the length of Ophiucus huge
In th' Artick Sky, and from his horrid hair
Shakes Pestilence and Warr. Each at the Head

712. Level'd his deadly aime; thir fatall hands
No second stroke intend, and such a frown

714. Each cast at th' other, as when two black Clouds
With Heav'ns Artillery fraught, come rattling on
Over the Caspian, then stand front to front
Hov'ring a space, till Winds the signal blow
To join thir dark Encounter in mid air:
So frownd the mighty Combatants, that Hell
Grew darker at thir frown, so matcht they stood;

721. For never but once more was either like

722. To meet so great a foe: and now great deeds
Had been achiev'd, whereof all Hell had rung,
Had not the Snakie Sorceress that sat

725. Fast by Hell Gate, and kept the fatal Key,
Ris'n, and with hideous outcry rush'd between.

681.   He said, *"What and who do you think you are, blocking my way to those gates?*

684.   *I don't need your permission to pass, so get out of my way or I'll make you sorry you messed with one of Heaven's angels."*

689.   The creature said, *"Aren't you that traitor who led one third of Heaven's angels against God?*

693.   *And didn't he throw out the bunch of you to suffer here forever?*

696.   *What makes you think you have any link with Heaven left?*
697.   *Don't get tough with me. I am your king around here!*

699.   *Get back to your prison, and move fast or I'll let you taste a whip of scorpions and stab you with this dart and give you pain like you never felt before."*

704.   The shape looked very scary as he spoke.

706.   But Satan wasn't afraid. He was as angry as a comet.

712.   They got ready to fight each other, each one intending to kill the other one.
714.   Their faces were like dark clouds coming together before a storm.

721.   Neither one was likely to meet a greater enemy until they faced God.
722.   Now there would have been a major fight, if the woman hadn't jumped between them.
725.   She was the one whose job it was to sit by the gates and keep the key.

727.   O Father, what intends thy hand, she cry'd,
            Against thy only Son? What fury O Son,
            Possesses thee to bend that mortal Dart
            Against thy Fathers head? and know'st for whom;
731.   For him who sits above and laughs the while
        At thee ordain'd his drudge, to execute
        What e're his wrath, which he calls Justice, bids,
734.   His wrath which one day will destroy ye both.
735.   She spake, and at her words the hellish Pest
        Forbore, then these to her Satan return'd:
            So strange thy outcry, and thy words so strange
        Thou interposest, that my sudden hand
        Prevented spares to tell thee yet by deeds
        What it intends; till first I know of thee,
        What thing thou art, thus double-form'd, and why
        In this infernal Vaile first met thou call'st
        Me Father, and that Fantasm call'st my Son?
744.   I know thee not, nor ever saw till now
        Sight more detestable then him and thee.
            T' whom thus the Portress of Hell Gate reply'd;
747.   Hast thou forgot me then, and do I seem
        Now in thine eye so foul, once deemd so fair
749.   In Heav'n, when at th' Assembly, and in sight
        Of all the Seraphim with thee combin'd
        In bold conspiracy against Heav'ns King,
        All on a sudden miserable pain
        Surprisd thee, dim thine eyes, and dizzie swumm
        In darkness, while thy head flames thick and fast
        Threw forth, till on the left side op'ning wide,
        Likest to thee in shape and count'nance bright,
757.   Then shining Heav'nly fair, a Goddess arm'd
758.   Out of thy head I sprung; amazement seis'd
        All th' Host of Heav'n back they recoild affraid
        At first, and call'd me Sin, and for a Sign
761.   Portentous held me; but familiar grown,
        I pleas'd, and with attractive graces won
        The most averse, thee chiefly, who full oft
        Thy self in me thy perfect image viewing
765.   Becam'st enamour'd, and such joy thou took'st
        With me in secret, that my womb conceiv'd
767.   A growing burden. Mean while Warr arose,
        And fields were fought in Heav'n; wherein remain
        (For what could else) to our Almighty Foe
        Cleer Victory, to our part loss and rout
771.   Through all the Empyrean: down they fell
        Driv'n headlong from the Pitch of Heaven, down
        Into this Deep, and in the general fall
774.   I also; at which time this powerful Key
        Into my hand was giv'n, with charge to keep

727.   She cried, "*Father, why do you want to harm your only son? Son, why are you aiming your dagger at your father's head?*

731.   *God is laughing at both of you, while you stupidly do his dirty work—and satisfy what he calls justice!*

734.   *Someday he'll kill you both."*

735.   The two of them were stunned. Satan said, "*I'll hold off my attack long enough for you to tell me what the hell you are and why you call me 'father' and call that creep my son.*

744.   *I don't know you. I never saw a more disgusting sight than the two of you."*

747.   The woman answered, "*So you don't remember me. Am I that ugly? You didn't used to think so.*

749.   *When you first planned your rebellion in Heaven with all your followers, you suddenly felt intense pain and your head flew open in flames.*

757.   *I came out of the left side of your head. I was like a goddess, as beautiful as you were.*

758.   *It shocked everybody. They called me 'Sin' and were afraid at first.*

761.   *But I was beautiful and they all began to like me, especially you.*

765.   *You loved me. We had sex and I got pregnant.*

767.   *Meanwhile war broke out and, naturally, you lost.*

771.   *I fell into this pit with the rest of you.*

774.   *They gave me this key and told me I had to keep these gates shut forever.*

These Gates for ever shut, which none can pass
Without my op'ning. Pensive here I sat
778. Alone, but long I sat not, till my womb
Pregnant by thee, and now excessive grown
Prodigious motion felt and rueful throes.
At last this odious offspring whom thou seest
782. Thine own begotten, breaking violent way
Tore through my entrails, that with fear and pain
784. Distorted, all my nether shape thus grew
785. Transform'd: but he my inbred enemie
Forth issu'd, brandishing his fatal Dart
787. Made to destroy: I fled, and cry'd out Death;
Hell trembl'd at the hideous Name, and sigh'd
From all her Caves, and back resounded Death.
790. I fled, but he pursu'd (though more, it seems,
Inflam'd with lust then rage) and swifter far,
Mee overtook his mother all dismaid,
And in embraces forcible and foule
794. Ingendring with me, of that rape begot
These yelling Monsters that with ceasless cry
796. Surround me, as thou sawst, hourly conceiv'd
And hourly born, with sorrow infinite
To me, for when they list into the womb
That bred them they return, and howle and gnaw
800. My Bowels, thir repast; then bursting forth
A fresh with conscious terrours vex me round,
That rest or intermission none I find.
803. Before mine eyes in opposition sits
Grim Death my Son and foe, who sets them on,
And me his Parent would full soon devour
For want of other prey, but that he knows
His end with mine involvd; and knows that I
Should prove a bitter Morsel, and his bane,
Whenever that shall be; so Fate pronounc'd.
810. But thou O Father, I forewarn thee, shun
His deadly arrow; neither vainly hope
To be invulnerable in those bright Arms,
Though temper'd heav'nly, for that mortal dint,
814. Save he who reigns above, none can resist.
     She finish'd, and the suttle Fiend his lore
816. Soon learnd, now milder, and thus answerd smooth.
Dear Daughter, since thou claim'st me for thy Sire,
And my fair Son here showst me, the dear pledge
819. Of dalliance had with thee in Heav'n, and joys
Then sweet, now sad to mention, through dire change
Befalln us unforeseen, unthought of, know
822. I come no enemie, but to set free
From out this dark and dismal house of pain,
Both him and thee, and all the heav'nly Host

778. *Before long I went into labor and gave birth to this repulsive offspring you see.*

782. *It was a violent delivery. He tore up my intestines coming out.*

784. *That's how I got this snake's shape below.*
785. *He came out waving his dart and scared the hell out of me.*

787. *I screamed 'Death' and Hell echoed the word from all the caves.*
790. *I ran and he chased me. He was too fast for me. He caught me and raped me.*

794. *From that rape came more offspring—these monstrous dogs that surround me.*
796. *They never leave. They go back inside me whenever they want and howl and chew my insides.*

800. *Then I give birth to them again and again.*

803. *My no good son over there would just as soon kill me and eat me, since there's nothing else for him to eat. But he knows it would probably kill him too.*

810. *But watch out for his dart. Even your armor wouldn't protect you from its deadly sting.*

814. *God is the only one who can't be killed by it."*

816.   Satan calmed down. He said, "*So you're my daughter and this is my son.*

819. *And this is the result of the pleasure we had in Heaven, which has turned unexpectedly into sadness.*

822. *I'm not an enemy. I'm here to set free you and all my followers.*

Of Spirits that in our just pretenses arm'd
826. Fell with us from on high: from them I go
This uncouth errand sole, and one for all
Myself expose, with lonely steps to tread
Th' unfounded deep, and through the void immense
To search with wandring quest a place foretold
Should be, and, by concurring signs, ere now
Created vast and round, a place of bliss
In the Purlieues of Heav'n, and therein plac't
834. A race of upstart Creatures, to supply
835. Perhaps our vacant room, though more remov'd,
Least Heav'n surcharg'd with potent multitude
837. Might hap to move new broiles: Be this or aught
Then this more secret now design'd, I haste
To know, and this once known, shall soon return,
And bring ye to the place where Thou and Death
Shall dwell at ease, and up and down unseen
Wing silently the buxom Air, imbalm'd
With odours; there ye shall be fed and fill'd
Immeasurably, all things shall be your prey.
845.   He ceas'd, for both seem'd highly pleasd, and Death
846. Grinnd horrible a gastly smile, to hear
His famine should be fill'd, and blest his mawe
Destin'd to that good hour: no less rejoyc'd
His mother bad, and thus bespake her Sire.
850. The key of this infernal Pit by due,
And by command of Heav'ns all-powerful King
I keep, by him forbidden to unlock
These Adamantine Gates; against all force
Death ready stands to interpose his dart,
Fearless to be o'rmatcht by living might.
856. But what ow I to his commands above
857. Who hates me, and hath hither thrust me down
Into this gloom of Tartarus profound,
To sit in hateful Office here confin'd,
Inhabitant of Heav'n, and heav'nlie-born,
Here in perpetual agonie and pain,
With terrors and with clamors compasst round
Of mine own brood, that on my bowels feed:
864. Thou art my Father, thou my Author, thou
My being gav'st me; whom should I obey
866. But thee, whom follow? thou wilt bring me soon
To that new world of light and bliss, among
The Gods who live at ease, where I shall Reign
At thy right hand voluptuous, as beseems
Thy daughter and thy darling, without end.
871.   Thus saying, from her side the fatal Key,
Sad instrument of all our woe, she took;
And towards the Gate rouling her bestial train,

826. *I'm going out there alone to search for a new place that's said to be near Heaven.*

834. *There should be some new creatures there that are supposed to take our place.*
835. *He probably put them outside Heaven so there wouldn't be a chance of new uprisings due to overpopulation.*
837. *Anyway, I'll find out whatever's out there. Then I'll bring you and Death there, where you can fly around, invisible, and live comfortably and have plenty to eat—in fact, you can have everything."*

845.   The mother and son were overjoyed.
846. Death grinned and rubbed his stomach.

850. Sin said, "*I'm supposed to keep these gates locked, and Death is supposed to kill whoever tries to get past.*

856. *But why should I obey God's orders?*
857. *He hates me. He threw me in this pit and created all my suffering.*

864. *You're my father. You're the one I should obey.*

866. *Soon we'll be together in that new world of pleasure. We'll be like king and queen. I'll be your daughter and your lover, forever."*

871.   She took the key from her side. She rolled over to the gate. She pulled up the heavy grating, which nobody else could have moved.

Forthwith the huge Porcullis high up drew,
Which but her self not all the Stygian powers
876. Could once have mov'd; then in the key-hole turns
Th' intricate wards, and every Bolt and Bar
Of massie Iron or sollid Rock with ease
Unfast'ns: on a sudden op'n flie
With impetuous recoile and jarring sound
Th' infernal dores, and on thir hinges grate
Harsh Thunder, that the lowest bottom shook
883. Of Erebus. She op'nd, but to shut
884. Excel'd her power; the Gates wide op'n stood,
That with extended wings a Bannerd Host
Under spread Ensigns marching might pass through
With Horse and Chariots rankt in loose array;
888. So wide they stood, and like a Furnace mouth
Cast forth redounding smoak and ruddy flame.
890. Before thir eyes in sudden view appear
The secrets of the hoarie deep, a dark
Illimitable Ocean without bound,
893. Without dimension, where length, breadth, & highth,
And time and place are lost; where eldest Night
And Chaos, Ancestors of Nature, hold
Eternal Anarchie, amidst the noise
Of endless Warrs, and by confusion stand.
For hot, cold, moist, and dry, four Champions fierce
899. Strive here for Maistrie, and to Battel bring
Thir embryon Atoms; they around the flag
Of each his faction, in thir several Clanns,
Light-arm'd or heavy, sharp, smooth, swift or slow,
Swarm populous, unnumber'd as the Sands
Of Barca or Cyrene's torrid soil,
Levied to side with warring Winds, and poise
Thir lighter wings. To whom these most adhere,
907. Hee rules a moment; Chaos Umpire sits,
And by decision more imbroiles the fray
By which he Reigns: next him high Arbiter
Chance governs all. Into this wilde Abyss,
911. The Womb of nature and perhaps her Grave,
Of neither Sea, nor Shore, nor Air, nor Fire,
But all these in thir pregnant causes mixt
Confus'dly, and which thus must ever fight,
915. Unless th' Almighty Maker them ordain
His dark materials to create more Worlds,
917. Into this wild Abyss the warie fiend
Stood on the brink of Hell and look'd a while,
919. Pondering his Voyage: for no narrow frith
920. He had to cross. Nor was his eare less peal'd
With noises loud and ruinous (to compare
Great things with small) then when Bellona storms,

876. She put the key in the lock, and the bolts unlocked and the gates flew open, making a loud grating sound.

883. She didn't have the power to ever close them again.
884. They were open wide enough for a whole army to march through easily.

888. The opening blew out smoke and flames like a furnace.

890. The three of them looked out and saw a wild mix of confusion, all dark and noisy. Wild winds blew everything all around.

893. There was no space or time, just Night and Chaos, which would someday produce Nature.

899. All kinds of atoms were battling each other like a desert sandstorm.

907. Everything was ruled by Chaos and Chance.

911. This was where all things were born and where they ended up after they died.

915. These were the raw elements God used to create worlds.

917. Satan stood there awhile, watching.

919. He saw that this was going to be a tough journey.
920. The sound was as loud as if the Earth exploded.

With all her battering Engines bent to rase
Som Capital City; or less then if this frame
Of Heav'n were falling, and these Elements
In mutinie had from her Axle torn

927. The stedfast Earth. At last his Sail-broad Vannes
He spreads for flight, and in the surging smoak

929. Uplifted spurns the ground, thence many a League
As in a cloudy Chair ascending rides

931. Audacious, but that seat soon failing, meets
A vast vacuitie: all unawares
Fluttring his pennons vain plumb down he drops

934. Ten thousand fadom deep, and to this hour
Down had been falling, had not by ill chance
The strong rebuff of som tumultuous cloud
Instinct with Fire and Nitre hurried him

938. As many miles aloft: that furie stay'd,
Quencht in a Boggy Syrtis, neither Sea,
Nor good dry Land: nigh founderd on he fares,
Treading the crude consistence, half on foot,
Half flying; behoves him now both Oare and Saile.

943. As when a Gryfon through the Wilderness
With winged course ore Hill or moarie Dale,
Pursues the Arimaspian, who by stelth
Had from his wakeful custody purloind
The guarded Gold: So eagerly the fiend

948. Ore bog or steep, through strait, rough, dense, or rare,
With head, hands, wings, or feet pursues his way,
And swims or sinks, or wades, or creeps, or flyes:

951. At length a universal hubbub wilde
Of stunning sounds and voices all confus'd
Borne through the hollow dark assaults his eare

954. With loudest vehemence: thither he plyes,
Undaunted to meet there what ever power
Or Spirit of the nethermost Abyss
Might in that noise reside, of whom to ask
Which way the neerest coast of darkness lyes
Bordering on light; when strait behold the Throne

960. Of Chaos, and his dark Pavilion spread
Wide on the wasteful Deep; with him Enthron'd
Sat Sable-vested Night, eldest of things,
The Consort of his Reign; and by them stood

964. Orcus and Ades, and the dreaded name
Of Demogorgon; Rumor next and Chance,
And Tumult and Confusion all imbroild,
And Discord with a thousand various mouths.
    T' whom Satan turning boldly, thus. Ye Powers

969. And Spirits of this nethermost Abyss,
Chaos and ancient Night, I come no Spy,
With purpose to explore or to disturb

927. Finally, he spread his wings and flew out into it.

929. He flew up many miles.

931. He unexpectedly flew into a vacuum and started to fall.

934. He might have fallen forever, but a sudden strong wind blew him back up again.

938. Next, he ended up in an area that was like quicksand. He could barely make it through. He had to half fly and half walk.

943. He looked like a griffin chasing some thieves who stole his gold.

948. He flew or crept or swam or whatever he needed to do to get through all the different kinds of materials.

951. After a while he heard some kind of noisy racket.

954. He went to see who it was. Maybe they could give him directions.

960. It was King Chaos. Next to him sat Night.

964. There was also Rumor, Chance, Tumult, Confusion, and Discord—all yelling at each other.

969.   Satan explained to them that he didn't mean to disturb their home.

The secrets of your Realm, but by constraint
973. Wandring this darksome Desart, as my way
Lies through your spacious Empire up to light,
Alone, and without guide, half lost, I seek
What readiest path leads where your gloomie bounds
Confine with Heav'n; or if som other place
From your Dominion won, th' Ethereal King
Possesses lately, thither to arrive
980. I travel this profound, direct my course;
Directed no mean recompence it brings
982. To your behoof, if I that Region lost,
All usurpation thence expell'd, reduce
To her original darkness and your sway
(Which is my present journey) and once more
Erect the Standard there of ancient Night;
987. Yours be th' advantage all, mine the revenge.
988.   Thus Satan; and him thus the Anarch old
With faultring speech and visage incompos'd
Answer'd. I know thee, stranger, who thou art,
That mighty leading Angel, who of late
Made head against Heav'ns King, though overthrown.
993. I saw and heard, for such a numerous Host
Fled not in silence through the frighted deep
With ruin upon ruin, rout on rout,
Confusion worse confounded; and Heav'n Gates
Pourd out by millions her victorious Bands
Pursuing. I upon my Frontieres here
999. Keep residence; if all I can will serve,
That little which is left so to defend
Encroacht on still through our intestine broiles
Weakning the Scepter of old Night: first Hell
Your dungeon stretching far and wide beneath;
Now lately Heaven and Earth, another World
Hung ore my Realm, link'd in a golden Chain
To that side Heav'n from whence your Legions fell:
1007. If that way be your walk, you have not farr;
So much the neerer danger; go and speed;
Havock and spoil and ruin are my gain.
    He ceas'd; and Satan staid not to reply,
But glad that now his Sea should find a shore,
1012. With fresh alacritie and force renew'd
1013. Springs upward like a Pyramid of fire
Into the wilde expanse, and through the shock
Of fighting Elements, on all sides round
Environ'd wins his way; harder beset
1017. And more endanger'd, then when Argo pass'd
Through Bosporus betwixt the justling Rocks:
Or when Ulysses on the Larbord shunnd
Charybdis, and by th' other whirlpool steard.

973.   *"I was just passing through and got lost. I'm trying to find the way out of here, where your property ends and Heaven's light begins.*

980.   *If you can direct me there, there may be something in it for both of us.*

982.   *When I get there I'll win some of that area back for you.*

987.   *That way I'll get my revenge."*

988.   Chaos answered, *"I know all about you and your war.*

993.   *It was hard to miss your army being chased out of Heaven and all falling down into Hell, with all the racket you made. I saw and heard it all.*

999.   *I'm fed up with my domain being taken over—first by Hell, now by another whole universe that hangs by a chain from the Heaven you fell from.*

1007. *You don't have far to go. Go do what you have to do. It's all the better for me."*

1012. Satan regained his enthusiasm.

1013. He took off like a shot.

1017. He was facing worse dangers than Jason or Ulysses.

So he with difficulty and labour hard
1022. Mov'd on, with difficulty and labour hee;
But hee once past, soon after when man fell,
Strange alteration! Sin and Death amain
Following his track, such was the will of Heav'n,
Pav'd after him a broad and beat'n way
Over the dark Abyss, whose boiling Gulf
Tamely endur'd a Bridge of wondrous length
From Hell continu'd reaching th' utmost Orbe
Of this frail World; by which the Spirits perverse
With easie intercourse pass to and fro
To tempt or punish mortals, except whom
God and good Angels guard by special grace.
1034. But now at last the sacred influence
Of light appears, and from the walls of Heav'n
Shoots farr into the bosom of dim Night
A glimmering dawn; here Nature first begins
Her fardest verge, and Chaos to retire
As from her outmost works a brok'n foe
With tumult less and with less hostile din,
1041. That Satan with less toil, and now with ease
Wafts on the calmer wave by dubious light
1043. And like a weather-beaten Vessel holds
Gladly the Port, though Shrouds and Tackle torn;
Or in the emptier waste, resembling Air,
1046. Weighs his spread wings, at leasure to behold
Farr off th' Empyreal Heav'n, extended wide
In circuit, undetermind square or round,
1049. With Opal Towrs and Battlements adorn'd
Of living Saphire, once his native Seat;
1051. And fast by hanging in a golden Chain
1052. This pendant world, in bigness as a Starr
Of smallest Magnitude close by the Moon.
1054. Thither full fraught with mischievous revenge,
Accurst, and in a cursed hour he hies.

1022.   His journey was hard, but later Sin and Death would build a highway from Hell to Earth to be used by all the bad angels.

1034.   Satan began to see some of Heaven's light, and things started to get calmer.

1041.   Traveling got easier.

1043.   He was like a weather-beaten ship coming to shore.

1046.   He stopped to look at Heaven.

1049.   You could see towers made of gems.

1051.   Our little universe hung on a chain from Heaven.

1052.   It looked like a star next to the moon.

1054.   So that's exactly where Satan headed, with bad intentions.

Book III

1.   Hail holy light, ofspring of Heav'n first-born,
Or of th' Eternal Coeternal beam
May I express thee unblam'd? since God is light,
And never but in unapproached light
Dwelt from Eternitie, dwelt then in thee,
Bright effluence of bright essence increate.
Or hear'st thou rather pure Ethereal stream,

8.   Whose Fountain who shall tell? before the Sun,

9.   Before the Heavens thou wert, and at the voice
Of God, as with a Mantle didst invest
The rising world of waters dark and deep,
Won from the void and formless infinite.

13.   Thee I re-visit now with bolder wing,
Escap't the Stygian Pool, though long detain'd
In that obscure sojourn, while in my flight
Through utter and through middle darkness borne
With other notes then to th' Orphean Lyre
I sung of Chaos and Eternal Night,
Taught by the heav'nly Muse to venture down
The dark descent, and up to reascend,

21.   Though hard and rare: thee I revisit safe,
And feel thy sovran vital Lamp; but thou

23.   Revisit'st not these eyes, that rowle in vain
To find thy piercing ray, and find no dawn;
So thick a drop serene hath quencht thir Orbs,
Or dim suffusion veild. Yet not the more
Cease I to wander where the Muses haunt
Cleer Spring, or shadie Grove, or Sunnie Hill,

29.   Smit with the love of sacred Song; but chief
Thee Sion and the flowrie Brooks beneath
That wash thy hallowd feet, and warbling flow,

32.   Nightly I visit: nor somtimes forget
Those other two equal'd with me in Fate,
So were I equal'd with them in renown,
Blind Thamyris and blind Mæonides,
And Tiresias and Phineus Prophets old.
Then feed on thoughts, that voluntarie move

38.   Harmonious numbers; as the wakeful Bird
Sings darkling, and in shadiest Covert hid

40.   Tunes her nocturnal Note. Thus with the Year
Seasons return, but not to me returns
Day, or the sweet approach of Ev'n or Morn,

Chapter 3

IN PLAIN ENGLISH

1.   Hail, holy light. You were here forever, like God.

8. You were here before the sun.
9. When God said, "*Let there be light*," you came to light up the creation of the world.

13. I'm finished talking about Hell for a while.

21. Now I'm asking your light to shine on me.

23. I'm blind, so it won't help my eyes, but that doesn't stop me from enjoying hearing about beautiful places.

29. I love poetry, especially in the Bible.

32. There were many blind men in history and in legend who had great thoughts and wrote great poetry.

38. The nightingale sings beautifully in the dark.

40. The seasons change, day turns to night, there are flowers, birds, and beautiful faces. But I can't see any of it.

Or sight of vernal bloom, or Summers Rose,
Or flocks, or heards, or human face divine;
45. But cloud in stead, and ever-during dark
Surrounds me, from the chearful wayes of men
Cut off, and for the Book of knowledg fair
Presented with a Universal blanc
Of Nature's works to mee expung'd and ras'd,
And wisdome at one entrance quite shut out.
51. So much the rather thou Celestial light
Shine inward, and the mind through all her powers
Irradiate, there plant eyes, all mist from thence
Purge and disperse, that I may see and tell
Of things invisible to mortal sight.
56.   Now had the Almighty Father from above,
From the pure Empyrean where he sits
High Thron'd above all highth, bent down his eye,
His own works and their works at once to view:
60. About him all the Sanctities of Heaven
Stood thick as Starrs, and from his sight receiv'd
62. Beatitude past utterance; on his right
The radiant image of his Glory sat,
64. His onely Son; On Earth he first beheld
Our two first Parents, yet the onely two
Of mankind, in the happie Garden plac't,
Reaping immortal fruits of joy and love,
Uninterrupted joy, unrivald love
69. In blissful solitude; he then survey'd
Hell and the Gulf between, and Satan there
Coasting the wall of Heav'n on this side Night
In the dun Air sublime, and ready now
To stoop with wearied wings, and willing feet
On the bare outside of this World, that seem'd
75. Firm land imbosom'd without Firmament,
Uncertain which, in Ocean or in Air.
77. Him God beholding from his prospect high,
Wherein past, present, future he beholds,
Thus to his onely Son foreseeing spake.
80.   Onely begotten Son, seest thou what rage
Transports our adversarie, whom no bounds
Prescrib'd, no barrs of Hell, nor all the chains
Heapt on him there, nor yet the main Abyss
84. Wide interrupt can hold; so bent he seems
On desparate reveng, that shall redound
86. Upon his own rebellious head. And now
Through all restraint broke loose he wings his way
Not farr off Heav'n, in the Precincts of light,
Directly towards the new created World,
And Man there plac't, with purpose to assay
If him by force he can destroy, or worse,
92. By some false guile pervert; and shall pervert

45.   I can't learn anything by looking around.

51.   So please shine your light inside me so I'll be able to see and tell about things people can't see.

56.   Now I'm imagining how God looked down on his creation from Heaven.

60.   All the angels were gathered around him. They were greatly blessed just by being in his presence.

62.   His son, Messiah, sat on his right side.

64.   God saw Adam and Eve enjoying the Garden of Eden.

69.   He looked down into Hell and all the way up to the dark side of Heaven. There he saw Satan getting ready to land on the outer shell of our universe.

75.   It looked like a big globe full of water or air.

77.   God watched Satan and knew everything, past, present, and future.

80.   He said to his son, *"See how angry Satan is. Neither the prison of Hell, nor the wildness of chaos can stop him.*

84.   *He's looking for revenge, but it will only fall back on him.*

86.   *He's headed for Earth. He wants to find out if he can destroy man by force or by trickery.*

92.   *He will succeed in tricking man, who will believe his lies and commit sin.*

For man will heark'n to his glozing lyes,
And easily transgress the sole Command,

95. Sole pledge of his obedience: So will fall,
Hee and his faithless Progenie: whose fault?

97. Whose but his own? ingrate, he had of mee
All he could have; I made him just and right,
Sufficient to have stood, though free to fall.

100. Such I created all th' Ethereal Powers
And Spirits, both them who stood and them who faild;
Freely they stood who stood, and fell who fell.

103. Not free, what proof could they have givn sincere
Of true allegiance, constant Faith or Love,
Where onely what they needs must do, appeard,
Not what they would? what praise could they receive?

107. What pleasure I from such obedience paid,
When Will and Reason (Reason also is choice)
Useless and vain, of freedom both despoild,
Made passive both, had servd necessitie,
Not mee. They therefore as to right belongd,

112. So were created, nor can justly accuse
Thir maker, or thir making, or thir Fate,
As if predestination over-rul'd
Thir will, dispos'd by absolute Decree
Or high foreknowledge; they themselves decreed

117. Thir own revolt, not I: if I foreknew,
Foreknowledge had no influence on their fault,
Which had no less prov'd certain unforeknown.
So without least impulse or shadow of Fate,
Or aught by me immutablie foreseen,

122. They trespass, Authors to themselves in all
Both what they judge and what they choose; for so

124. I formd them free, and free they must remain,

125. Till they enthrall themselves: I else must change
Thir nature, and revoke the high Decree
Unchangeable, Eternal, which ordain'd

128. Thir freedom, they themselves ordain'd thir fall.
The first sort by thir own suggestion fell,
Self-tempted, self-deprav'd: Man falls deceiv'd

131. By the other first: Man therefore shall find grace,

132. The other none: in Mercy and Justice both,
Through Heav'n and Earth, so shall my glorie excel,
But Mercy first and last shall brightest shine.

135.   Thus while God spake, ambrosial fragrance fill'd
All Heav'n, and in the blessed Spirits elect
Sense of new joy ineffable diffus'd:

138. Beyond compare the Son of God was seen
Most glorious, in him all his Father shon
Substantially express'd, and in his face
Divine compassion visibly appeerd,
Love without end, and without measure Grace,

95. *Man will fall and cause the downfall of all future men.*

97. *It will be his own fault. I gave him every chance to succeed.*

100. *I gave the same freedom to all the angels—the ones who succeeded, as well as the ones who fell.*

103. *Without freedom, how could they prove their faith or love? They would only be doing what they were forced to do.*

107. *What pleasure would I get from that?*

112. *They can't blame me for their failure.*

117. *The fact that I can see the future has no effect on their free will.*

122. *They are responsible for all their thoughts and actions.*

124. *I created them free and they will remain free unless they become slaves to sin.*

125. *To prevent this, I would have to change their nature, and take away their freedom.*

128. *They changed themselves—Satan and his followers by their own plan—Adam and Eve by being tricked and lied to.*

131. *So I will forgive them, but not Satan.*

132. *I will give justice and mercy, but mostly mercy."*

135. When God spoke, the air was filled with sweet fragrance and the angels felt happy.

138. God's son looked glorious. His face showed kindness and unlimited love. He expressed this in his words also.

Which uttering thus he to his Father spake.

144.   O Father, gracious was that word which clos'd
Thy sovran sentence, that Man should find grace;
For which both Heav'n and Earth shall high extoll
Thy praises, with th' innumerable sound
Of Hymns and sacred Songs, wherewith thy Throne
Encompass'd shall resound thee ever blest.

150. For should Man finally be lost, should Man
Thy creature late so lov'd, thy youngest Son
Fall circumvented thus by fraud, though joynd
With his own folly? that be from thee farr,
That farr be from thee, Father, who art Judg
Of all things made, and judgest onely right.

156. Or shall the Adversarie thus obtain
His end, and frustrate thine, shall he fulfill
His malice, and thy goodness bring to naught,
Or proud return though to his heavier doom,
Yet with revenge accomplish't and to Hell
Draw after him the whole Race of mankind,

162. By him corrupted? or wilt thou thy self
Abolish thy Creation, and unmake,
For him, what for thy glorie thou hast made?

165. So should thy goodness and thy greatness both
Be questiond and blaspheam'd without defence.

167.   To whom the great Creatour thus reply'd.
O Son, in whom my Soul hath chief delight,
Son of my bosom, Son who art alone
My word, my wisdom, and effectual might,

171. All hast thou spok'n as my thoughts are, all
As my Eternal purpose hath decreed:

173. Man shall not quite be lost, but sav'd who will,
Yet not of will in him, but grace in me
Freely voutsaft; once more I will renew
His lapsed powers, though forfeit and enthrall'd
By sin to foul exorbitant desires;
Upheld by me, yet once more he shall stand
On even ground against his mortal foe,

180. By me upheld, that he may know how frail
His fall'n condition is, and to me ow
All his deliv'rance, and to none but me.

183. Some I have chosen of peculiar grace
Elect above the rest; so is my will:

185. The rest shall hear me call, and oft be warnd
Thir sinful state, and to appease betimes
Th' incensed Deitie while offerd grace
Invites; for I will cleer thir senses dark,
What may suffice, and soft'n stonie hearts
To pray, repent, and bring obedience due.
To Prayer, repentance, and obedience due,
Though but endevord with sincere intent,

144.   "*Father, you will be highly praised with songs in Heaven and Earth for promising to forgive man.*

150.   *After all, why should you give up on man because he was tricked into sinning? You love him, and you always do the right thing.*

156.   *And we certainly don't want Satan to succeed and ruin all your hopes for man, and proudly return to Hell, where he would like to bring the whole human race.*

162.   *And of course you wouldn't want to destroy your own whole creation yourself out of anger.*

165.   *That would make everybody mad at you, and who could blame them?"*

167.   "*Son,*" answered the father, "*You know I love you most. You're the only one who has the same wisdom and power as I have.*

171.   *Everything you said is the same as what I was thinking.*

173.   *Some men will be saved if they want to be—but only because I give them the power to fight Satan's evil.*

180.   *Man is weak, and he will learn that he needs me. Nobody else can save him.*

183.   *I will pick some of them as my favorites.*

185.   *I'll warn the rest that they better repent while there's still time.*

193. Mine ear shall not be slow, mine eye not shut.
194. And I will place within them as a guide
      My Umpire Conscience, whom if they will hear,
      Light after light well us'd they shall attain,
      And to the end persisting, safe arrive.
198. This my long sufferance and my day of grace
      They who neglect and scorn, shall never taste;
      But hard be hard'nd, blind be blinded more,
      That they may stumble on, and deeper fall;
      And none but such from mercy I exclude.
203. But yet all is not don; Man disobeying,
      Disloyal breaks his fealtie, and sinns
      Against the high Supremacie of Heav'n,
      Affecting God-head, and so loosing all,
      To expiate his Treason hath naught left,
      But to destruction sacred and devote,
      He with his whole posteritie must dye,
210. Dye hee or Justice must; unless for him
      Som other able, and as willing, pay
      The rigid satisfaction, death for death.
213. Say Heav'nly Powers, where shall we find such love,
214. Which of ye will be mortal to redeem
      Mans mortal crime, and just th' unjust to save,
      Dwels in all Heaven charitie so deare?
          He ask'd, but all the Heav'nly Quire stood mute,
218. And silence was in Heav'n: on mans behalf
      Patron or Intercessor none appeerd,
      Much less that durst upon his own head draw
      The deadly forfeiture, and ransom set.
222. And now without redemption all mankind
      Must have bin lost, adjudg'd to Death and Hell
      By doom severe, had not the Son of God,
      In whom the fulness dwells of love divine,
      His dearest mediation thus renewd.
227.   Father, thy word is past, man shall find grace;
      And shall grace not find means, that finds her way,
      The speediest of thy winged messengers,
230. To visit all thy creatures, and to all
      Comes unprevented, unimplor'd, unsought,
232. Happie for man, so coming; he her aide
      Can never seek, once dead in sins and lost;
      Attonement for himself or offering meet,
      Indebted and undon, hath none to bring:
236. Behold mee then, mee for him, life for life
      I offer, on mee let thine anger fall;
238. Account mee man; I for his sake will leave
      Thy bosom, and this glorie next to thee
      Freely put off, and for him lastly dye
      Well pleas'd, on me let Death wreck all his rage;
242. Under his gloomie power I shall not long

193. *I will pay attention to their prayers if they are sincere.*

194. *I'll give them a conscience that will protect and guide them, if they listen.*

198. *Those who won't listen will sink deeper into trouble and get no mercy from me.*

203. *But there's something else to consider. After man sins against me, there would be nothing left for me to do but kill him.*

210. *If I didn't kill him, I would be killing justice—unless somebody else is willing to take his place, become human and die for him.*

213. *Is any one of you up to it?"*

214.   Nobody stepped up.

218. None of the angels even spoke up on man's behalf, let alone offered to die for him.

222. So now the whole human race would have died and gone to Hell if the Son of God hadn't come forward.

227.   *"Father,"* he said, *"you said man will find grace, so there's no doubt it will happen.*

230. *You send grace to everybody without being asked.*

232. *But in the shape he'll be in, he couldn't even ask.*

236. *Okay then, I'll do it. I'll offer my life. You can pretend I'm man and be angry at me.*

238. *I'll give up Heaven. I'll become human and let Death have his way with me.*

242. *I won't suffer long. You gave me eternal life. As much of me as can die will die, but you won't leave me in the grave.*

Lie vanquisht; thou hast givn me to possess
Life in my self for ever, by thee I live,
Though now to Death I yield, and am his due
All that of me can die, yet that debt paid,
Thou wilt not leave me in the loathsom grave
His prey, nor suffer my unspotted Soule
For ever with corruption there to dwell;
250. But I shall rise Victorious, and subdue
My Vanquisher, spoild of his vanted spoile;
Death his deaths wound shall then receive, and stoop
Inglorious, of his mortal sting disarm'd.
254. I through the ample Air in Triumph high
Shall lead Hell Captive maugre Hell, and show
256. The powers of darkness bound. Thou at the sight
Pleas'd, out of Heaven shalt look down and smile,
258. While by thee rais'd I ruin all my Foes,
Death last, and with his Carcass glut the Grave:
260. Then with the multitude of my redeemd
Shall enter Heaven long absent, and returne,
262. Father, to see thy face, wherein no cloud
Of anger shall remain, but peace assur'd,
And reconcilement; wrauth shall be no more
Thenceforth, but in thy presence Joy entire.
266.   His words here ended, but his meek aspect
Silent yet spake, and breath'd immortal love
To mortal men, above which only shon
Filial obedience: as a sacrifice
Glad to be offer'd, he attends the will
271. Of his great Father. Admiration seis'd
All Heav'n, what this might mean, and whither tend
Wondring; but soon th' Almighty thus reply'd:
274.   O thou in Heav'n and Earth the only peace
Found out for mankind under wrauth, O thou
My sole complacence! well thou know'st how dear,
To me are all my works, nor Man the least
278. Though last created, that for him I spare
Thee from my bosom and right hand, to save,
By loosing thee a while, the whole Race lost.
281. Thou therefore whom thou only canst redeem,
Thir Nature also to thy Nature joyn;
And be thy self Man among men on Earth,
284. Made flesh, when time shall be, of Virgin seed,
285. By wondrous birth: Be thou in Adams room
The Head of all mankind, though Adams Son.
As in him perish all men, so in thee
As from a second root shall be restor'd,
As many as are restor'd, without thee none.
290. His crime makes guiltie all his Sons, thy merit
Imputed shall absolve them who renounce
Thir own both righteous and unrighteous deeds,

250. *I will rise up and kill Death.*

254. *I'll seal up Hell and end all its powers.*

256. *You'll like that.*

258. *I'll kill all my enemies and use Death's body to seal up their grave.*

260. *Then I'll bring all the saved souls up to Heaven.*

262. *We'll be reunited and you won't be angry anymore. You'll be spreading peace and joy."*

266.   He was glad to make this sacrifice out of love for mankind, but mostly to please his father.

271. The angels admired him. They wondered what the end result of all this would be.

274.   God said, "*You are mankind's only hope. You put my mind at ease, knowing how precious all my works are to me, especially mankind.*

278. *You will leave me for a while, but the whole human race will be saved.*

281. *Only you can save them, so go and become one of them, when the time is right.*

284. *You will magically be born from a virgin.*

285. *You'll take Adam's place as head of all mankind. Where he was the cause of their destruction, you will be their second chance for salvation.*

290. *They all share his guilt, but if they become reborn in you, they will be forgiven.*

And live in thee transplanted, and from thee
294. Receive new life. So Man, as is most just,
Shall satisfie for Man, be judg'd and die,
And dying rise, and rising with him raise
His Brethren, ransomd with his own dear life.
So Heav'nly love shall outdoo Hellish hate,
Giving to death, and dying to redeeme,
300. So dearly to redeem what Hellish hate
So easily destroy'd, and still destroyes
In those who, when they may, accept not grace.
303. Nor shalt thou by descending to assume
Mans Nature, less'n or degrade thine owne.
305. Because thou hast, though Thron'd in highest bliss
Equal to God, and equally enjoying
God-like fruition, quitted all to save
A World from utter loss, and hast been found
By Merit more then Birthright Son of God,
Found worthiest to be so by being Good,
Farr more then Great or High; because in thee
Love hath abounded more then Glory abounds,
313. Therefore thy Humiliation shall exalt
With thee thy Manhood also to this Throne;
Here shalt thou sit incarnate, here shalt Reign
Both God and Man, Son both of God and Man,
317. Anointed universal King, all Power
I give thee, reign for ever, and assume
Thy Merits; under thee as Head Supream
Thrones, Princedoms, Powers, Dominions I reduce:
All knees to thee shall bow, of them that bide
In Heaven, or Earth, or under Earth in Hell;
323. When thou attended gloriously from Heav'n
Shalt in the Sky appeer, and from thee send
The summoning Arch-Angels to proclaime
Thy dread Tribunal: forthwith from all Windes
The living, and forthwith the cited dead
Of all past Ages to the general Doom
Shall hast'n, such a peal shall rouse thir sleep.
330. Then all thy Saints assembl'd, thou shalt judge
Bad men and Angels, they arraignd shall sink
Beneath thy Sentence; Hell her numbers full,
Thenceforth shall be for ever shut. Mean while
334. The World shall burn, and from her ashes spring
New Heav'n and Earth, wherein the just shall dwell
336. And after all thir tribulations long
See golden days, fruitful of golden deeds,
With Joy and Love triumphing, and fair Truth.
339. Then thou thy regal Scepter shalt lay by,
For regal Scepter then no more shall need,
341. God shall be All in All. But all ye Gods,
Adore him, who to compass all this dies,

294. *Only a man can stand for mankind, so go and be judged as a man, die, and rise up again, and save everybody that way.*

300. *You can undo all the damage that Hell does, except for those who refuse your help.*

303. *Don't think that because you become a human your glory will be lessened.*

305. *By giving up your place in Heaven to save the world, you show yourself to be even more worthy to be the Son of God.*

313. *When you come back to Heaven, you will keep your human form forever.*

317. *I will give you all the power to reign as king over Heaven and Earth and Hell, forever.*

323. *When doomsday comes, you'll appear in the sky and all the dead of past ages will come to be judged.*

330. *You'll send all the bad men and angels to fill up Hell, and seal it up forever.*

334. *The Earth will burn, and out of the ashes a new heavenly Earth will grow where all the good souls will live forever.*

336. *After all their hard times, everybody will enjoy peace and happiness.*

339. *You won't even have to act like a king anymore, because everybody will be a part of you.*

341. *Now all you angels, let me hear you give my son the praise he deserves."*

Adore the Son, and honour him as mee.

344.   No sooner had th' Almighty ceas't, but all
The multitude of Angels with a shout
Loud as from numbers without number, sweet
As from blest voices, uttering joy, Heav'n rung
With Jubilee, and loud Hosanna's filld
Th' eternal Regions: lowly reverent

350. Towards either Throne they bow, and to the ground
With solemn adoration down they cast
Thir Crowns inwove with Amarant and Gold,

353. Immortal Amarant, a Flour which once
In Paradise, fast by the Tree of Life
Began to bloom, but soon for mans offence
To Heav'n remov'd where first it grew, there grows,
And flours aloft shading the Fount of Life,
And where the river of Bliss through midst of Heavn
Rowls o're Elisian Flours her Amber stream;

360. With these that never fade the Spirits elect
Bind thir resplendent locks inwreath'd with beams,

362. Now in loose Garlands thick thrown off, the bright
Pavement that like a Sea of Jasper shon
Impurpl'd with Celestial Roses smil'd.

365. Then Crown'd again thir gold'n Harps they took,
Harps ever tun'd, that glittering by thir side
Like Quivers hung, and with Præamble sweet
Of charming symphonie they introduce
Thir sacred Song, and waken raptures high;

370. No voice exempt, no voice but well could joine
Melodious part, such concord is in Heav'n.

372.   Thee Father first they sung Omnipotent,
Immutable, Immortal, Infinite,
Eternal King; thee Author of all being,
Fountain of Light, thy self invisible
Amidst the glorious brightness where thou sit'st
Thron'd inaccessible, but when thou shad'st
The full blaze of thy beams, and through a cloud
Drawn round about thee like a radiant Shrine,
Dark with excessive bright thy skirts appeer,
Yet dazle Heav'n, that brightest Seraphim
Approach not, but with both wings veil thir eyes,

383. Thee next they sang of all Creation first,
Begotten Son, Divine Similitude,
In whose conspicuous count'nance, without cloud
Made visible, th' Almighty Father shines,
Whom else no Creature can behold; on thee
Impresst the effulgence of his Glorie abides,
Transfus'd on thee his ample Spirit rests.

390. Hee Heav'n of Heavens and all the Powers therein
By thee created, and by thee threw down
Th' Aspiring Dominations: thou that day

344.   The angels cheered loudly.

350.   They bowed to each throne and threw the gold crowns they wore on the ground.

353.   The crowns were decorated with a flower that used to grow in the Garden of Eden. But after man sinned it was removed from Earth and brought back to Heaven where it came from.

360.   These flowers never fade. The angels use them to tie up their hair.

362.   Now they were all over the ground, making it look like a sea of green jewels.

365.   They picked them all up and put the crowns back on their heads and took the harps they carried and started to play.

370.   They all started to sing in perfect harmony.

372.   They sang about how God's brightness was so bright they could only look at him when he was in a mist, and how even then they had to shade their eyes with their wings.

383.   Then they sang about the Son, who they could see, even though he had all the same bright glory as his father.

390.   They sang about how God sent his Son to fight the bad angels in his chariot.

Thy Fathers dreadful Thunder didst not spare,
Nor stop thy flaming Chariot wheels, that shook
Heav'ns everlasting Frame, while o're the necks
Thou drov'st of warring Angels disarraid.
Back from pursuit thy Powers with loud acclaime
Thee only extoll'd, Son of thy Fathers might,
To execute fierce vengeance on his foes,
400. Not so on Man; him through their malice fall'n,
Father of Mercie and Grace, thou didst not doome
So strictly, but much more to pitie encline:
403. No sooner did thy dear and onely Son
Perceive thee purpos'd not to doom frail Man
So strictly, but much more to pitie enclin'd,
He to appease thy wrauth, and end the strife
Of Mercy and Justice in thy face discern'd,
Regardless of the Bliss wherein hee sat
Second to thee, offerd himself to die
410. For mans offence. O unexampl'd love,
Love no where to be found less then Divine!
Hail Son of God, Saviour of Men, thy Name
Shall be the copious matter of my Song
Henceforth, and never shall my Harp thy praise
Forget, nor from thy Fathers praise disjoine.
416.   Thus they in Heav'n, above the starry Sphear,
Thir happie hours in joy and hymning spent.
Mean while upon the firm opacous Globe
Of this round World, whose first convex divides
The luminous inferior Orbs, enclos'd
From Chaos and th' inroad of Darkness old,
422. Satan alighted walks: a Globe farr off
It seem'd, now seems a boundless Continent
Dark, waste, and wild, under the frown of Night
Starless expos'd, and ever-threatning storms
Of Chaos blustring round, inclement skie;
427. Save on that side which from the wall of Heav'n
Though distant farr some small reflection gaines
Of glimmering air less vext with tempest loud:
430. Here walk'd the Fiend at large in spacious field.
As when a Vultur on Imaus bred,
Whose snowie ridge the roving Tartar bounds,
Dislodging from a Region scarce of prey
To gorge the flesh of Lambs or yeanling Kids
On Hills where Flocks are fed, flies toward the Springs
Of Ganges or Hydaspes, Indian streams;
But in his way lights on the barren Plaines
Of Sericana, where Chineses drive
With Sails and Wind thir canie Waggons light:
440. So on this windie Sea of Land, the Fiend
Walk'd up and down alone bent on his prey,
442. Alone, for other Creature in this place

400. They sang about his merciful attitude toward man.

403. They sang about the Son's offer to sacrifice himself.

410. They sang praises to the Son's great love, and swore never to stop praising him, as well as his father.

416.   While they were celebrating in Heaven, Satan was walking on the surface of the globe that contained the universe.

422. It looked like a big, dark, endless land. There were wild storms all around.

427. In the distance some of the light from Heaven reflected down on it, and it seemed a little calmer there.

430. Satan was like a vulture that came from the mountains where Genghis Kahn roamed, where there was no prey, and was headed towards the hills by the rivers in India where it could find lambs and goats, but on its way it landed on the barren plains in China, where it was so windy the people traveled in sail-powered wagons.

440. Satan walked up and down on the windy land.

442. He was completely alone.

Living or liveless to be found was none,

444. None yet, but store hereafter from the earth
Up hither like Aereal vapours flew
Of all things transitorie and vain, when Sin
With vanity had filld the works of men:
Both all things vain, and all who in vain things
Built thir fond hopes of Glorie or lasting fame,
Or happiness in this or th' other life;
All who have thir reward on Earth, the fruits
Of painful Superstition and blind Zeal,
Naught seeking but the praise of men, here find
Fit retribution, emptie as thir deeds;

455. All th' unaccomplisht works of Natures hand,
Abortive, monstrous, or unkindly mixt,
Dissolvd on earth, fleet hither, and in vain,

458. Till final dissolution, wander here,
Not in the neighbouring Moon, as some have dreamd;

460. Those argent Fields more likely habitants,
Translated Saints, or middle Spirits hold
Betwixt th' Angelical and Human kinde:

463. Hither of ill-joynd Sons and Daughters born
First from the ancient World those Giants came
With many a vain exploit, though then renownd:
The builders next of Babel on the Plain
Of Sennaar, and still with vain designe
New Babels, had they wherewithall, would build:

469. Others came single; he who to be deem'd
A God, leap'd fondly into Ætna flames
Empedocles, and hee who to enjoy
Plato's Elysium, leap'd into the Sea,
Cleombrotus, and many more too long,
Embryo's and Idiots, Eremits and Friers
White, Black and Grey, with all thir trumperie.
Here Pilgrims roam, that stray'd so farr to seek
In Golgotha him dead, who lives in Heav'n;

478. And they who to be sure of Paradise
Dying put on the weeds of Dominic,
Or in Franciscan think to pass disguis'd;

481. They pass the Planets seven, and pass the fixt,
And that Crystalline Sphear whose ballance weighs
The Trepidation talkt, and that first mov'd;
And now Saint Peter at Heav'ns Wicket seems
To wait them with his Keys, and now at foot

486. Of Heav'ns ascent they lift thir Feet, when loe
A violent cross wind from either Coast
Blows them transverse ten thousand Leagues awry
Into the devious Air; then might ye see

490. Cowles, Hoods and Habits with thir wearers tost
And flutterd into Raggs, then Reliques, Beads,
Indulgences, Dispenses, Pardons, Bulls,

444. But someday this land would be full of people who had stupidly based their lives on fame or fortune on Earth.

455. Here they would find nature in a mixed up, empty state, just like their worthless lives.

458. Here's where they'd be wandering until God was ready to deal with them—not on the moon, like some people think.

460. The moon was more likely a stopping place for certain people who were allowed to come to Heaven in their human bodies.

463. But this dark plain was for the giants who were born half-angel and half-human, and the ones who built the Tower of Babel.

469. There would also be all the stupid philosophers who committed suicide because they thought they were like gods, and all the phony Christian orders with all their showy nonsense, and those who make pilgrimages to the hill where the crucifixion took place, as if Jesus was still there.

478. Some would disguise themselves as followers of Saint Dominic or Saint Francis, to get into Heaven.

481. They would get past the seven planets and the sun all right, right up to where Saint Peter would seem to wait for them at Heaven's gate with his keys.

486. But as soon as they lifted a foot to step on the ladder to Heaven, a violent crosswind would blow them thousands of miles sideways.

490. Their hoods and robes, Rosaries and various religious documents would be torn and scattered all over the place.

493. The sport of Winds: all these upwhirld aloft
      Fly o're the backside of the World farr off
      Into a Limbo large and broad, since calld
      The Paradise of Fools, to few unknown
      Long after, now unpeopl'd, and untrod;
498. All this dark Globe the Fiend found as he pass'd,
499. And long he wanderd, till at last a gleame
      Of dawning light turnd thither-ward in haste
501. His travell'd steps; farr distant he descries
      Ascending by degrees magnificent
      Up to the wall of Heaven a Structure high,
      At top whereof, but farr more rich appeer'd
      The work as of a Kingly Palace Gate
      With Frontispice of Diamond and Gold
      Imbellisht, thick with sparkling orient Gemmes
      The Portal shon, inimitable on Earth
509. By Model, or by shading Pencil drawn.
510. The Stairs were such as whereon Jacob saw
      Angels ascending and descending, bands
      Of Guardians bright, when he from Esau fled
      To Padan-Aram in the field of Luz,
      Dreaming by night under the open Skie,
      And waking cri'd, This is the Gate of Heav'n
516. Each Stair mysteriously was meant, nor stood
517. There alwayes, but drawn up to Heav'n somtimes
518. Viewless, and underneath a bright Sea flow'd
      Of Jasper, or of liquid Pearle, whereon
520. Who after came from Earth, sayling arriv'd,
      Wafted by Angels, or flew o're the Lake
      Rapt in a Chariot drawn by fiery Steeds.
523. The Stairs were then let down, whether to dare
      The Fiend by easie ascent, or aggravate
      His sad exclusion from the dores of Bliss.
526. Direct against which opn'd from beneath,
      Just o're the blissful seat of Paradise,
      A passage down to th' Earth, a passage wide,
529. Wider by farr then that of after-times
      Over Mount Sion, and, though that were large,
      Over the Promis'd Land to God so dear,
      By which, to visit oft those happy Tribes,
      On high behests his Angels to and fro
      Pass'd frequent, and his eye with choice regard
      From Paneas the fount of Jordans flood
      To Beersaba, where the Holy Land
      Borders on Ægypt and th' Arabian shoare;
538. So wide the op'ning seemd, where bounds were set
      To darkness, such as bound the Ocean wave.
540. Satan from hence now on the lower stair
      That scal'd by steps of Gold to Heav'n Gate
      Looks down with wonder at the sudden view

493. These are all the souls that would be thrown into this place they would call Limbo or the Paradise of Fools.

498. But it was all empty now as Satan wandered around.
499. Finally he saw a glimmer of light in the distance and ran towards it.
501. He found a magnificent staircase leading up to the wall of Heaven. There was a palace gate at the top full of diamonds and gold and other jewels.

509. There was never anything like it on Earth, not even in paintings.
510. This is where Jacob thought he saw angels going up and down a ladder.

516. Each step on the staircase had a secret meaning.
517. The staircase would be hidden up in Heaven, to be let down when needed.
518. A pearl colored sea was underneath it.

520. Whoever came from Earth would come floating on or above the sea in chariots.

523. Now the stairs were down, either to dare Satan to try to climb them, or to taunt him by showing him where he could not go.

526. Right under the stairs was a big opening down into the interior of the globe of the universe.

529. It was much wider than the one over Mount Zion, where God would later send his angels on many missions to Earth.

538. It kept chaos out the way a dam holds back the sea.

540. Satan stood on the bottom step of Heaven's staircase and looked down into the universe.

543. Of all this World at once. As when a Scout
     Through dark and desart wayes with peril gone
     All night; at last by break of chearful dawne
     Obtains the brow of some high-climbing Hill,
     Which to his eye discovers unaware
     The goodly prospect of some forein land
     First-seen, or some renown'd Metropolis
     With glistering Spires and Pinnacles adorn'd,
     Which now the Rising Sun guilds with his beams.
552. Such wonder seis'd, though after Heaven seen,
     The Spirit maligne, but much more envy seis'd
     At sight of all this World beheld so faire.
555. Round he surveys, and well might, where he stood
     So high above the circling Canopie
     Of Nights extended shade; from Eastern Point
     Of Libra to the fleecie Starr that bears
     Andromeda farr off Atlantic Seas
     Beyond th' Horizon; then from Pole to Pole
561. He views in bredth, and without longer pause
     Down right into the Worlds first Region throws
563. His flight precipitant, and windes with ease
     Through the pure marble Air his oblique way
565. Amongst innumerable Starrs, that shon
     Stars distant, but nigh hand seemd other Worlds,
     Or other Worlds they seemd, or happy Iles,
     Like those Hesperian Gardens fam'd of old,
     Fortunate Fields, and Groves and flourie Vales,
570. Thrice happy Iles, but who dwelt happy there
571. He stayd not to enquire: above them all
     The golden Sun in splendor likest Heaven
573. Allur'd his eye: Thither his course he bends
     Through the calm Firmament; but up or downe
     By center, or eccentric, hard to tell,
     Or Longitude, where the great Luminarie
     Alooff the vulgar Constellations thick,
     That from his Lordly eye keep distance due,
579. Dispenses Light from farr; they as they move
     Thir Starry dance in numbers that compute
     Days, months, & years, towards his all-chearing Lamp
     Turn swift thir various motions, or are turnd
583. By his Magnetic beam, that gently warms
     The Univers, and to each inward part
     With gentle penetration, though unseen,
     Shoots invisible vertue even to the deep:
     So wondrously was set his Station bright.
588. There lands the Fiend, a spot like which perhaps
     Astronomer in the Sun's lucent Orbe
     Through his glaz'd Optic Tube yet never saw.
591. The place he found beyond expression bright,
592. Compar'd with aught on Earth, Medal or Stone;

543. It was like when a scout climbs a high hill by the morning light and is surprised to see a spectacular view of some undiscovered city.

552. Satan felt intense jealousy.

555. He took in the whole panoramic view of the cosmos from Libra to Andromeda.

561. He flew down into the universe.

563. It was easy to fly through the clear air.

565. He passed innumerable stars. They were pinpoints in the distance, but close up were like whole worlds that could provide pleasant habitats.

570. But he wasn't interested in any of them.
571. His attention was on the brightest one—the sun that shined like Heaven.
573. He headed there, but it's hard to explain what direction he took.

579. The stars moved around the sun. They would be used to count days, months, and years.

583. The sun's warm rays penetrated every part of the universe.

588. Satan landed on the sun, on a spot no astronomer probably ever saw.
591. It was very bright.
592. Everything on the sun's surface glowed, like all kinds of precious metals and precious stones.

Not all parts like, but all alike informd
With radiant light, as glowing Iron with fire;
If mettal, part seemd Gold, part Silver cleer;
If stone, Carbuncle most or Chrysolite,
Rubie or Topaz, to the Twelve that shon

598. In Aarons Brest-plate, and a stone besides
Imagind rather oft then elsewhere seen,
That stone, or like to that which here below
Philosophers in vain so long have sought,
In vain, though by thir powerful Art they binde
Volatil Hermes, and call up unbound
In various shapes old Proteus from the Sea,
Draind through a Limbec to his Native forme.

606. What wonder then if fields and region here
Breathe forth Elixir pure, and Rivers run
Potable Gold, when with one vertuous touch
Th' Arch-chimic Sun so farr from us remote
Produces with Terrestrial Humor mixt
Here in the dark so many precious things
Of colour glorious and effect so rare?

613. Here matter new to gaze the Devil met
Undazl'd, farr and wide his eye commands,

615. For sight no obstacle found here, nor shade,

616. But all Sun-shine, as when his Beams at Noon
Culminate from th' Æquator, as they now

618. Shot upward still direct, whence no way round
Shadow from body opaque can fall, and the Aire,

620. No where so cleer, sharp'nd his visual ray

621. To objects distant farr, whereby he soon
Saw within kenn a glorious Angel stand,
The same whom John saw also in the Sun:
His back was turnd, but not his brightness hid;
Of beaming sunnie Raies, a golden tiar
Circl'd his Head, nor less his Locks behind
Illustrious on his Shoulders fledge with wings
Lay waving round; on som great charge imploy'd

629. He seemd, or fixt in cogitation deep.

630. Glad was the Spirit impure as now in hope
To find who might direct his wandring flight
To Paradise the happie seat of Man,
His journies end and our beginning woe.
But first he casts to change his proper shape,
Which else might work him danger or delay:

636. And now a stripling Cherube he appeers,
Not of the prime, yet such as in his face
Youth smil'd Celestial, and to every Limb
Sutable grace diffus'd, so well he feign'd;
Under a Coronet his flowing haire

641. In curles on either cheek plaid, wings he wore
Of many a colourd plume sprinkl'd with Gold,

598. You might even find something like the famous magic "philos-
opher's stone" that turned metals into gold.

606. When you think how the sun's rays produce such colorful
plants and flowers from so far away, it's no wonder you can
find things like rivers of gold on the sun.

613. Looking around, Satan saw things he never saw before, but
the brightness didn't hurt his eyes.
615. Nothing blocked his view.
616. It was like being on Earth at the equator at high noon.

618. The sun's beams shot upward here, instead of downward, as
on Earth. So there couldn't be any shadows.
620. The air was so clear that he could see very far.
621. In the distance he saw a bright angel with a gold halo stand-
ing with his back to him.

629. He seemed to be in deep thought, while holding some impor-
tant post.
630. Satan became excited and immediately began to plot how to
get this angel to direct him where to find man.

636. He changed his shape into a charming, curly-haired, young
cherub.

641. He had multi-colored wings, sprinkled with gold, and held a
silver wand.

His habit fit for speed succinct, and held
Before his decent steps a Silver wand.

645. He drew not nigh unheard, the Angel bright,
Ere he drew nigh, his radiant visage turnd,
Admonisht by his ear, and strait was known

648. Th' Arch-Angel Uriel, one of the seav'n
Who in God's presence, neerest to his Throne
Stand ready at command, and are his Eyes
That run through all the Heav'ns, or down to th' Earth
Bear his swift errands over moist and dry,
O're Sea and Land; him Satan thus accostes;

654.   Uriel, for thou of those seav'n Spirits that stand
In sight of God's high Throne, gloriously bright,
The first art wont his great authentic will
Interpreter through highest Heav'n to bring,
Where all his Sons thy Embassie attend;
And here art likeliest by supream decree
Like honor to obtain, and as his Eye
To visit oft this new Creation round;

662. Unspeakable desire to see, and know
All these his wondrous works, but chiefly Man,
His chief delight and favour, him for whom
All these his works so wondrous he ordaind,
Hath brought me from the Quires of Cherubim

667. Alone thus wandring. Brightest Seraph tell
In which of all these shining Orbes hath Man
His fixed seat, or fixed seat hath none,
But all these shining Orbes his choice to dwell;

671. That I may find him, and with secret gaze,
Or open admiration him behold
On whom the great Creator hath bestowd
Worlds, and on whom hath all these graces powrd;
That both in him and all things, as is meet,
The Universal Maker we may praise;
Who justly hath driv'n out his Rebell Foes
To deepest Hell, and to repair that loss
Created this new happie Race of Men
To serve him better: wise are all his wayes.

681.   So spake the false dissembler unperceivd;
For neither Man nor Angel can discern
Hypocrisie, the onely evil that walks
Invisible, except to God alone,
By his permissive will, through Heav'n and Earth:
And oft though wisdom wake, suspicion sleeps
At wisdoms Gate, and to simplicitie
Resigns her charge, while goodness thinks no ill
Where no ill seems: Which now for once beguil'd
Uriel, though Regent of the Sun, and held
The sharpest sighted Spirit of all in Heav'n;
Who to the fraudulent Impostor foule

645. The bright angel turned when he heard Satan approach.

648. Satan recognize Uriel, who was one of God's seven archangels that stand watch all over Heaven and Earth.

654.   "*Uriel,*" said Satan, "*you stand here as God's eye, watching over his new creation.*

662. *I came to see this amazing creation, and to see the creature, man, that it was created for.*

667. *Can you tell me which one of these stars he lives on?*

671. *Maybe I will watch him secretly, or maybe I will meet him and express my admiration and praise for his maker.*"

681.   Uriel was fooled by Satan's act.

In his uprightness answer thus returnd.

694.   Faire Angel, thy desire which tends to know
The works of God, thereby to glorifie
The great Work-Maister, leads to no excess
That reaches blame, but rather merits praise
The more it seems excess, that led thee hither
From thy Empyreal Mansion thus alone,
To witness with thine eyes what some perhaps
Contented with report hear onely in heav'n:

702. For wonderful indeed are all his works,
Pleasant to know, and worthiest to be all
Had in remembrance alwayes with delight;

705. But what created mind can comprehend
Thir number, or the wisdom infinite
That brought them forth, but hid thir causes deep.

708. I saw when at his Word the formless Mass,
This worlds material mould, came to a heap:

710. Confusion heard his voice, and wilde uproar
Stood rul'd, stood vast infinitude confin'd;
Till at his second bidding darkness fled,
Light shon, and order from disorder sprung:

714. Swift to thir several Quarters hasted then
The cumbrous Elements, Earth, Flood, Aire, Fire,
And this Ethereal quintessence of Heav'n
Flew upward, spirited with various forms,
That rowld orbicular, and turnd to Starrs
Numberless, as thou seest, and how they move;
Each had his place appointed, each his course,
The rest in circuit walles this Universe.

722. Look downward on that Globe whose hither side
With light from hence, though but reflected, shines;

724. That place is Earth the seat of Man, that light

725. His day, which else as th' other Hemisphere

726. Night would invade, but there the neighbouring Moon
(So call that opposite fair Starr) her aide
Timely interposes, and her monthly round
Still ending, still renewing through mid Heav'n,
With borrowd light her countenance triform
Hence fills and empties to enlighten th' Earth,
And in her pale dominion checks the night.

733. That spot to which I point is Paradise,
Adams abode, those loftie shades his Bowre.
Thy way thou canst not miss, me mine requires.

736.   Thus said, he turnd, and Satan bowing low,
As to superior Spirits is wont in Heaven,
Where honour due and reverence none neglects,

739. Took leave, and toward the coast of Earth beneath,
Down from th' Ecliptic, sped with hop'd success,
Throws his steep flight in many an Aerie wheele,
Nor staid, till on Niphates top he lights.

694.   He praised him for coming to see with his own eyes what others were satisfied just to hear about.

702. *"God's work is wonderful to see and remember,"* said Uriel.

705. *"But nobody can really understand it.*

708. *I was there when God created the world.*

710. *I saw when he made wild confusion turn into order, and light shine.*

714. *Earth, water, air and fire all came together and turned into millions of stars that moved in orderly pathways.*

722. *Look down at that globe that shines with light reflected from here.*
724. *That's the Earth, where man lives.*
725. *The light is his day. On the other hemisphere is night.*
726. *The small star you see over there is the moon, which reflects light from here and sends it to Earth. It lessens night's darkness periodically as it orbits the Earth each month.*

733. *The spot I'm pointing to is Paradise. That shelter is Adam's home, which you will easily find."*

736.   Uriel returned to his post as Satan bowed respectfully.

739. Satan flew speedily straight down to Earth and landed on Mt. Niphates.

Book IV

PARADISE LOST

1.   O for that warning voice, which he who saw
Th' Apocalyps, heard cry in Heaven aloud,
Then when the Dragon, put to second rout,
Came furious down to be reveng'd on men,
Wo to the inhabitants on Earth! that now,

6. While time was, our first-Parents had bin warnd
The coming of thir secret foe, and scap'd
Haply so scap'd his mortal snare; for now

9. Satan, now first inflam'd with rage, came down,
The Tempter ere th' Accuser of man-kind,
To wreck on innocent frail man his loss
Of that first Battel, and his flight to Hell:

13. Yet not rejoycing in his speed, though bold,
Far off and fearless, nor with cause to boast,
Begins his dire attempt, which nigh the birth

16. Now rowling, boiles in his tumultuous brest,
And like a devillish Engine back recoiles
Upon himself; horror and doubt distract

19. His troubl'd thoughts, and from the bottom stirr
The Hell within him, for within him Hell
He brings, and round about him, nor from Hell
One step no more then from himself can fly

23. By change of place: Now conscience wakes despair
That slumberd, wakes the bitter memorie
Of what he was, what is, and what must be
Worse; of worse deeds worse sufferings must ensue.
Sometimes towards Eden which now in his view
Lay pleasant, his grievd look he fixes sad,

29. Sometimes towards Heav'n and the full-blazing Sun,
Which now sat high in his Meridian Towre:

31. Then much revolving, thus in sighs began.
O thou that with surpassing Glory crownd,
Look'st from thy sole Dominion like the God
Of this new World; at whose sight all the Starrs

35. Hide thir diminisht heads; to thee I call,
But with no friendly voice, and add thy name
O Sun, to tell thee how I hate thy beams
That bring to my remembrance from what state
I fell, how glorious once above thy Spheare;

40. Till Pride and worse Ambition threw me down
Warring in Heav'n against Heav'ns matchless King:
Ah wherefore! he deservd no such return

Chapter 4

IN PLAIN ENGLISH

1.   I wish somebody had warned Adam and Eve, the way St. John warned everybody about Satan in the Book of Revelation.

6. Then maybe they could've been saved.

9. Satan was coming to Earth to take revenge on them for losing the war and being thrown into Hell.

13. But he was feeling less sure of himself than when he began his mission.

16. He was feeling nervous.

19. He couldn't escape the feeling that he was still in Hell.

23. He was suddenly overwhelmed by painful memories of the glory he once had and how terrible his situation had become.

29. He looked down at Eden, which was beautiful. Then he looked up at the full shining sun.

31.   He said to the sun, "*You look like the god of this new world. All the stars hide when you come out.*

35. *But I hate you. I hate how you remind me of how glorious I once was—even more glorious than you.*

40. *Pride and ambition caused me to go against God. But why? He's the one who gave me my glory. He was kind to me. And he didn't ask much in return.*

　　　　From me, whom he created what I was
　　　　In that bright eminence, and with his good
　　　　Upbraided none; nor was his service hard.
46.　What could be less then to afford him praise,
　　　　The easiest recompence, and pay him thanks,
48.　How due! yet all his good prov'd ill in me,
49.　And wrought but malice; lifted up so high
　　　　I 'sdeind subjection, and thought one step higher
　　　　Would set me highest, and in a moment quit
52.　The debt immense of endless gratitude,
　　　　So burthensome, still paying, still to ow;
54.　Forgetful what from him I still receivd,
55.　And understood not that a grateful mind
　　　　By owing owes not, but still pays, at once
　　　　Indebted and dischargd; what burden then?
58.　O had his powerful Destiny ordaind
　　　　Me some inferiour Angel, I had stood
　　　　Then happie; no unbounded hope had rais'd
61.　Ambition. Yet why not? som other Power
　　　　As great might have aspir'd, and me though mean
63.　Drawn to his part; but other Powers as great
　　　　Fell not, but stand unshak'n, from within
　　　　Or from without, to all temptations arm'd.
66.　Hadst thou the same free Will and Power to stand?
　　　　Thou hadst: whom hast thou then or what to accuse,
68.　But Heav'ns free Love dealt equally to all?
　　　　Be then his Love accurst, since love or hate,
　　　　To me alike, it deals eternal woe.
71.　Nay curs'd be thou; since against his thy will
　　　　Chose freely what it now so justly rues.
73.　Me miserable! which way shall I flie
　　　　Infinite wrauth, and infinite despaire?
　　　　Which way I flie is Hell; my self am Hell;
76.　And in the lowest deep a lower deep
　　　　Still threatning to devour me opens wide,
　　　　To which the Hell I suffer seems a Heav'n.
79.　O then at last relent: is there no place
　　　　Left for Repentance, none for Pardon left?
　　　　None left but by submission; and that word
82.　Disdain forbids me, and my dread of shame
83.　Among the Spirits beneath, whom I seduc'd
　　　　With other promises and other vaunts
　　　　Then to submit, boasting I could subdue
86.　Th' Omnipotent. Ay me, they little know
　　　　How dearly I abide that boast so vaine,
　　　　Under what torments inwardly I groane:
　　　　While they adore me on the Throne of Hell,
　　　　With Diadem and Sceptre high advanc'd
91.　The lower still I fall, onely Supream

46. *What was so hard about giving him the praise and thanks that he deserved?*
48. *But all his goodness only made me bad.*
49. *I was in a high position, but it just made me want to be higher.*

52. *I got sick of always saying thank you.*

54. *I guess I forgot all that he continually gave.*
55. *I didn't see that feeling gratitude does not need to be expressed in words. So what was the problem?*

58. *Maybe it would have been better if he had made me a lesser angel. Then I wouldn't have become so ambitious.*

61. *But then maybe another high angel would've done what I did. And I would end up one of his followers.*

63. *But there were other angels as powerful as me, yet they never rebelled.*

66. *I had the same free will as they did. So what do I have to blame for my fall?*

68. *Nothing but God's love that he gives equally to everybody. Then damn his love! Since it makes no difference whether he loves me or hates me. Here's where I end up.*

71. *No, damn myself. Since I freely chose to do what I did, and now sadly regret.*

73. *I feel like Hell. Wherever I go is Hell. Infinite Hell, infinite hate, infinite despair.*

76. *And yet I'm afraid an even worse Hell waits for me—one so bad that, compared to it, this is like Heaven.*

79. *What can I do? Is there any way out of this? Yes, I can beg forgiveness, but the thought of it makes me sick.*

82. *How ashamed I would feel before all my followers.*
83. *I led them to this, with promises and bragging how I could beat God.*

86. *They should only know how I now eat those words, and what terror I feel while they worship me as their king.*

91. *King of misery, that's me. Still falling into worse misery.*

In miserie; such joy Ambition findes.

93. But say I could repent and could obtaine
By Act of Grace my former state; how soon
Would higth recall high thoughts, how soon unsay
What feign'd submission swore: ease would recant
Vows made in pain, as violent and void.

98. For never can true reconcilement grow
Where wounds of deadly hate have peirc'd so deep:

100. Which would but lead me to a worse relapse
And heavier fall: so should I purchase deare
Short intermission bought with double smart.

103. This knows my punisher; therefore as farr
From granting hee, as I from begging peace:

105. All hope excluded thus, behold in stead
Of us out-cast, exil'd, his new delight,
Mankind created, and for him this World.

108. So farewel Hope, and with Hope farewel Fear,

109. Farewel Remorse: all Good to me is lost;
Evil be thou my Good; by thee at least
Divided Empire with Heav'ns King I hold
By thee, and more then half perhaps will reigne;
As Man ere long, and this new World shall know.

114.   Thus while he spake, each passion dimm'd his face
Thrice chang'd with pale, ire, envie and despair,
Which marrd his borrow'd visage, and betraid
Him counterfet, if any eye beheld.
For heav'nly mindes from such distempers foule

119. Are ever cleer. Whereof hee soon aware,
Each perturbation smooth'd with outward calme,
Artificer of fraud; and was the first
That practisd falshood under saintly shew,
Deep malice to conceale, couch't with revenge:

124. Yet not anough had practisd to deceive
Uriel once warnd; whose eye pursu'd him down
The way he went, and on th' Assyrian mount
Saw him disfigur'd, more then could befall
Spirit of happie sort: his gestures fierce
He markd and mad demeanour, then alone,
As he suppos'd all unobserv'd, unseen.

131. So on he fares, and to the border comes

132. Of Eden, where delicious Paradise,
Now nearer, Crowns with her enclosure green,
As with a rural mound the champain head

135. Of a steep wilderness, whose hairie sides
With thicket overgrown, grottesque and wilde,

137. Access deni'd; and over head up grew
Insuperable highth of loftiest shade,
Cedar, and Pine, and Firr, and branching Palm
A Silvan Scene, and as the ranks ascend

93. *Even if I could be forgiven, how long could I keep up the insincere apologies I made in pain, once I was back in my comfortable old high place.*

98. *Things have gone way too far. There's too much hatred to ever be undone.*
100. *I would only relapse into worse hatred and worse rebellion. Any reconcilement would be short-lived.*

103. *God knows all this. He's as unlikely to forgive me as I am to ask him to.*
105. *He's given up on us and created this new world of man to take our place.*

108. *So all hope is gone, and with it, fear and regret as well.*
109. *All good is lost to me. Evil will become my good. Let God rule over the world of good. I will rule over evil—and maybe my half will turn out to be bigger than his, as mankind may soon find out."*
114.   While he spoke, his evil emotions showed on his face. If anybody had seen him, it would have given away his phony cherub's disguise, since they never have such bad thoughts.

119. Realizing this, he quickly changed his expression. He was the first one ever to pretend to be saintly, while hiding his true evil intent.

124. But he was too late. Uriel had been watching him the whole time.

131. So Satan moved on, and soon he was at the border of Eden.
132. Paradise was at the top of a steep hill on the open plain.

135. The sides of the hill were full of thick, wild plants that you couldn't walk through.
137. All kinds of very tall trees shaded the area and were very attractive.

Shade above shade, a woodie Theatre

142. Of stateliest view. Yet higher then thir tops
The verdurous wall of paradise up sprung:

144. Which to our general Sire gave prospect large
Into his neather Empire neighbouring round.

146. And higher then that Wall a circling row
Of goodliest Trees loaden with fairest Fruit,
Blossoms and Fruits at once of golden hue
Appeerd, with gay enameld colours mixt:

150. On which the Sun more glad impress'd his beams
Then in fair Evening Cloud, or humid Bow,
When God hath showrd the earth; so lovely seemd

153. That Lantskip: And of pure now purer aire
Meets his approach, and to the heart inspires
Vernal delight and joy, able to drive
All sadness but despair: now gentle gales
Fanning thir odoriferous wings dispense

158. Native perfumes, and whisper whence they stole

159. Those balmie spoiles. As when to them who saile
Beyond the Cape of Hope, and now are past
Mozambic, off at Sea North-East windes blow
Sabean Odours from the spicie shoare
Of Arabie the blest, with such delay
Well pleas'd they slack thir course, and many a League
Chear'd with the grateful smell old Ocean smiles.

166. So entertaind those odorous sweets the Fiend

167. Who came thir bane, though with them better pleas'd
Then Asmodeus with the fishie fume,
That drove him, though enamourd, from the Spouse
Of Tobits Son, and with a vengeance sent
From Media post to Ægypt, there fast bound.

172.   Now to th' ascent of that steep savage Hill
Satan had journied on, pensive and slow;
But further way found none, so thick entwin'd,
As one continu'd brake, the undergrowth
Of shrubs and tangling bushes had perplext
All path of Man or Beast that past that way:

178. One Gate there only was, and that look'd East
On th' other side: which when th' arch-fellon saw

180. Due entrance he disdaind, and in contempt,
At one slight bound high over leap'd all bound
Of Hill or highest Wall, and sheer within

183. Lights on his feet. As when a prowling Wolfe,
Whom hunger drives to seek new haunt for prey,
Watching where Shepherds pen thir Flocks at eeve
In hurdl'd Cotes amid the field secure,
Leaps o're the fence with ease into the Fould:
Or as a Thief bent to unhoord the cash
Of some rich Burgher, whose substantial dores,

142. Way up higher than the tops of the trees was a vine covered wall that enclosed Paradise.
144. From inside the wall you could view all the surrounding land outside Paradise.
146. Above the wall Satan saw beautiful trees full of colorful blossoms and fruit.

150. The sight was prettier than a sunset or a rainbow.

153. As Satan approached the garden, the air became so pure it could cheer a person up—if he wasn't too far gone.

158. Gentle winds blew various pleasant smells from the garden.
159. It was like when ships sailing around the Cape of Good Hope, past Mozambique, slow down to enjoy the sweet spicy smells blowing from the southern shore of Araby (which is now Yemen).

166. But the garden aromas were inviting the person who was going to destroy the garden.
167. Too bad he wasn't driven away by the bad smells of burnt fish, like the demon murderer Asmodeus, who fled from his lover's side to Egypt, where he was captured.

172.   Satan cautiously started up the hill, but soon the undergrowth became too thick for anyone, even animals, to pass through.

178. There was only one gate, on the other side.

180. Satan didn't care. He just jumped over the whole thing and landed inside the wall.

183. He was like a wolf jumping into a sheep's pen, or a burglar climbing in a window.

      Cross-barrd and bolted fast, fear no assault,
      In at the window climbs, or o're the tiles;
192. So clomb this first grand Thief into Gods Fould:
      So since into his Church lewd Hirelings climbe.
194. Thence up he flew, and on the Tree of Life,
      The middle Tree and highest there that grew,
196. Sat like a Cormorant; yet not true Life
      Thereby regaind, but sat devising Death
198. To them who liv'd; nor on the vertue thought
      Of that life-giving Plant, but only us'd
      For prospect, what well us'd had bin the pledge
201. Of immortality. So little knows
      Any, but God alone, to value right
      The good before him, but perverts best things
      To worst abuse, or to thir meanest use.
205. Beneath him with new wonder now he views
      To all delight of human sense expos'd
      In narrow room Natures whole wealth, yea more,
      A Heaven on Earth, for blissful Paradise
209. Of God the Garden was, by him in the East
      Of Eden planted; Eden stretchd her Line
      From Auran Eastward to the Royal Towrs
      Of Great Seleucia, built by Grecian Kings,
      Or where the Sons of Eden long before
      Dwelt in Telassar: in this pleasant soile
      His farr more pleasant Garden God ordaind;
216. Out of the fertil ground he caus'd to grow
      All Trees of noblest kind for sight, smell, taste;
218. And all amid them stood the Tree of Life,
      High eminent, blooming Ambrosial Fruit
220. Of vegetable Gold; and next to Life
      Our Death the Tree of Knowledge grew fast by,
      Knowledge of Good bought dear by knowing ill.
223. Southward through Eden went a River large,
224. Nor chang'd his course, but through the shaggie hill
225. Pass'd underneath ingulft, for God had thrown
      That Mountain as his Garden mould high rais'd
      Upon the rapid current, which through veins
      Of porous Earth with kindly thirst up drawn,
      Rose a fresh Fountain, and with many a rill
230. Waterd the Garden; thence united fell
      Down the steep glade, and met the neather Flood,
      Which from his darksom passage now appeers,
      And now divided into four main Streams,
      Runs divers, wandring many a famous Realme
      And Country whereof here needs no account,
236. But rather to tell how, if Art could tell,
      How from that Saphire Fount the crisped Brooks,
      Rowling on Orient Pearl and sands of Gold,

192. He snuck into God's garden like his accomplices would later sneak into God's church.
194. Then he flew up into the Tree of Life in the middle of the garden, the highest tree there.
196. He sat there like a vulture.
198. The tree had the power to give eternal life, but he didn't care about that. He just wanted a good place to view the whole garden.
201. But don't we all misuse God's gifts in ways that show we don't appreciate their real value?

205. He was impressed by his view of the garden. It was like a Heaven on Earth.

209. God placed his beautiful garden in the eastern part of Eden—which is today Iraq.

216. There were all the trees that are the best looking, smelling, and tasting.
218. And in the middle was the Tree of Life, the tallest tree. It's fruit was gold colored.
220. Right next to it was the Tree of Knowledge, which would eventually bring death into the world.
223. There was a big river that flowed southward through Eden.
224. It didn't go around the hill where the garden was. It went into the ground underneath it and came out on the other side.
225. God arranged it so the water would be drawn up into the garden as a spring and water all the plants.

230. The leftover water flowed back into the river on the other side and the river divided into four rivers and continued on into different countries.

236. The water was like magical nectar, producing the most beautiful flowers.

With mazie error under pendant shades
Ran Nectar, visiting each plant, and fed
241. Flours worthy of Paradise which not nice Art
In Beds and curious Knots, but Nature boon
Powrd forth profuse on Hill and Dale and Plaine,
Both where the morning Sun first warmly smote
The open field, and where the unpierc't shade
Imbround the noontide Bowrs: Thus was this place,
A happy rural seat of various view;
Groves whose rich Trees wept odorous Gumms and Balme,
Others whose fruit burnisht with Golden Rinde
250. Hung amiable, Hesperian Fables true,
If true, here only, and of delicious taste:
252. Betwixt them Lawns, or level Downs, and Flocks
Grasing the tender herb, were interpos'd,
254. Or palmie hilloc, or the flourie lap
Of som irriguous Valley spred her store,
256. Flours of all hue, and without Thorn the Rose:
257. Another side, umbrageous Grots and Caves
Of coole recess, o're which the mantling vine
Layes forth her purple Grape, and gently creeps
260. Luxuriant; mean while murmuring waters fall
Down the slope hills, disperst, or in a Lake,
That to the fringed Bank with Myrtle crownd,
Her chrystal mirror holds, unite thir streams.
264. The Birds thir quire apply; aires, vernal aires,
Breathing the smell of field and grove, attune
266. The trembling leaves, while Universal Pan
Knit with the Graces and the Hours in dance
268. Led on th' Eternal Spring. Not that faire field
Of Enna, where Proserpin gathering flours
Her self a fairer Floure by gloomie Dis
Was gatherd, which cost Ceres all that pain
To seek her through the world; nor that sweet Grove
Of Daphne by Orontes, and th' inspir'd
Castalian Spring, might with this Paradise
Of Eden strive; nor that Nyseian Ile
Girt with the River Triton, where old Cham,
Whom Gentiles Ammon call and Lybian Jove,
Hid Amalthea and her Florid Son
Young Bacchus from his Stepdame Rhea's eye;
280. Nor where Abassin Kings thir issue Guard,
Mount Amara, though this by som suppos'd
True Paradise under the Ethiop Line
By Nilus head, enclosd with shining Rock,
A whole days journy high, but wide remote
285. From this Assyrian Garden, where the Fiend
Saw undelighted all delight, all kind
Of living Creatures new to sight and strange:

241. They were not planted in neat little beds, but grew wild all over the hills and valleys—not only on the sunny plains, but even in shady spots.

250. The trees were as beautiful, with fruit as delicious as you only hear about in fairy tales, but here it was all true.
252. Between the groves there were grassy fields where animals grazed.
254. There were palm trees on the hills.
256. There were flowers of all colors in the valley. The roses didn't have thorns.
257. On another side there were cool caves with shady grapevines.

260. There were waterfalls and lakes.

264. Birds sang. The breezes rustled the leaves and smelled fresh.

266. Nature created a perpetual springtime here.

268. This paradise could not be compared to any that you might hear about in ancient myths;

280. ...nor the beautiful lands in Ethiopia.

285. Satan saw all this beauty and all kinds of animals he never saw before.

288. Two of far nobler shape erect and tall,
     Godlike erect, with native Honour clad
     In naked Majestie seemd Lords of all,
     And worthie seemd, for in thir looks Divine
     The image of thir glorious Maker shon,
     Truth, wisdome, Sanctitude severe and pure,
     Severe but in true filial freedom plac't;
     Whence true autority in men; though both
296. Not equal, as thir sex not equal seemd;
297. For contemplation hee and valour formd,
298. For softness shee and sweet attractive Grace,
299. Hee for God only, shee for God in him:
300. His fair large Front and Eye sublime declar'd
301. Absolute rule; and Hyacinthin Locks
     Round from his parted forelock manly hung
     Clustring, but not beneath his shoulders broad:
304. Shee as a vail down to the slender waste
     Her unadorned golden tresses wore
     Disheveld, but in wanton ringlets wav'd
     As the Vine curles her tendrils, which impli'd
308. Subjection, but requir'd with gentle sway,
309. And by her yielded, by him best receivd,
     Yielded with coy submission, modest pride,
     And sweet reluctant amorous delay.
312. Nor those mysterious parts were then conceald,
313. Then was not guiltie shame, dishonest shame
     Of natures works, honor dishonorable,
     Sin-bred, how have ye troubl'd all mankind
     With shews instead, meer shews of seeming pure,
317. And banisht from mans life his happiest life,
     Simplicitie and spotless innocence.
319. So passd they naked on, nor shund the sight
     Of God or Angel, for they thought no ill:
321. So hand in hand they passd, the lovliest pair
     That ever since in loves imbraces met,
     Adam the goodliest man of men since borne
     His Sons, the fairest of her Daughters Eve.
325. Under a tuft of shade that on a green
     Stood whispering soft, by a fresh Fountain side
327. They sat them down, and after no more toil
     Of thir sweet Gardning labour then suffic'd
     To recommend coole Zephyr, and made ease
     More easie, wholsom thirst and appetite
     More grateful, to thir Supper Fruits they fell,
     Nectarine Fruits which the compliant boughes
333. Yielded them, side-long as they sat recline
     On the soft downie Bank damaskt with flours:
     The savourie pulp they chew, and in the rinde
336. Still as they thirsted scoop the brimming stream;

288. Then he saw two that stood upright and resembled God.

296. But they were different from each other.
297. The male seemed intelligent and brave.
298. The female looked soft and pretty.
299. The male resembled God more than she did.
300. He had a high forehead and the eyes of a leader.
301. His dark wavy hair parted in the middle and hung almost to his shoulders.
304. She had long blonde hair down to her waist.

308. She would toss back her hair with a movement of her head.
309. The man liked to watch her. She pretended not to notice.

312. Their genitals were not covered.
313. There was nothing to be ashamed of then like there is now because of sin.

317. Man was happiest back then. Life was simple and innocent.

319. They walked around naked, even in front of God and the angels. They didn't see anything wrong with it.
321. They walked holding hands. They were the loveliest couple ever. Adam was the nicest man and Eve was the prettiest woman.

325. They sat down on the shady bank of a stream.

327. They had been working in the garden just long enough to make them enjoy resting in the cool breeze, and make them hungry and thirsty enough to enjoy lunch.

333. They leaned back among the flowers and ate nectarines from the trees.

336. They used the skins to scoop up water to drink.

Nor gentle purpose, nor endearing smiles
338. Wanted, nor youthful dalliance as beseems
Fair couple, linkt in happie nuptial League,
Alone as they. About them frisking playd
341. All Beasts of th' Earth, since wilde, and of all chase
In Wood or Wilderness, Forrest or Den;
343. Sporting the Lion rampd, and in his paw
344. Dandl'd the Kid; Bears, Tygers, Ounces, Pards
345. Gambold before them, th' unwieldy Elephant
To make them mirth us'd all his might, and wreathd
347. His Lithe Proboscis; close the Serpent sly
Insinuating, wove with Gordian twine
His breaded train, and of his fatal guile
350. Gave proof unheeded; others on the grass
Coucht, and now fild with pasture gazing sat,
352. Or Bedward ruminating: for the Sun
Declin'd was hasting now with prone carreer
To th' Ocean Iles, and in th' ascending Scale
Of Heav'n the Starrs that usher Evening rose:
356. When Satan still in gaze, as first he stood,
Scarce thus at length faild speech recoverd sad.
358.   O Hell! what doe mine eyes with grief behold,
359. Into our room of bliss thus high advanc't
Creatures of other mould, earth-born perhaps,
361. Not Spirits, yet to heav'nly Spirits bright
Little inferior; whom my thoughts pursue
With wonder, and could love, so lively shines
In them Divine resemblance, and such grace
The hand that formd them on thir shape hath pourd.
366. Ah gentle pair, yee little think how nigh
Your change approaches, when all these delights
Will vanish and deliver ye to woe,
369. More woe, the more your taste is now of joy;
370. Happie, but for so happie ill secur'd
Long to continue, and this high seat your Heav'n
Ill fenc't for Heav'n to keep out such a foe
373. As now is enterd; yet no purpos'd foe
To you whom I could pittie thus forlorne
375. Though I unpittied: League with you I seek,
And mutual amitie so streight, so close,
That I with you must dwell, or you with me
378. Henceforth; my dwelling haply may not please
Like this fair Paradise, your sense, yet such
Accept your Makers work; he gave it me,
381. Which I as freely give; Hell shall unfold,
To entertain you two, her widest Gates,
And send forth all her Kings; there will be room,
Not like these narrow limits, to receive
385. Your numerous ofspring; if no better place,

338. They flirted with each other and necked, like all young couples do.

341. All the animals were around them, tame and playing together.

343. A lion petted a young goat with his paw.
344. Bears, tigers and leopards were running and jumping all around them.
345. They laughed at the elephant curling his trunk.
347. A snake curled up nearby, but nobody guessed the trouble he would later cause.
350. Other creatures were laying in the field after having grazed. Some were going back to their dens to sleep.
352. The sun was setting and stars were starting to shine.

356. Satan stood staring speechless at the whole thing. He was not happy.
358.   *"What the hell is this I'm seeing!"* he said.
359. *"Who are all these strange creatures acting as happy as we once were?*
361. *They're not spirits, but they're just as beautiful. I could almost love them.*

366. *Ah, gentle pair, how little you know about the drastic change that's about to take place, when all this loveliness will disappear and be replaced with misery.*
369. *The happier you are now, the more miserable you will become.*
370. *You may be happy, but you're not so well protected here—not from me, anyway.*
373. *It wasn't my idea to become your enemy, you know.*
375. *I only wanted to be your friend—a close friend—so close that we should live together.*

378. *You might not like my home as much as this one, but it's the one God made for me, and now I'm going to share it with you.*

381. *Hell's gates will open wide and there will be lots of room—for you and all your children.*

385. *If you don't like it, blame God, not me.*

Thank him who puts me loath to this revenge
On you who wrong me not for him who wrongd.

388.   And should I at your harmless innocence
Melt, as I doe, yet public reason just,
Honour and Empire with revenge enlarg'd,
By conquering this new World, compels me now
To do what else though damnd I should abhorre.

393.   So spake the Fiend, and with necessitie,
The Tyrants plea, excus'd his devilish deeds.

395.   Then from his loftie stand on that high Tree
Down he alights among the sportful Herd

397.   Of those fourfooted kindes, himself now one,
Now other, as thir shape servd best his end
Neerer to view his prey, and unespi'd
To mark what of thir state he more might learn
By word or action markt: about them round

402.   A Lion now he stalkes with fierie glare,
Then as a Tyger, who by chance hath spi'd
In some Purlieu two gentle Fawnes at play,
Strait couches close, then rising changes oft
His couchant watch, as one who chose his ground
Whence rushing he might surest seize them both

408.   Gript in each paw: when Adam first of men
To first of women Eve thus moving speech,
Turnd him all eare to hear new utterance flow.

411.   Sole partner and sole part of all these joyes,
Dearer thy self then all; needs must the Power
That made us, and for us this ample World
Be infinitly good, and of his good
As liberal and free as infinite,

416.   That rais'd us from the dust and plac't us here
In all this happiness, who at his hand
Have nothing merited, nor can performe

419.   Aught whereof hee hath need, hee who requires
From us no other service then to keep

421.   This one, this easie charge, of all the Trees
In Paradise that bear delicious fruit
So various, not to taste that onely Tree
Of knowledge, planted by the Tree of Life,

425.   So neer grows Death to Life, what ere Death is,
Som dreadful thing no doubt; for well thou knowst
God hath pronounc't it death to taste that Tree,

428.   The only sign of our obedience left

429.   Among so many signes of power and rule
Conferrd upon us, and Dominion giv'n
Over all other Creatures that possess
Earth, Aire, and Sea. Then let us not think hard
One easie prohibition, who enjoy
Free leave so large to all things else, and choice

388. *I have nothing against you personally. But I have to do what I have to do."*

393.   Satan was trying to excuse his bad intentions.

395. He jumped down from the tree and mixed among the animals.

397. He became one of them, changing his shape as he moved from one kind to another, to get closer to the human couple to spy on them.

402. He took the shape of a lion, and then a tiger that looked like it was about to attack them.

408. He suddenly stopped and listened when Adam began to speak to Eve.

411.   *"Dear Eve, my one and only partner, isn't God good to us!*

416. *He made us and gave us all this happiness, even though we haven't done anything to deserve it.*

419. *And all he asks in return is for us to follow one easy rule.*

421. *Just don't eat the fruit from the Tree of Knowledge, planted next to the Tree of Life.*

425. *He said it would bring us death, whatever that means. It must be something bad.*

428. *That's all he asks.*
429. *He gives us power over all the creatures in the land and sea and air, and all the freedom to enjoy so many pleasures around here. We're certainly not going to complain about one little rule that's so easy to keep.*

Unlimited of manifold delights:
436. But let us ever praise him, and extoll
His bountie, following our delightful task
To prune these growing Plants, and tend these Flours,
Which were it toilsom, yet with thee were sweet.
440.   To whom thus Eve repli'd. O thou for whom
And from whom I was formd flesh of thy flesh,
And without whom am to no end, my Guide
443. And Head, what thou hast said is just and right.
For wee to him indeed all praises owe,
And daily thanks, I chiefly who enjoy
446. So farr the happier Lot, enjoying thee
Præeminent by so much odds, while thou
Like consort to thy self canst no where find.
449. That day I oft remember, when from sleep
I first awak't, and found my self repos'd
451. Under a shade of flours, much wondring where
And what I was, whence thither brought, and how.
453. Not distant far from thence a murmuring sound
Of waters issu'd from a Cave and spread
Into a liquid Plain, then stood unmov'd
Pure as th' expanse of Heav'n; I thither went
457. With unexperienc't thought, and laid me downe
On the green bank, to look into the cleer
Smooth Lake, that to me seemd another Skie.
460. As I bent down to look, just opposite,
A Shape within the watry gleam appeard
Bending to look on me, I started back,
463. It started back, but pleas'd I soon returnd,
Pleas'd it returnd as soon with answering looks
465. Of sympathie and love; there I had fixt
Mine eyes till now, and pin'd with vain desire,
467. Had not a voice thus warnd me, What thou seest,
What there thou seest fair Creature is thy self,
469. With thee it came and goes: but follow me,
And I will bring thee where no shadow staies
Thy coming, and thy soft imbraces, hee
472. Whose image thou art, him thou shalt enjoy
Inseparablie thine, to him shalt beare
Multitudes like thy self, and thence be call'd
Mother of human Race: what could I doe,
476. But follow strait, invisibly thus led?
477. Till I espi'd thee, fair indeed and tall,
478. Under a Platan, yet methought less faire,
Less winning soft, less amiablie milde,
480. Then that smooth watry image; back I turnd,
481. Thou following cryd'st aloud, Return faire Eve,
482. Whom fli'st thou? whom thou fli'st, of him thou art,
483. His flesh, his bone; to give thee being I lent

436. *Let's always thank him and praise him while we work in the garden, which is so enjoyable. But even if it was hard work, sharing it with you it would still be a pleasure."*

440. Eve said, *"Adam, I was made from you. You are my only reason for being here. You are my leader.*

443. *I agree with you, we owe God praise and thanks—especially me, since I have you, and you are so much higher than me.*

446. *But you, poor man, you have nobody equal to you for company.*

449. *I often think about when I first woke up in that shady spot, lying on the flowers.*

451. *I didn't know who I was, or where I was, or how I got there.*

453. *I heard the sound of water. I went and found a stream coming from a cave into a big peaceful lake.*

457. *It was all new to me. The lake looked like the sky. I got down on the bank and looked into it.*

460. *A person looked back at me. I jumped back.*

463. *It jumped back too. I looked again. She was sweet and lovely.*

465. *I fell in love with her. I think I would still be there if I didn't hear what I heard next.*

467. *'You're looking at yourself, beautiful woman' a voice said, 'It's just a reflection.*

469. *But come with me and I'll bring you to somebody you can put your arms around.*

472. *You'll be his forever. From you two will come millions like you. You will be the mother of the human race.'*

476. *I couldn't see anybody, but I followed the voice till I came to you.*

477. *You were standing under a plane tree, tall and handsome.*

478. *But you were not as sweet looking as the person in the lake.*

480. *So I turned to go back to her.*

481. *But you came after me and called out, 'Where are you going, Eve. Come back.*

482. *I'm the one you came from.*

483. *God took you out of my side. You're part of my soul. You're like my other half.'*

Out of my side to thee, neerest my heart
Substantial Life, to have thee by my side
Henceforth an individual solace dear;
Part of my Soul I seek thee, and thee claim
488. My other half: with that thy gentle hand
489. Seisd mine, I yielded, and from that time see
How beauty is excelld by manly grace
And wisdom, which alone is truly fair.
492.   So spake our general Mother, and with eyes
Of conjugal attraction unreprov'd,
494. And meek surrender, half imbracing leand
On our first Father, half her swelling Breast
Naked met his under the flowing Gold
497. Of her loose tresses hid: he in delight
Both of her Beauty and submissive Charms
499. Smil'd with superior Love, as Jupiter
On Juno smiles, when he impregns the Clouds
501. That shed May Flowers; and press'd her Matron lip
502. With kisses pure: aside the Devil turnd
For envie, yet with jealous leer maligne
Ey'd them askance, and to himself thus plaind.
505.   Sight hateful, sight tormenting! thus these two
506. Imparadis't in one anothers arms
The happier Eden, shall enjoy thir fill
Of bliss on bliss, while I to Hell am thrust,
Where neither joy nor love, but fierce desire,
Among our other torments not the least,
Still unfulfill'd with pain of longing pines;
512. Yet let me not forget what I have gain'd
513. From thir own mouths; all is not theirs it seems:
One fatal Tree there stands of Knowledge call'd,
Forbidden them to taste: Knowledge forbidd'n?
516. Suspicious, reasonless. Why should thir Lord
517. Envie them that? can it be sin to know,
Can it be death? and do they onely stand
By Ignorance, is that thir happie state,
The proof of thir obedience and thir faith?
521. O fair foundation laid whereon to build
Thir ruine! Hence I will excite thir minds
With more desire to know, and to reject
Envious commands, invented with designe
To keep them low whom knowledge might exalt
Equal with Gods; aspiring to be such,
527. They taste and die: what likelier can ensue?
528. But first with narrow search I must walk round
This Garden, and no corner leave unspi'd;
A chance but chance may lead where I may meet
Some wandring Spirit of Heav'n, by Fountain side,
Or in thick shade retir'd, from him to draw

488. *Then you gently took my hand.*
489. *Now I think a gentleman is more attractive than a pretty women."*

492.   Eve showed love in her eyes as she spoke.

494. She leaned against Adam. Her naked breast pressed against his chest. It was hidden by her long hair.

497. Adam smiled at her beauty, and because she made him feel superior.
499. They were like a god and goddess.

501. Adam kissed Eve.
502. Satan turned away and glared at them sideways, full of jealousy and hate.
505.   *"I can't stand this!"* he said to himself.
506. *"These two are enjoying heavenly pleasure in each other's arms, while I'm stuck in Hell, where there's no joy or love, only sexual desire that never gets satisfied.*

512. *But now I have some useful information.*
513. *Apparently, they are forbidden to eat from one of the trees, called Knowledge.*

516. *It doesn't make any sense. Why would God forbid them that? Can knowledge be a sin that kills you?*
517. *Is all their happiness based on their ignorance? Is that how God keeps them obedient?*
521. *This is almost too easy. All I have to do is stir up their curiosity, and convince them God is trying to prevent them from becoming great like him.*

527. *They'll eat the fruit and die. What else?*
528. *But first I'll case the area and see if there are any other angels hanging around. Maybe I can learn some more useful information.*

533. What further would be learnt. Live while ye may,
     Yet happie pair; enjoy, till I return,
     Short pleasures, for long woes are to succeed.

536.   So saying, his proud step he scornful turn'd,
     But with sly circumspection, and began
     Through wood, through waste, o're hill, o're dale his roam.

539. Mean while in utmost Longitude, where Heav'n
     With Earth and Ocean meets, the setting Sun

541. Slowly descended, and with right aspect
     Against the eastern Gate of Paradise

543. Leveld his eevning Rayes: it was a Rock
     Of Alablaster, pil'd up to the Clouds,

545. Conspicuous farr, winding with one ascent
     Accessible from Earth, one entrance high;

547. The rest was craggie cliff, that overhung
     Still as it rose, impossible to climbe.

549. Betwixt these rockie Pillars Gabriel sat
     Chief of th' Angelic Guards, awaiting night;

551. About him exercis'd Heroic Games
     Th' unarmed Youth of Heav'n, but nigh at hand

553. Celestial Armourie, Shields, Helmes, and Speares
     Hung high with Diamond flaming, and with Gold.

555. Thither came Uriel, gliding through the Eeven
     On a Sun beam, swift as a shooting Starr
     In Autumn thwarts the night, when vapors fir'd
     Impress the Air, and shews the Mariner
     From what point of his Compass to beware
     Impetuous winds: he thus began in haste.

561.   Gabriel, to thee thy course by Lot hath giv'n
     Charge and strict watch that to this happie place
     No evil thing approach or enter in;

564. This day at highth of Noon came to my Spheare
     A Spirit, zealous, as he seem'd, to know
     More of th' Almighties works, and chiefly Man

567. Gods latest Image: I describ'd his way
     Bent all on speed, and markt his Aerie Gate;

569. But in the Mount that lies from Eden North,
     Where he first lighted, soon discernd his looks
     Alien from Heav'n, with passions foul obscur'd:
     Mine eye pursu'd him still, but under shade

573. Lost sight of him; one of the banisht crew
     I fear, hath ventur'd from the Deep, to raise
     New troubles; him thy care must be to find.

576.   To whom the winged Warriour thus returnd:
     Uriel, no wonder if thy perfet sight,
     Amid the Suns bright circle where thou sitst,

579. See farr and wide: in at this Gate none pass
     The vigilance here plac't, but such as come
     Well known from Heav'n; and since Meridian hour

533. *Enjoy yourselves while you can, children, you've got a lot of misery coming your way."*

536.   Satan went off.

539. The sun was setting.

541. It shined on the east gate of Paradise.

543. The gate was big, with white rock columns.

545. There was only one way to get to it, on a winding path from below.

547. Everywhere else there was just a steep cliff that was impossible to climb.

549. Between the columns sat Gabriel, chief of the angelic guards.

551. Around him young angels exercised in athletic games.

553. Their shields and helmets and spears hung nearby. They were made of gold and diamonds.

555. Here's where Uriel came sliding down a sunbeam as fast as a shooting star, like the ones that show sailors which way the wind will blow.

561.   *"Gabriel," he said, excitedly, "I know your job is to guard this place, so listen.*

564. *Today, at noon, an angel came by my post. He was anxious to see the new world and man.*

567. *I directed him, and he landed on the mountain north of Eden.*

569. *But as I watched him, his behavior made me suspicious. I lost sight of him in the shadows.*

573. *I'm afraid one of the bad angels from Hell has come to stir up trouble. You better find him."*

576.   Gabriel said, *"I don't doubt you see everything from up there on the sun.*

579. *But nobody gets through these gates who we don't know. And nobody at all came since noon.*

582. No Creature thence: if Spirit of other sort,
So minded, have oreleapt these earthie bounds
On purpose, hard thou knowst it to exclude
Spiritual substance with corporeal barr.

586. But if within the circuit of these walks,
In whatsoever shape he lurk, of whom
Thou tellst, by morrow dawning I shall know.

589.   So promis'd hee, and Uriel to his charge
Returnd on that bright beam, whose point now rais'd
Bore him slope downward to the Sun now fall'n
Beneath th' Azores; whither the prime Orb,
Incredible how swift, had thither rowl'd

594. Diurnal, or this less volubil Earth
By shorter flight to th' East, had left him there
Arraying with reflected Purple and Gold

597. The Clouds that on his Western Throne attend:
Now came still Eevning on, and Twilight gray

599. Had in her sober Liverie all things clad;

600. Silence accompanied, for Beast and Bird,
They to thir grassie Couch, these to thir Nests

602. Were slunk, all but the wakeful Nightingale;
She all night long her amorous descant sung;

604. Silence was pleas'd: now glow'd the Firmament
With living Saphirs: Hesperus that led
The starrie Host, rode brightest, till the Moon
Rising in clouded Majestie, at length
Apparent Queen unvaild her peerless light,
And o're the dark her Silver Mantle threw.

610.   When Adam thus to Eve: Fair Consort, th' hour
Of night, and all things now retir'd to rest

612. Mind us of like repose, since God hath set
Labour and rest, as day and night to men
Successive, and the timely dew of sleep
Now falling with soft slumbrous weight inclines
Our eye-lids; other Creatures all day long
Rove idle unimploid, and less need rest;
Man hath his daily work of body or mind
Appointed, which declares his Dignitie,
And the regard of Heav'n on all his waies;
While other Animals unactive range,
And of thir doings God takes no account.

623. To morrow ere fresh Morning streak the East
With first approach of light, we must be ris'n,
And at our pleasant labour, to reform
Yon flourie Arbors, yonder Allies green,

627. Our walk at noon, with branches overgrown,
That mock our scant manuring, and require
More hands then ours to lop thir wanton growth:
Those Blossoms also, and those dropping Gumms,

582. *But you know we can't keep spirits out of this Garden with physical walls.*

586. *If this angel you describe is here, we'll find him before morning."*

589.   Uriel slid back down to the sun on the sunbeam. It was sloped downward now because now the sun was lower than the Earth.

594. Or maybe the Earth just spun to the East—I'm not sure.

597. The clouds near the sun were purple and gold.

599. The evening twilight made everything else look gray.
600. All the animals and birds silently went to bed.

602. Only a nightingale stayed awake, singing all night long.

604. The stars came out, and then the moon.

610.   Adam said to Eve, "*It's getting late. We should go to bed.*

612. *God wants us to rest after our day's work, which exercises our bodies and minds, unlike the animals who just roam around doing nothing.*

623. *Tomorrow we have to be up and at it again early.*

627. *We have to clear all our paths of leaves and cut the overgrown branches. It's almost more than the two of us can handle.*

That lie bestrowne unsightly and unsmooth,
Ask riddance, if we mean to tread with ease;
633. Mean while, as Nature wills, Night bids us rest.
634.   To whom thus Eve with perfet beauty adornd.
My Author and Disposer, what thou bidst
Unargu'd I obey; so God ordains,
God is thy Law, thou mine: to know no more
Is womans happiest knowledge and her praise.
639. With thee conversing I forget all time,
640. All seasons and thir change, all please alike.
Sweet is the breath of morn, her rising sweet,
With charm of earliest Birds; pleasant the Sun
When first on this delightful Land he spreads
His orient Beams, on herb, tree, fruit, and flour,
Glistring with dew; fragrant the fertil earth
646. After soft showers; and sweet the coming on
Of grateful Eevning milde, then silent Night
With this her solemn Bird and this fair Moon,
And these the Gemms of Heav'n, her starrie train:
650. But neither breath of Morn when she ascends
With charm of earliest Birds, nor rising Sun
On this delightful land, nor herb, fruit, floure,
Glistring with dew, nor fragrance after showers,
654. Nor grateful Eevning mild, nor silent Night
With this her solemn Bird, nor walk by Moon,
Or glittering Starr-light without thee is sweet.
657. But wherfore all night long shine these, for whom
This glorious sight, when sleep hath shut all eyes?
    To whom our general Ancestor repli'd.
660. Daughter of God and Man, accomplisht Eve,
Those have thir course to finish, round the Earth,
By morrow Eevning, and from Land to Land
In order, though to Nations yet unborn,
664. Ministring light prepar'd, they set and rise;
Least total darkness should by Night regaine
Her old possession, and extinguish life
In Nature and all things, which these soft fires
Not only enlighten, but with kindly heate
Of various influence foment and warme,
Temper or nourish, or in part shed down
Thir stellar vertue on all kinds that grow
On Earth, made hereby apter to receive
Perfection from the Suns more potent Ray.
These then, though unbeheld in deep of night,
675. Shine not in vain, nor think, though men were none,
That heav'n would want spectators, God want praise;
Millions of spiritual Creatures walk the Earth
Unseen, both when we wake, and when we sleep:
All these with ceasless praise his works behold

633.   *We need our rest."*
634.   *"You're the boss, Adam,"* said Eve, *"That's how God wants it, and it's fine with me.*

639.   *When I'm talking with you, I forget what time it is.*
640.   *I love every time of day: the birds singing in the morning, the sun rising on all the fruit trees and flowers, the smell of the ground after a shower.*

646.   *And then the quiet nights, the nightingale, and the moon and stars.*

650.   *But none of that would be worth much without you.*

654.   *What would a walk under the moon and stars be without you?*

657.   *I have a question. Why do these stars shine all night long if nobody's awake here to see them?"*

660.   *"Well, Eve,"* replied Adam, *"the stars will go once around the Earth and be back by tomorrow evening.*

664.   *They keep life going on all over the Earth by their soft light and heat at night so everything that grows will be ready to receive their full dose of energy from the sun.*

675.   *Even if there were no people, millions of invisible angels are always around, day and night, admiring the stars and everything.*

680. Both day and night: how often from the steep
     Of echoing Hill or Thicket have we heard
     Celestial voices to the midnight air,
     Sole, or responsive each to others note
     Singing thir great Creator: oft in bands
     While they keep watch, or nightly rounding walk,
     With Heav'nly touch of instrumental sounds
     In full harmonic number joind, thir songs
     Divide the night, and lift our thoughts to Heaven.
689.   Thus talking hand in hand alone they pass'd
690. On to thir blissful Bower; it was a place
     Chos'n by the sovran Planter, when he fram'd
692. All things to mans delightful use; the roofe
     Of thickest covert was inwoven shade
     Laurel and Mirtle, and what higher grew
     Of firm and fragrant leaf; on either side
     Acanthus, and each odorous bushie shrub
     Fenc'd up the verdant wall; each beauteous flour,
     Iris all hues, Roses, and Gessamin
     Rear'd high thir flourisht heads between, and wrought
700. Mosaic; underfoot the Violet,
     Crocus, and Hyacinth with rich inlay
     Broiderd the ground, more colour'd then with stone
703. Of costliest Emblem: other Creature here
     Beast, Bird, Insect, or Worm durst enter none;
     Such was thir awe of Man. In shadie Bower
706. More sacred and sequesterd, though but feignd,
     Pan or Silvanus never slept, nor Nymph,
708. Nor Faunus haunted. Here in close recess
     With Flowers, Garlands, and sweet-smelling Herbs
     Espoused Eve deckt first her Nuptial Bed,
     And heav'nlyly Quires the Hymenæan sung,
     What day the genial Angel to our Sire
713. Brought her in naked beauty more adorn'd
     More lovely then Pandora, whom the Gods
715. Endowd with all thir gifts, and O too like
     In sad event, when to the unwiser Son
     Of Japhet brought by Hermes, she ensnar'd
     Mankind with her faire looks, to be aveng'd
     On him who had stole Joves authentic fire.
720.   Thus at thir shadie Lodge arriv'd, both stood
     Both turnd, and under op'n Skie ador'd
     The God that made both Skie, Air, Earth and Heav'n
     Which they beheld, the Moons resplendent Globe
724. And starrie Pole: Thou also mad'st the Night,
     Maker Omnipotent, and thou the Day,
726. Which we in our appointed work imployd
727. Have finisht happie in our mutual help
     And mutual love, the Crown of all our bliss

680. *Haven't you noticed the heavenly voices that echo in the hills at night, singing and playing music while they guard us?"*

689.   They went home.
690. It was a rustic shelter that God designed for them.

692. The walls and roof were made of pleasant smelling plants and flowers.

700. On the ground violets and crocuses looked better than an expensive carpet.

703. No animals or insects would enter their home.

706. It was as nice a home as any mythological woodland creature ever had.
708. This is where Eve decorated their wedding bed with flowers and herbs, and angels sang, the day she was first brought to Adam.

713. Her naked beauty was like wearing beautiful clothes. She was more beautiful than Pandora.
715. Unfortunately, she brought us all big troubles, just like Pandora.

720.   Adam and Eve looked at the night sky from their doorway and said their evening prayers:

724. *"You made day and night, Lord.*

726. *We have finished our day's work.*
727. *We enjoyed our companionship, thanks to you.*

729. Ordaind by thee, and this delicious place
       For us too large, where thy abundance wants
       Partakers, and uncropt falls to the ground.
732. But thou hast promis'd from us two a Race
733. To fill the Earth, who shall with us extoll
       Thy goodness infinite, both when we wake,
       And when we seek, as now, thy gift of sleep.
736.   This said unanimous, and other Rites
       Observing none, but adoration pure
738. Which God likes best, into thir inmost bowre
       Handed they went; and eas'd the putting off
       These troublesom disguises which wee wear,
741. Strait side by side were laid, nor turnd I weene
       Adam from his fair Spouse, nor Eve the Rites
       Mysterious of connubial Love refus'd:
744. Whatever Hypocrites austerely talk
       Of puritie and place and innocence,
746. Defaming as impure what God declares
       Pure, and commands to som, leaves free to all.
748. Our Maker bids increase, who bids abstain
       But our Destroyer, foe to God and Man?
750. Haile wedded Love, mysterious Law, true source
       Of human ofspring, sole propriety,
752. In Paradise of all things common else.
753. By thee adulterous lust was driv'n from men
       Among the bestial herds to raunge, by thee
755. Founded in Reason, Loyal, Just, and Pure,
       Relations dear, and all the Charities
       Of Father, Son, and Brother first were known.
758. Farr be it, that I should write thee sin or blame,
       Or think thee unbefitting holiest place,
760. Perpetual Fountain of Domestic sweets,
       Whose bed is undefil'd and chaste pronounc't,
       Present, or past, as Saints and Patriarchs us'd.
763. Here Love his golden shafts imploies, here lights
       His constant Lamp, and waves his purple wings,
765. Reigns here and revels; not in the bought smile
       Of Harlots, loveless, joyless, unindeard,
       Casual fruition, nor in Court Amours
       Mixt Dance, or wanton Mask, or Midnight Bal,
       Or Serenate, which the starv'd Lover sings
       To his proud fair, best quitted with disdain.
771. These lulld by Nightingales imbraceing slept,
       And on thir naked limbs the flourie roof
       Showrd Roses, which the Morn repair'd. Sleep on
774. Blest pair; and O yet happiest if ye seek
       No happier state, and know to know no more.
776.   Now had night measur'd with her shaddowie Cone
       Half way up Hill this vast Sublunar Vault,

729. *This place is nice, but it's too big for us.*

732. *But you promised us many people would come out of us and share it with us.*
733. *They'll join us in praising you in our morning and evening prayers."*
736.   They prayed together like one person.
738. When they went inside they didn't need to bother undressing like we do.

741. They went to bed and didn't hesitate to make love.

744. It's stupid to think they didn't have sex.

746. God married them and told them to have children.

748. You'd have to be a hypocrite to say there shouldn't be sex in Paradise—or the Devil himself.
750. Hooray for love and marriage! This is where babies come from.

752. This is the only thing in Paradise that's private. Everything else is free to all.
753. Free sex is only okay among the animals.
755. Marriage is all about trust and faithfulness and family.

758. Marital love is perfectly acceptable even in the holiest places.

760. There's nothing shameful about the pleasures of the marriage bed. It's been used by holy men and saints.
763. This is where the beauty of love really shines.

765. Not in casual sex with strangers and whores. Not in silly love songs.

771. The couple fell asleep while nightingales sang and rose petals fell on them.

774. If only they knew enough to appreciate their blessings and not risk everything to know more.
776.   At 9 p.m. the armed angels came out for the changing of the guard.

And from thir Ivorie Port the Cherubim
Forth issuing at th' accustomd hour stood armd
To thir night watches in warlike Parade,
781. When Gabriel to his next in power thus spake.
    Uzziel, half these draw off, and coast the South
With strictest watch; these other wheel the North,
Our circuit meets full West. As flame they part
Half wheeling to the Shield, half to the Spear.
786. From these, two strong and suttle Spirits he calld
That neer him stood, and gave them thus in charge.
    Ithuriel and Zephon, with wingd speed
Search through this Garden, leave unsearcht no nook,
But chiefly where those two fair Creatures Lodge,
Now laid perhaps asleep secure of harme.
792. This Eevning from the Sun's decline arriv'd
Who tells of som infernal Spirit seen
Hitherward bent (who could have thought?) escap'd
The barrs of Hell, on errand bad no doubt:
796. Such where ye find, seise fast, and hither bring.
797.   So saying, on he led his radiant Files,
Daz'ling the Moon; these to the Bower direct
799. In search of whom they sought: him there they found
Squat like a Toad, close at the eare of Eve;
801. Assaying by his Devilish art to reach
The Organs of her Fancie, and with them forge
Illusions as he list, Phantasms and Dreams,
Or if, inspiring venom, he might taint
Th' animal spirits that from pure blood arise
Like gentle breaths from Rivers pure, thence raise
At least distemperd, discontented thoughts,
Vaine hopes, vaine aimes, inordinate desires
Blown up with high conceits ingendring pride.
810. Him thus intent Ithuriel with his Spear
Touch'd lightly; for no falshood can endure
812. Touch of Celestial temper, but returns
Of force to its own likeness: up he starts
Discoverd and surpriz'd. As when a spark
Lights on a heap of nitrous Powder, laid
Fit for the Tun som Magazin to store
Against a rumord Warr, the Smuttie graine
With sudden blaze diffus'd, inflames the Aire:
So started up in his own shape the Fiend.
820. Back stept those two fair Angels half amaz'd
So sudden to behold the grieslie King;
Yet thus, unmovd with fear, accost him soon.
823.   Which of those rebell Spirits adjudg'd to Hell
Com'st thou, escap'd thy prison, and transform'd,
Why satst thou like an enemie in waite
Here watching at the head of these that sleep?

781.   Gabriel said to his next in rank, "*Uzziel, take half of these men and patrol the south side of the garden. I'll take the rest along the north side. We'll meet at the west end.*"

786.   Then he told Ithuriel and Zephon, "*You two search the interior of the garden. Look everywhere, especially around Adam and Eve's house, where they're probably sleeping peacefully.*

792.   *This evening I received news that a devil has escaped from Hell and is headed here.*

796.   *If you find him, arrest him and bring him to me.*"

797.   Gabriel led his men away, and the two angels went to Adam's home.

799.   They found Satan there, squatting like a frog, whispering into Eve's ear while she was sleeping.

801.   He was trying to put bad thoughts into her dreams.

810.   Ithuriel touched him lightly with his spear.

812.   Satan jumped up like a heap of gunpowder lit by a spark, and changed back into his normal shape.

820.   The two angels stepped back in surprise.

823.   One of them said, "*Who are you and what are you doing here?*"

827.   Know ye not then said Satan, fill'd with scorn
        Know ye not mee? ye knew me once no mate
        For you, there sitting where ye durst not soare;
830.   Not to know mee argues your selves unknown,
831.   The lowest of your throng; or if ye know,
        Why ask ye, and superfluous begin
        Your message, like to end as much in vain?
834.   To whom thus Zephon, answering scorn with scorn.
        Think not, revolted Spirit, thy shape the same,
        Or undiminisht brightness, to be known
        As when thou stoodst in Heav'n upright and pure;
        That Glorie then, when thou no more wast good,
        Departed from thee, and thou resembl'st now
        Thy sin and place of doom obscure and foule.
841.   But come, for thou, be sure, shalt give account
        To him who sent us, whose charge is to keep
        This place inviolable, and these from harm.
          So spake the Cherube, and his grave rebuke
        Severe in youthful beautie, added grace
846.   Invincible: abasht the Devil stood,
        And felt how awful goodness is, and saw
        Vertue in her shape how lovly, saw, and pin'd
        His loss; but chiefly to find here observd
        His lustre visibly impair'd; yet seemd
851.   Undaunted. If I must contend, said he,
        Best with the best, the Sender not the sent,
        Or all at once; more glorie will be wonn,
854.   Or less be lost. Thy fear, said Zephon bold,
        Will save us trial what the least can doe
        Single against thee wicked, and thence weak.
857.   The Fiend repli'd not, overcome with rage;
858.   But like a proud Steed reind, went hautie on,
        Chaumping his iron curb: to strive or flie
        He held it vain; awe from above had quelld
861.   His heart, not else dismai'd. Now drew they nigh
        The western Point, where those half-rounding guards
        Just met, and closing stood in squadron joind
        Awaiting next command. To whom thir Chief
865.   Gabriel from the Front thus calld aloud.
          O friends, I hear the tread of nimble feet
        Hasting this way, and now by glimps discerne
        Ithuriel and Zephon through the shade,
869.   And with them comes a third of Regal port,
        But faded splendor wan; who by his gate
        And fierce demeanour seems the Prince of Hell,
        Not likely to part hence without contest;
        Stand firm, for in his look defiance lours.
874.   He scarce had ended, when those two approachd
        And brief related whom they brought, where found,

827.   *"Don't you recognize me?"* said Satan, *"You once knew me well enough to stay clear of me.*

830.   *If you really don't know me it just goes to show what nobodies you are.*

831.   *And if you do know me why waste my time with stupid questions."*

834.   Zephon said, *"Do you think you look the same as you did in Heaven? When you turned bad you lost your looks. Now you look as repulsive as the place you came from.*

841.   *Anyway, get moving. If you won't talk here, you'll talk to our captain."*

846.   Satan was humiliated to find out that he had become ugly.

851.   He said, *"Good. Let me deal with the top man, not a pair of messengers. Or maybe I'll deal with all of you at once."*

854.   Zephon said, *"Well, that saves us the trouble of showing you what 'messengers' can do to weak, evil people."*

857.   Satan was too angry to say any more.

858.   He knew it was useless to resist, so he went along with them, trying to keep his pride.

861.   They came to where Gabriel's troops had met at the western end.

865.   Gabriel called out, *"Here come Ithuriel and Zephon.*

869.   *They're bringing somebody who looks like the Prince of Hell. Be ready for trouble."*

874.   The two angels came and told Gabriel what had happened.

How busied, in what form and posture coucht.
877.   To whom with stern regard thus Gabriel spake.
Why hast thou, Satan, broke the bounds prescrib'd
To thy transgressions, and disturbd the charge
Of others, who approve not to transgress
By thy example, but have power and right
To question thy bold entrance on this place;
Imploi'd it seems to violate sleep, and those
Whose dwelling God hath planted here in bliss?
885.   To whom thus Satan with contemptuous brow.
Gabriel, thou hadst in Heav'n th' esteem of wise,
And such I held thee; but this question askt
888. Puts me in doubt. Lives ther who loves his pain?
Who would not, finding way, break loose from Hell,
Though thither doomd? Thou wouldst thyself, no doubt,
891. And boldly venture to whatever place
Farthest from pain, where thou mightst hope to change
Torment with ease, and; soonest recompence
Dole with delight, which in this place I sought;
To thee no reason; who knowst only good,
But evil hast not tri'd: and wilt object
897. His will who bound us? let him surer barr
His Iron Gates, if he intends our stay
In that dark durance: thus much what was askt.
900. The rest is true, they found me where they say;
901. But that implies not violence or harme.
902.   Thus he in scorn. The warlike Angel mov'd,
Disdainfully half smiling thus repli'd.
O loss of one in Heav'n to judge of wise,
Since Satan fell, whom follie overthrew,
And now returns him from his prison scap't,
Gravely in doubt whether to hold them wise
Or not, who ask what boldness brought him hither
Unlicenc't from his bounds in Hell prescrib'd;
910. So wise he judges it to fly from pain
However, and to scape his punishment.
So judge thou still, presumptuous, till the wrauth,
Which thou incurr'st by flying, meet thy flight
Seavenfold, and scourge that wisdom back to Hell,
915. Which taught thee yet no better, that no pain
Can equal anger infinite provok't.
917. But wherefore thou alone? wherefore with thee
Came not all Hell broke loose? is pain to them
Less pain, less to be fled, or thou then they
Less hardie to endure? courageous Chief,
The first in flight from pain, hadst thou alleg'd
To thy deserted host this cause of flight,
Thou surely hadst not come sole fugitive.
924.   To which the Fiend thus answerd frowning stern.

877.   Gabriel said, "*Satan, why did you escape from Hell and trespass here, apparently trying to disturb the sleeping couple at their home?*"

885.   Satan said, "*I thought you were smarter than that, Gabriel.*

888.   *Who wouldn't escape from Hell if he could? You would, yourself.*

891.   *And you'd look for a better place, like this, just like I did.*

897.   *If God wants to keep us in Hell, he'll have to build stronger gates.*

900.   *The rest is true, they found me where they say.*
901.   *But that doesn't mean I intended any violence or harm.*"
902.   With a wry smile, Gabriel said, "*So you think my question was stupid?*

910.   *And you consider yourself smart to try to escape God's punishment and anger him all the more?*

915.   *Being in Hell hasn't taught you much, has it?*

917.   *But, wait a minute, how come you escaped all alone? Do the rest of your friends like it in Hell? Or are you just too soft to handle it like the others?*"

924.   Satan said, "*You know better than that. Remember the war? You couldn't beat me with your worst attack, till God helped you.*

Not that I less endure, or shrink from pain,
Insulting Angel, well thou knowst I stood
Thy fiercest, when in Battel to thy aide
The blasting volied Thunder made all speed
And seconded thy else not dreaded Spear.
930. But still thy words at random, as before,
Argue thy inexperience what behooves
From hard assaies and ill successes past
A faithful Leader, not to hazard all
Through wayes of danger by himself untri'd,
935. I therefore, I alone first undertook
To wing the desolate Abyss, and spie
This new created World, whereof in Hell
Fame is not silent, here in hope to find
Better abode, and my afflicted Powers
To settle here on Earth, or in mid Aire;
941. Though for possession put to try once more
What thou and thy gay Legions dare against;
Whose easier business were to serve thir Lord
High up in Heav'n, with songs to hymne his Throne,
And practis'd distances to cringe, not fight.
946.   To whom the warriour Angel, soon repli'd.
To say and strait unsay, pretending first
Wise to flie pain, professing next the Spie,
Argues no Leader, but a lyar trac't,
Satan, and couldst thou faithful add? O name,
O sacred name of faithfulness profan'd!
Faithful to whom? to thy rebellious crew?
Armie of Fiends, fit body to fit head;
Was this your discipline and faith ingag'd,
Your military obedience, to dissolve
Allegeance to th' acknowledg'd Power supream?
And thou sly hypocrite, who now wouldst seem
958. Patron of liberty, who more then thou
Once fawn'd, and cring'd, and servilly ador'd
Heav'ns awful Monarch? wherefore but in hope
To dispossess him, and thy self to reigne?
962. But mark what I arreede thee now, avant;
963. Flie thither whence thou fledst: if from this houre
Within these hallowd limits thou appeer,
Back to th' infernal pit I drag thee chaind,
And Seale thee so, as henceforth not to scorne
The facil gates of hell too slightly barrd.
968.   So threatn'd hee, but Satan to no threats
Gave heed, but waxing more in rage repli'd.
970.   Then when I am thy captive talk of chaines,
Proud limitarie Cherube, but ere then
Farr heavier load thy self expect to feel
973. From my prevailing arme, though Heavens King

930. *This just shows how dumb you are. A leader doesn't lead all his men into an unknown situation without checking it out first himself.*

935. *I made this journey alone to find a better place for my people to live.*

941. *And to see what we might be up against—these fancy dressed legions of yours. They look better suited to bowing and kneeling and singing for their master."*

946.   Gabriel said, "*You contradict yourself all over the place— first you're escaping, then you're exploring. On top of it all, you call yourself a faithful leader. You're a hypocrite and a liar!*

958. *Nobody bowed and scraped before God more than you did, all the while planning to revolt and take over as king.*

962. *Now you listen to me. Get out of here now! Go back where you came from.*

963. *If you're not gone from this sacred garden in less than an hour, I will personally drag you back to Hell in chains and see to it you think twice about leaving there again."*

968.   Satan got very angry.

970.   He said, "*When you have me captive, then you can talk about chains. Right now let me show you my power.*

973. *I don't care if you get God to help you."*

       Ride on thy wings, and thou with thy Compeers,
       Us'd to the yoak, draw'st his triumphant wheels
       In progress through the rode of Heav'n Star-pav'd.
977.   While thus he spake, th' Angelic Squadron bright
       Turnd fierie red, sharpning in mooned hornes
       Thir Phalanx, and began to hemm him round
980. With ported Spears, as thick as when a field
       Of Ceres ripe for harvest waving bends
       Her bearded Grove of ears, which way the wind
       Swayes them; the careful Plowman doubting stands
       Least on the threshing floore his hopeful sheaves
985. Prove chaff. On th' other side Satan allarm'd
       Collecting all his might dilated stood,
987. Like Teneriff or Atlas unremov'd:
       His stature reacht the Skie, and on his Crest
       Sat horror Plum'd; nor wanted in his graspe
990. What seemd both Spear and Shield: now dreadful deeds
       Might have ensu'd, nor onely Paradise
       In this commotion, but the Starrie Cope
       Of Heav'n perhaps, or all the Elements
       At least had gon to rack, disturbd and torne
       With violence of this conflict, had not soon
996. Th' Eternal to prevent such horrid fray
       Hung forth in Heav'n his golden Scales, yet seen
       Betwixt Astrea and the Scorpion signe,
       Wherein all things created first he weighd,
       The pendulous round Earth with balanc't Aire
       In counterpoise, now ponders all events,
1002. Battels and Realms: in these he put two weights
       The sequel each of parting and of fight;
1004. The latter quick up flew, and kickt the beam;
       Which Gabriel spying, thus bespake the Fiend.
1006.   Satan, I know thy strength, and thou know'st mine,
1007. Neither our own but giv'n; what follie then
       To boast what Arms can doe, since thine no more
1009. Then Heav'n permits, nor mine, though doubld now
1010. To trample thee as mire: for proof look up,
       And read thy Lot in yon celestial Sign
       Where thou art weigh'd, and shown how light, how weak,
1013. If thou resist. The Fiend lookt up and knew
1014. His mounted scale aloft: nor more; but fled
1015. Murmuring, and with him fled the shades of night.

977.   As he spoke, the angels circled him and began to close in, pointing their spears at him.

980. They looked like a big field of wheat waving in the wind.

985. Satan braced himself.

987. He seemed to get bigger, like a mountain that could not be budged.

990. Now a violent battle might have taken place—enough to shake up the whole universe.

996. God decided to prevent it by sending an astrological message in the sky.

1002. Libra, or the scales, weighed the consequences of what would happen if Satan resisted, or if he just went away.

1004. You could see the choice to fight was the one that would fail.

1006.   "*Satan,*" said Gabriel, "*I know your strength and you know mine.*

1007. *Both are controlled by God. It's silly to brag, since neither one of us can do anything more than God permits.*

1009. *(By the way, I'm twice as strong as usual and can trample you like mud.)*

1010. *But if you want proof, just look up at that sign in the Zodiac and see what'll happen if you try to fight me.*"

1013. Satan looked up and saw the bad news.

1014. He took off, mumbling to himself.

1015. Meanwhile, dawn was breaking.

Book V

PARADISE LOST

1.   Now Morn her rosie steps in th' Eastern Clime
Advancing, sow'd the earth with Orient Pearle,
When Adam wak't, so customd, for his sleep
4. Was Aerie light, from pure digestion bred,
And temperat vapors bland, which th' only sound leaves and
fuming rills, Aurora's fan,
Lightly dispers'd, and the shrill Matin Song
Of Birds on every bough; so much the more
9. His wonder was to find unwak'nd Eve
With Tresses discompos'd, and glowing Cheek,
As through unquiet rest: he on his side
12. Leaning half-rais'd, with looks of cordial Love
Hung over her enamour'd, and beheld
Beautie, which whether waking or asleep,
Shot forth peculiar graces; then with voice
Milde, as when Zephyrus on Flora breathes,
17. Her hand soft touching, whisperd thus. Awake
My fairest, my espous'd, my latest found,
Heav'ns last best gift, my ever new delight,
Awake, the morning shines, and the fresh field
Calls us, we lose the prime, to mark how spring
22. Our tended Plants, how blows the Citron Grove,
What drops the Myrrhe, and what the balmie Reed,
How Nature paints her colours, how the Bee
Sits on the Bloom extracting liquid sweet.
26.   Such whispering wak'd her, but with startl'd eye
On Adam, whom imbracing, thus she spake.
28.   O Sole in whom my thoughts find all repose,
My Glorie, my Perfection, glad I see
Thy face, and Morn return'd, for I this Night,
31. Such night till this I never pass'd, have dream'd,
If dream'd, not as I oft am wont, of thee,
Works of day pass't, or morrows next designe,
But of offense and trouble, which my mind
Knew never till this irksom night; methought
36. Close at mine ear one call'd me forth to walk
With gentle voice, I thought it thine; it said,
38. Why sleepst thou Eve? now is the pleasant time,
The cool, the silent, save where silence yields
To the night-warbling Bird, that now awake
Tunes sweetest his love-labor'd song; now reignes
Full Orb'd the Moon, and with more pleasing light

Chapter 5

IN PLAIN ENGLISH

1. It was sunrise when Adam woke up.

4. His healthy environment caused him to sleep light, so just the sound of rustling leaves or birds would wake him up.

9. So he was surprised to see Eve still asleep with her hair in a mess and with a troubled expression on her face.

12. He raised himself up on his elbow and stared at her, admiring her.

17. He whispered, "*Wake up, Eve, before the beauty of the early morning is gone.*

22. *You don't want to miss the citrus blooms, the colors and the fragrance, and the bees collecting their pollen.*"

26. She woke up with a start.

28. "*Oh, Adam,*" she said, "*I'm so glad to see your perfect face.*

31. *I had a dream, but not as I usually dream, about you and pleasant things, but bad things I never thought about before.*

36. *I thought I heard you talking in my ear, telling me to go with you.*

38. *You talked about how beautiful the night was, the birds that sing at night, and how the moonlight from the full moon made everything beautiful, but nobody was there to see it.*

       Shadowie sets off the face of things; in vain,

44. If none regard; Heav'n wakes with all his eyes,
       Whom to behold but thee, Natures desire,
       In whose sight all things joy, with ravishment
       Attracted by thy beauty still to gaze.

48. I rose as at thy call, but found thee not;

49. To find thee I directed then my walk;
       And on, methought, alone I pass'd through ways
       That brought me on a sudden to the Tree

52. Of interdicted Knowledge: fair it seem'd,
       Much fairer to my Fancie then by day:

54. And as I wondring lookt, beside it stood
       One shap'd and wing'd like one of those from Heav'n
       By us oft seen; his dewie locks distill'd
       Ambrosia; on that Tree he also gaz'd;

58. And O fair Plant, said he, with fruit surcharg'd,
       Deigns none to ease thy load and taste thy sweet,
       Nor God, nor Man; is Knowledge so despis'd?
       Or envie, or what reserve forbids to taste?
       Forbid who will, none shall from me withhold
       Longer thy offerd good, why else set here?

64. This said he paus'd not, but with ventrous Arme
       He pluckt, he tasted; mee damp horror chil'd
       At such bold words voucht with a deed so bold:

67. But he thus overjoy'd, O Fruit Divine,
       Sweet of thy self, but much more sweet thus cropt,
       Forbidd'n here, it seems, as onely fit
       For God's, yet able to make Gods of Men:
       And why not Gods of Men, since good, the more
       Communicated, more abundant growes,
       The Author not impair'd, but honourd more?

74. Here, happie Creature, fair Angelic Eve,
       Partake thou also; happie though thou art,
       Happier thou mayst be, worthier canst not be:
       Taste this, and be henceforth among the Gods
       Thy self a Goddess, not to Earth confind,
       But somtimes in the Air, as wee, somtimes
       Ascend to Heav'n, by merit thine, and see
       What life the Gods live there, and such live thou.

82. So saying, he drew nigh, and to me held,
       Even to my mouth of that same fruit held part
       Which he had pluckt; the pleasant savourie smell
       So quick'nd appetite, that I, methought,

86. Could not but taste. Forthwith up to the Clouds
       With him I flew, and underneath beheld
       The Earth outstretcht immense, a prospect wide
       And various: wondring at my flight and change
       To this high exaltation; suddenly
       My Guide was gon, and I, me thought, sunk down,

44. *You said the stars were like eyes waiting to enjoy my beauty.*

48. *I got up to follow you, but you weren't there.*
49. *I went to look for you and I came to the tree with the forbidden fruit.*

52. *It looked beautiful, much more than it does in daytime.*

54. *Suddenly I noticed an angel standing beside it.*

58. *'What beautiful fruit!' he said, 'and nobody wants to taste it? Well, nobody's going to stop me from eating it. What else is it here for?'*

64. *Then he picked a piece of fruit and ate it. I was shocked.*

67. *He said 'Wonderful fruit! Good to look at, better to taste. It's supposed to be only for the gods, but it's able to turn men into gods. And why not? Why not spread the good? That would honor God all the more.'*

74. *Then he told me I should eat the fruit too. He said it would make me even happier than I am and turn me into a goddess.*

82. *Then he put the fruit near my mouth. It smelled so good, I couldn't help myself. I ate it.*

86. *Suddenly we both flew up into the sky. Then he was gone and I sank back down into sleep.*

92. And fell asleep; but O how glad I wak'd
    To find this but a dream! Thus Eve her Night
    Related, and thus Adam answerd sad.

95.   Best Image of my self and dearer half,
    The trouble of thy thoughts this night in sleep
    Affects me equally; nor can I like
    This uncouth dream, of evil sprung I fear;

99. Yet evil whence? in thee can harbour none,
    Created pure. But know that in the Soule

101. Are many lesser Faculties that serve
    Reason as chief; among these Fansie next
    Her office holds; of all external things,

106. Which the five watchful Senses represent,
    She forms Imaginations, Aerie shapes,
    Which Reason joyning or disjoyning, frames
    All what we affirm or what deny, and call
    Our knowledge or opinion; then retires
    Into her private Cell when Nature rests.
    Oft in her absence mimic Fansie wakes

111. To imitate her; but misjoyning shapes,
    Wilde work produces oft, and most in dreams,
    Ill matching words and deeds long past or late.

114. Som such resemblances methinks I find
    Of our last Eevnings talk, in this thy dream,

116. But with addition strange; yet be not sad.
    Evil into the mind of God or Man
    May come and go, so unapprov'd, and leave

119. No spot or blame behind: Which gives me hope
    That what in sleep thou didst abhorr to dream,
    Waking thou never wilt consent to do.

122. Be not disheart'nd then, nor cloud those looks
    That wont to be more chearful and serene
    Then when fair Morning first smiles on the World,
    And let us to our fresh imployments rise
    Among the Groves, the Fountains, and the Flours
    That open now thir choicest bosom'd smells
    Reservd from night, and kept for thee in store.
        So cheard he his fair Spouse, and she was cheard,

130. But silently a gentle tear let fall
    From either eye, and wip'd them with her haire;
    Two other precious drops that ready stood,
    Each in thir Chrystal sluce, hee ere they fell
    Kiss'd as the gracious signs of sweet remorse
    And pious awe, that feard to have offended.

136.   So all was cleard, and to the Field they haste.
    But first from under shadie arborous roof,

138. Soon as they forth were come to open sight
    Of day-spring, and the Sun, who scarce up risen
    With wheels yet hov'ring o're the Ocean brim,

92. *I'm so relieved to find out it was just a dream!"*

95.   Adam said, *"I don't like this dream. It comes from some unknown evil.*

99. *But where could it come from? There is no evil in you. You were created pure.*

101. *But in addition to our five senses, we have imagination.*

106. *Our conscious mind holds our knowledge, but when we sleep our imagination takes over.*

111. *Imagination sometimes mixes up our memories in our dreams.*

114. *I think I see some of what we talked about last night in your dream, with some more strange stuff.*

116. *But don't worry. We might get bad thoughts, but no harm is done. They're only thoughts.*

119. *The fact that you're so upset at what you dreamed shows us that it's something you would never do in real life.*

122. *So cheer up, and let's get to work in the garden. The morning blossoms smell so good."*

130.   She felt better that she hadn't offended God. She wiped some tears with her hair, and Adam kissed away the ones forming in her eyes.

136.   Before they went out into the fields, they said their morning prayers.

138. From their doorway they could see the sunrise lighting up the whole landscape.

Shot paralel to the earth his dewie ray,
Discovering in wide Lantskip all the East
Of Paradise and Edens happie Plains,

144. Lowly they bow'd adoring, and began
Thir Orisons, each Morning duly paid
In various style, for neither various style
Nor holy rapture wanted they to praise
Thir Maker, in fit strains pronounc't or sung
Unmeditated, such prompt eloquence
Flowd from thir lips, in Prose or numerous Verse,

151. More tuneable then needed Lute or Harp
To add more sweetness, and they thus began.

153.   These are thy glorious works, Parent of good,
Almightie, thine this universal Frame,
Thus wondrous fair; thy self how wondrous then!

157. Unspeakable, who sitts above these Heavens
To us invisible or dimly seen
In these thy lowest works, yet these declare
Thy goodness beyond thought, and Power Divine:

160. Speak yee who best can tell, ye Sons of Light,
Angels, for yee behold him, and with songs
And choral symphonies, Day without Night,
Circle his Throne rejoycing, yee in Heav'n,
On Earth joyn all ye Creatures to extoll
Him first, him last, him midst, and without end.

166. Fairest of Starrs, last in the train of Night,
If better thou belong not to the dawn,
Sure pledge of day, that crownst the smiling Morn
With thy bright Circlet, praise him in thy Spheare
While day arises, that sweet hour of Prime.

171. Thou Sun, of this great World both Eye and Soule,
Acknowledge him thy Greater, sound his praise
In thy eternal course, both when thou climb'st,
And when high Noon hast gaind, and when thou fallst.

175. Moon, that now meetst the orient Sun, now fli'st
With the fixt Starrs, fixt in thir Orb that flies,
And yee five other wandring Fires that move
In mystic Dance not without Song, resound
His praise, who out of Darkness call'd up Light.

180. Aire, and ye Elements the eldest birth
Of Natures Womb, that in quaternion run
Perpetual Circle, multiform; and mix
And nourish all things, let your ceasless change
Varie to our great Maker still new praise.

185. Ye Mists and Exhalations that now rise
From Hill or steaming Lake, duskie or grey,
Till the Sun paint your fleecie skirts with Gold,
In honour to the Worlds great Author rise,
Whether to deck with Clouds th' uncolourd skie,

144. They began to pray. They were very good at making up different kinds of beautiful prayers every morning.

151. They didn't need any background music.

153.   They began, "*Dear God, how wonderful you are, to have created this wonderful world.*

157. *You are invisible, but we can see you in your beautiful creation.*

160. *Angels, you who know him best, join us in praising him.*

166. *And you, morning star, praise him as you shine.*

171. *And you, sun, praise him as you rise and fall.*

175. *And you, moon and planets, praise the one who made light.*

180. *Air and fire and water and earth, that mix and change, give God different praise.*

185. *You mists that rise up from land and water, also praise him as you make clouds and rain.*

Or wet the thirstie Earth with falling showers,
Rising or falling still advance his praise.

192. His praise ye Winds, that from four Quarters blow,
Breathe soft or loud; and wave your tops, ye Pines,
With every Plant, in sign of Worship wave.

195. Fountains and yee, that warble, as ye flow,
Melodious murmurs, warbling tune his praise.

197. Joyn voices all ye living Souls; ye Birds,
That singing up to Heaven Gate ascend,
Bear on your wings and in your notes his praise;
Yee that in Waters glide, and yee that walk
The Earth, and stately tread, or lowly creep;
Witness if I be silent, Morn or Eeven,
To Hill, or Valley, Fountain, or fresh shade
Made vocal by my Song, and taught his praise.

205. Hail universal Lord, be bounteous still
To give us onely good; and if the night
Have gathered aught of evil or conceald,
Disperse it, as now light dispels the dark.

209.   So pray'd they innocent, and to thir thoughts
Firm peace recoverd soon and wonted calm.

211. On to thir mornings rural work they haste
Among sweet dewes and flours; where any row

213. Of Fruit-trees overwoodie reachd too farr
Thir pamperd boughes, and needed hands to check
Fruitless imbraces: or they led the Vine
To wed her Elm; she spous'd about him twines
Her marriageable arms, and with her brings
Her dowr th' adopted Clusters, to adorn

219. His barren leaves. Them thus imploid beheld

220. With pittie Heav'ns high King, and to him call'd
Raphael, the sociable Spirit, that deign'd
To travel with Tobias, and secur'd
His marriage with the seaventimes-wedded Maid.

224.   Raphael, said hee, thou hear'st what stir on Earth
Satan from Hell scap't through the darksom Gulf
Hath raisd in Paradise, and how disturbd
This night the human pair, how he designes
In them at once to ruin all mankind.

229. Go therefore, half this day as friend with friend
Converse with Adam, in what Bowre or shade
Thou find'st him from the heat of Noon retir'd,
To respit his day-labour with repast,

233. Or with repose; and such discourse bring on,
As may advise him of his happie state,
Happiness in his power left free to will,
Left to his own free Will, his Will though free,

237. Yet mutable; whence warne him to beware
He swerve not too secure: tell him withall

192. *Wind, blow the treetops and make them wave praise to him.*

195. *Waterfalls and rippling brooks, sing his praise.*

197. *All birds and beasts, learn from us to praise God.*

205. *Dear God, please continue to give us good things, and chase away any evil things that may have come in the night."*

209.   They felt better after they prayed.

211. They hurried off to work.

213. They pruned the fruit trees and guided the wild vines up the elm trees.

219. God was watching them. He felt bad about what was in store for them.

220. He called Raphael, a friendly angel who once saved Tobias, Sara's husband, from a demon who had murdered her seven former husbands.

224.   *"Raphael,"* said God, *"Did you hear what Satan did? He bothered Eve in her sleep and now he's planning to ruin all mankind.*

229. *I want you to go down to Earth at noontime and find Adam and talk to him.*

233. *Explain to him that his happiness depends on how he uses his free will.*

237. *Warn him not to be too sure of his safety. Tell him about how Satan is after him.*

His danger, and from whom, what enemie
Late falln himself from Heav'n, is plotting now
The fall of others from like state of bliss;
242. By violence, no, for that shall be withstood,
243. But by deceit and lies; this let him know,
Lest wilfully transgressing he pretend
Surprisal, unadmonisht, unforewarnd.
246.   So spake th' Eternal Father, and fulfilld
All Justice: nor delaid the winged Saint
After his charge receivd; but from among
249. Thousand Celestial Ardors, where he stood
Vaild with his gorgeous wings, up springing light
Flew through the midst of Heav'n; th' angelic Quires
On each hand parting, to his speed gave way
253. Through all th' Empyreal road; till at the Gate
Of Heav'n arriv'd, the gate self-opend wide
On golden Hinges turning, as by work
Divine the sov'ran Architect had fram'd.
257. From hence, no cloud, or, to obstruct his sight,
Starr interpos'd, however small he sees,
Not unconform to other shining Globes,
Earth and the Gard'n of God, with Cedars crownd
261. Above all Hills. As when by night the Glass
Of Galileo, less assur'd, observes
Imagind Lands and Regions in the Moon:
Or Pilot from amidst the Cyclades
Delos or Samos first appeering kenns
266. A cloudy spot. Down thither prone in flight
He speeds, and through the vast Ethereal Skie
Sailes between worlds and worlds, with steddie wing
Now on the polar windes, then with quick Fann
270. Winnows the buxom Air; till within soare
271. Of Towring Eagles, to all the Fowles he seems
A Phœnix, gaz'd by all, as that sole Bird
When to enshrine his reliques in the Sun's
Bright Temple, to Ægyptian Theb's he flies.
275. At once on th' Eastern cliff of Paradise
He lights, and to his proper shape returns
277. A Seraph wingd; six wings he wore, to shade
His lineaments Divine; the pair that clad
Each shoulder broad, came mantling o're his brest
With regal Ornament; the middle pair
Girt like a Starrie Zone his waste, and round
282. Skirted his loines and thighes with downie Gold
And colours dipt in Heav'n; the third his feet
Shaddowd from either heele with featherd maile
Skie-tinctur'd grain. Like Maia's son he stood,
And shook his Plumes, that Heav'nly fragrance filld
287. The circuit wide. Strait knew him all the Bands

242. *Explain that Satan can't hurt him by violence—that he's planning to bring him down using deceit and lies.*

243. *I want him to understand all this so he can't say nobody warned him when he sins."*

246.   So God was covered.

249. A thousand angels cleared the way for Raphael to pass on his way to the gate of Heaven.

253. The gate opened by itself.

257. From there his angel eyes could see all the way down into the universe, to Earth and the Garden of Eden.

261. He was like Galileo looking through his telescope at new places on the moon, or a ship's pilot spying the mist of a distant island while sailing among many islands.

266. He dove straight down.

270. When he came into the Earth's atmosphere, he flapped his wings.

271. He looked like a phoenix.

275. He landed on the eastern cliff of Paradise.

277. He had six wings—two at his shoulders, two gold and multicolored ones at his waist, and two sky blue ones on the heels of his feet, like Mercury.

282. Perfume came out of the feathers when he shook them.

287. The angels on guard recognized him right away. They stood up out of respect as he passed.

Of Angels under watch; and to his state,
And to his message high in honour rise;
For on Som message high they guessd him bound.

291. Thir glittering Tents he passd, and now is come
Into the blissful field, through Groves of Myrrhe,
And flouring Odours, Cassia, Nard, and Balme;
A Wilderness of sweets; for Nature here
Wantond as in her prime, and plaid at will
Her Virgin Fancies, pouring forth more sweet,
Wilde above Rule or Art; enormous bliss.

298. Him through the spicie Forrest onward com
Adam discernd, as in the dore he sat
Of his coole Bowre, while now the mounted Sun
Shot down direct his fervid Raies, to warme
Earths inmost womb, more warmth then Adam needs;

303. And Eve within, due at her hour prepar'd
For dinner savourie fruits, of taste to please
True appetite, and not disrelish thirst
Of nectarous draughts between, from milkie stream,

307. Berrie or Grape: to whom thus Adam call'd.
Haste hither Eve, and worth thy sight behold
Eastward among those Trees, what glorious shape
Comes this way moving; seems another Morn

311. Ris'n on mid-noon; Som great behest from Heav'n

312. To us perhaps he brings, and will voutsafe
This day to be our Guest. But goe with speed,
And what thy stores contain, bring forth and poure
Abundance, fit to honour and receive
Our Heav'nly stranger; well we may afford
Our givers thir own gifts, and large bestow
From large bestowd, where Nature multiplies
Her fertil growth, and by disburd'ning grows
More fruitful, which instructs us not to spare.

321. To whom thus Eve. Adam, earths hallowd mould,
Of God inspir'd, small store will serve, where store,
All seasons, ripe for use hangs on the stalk;
Save what by frugal storing firmness gains
To nourish, and superfluous moist consumes:

326. But I will haste and from each bough and break,
Each Plant and juiciest Gourd will pluck such choice
To entertain our Angel guest, as hee
Beholding shall confess that here on Earth
God hath dispenst his bounties as in Heav'n.

331. So saying, with dispatchful looks in haste
She turns, on hospitable thoughts intent
What choice to chuse for delicacie best,
What order, so contriv'd as not to mix
Tastes, not well joynd, inelegant, but bring
Taste after taste upheld with kindliest change,

291. He went by their station and into a forest of many sweet smelling spices.

298. Adam was sitting in the doorway of his shelter, away from the hot noon sun. He saw the angel coming.

303. Eve was inside preparing fruit for lunch, and squeezing drinks from berries and grapes.

307. Adam cried, "*Eve, hurry! Look at that bright shape coming from among those trees. He's as bright as the sun!*

311. *He must be bringing us some message from God.*
312. *Maybe he'll be our guest. Hurry and bring out all our best refreshments. Let's give back to this visitor from God what God has so generously given to us."*

321. Eve said, "*I really don't store that much, Adam, since there's always so many fresh fruits and vegetables growing all around us.*

326. *But I'll hurry up and go pick the best fruits I can find. We'll impress our guest with what God gave us."*

331. She hurried out and brought back an assortment of fruits that she knew would taste good in combination.

Bestirs her then, and from each tender stalk
338. Whatever Earth all-bearing Mother yields
In India East or West, or middle shoare
In Pontus or the Punic Coast, or where
Alcinous reign'd, fruit of all kindes, in coate,
Rough, or smooth rin'd, or bearded husk, or shell
She gathers, Tribute large, and on the board
Heaps with unsparing hand; for drink the Grape
345. She crushes, inoffensive moust, and meathes
From many a berrie, and from sweet kernels prest
She tempers dulcet creams, nor these to hold
348. Wants her fit vessels pure, then strews the ground
With Rose and Odours from the shrub unfum'd.
350. Mean while our Primitive great Sire, to meet
His god-like Guest, walks forth, without more train
352. Accompanied then with his own compleat
Perfections; in himself was all his state,
More solemn then the tedious pomp that waits
On Princes, when thir rich Retinue long
Of Horses led, and Grooms besmeard with Gold
Dazles the croud, and sets them all agape.
358. Neerer his presence Adam though not awd,
Yet with submiss approach and reverence meek,
As to a superior Nature, bowing low,
361.   Thus said. Native of Heav'n, for other place
None can then Heav'n such glorious shape contain;
363. Since by descending from the Thrones above,
Those happie places thou hast deignd a while
To want, and honour these, voutsafe with us
Two onely, who yet by sov'ran gift possess
This spacious ground, in yonder shadie Bowre
To rest, and what the Garden choicest bears
To sit and taste, till this meridian heat
Be over, and the Sun more coole decline.
371.   Whom thus the Angelic Vertue answerd milde.
Adam, I therefore came, nor art thou such
Created, or such place hast here to dwell,
As may not oft invite, though Spirits of Heav'n
To visit thee; lead on then where thy Bowre
Oreshades; for these mid-hours, till Eevning rise
I have at will. So to the Silvan Lodge
378. They came, that like Pomona's Arbour smil'd
With flourets deck't and fragrant smells; but Eve
380. Undeckt, save with her self more lovely fair
Then Wood-Nymph, or the fairest Goddess feign'd
Of three that in Mount Ida naked strove,
Stood to entertain her guest from Heav'n; no vaile
Shee needed, Vertue-proof, no thought infirme
385. Alterd her cheek. On whom the Angel Haile

338. All the delicious foods we find all over the world were once all here in the Garden of Eden.

345. She squeezed grapes and berries for drinks and made sweet creams and put them in pretty containers.

348. She spread rose petals and other pleasant smelling leaves on the ground.

350. Meanwhile, Adam went to meet the angel.

352. Even without any clothes on, Adam looked more royal than a prince with a long procession of fancy attendants on horse-back.

358. Adam was not afraid, but he bowed out of respect.

361.   He said, "*You look so glorious, you must be from Heaven.*

363. *Since you're honoring us by leaving Heaven for a while, come and enjoy some refreshments with us in our cool shelter this afternoon."*

371.   The angel said, "*That's what I came for, Adam. Your home is inviting, even to spirits of Heaven, and I'm free to stay till evening."*

378. They came to the shelter, which was covered with sweet smelling flowers.

380. But Eve, whose body was uncovered, was more lovely than Venus. She didn't need to be covered because her thoughts were all pure.

385.   The angel said, "*Hail, Eve,*" (the same way we would later pray to Mary, the second Eve) "*Mother of Mankind, you're going to fill the world with more sons than all the fruit God has given you here."*

Bestowd, the holy salutation us'd
Long after to blest Marie, second Eve.
    Haile Mother of Mankind, whose fruitful Womb
Shall fill the World more numerous with thy Sons
Then with these various fruits the Trees of God

391. Have heap'd this Table. Rais'd of grassie terf
Thir Table was, and mossie seats had round,
And on her ample Square from side to side
All Autumn pil'd, though Spring and Autumn here

395. Danc'd hand in hand. A while discourse they hold;
No fear lest Dinner coole; when thus began

397. Our Authour. Heav'nly stranger, please to taste
These bounties which our Nourisher, from whom
All perfet good unmeasur'd out, descends,
To us for food and for delight hath caus'd
The Earth to yeild; unsavourie food perhaps
To spiritual Natures; only this I know,
That one Celestial Father gives to all.

404.   To whom the Angel. Therefore what he gives
(Whose praise be ever sung) to man in part
Spiritual, may of purest Spirits be found

407. No ingrateful food: and food alike those pure
Intelligential substances require
As doth your Rational; and both contain
Within them every lower facultie
Of sense, whereby they hear, see, smell, touch, taste,
Tasting concoct, digest, assimilate,
And corporeal to incorporeal turn.

414. For know, whatever was created, needs
To be sustaind and fed; of Elements
The grosser feeds the purer, Earth the Sea,
Earth and the Sea feed Air, the Air those Fires
Ethereal, and as lowest first the Moon;
Whence in her visage round those spots, unpurg'd
Vapours not yet into her substance turnd.
Nor doth the Moon no nourishment exhale
From her moist Continent to higher Orbes.
The Sun that light imparts to all, receives
From all his alimental recompence
In humid exhalations, and at Even

426. Sups with the Ocean: though in Heav'n the Trees
Of life ambrosial frutage bear, and vines
Yield Nectar, though from off the boughs each Morn
We brush mellifluous Dewes, and find the ground
Cover'd with pearly grain: yet God hath here
Varied his bounty so with new delights,
As may compare with Heaven; and to taste

433. Think not I shall be nice. So down they sat,
And to thir viands fell, nor seemingly

391. The table and chairs were made of grass and moss. The table was piled full of fruit that was always in season.

395. There was no hurry to eat. This meal would not grow cold. So they could talk awhile.

397. Adam began by saying he wondered whether angels could enjoy human food.

404.   The angel answered, "*Man is also part spiritual, so what God gives you can't be bad for us.*

407. *Both you and I need nourishment to feed our bodies and souls.*

414. *Everything that was created needs nourishment. The earth and sea feed the air, the air feeds the moon, which feeds the stars. The sun, which gives light to everything, is rewarded with nourishing evening mist from the ocean.*

426. *In Heaven there are also trees and vines with delicious fruit, but here on Earth God has added new tasty looking varieties, which I wouldn't hesitate to try."*

433. So they sat down and started to eat.

435. The Angel, nor in mist, the common gloss
    Of Theologians, but with keen dispatch
    Of real hunger, and concoctive heate
438. To transubstantiate; what redounds, transpires
439. Through Spirits with ease; nor wonder; if by fire
    Of sooty coal the Empiric Alchimist
    Can turn, or holds it possible to turn
    Metals of drossiest Ore to perfet Gold
443. As from the Mine. Mean while at Table Eve
    Ministerd naked, and thir flowing cups
445. With pleasant liquors crown'd: O innocence
    Deserving Paradise! if ever, then,
    Then had the Sons of God excuse to have bin
    Enamour'd at that sight; but in those hearts
    Love unlibidinous reign'd, nor jealousie
    Was understood, the injur'd Lovers Hell.
451.   Thus when with meats and drinks they had suffic'd
    Not burd'nd Nature, sudden mind arose
    In Adam, not to let th' occasion pass
    Given him by this great Conference to know
    Of things above his World, and of thir being
    Who dwell in Heav'n, whose excellence he saw
    Transcend his own so farr, whose radiant forms
    Divine effulgence, whose high Power so far
    Exceeded human, and his wary speech
460. Thus to th' Empyreal Minister he fram'd.
    Inhabitant with God, now know I well
    Thy favour, in this honour done to man,
    Under whose lowly roof thou hast voutsaft
    To enter, and these earthly fruits to taste,
468. Food not of Angels, yet accepted so,
    As that more willingly thou couldst not seem
    At Heav'n's high feasts to have fed: yet what compare?
    To whom the winged Hierarch repli'd.
    O Adam, one Almightie is, from whom
    All things proceed, and up to him return,
    If not deprav'd from good, created all
472. Such to perfection, one first matter all,
    Indu'd with various forms, various degrees
    Of substance, and in things that live, of life;
475. But more refin'd, more spiritous, and pure,
    As neerer to him plac't or neerer tending
    Each in thir several active Sphears assignd,
    Till body up to spirit work, in bounds
479. Proportiond to each kind. So from the root
    Springs lighter the green stalk, from thence the leaves
    More aerie, last the bright consummate floure
    Spirits odorous breathes: flours and thir fruit
483. Mans nourishment, by gradual scale sublim'd

435. The angel ate like a real person. He was actually hungry. And his body could really digest food.

438. He never needed to go to the bathroom like us, though. The part he couldn't digest would just evaporate through his pores.

439. That's not so surprising when you consider how it's possible to turn crude ore from a mine into shiny gold by using fire.

443. Eve served the meal and poured drinks. She was naked.

445. If there ever was a sight to arouse lust, that was it. But in Paradise love was pure and innocent, and nobody knew how to be jealous.

451. When they finished eating (without overeating) Adam wanted to satisfy his curiosity about angels and Heaven.

460. He began, a little shyly, *"Raphael, I can't get over how you seem to enjoy this meal so much, when it can't possibly compare with the feasts you must have in Heaven."*

468. Raphael said, *"Adam, everything comes from God, and returns to him, if it's not corrupted by evil.*

472. *Everything he makes comes from the same basic material. He makes it into various forms and he gives life to some of them.*

475. *The closer each life grows to God, the purer and more refined it becomes, from body to spirit.*

479. *For example, from roots in the ground, a green stalk grows—from that, the more graceful leaves—then the delicate flower—and finally the sweet smelling perfume.*

483. *The fruit you eat nourishes your body, your blood, and finally your mind and soul.*

To vital Spirits aspire, to animal,
To intellectual, give both life and sense,
Fansie and understanding, whence the Soule
Reason receives, and reason is her being,

488. Discursive, or Intuitive; discourse
Is oftest yours, the latter most is ours,
Differing but in degree, of kind the same.

491. Wonder not then, what God for you saw good
If I refuse not, but convert, as you,

493. To proper substance; time may come when men
With Angels may participate, and find
No inconvenient Diet, nor too light Fare:
And from these corporal nutriments perhaps
Your bodies may at last turn all to Spirit,

498. Improv'd by tract of time, and wingd ascend
Ethereal, as wee, or may at choice
Here or in Heav'nly Paradises dwell;
If ye be found obedient, and retain
Unalterably firm his love entire

503. Whose progenie you are. Mean while enjoy
Your fill what happiness this happie state
Can comprehend, incapable of more.

506.   To whom the Patriarch of mankind repli'd,
O favourable spirit, propitious guest,
Well hast thou taught the way that might direct
Our knowledge, and the scale of Nature set
From center to circumference, whereon
In contemplation of created things
By steps we may ascend to God. But say,

513. What meant that caution joind, if ye be found
Obedient? can we want obedience then
To him, or possibly his love desert
Who formd us from the dust, and plac'd us here
Full to the utmost measure of what bliss
Human desires can seek or apprehend?

519.   To whom the Angel. Son of Heav'n and Earth,
Attend: That thou art happie, owe to God;
That thou continu'st such, owe to thy self,
That is, to thy obedience; therein stand.
This was that caution giv'n thee; be advis'd.

524. God made thee perfet, not immutable;
And good he made thee, but to persevere
He left it in thy power, ordaind thy will
By nature free, not over-rul'd by Fate
Inextricable, or strict necessity;

529. Our voluntarie service he requires,
Not our necessitated, such with him
Finds no acceptance, nor can find, for how
Can hearts, not free, be tri'd whether they serve

488. *You think by reasoning, we think intuitively. They are different degrees of the same thing.*

491. *So don't be surprised that I like your food. My spirit digests it in its own way.*

493. *Someday you may get to taste our kind of food. And from those nutrients you may finally become all spirit.*

498. *You'll be able to fly like us, and live here or in Heaven, which-ever you choose—but only if you continue to obey God.*

503. *For now, enjoy the happiness you have here."*

506.   Adam said, "*Very interesting!*

513. *But what do you mean, 'if we continue to obey God?' Haven't we been obedient enough? Are you saying he might stop loving us?"*

519.   Raphael said, "*I want you to listen very carefully to what I'm about to tell you. God gave you perfect happiness. But whether you stay happy or not depends entirely on you—and on your obedience.*

524. *He made you perfectly good, but he left it up to you if you want to stay that way. You have the freedom to be whatever you want to be.*

529. *It's the same with us. Angels stay welcome in Heaven as long as we stay obedient and serve of our own free will.*

Willing or no, who will but what they must
By Destinie, and can no other choose?
Myself and all th' Angelic Host that stand
In sight of God enthron'd, our happie state
Hold, as you yours, while our obedience holds;
On other surety none; freely we serve
Because we freely love, as in our will
To love or not; in this we stand or fall:

541. And Som are fall'n, to disobedience fall'n,
And so from Heav'n to deepest Hell; O fall
From what high state of bliss into what woe!

544.   To whom our great Progenitor. Thy words
Attentive, and with more delighted eare
Divine instructer, I have heard, then when
Cherubic Songs by night from neighbouring Hills
Aereal Music send: nor knew I not
To be both will and deed created free;

550. Yet that we never shall forget to love
Our maker, and obey him whose command
Single, is yet so just, my constant thoughts

553. Assur'd me and still assure: though what thou tellst
Hath past in Heav'n, Som doubt within me move,
But more desire to hear, if thou consent,
The full relation, which must needs be strange,
Worthy of Sacred silence to be heard;
And we have yet large day, for scarce the Sun
Hath finisht half his journey, and scarce begins
His other half in the great Zone of Heav'n.
    Thus Adam made request, and Raphael

562. After short pause assenting, thus began.
    High matter thou injoinst me, O prime of men,
Sad task and hard, for how shall I relate
To human sense th' invisible exploits
Of warring Spirits; how without remorse
The ruin of so many glorious once
And perfet while they stood; how last unfould
The secrets of another World, perhaps

570. Not lawful to reveal? yet for thy good
This is dispenc't, and what surmounts the reach
Of human sense, I shall delineate so,
By lik'ning spiritual to corporal forms,

574. As may express them best, though what if Earth
Be but the shaddow of Heav'n, and things therein
Each to other like, more then on earth is thought?

577.   As yet this World was not, and Chaos Wilde
Reignd where these Heav'ns now rowl, where Earth now rests
Upon her Center pois'd, when on a day
(For Time, though in Eternitie, appli'd
To motion, measures all things durable

541. *There are some angels who decided not to obey, and were kicked out of Heaven and thrown into Hell, and into such misery as you can't imagine."*

544.   "*I get it,*" said Adam. "*It feels good to hear you say it, but I already knew I was created with free will.*

550. *And, believe me, we have no intention of disobeying God, after he's been so kind to us.*

553. *But what was that thing you said about angels being kicked out of Heaven? I'd like to hear more about that. We have all afternoon. Would you tell me the whole story?"*

562.   Raphael said, "*You ask a lot, Adam. How can I make you understand how angels wage war? Just remembering how many angels were lost breaks my heart. These are things humans are not meant to understand.*

570. *But God has made an exception in your case. He's allowing me to reveal it all to you in ways you can understand, by describeing angels as if they were human.*

574. *Imagine if Heaven was just like Earth. (Maybe it is—more so than you might think). . .*

577.   One day, before this world was created, there was an official gathering in Heaven.

By present, past, and future) on such day
As Heav'ns great Year brings forth, th' Empyreal Host
584. Of Angels by Imperial summons call'd,
Innumerable before th' Almighties Throne
Forthwith from all the ends of Heav'n appeerd
Under thir Hierarchs in orders bright
588. Ten thousand thousand Ensignes high advanc'd,
Standards and Gonfalons twixt Van and Reare
Streame in the Aire, and for distinction serve
Of Hierarchies, of Orders, and Degrees;
Or in thir glittering Tissues bear imblaz'd
Holy Memorials, acts of Zeale and Love
594. Recorded eminent. Thus when in Orbes
Of circuit inexpressible they stood,
Orb within Orb, the Father infinite,
By whom in bliss imbosom'd sat the Son,
Amidst as from a flaming Mount, whose top
Brightness had made invisible, thus spake.
600.   Hear all ye Angels, Progenie of Light,
Thrones, Dominations, Princedoms, Vertues, Powers,
Hear my Decree, which unrevok't shall stand.
603. This day I have begot whom I declare
My onely Son, and on this holy Hill
Him have anointed, whom ye now behold
606. At my right hand; your Head I him appoint;
And by my Self have sworn to him shall bow
All knees in Heav'n, and shall confess him Lord:
Under his great Vice-gerent Reign abide
United as one individual Soule
611. For ever happie: him who disobeyes
Mee disobeyes, breaks union, and that day
Cast out from God and blessed vision, falls
Into utter darkness, deep ingulft, his place
Ordaind without redemption, without end.
616.   So spake th' Omnipotent, and with his words
All seemd well pleas'd, all seem'd, but were not all.
618. That day, as other solemn dayes, they spent
In song and dance about the sacred Hill,
620. Mystical dance, which yonder starrie Spheare
Of Planets and of fixt in all her Wheeles
Resembles nearest, mazes intricate,
Eccentric, intervolv'd, yet regular
Then most, when most irregular they seem,
And in thir motions harmonie Divine
626. So smooths her charming tones, that Gods own ear
627. Listens delighted. Eevning now approach'd
(For wee have also our Eevning and our Morn,
Wee ours for change delectable, not need)
630. Forthwith from dance to sweet repast they turn

584. All the angels were called together.

588. Thousands and thousands came, all in order according to rank. Their flags and banners showed their ranks.

594. They formed great circles around God, who sat on a mountain top with his Son beside him. The brightness around the two of them made them almost invisible.

600.   "*All you angels, take note,*" said God. "*This is my Son.*

603. *I hereby appoint him equal to me.*

606. *Consider him your Lord from now on, and worship him the same as you do me, and you will be happy forever.*

611. *If you disobey him, it's the same as if you were disobeying me, and you will be thrown out of Heaven into darkness forever.*"

616.   Everybody seemed happy, but some weren't.

618. They spent the rest of the day celebrating, singing and dancing.

620. Their music was as complicated as the movements of the stars and planets.

626. Even God enjoyed it.
627. Evening came. (Yes, we have evening in Heaven too, not because we need it, but because we like it.)
630. It was time to feast. Tables were piled with angel's food, and gold cups decorated with jewels were filled with nectar.

Desirous, all in Circles as they stood,
Tables are set, and on a sudden pil'd
With Angels Food, and rubied Nectar flows
In Pearl, in Diamond, and massie Gold,
Fruit of delicious Vines, the growth of Heav'n.

636. On flours repos'd, and with fresh flourets crownd,

637. They eate, they drink, and in communion sweet
Quaff immortalitie and joy, secure
Of surfet where full measure onely bounds
Excess, before th' all bounteous King, who showrd
With copious hand, rejoycing in thir joy.

642. Now when ambrosial Night with Clouds exhal'd
From that high mount of God, whence light & shade
Spring both, the face of brightest Heav'n had changd
To grateful Twilight (for Night comes not there

646. In darker veile) and roseat Dews dispos'd
All but the unsleeping eyes of God to rest,

648. Wide over all the Plain, and wider farr
Then all this globous Earth in Plain out spred,
(Such are the Courts of God) th' Angelic throng
Disperst in Bands and Files thir Camp extend
By living Streams among the Trees of Life,
Pavilions numberless, and sudden reard,
Celestial Tabernacles, where they slept

655. Fannd with coole Winds, save those who in thir course
Melodious Hymns about the sovran Throne

657. Alternate all night long: but not so wak'd

658. Satan, so call him now, his former name

659. Is heard no more in Heav'n; he of the first,
If not the first Arch-Angel, great in Power,

661. In favour and præeminence, yet fraught
With envie against the Son of God, that day
Honourd by his great Father, and proclaimd
Messiah King anointed, could not beare
Through pride that sight, & thought himself impaird.
Deep malice thence conceiving and disdain,

667. Soon as midnight brought on the duskie houre
Friendliest to sleep and silence, he resolv'd
With all his Legions to dislodge, and leave
Unworshipt, unobey'd the Throne supream
Contemptuous, and his next subordinate
Awak'ning, thus to him in secret spake.

673.   Sleepst thou, Companion dear, what sleep can close
Thy eye-lids? and remembrest what Decree
Of yesterday, so late hath past the lips

676. Of Heav'ns Almightie. Thou to me thy thoughts
Wast wont, I mine to thee was wont to impart;
Both waking we were one; how then can now

679. Thy sleep dissent? new Laws thou seest impos'd;

636. The angels sat and lay down on flowers and had crowns of flowers on their heads.
637. They ate and drank their fill and had a great time. God was happy to give it all to them.

642. The day was ending, but it never gets darker than twilight in Heaven.

646. Everybody was sleepy except God.

648. Open shelters that let in cool breezes sprung up magically all over for them. The area was bigger than all the plains on Earth combined.

655. They all went to sleep, except a few who sang hymns all night long.
657. But it wasn't those songs that kept Satan awake.
658. We call him Satan now. His former name isn't spoken in Heaven any more.
659. He used to be one of the highest, if not the highest archangel.
661. He was jealous of the Son of God.

667. At midnight he woke up his next in command and began to plot against God and his son.

673. *"How can you sleep after what you just heard from the mouth of the Almighty!"* he whispered.
676. *"I know we were both thinking the same thing.*

679. *Are you ready for a batch of new laws? Anyway, we can't talk here. Get all our men together. Tell them to meet me at our quarters in the north before daylight.*

New Laws from him who reigns, new minds may raise
In us who serve, new Counsels, to debate
What doubtful may ensue; more in this place
To utter is not safe. Assemble thou
Of all those Myriads which we lead the chief;
Tell them that by command, ere yet dim Night
Her shadowie Cloud withdraws, I am to haste,
And all who under me thir Banners wave,
Homeward with flying march where we possess
The Quarters of the North, there to prepare
690.   Fit entertainment to receive our King
The great Messiah, and his new commands,
Who speedily through all the Hierarchies
Intends to pass triumphant, and give Laws.
694.   So spake the false Arch-Angel, and infus'd
Bad influence into th' unwarie brest
Of his Associate; hee together calls,
Or several one by one, the Regent Powers,
Under him Regent, tells, as he was taught,
That the most High commanding, now ere Night,
Now ere dim Night had disincumberd Heav'n,
702.   The great Hierarchal Standard was to move;
Tells the suggested cause, and casts between
Ambiguous words and jealousies, to sound
704.   Or taint integritie; but all obey'd
The wonted signal, and superior voice
Of thir great Potentate; for great indeed
His name, and high was his degree in Heav'n;
His count'nance, as the Morning Starr that guides
The starrie flock, allur'd them, and with lyes
710.   Drew after him the third part of Heav'ns Host:
711.   Mean while th' Eternal eye, whose sight discernes
Abstrusest thoughts, from forth his holy Mount
And from within the golden Lamps that burne
Nightly before him, saw without thir light
Rebellion rising, saw in whom, how spred
Among the sons of Morn, what multitudes
Were banded to oppose his high Decree;
And smiling to his onely Son thus said.
719.   Son, thou in whom my glory I behold
In full resplendence, Heir of all my might,
Neerly it now concernes us to be sure
Of our Omnipotence, and with what Arms
We mean to hold what anciently we claim
Of Deitie or Empire, such a foe
Is rising, who intends to erect his Throne
Equal to ours, throughout the spacious North;
Nor so content, hath in his thought to try
In battel, what our Power is, or our right.

690. *We'll prepare a nice welcome party for our new king, the great Messiah, when he comes to flaunt his power over us."*

694.   Satan was a bad influence on his friend, who spread the message as he was told.

702. He chose his words carefully, to see how loyal Satan's men were, and to persuade them to go along with his cause.

704. None of them refused. Satan was a superstar in Heaven.

710. His followers made up one third of Heaven's population.

711. But God knows everything, even the deepest thoughts in everybody's minds.

719.   He said to his Son, "*We have an enemy who's trying to build a kingdom equal to ours, and what's worse, he's planning to wage war against us.*

729.   Let us advise, and to this hazard draw
       With speed what force is left, and all imploy
       In our defense, lest unawares we lose
       This our high place, our Sanctuarie, our Hill.
733.   To whom the Son with calm aspect and cleer
       Light'ning Divine, ineffable, serene,
       Made answer. Mightie Father, thou thy foes
       Justly hast in derision, and secure
       Laugh'st at thir vain designes and tumults vain,
       Matter to mee of Glory, whom thir hate
       Illustrates, when they see all Regal Power
       Giv'n me to quell thir pride, and in event
       Know whether I be dextrous to subdue
       Thy Rebels, or be found the worst in Heav'n.
743.   So spake the Son, but Satan with his Powers
       Far was advanc't on winged speed, an Host
       Innumerable as the Starrs of Night,
       Or Starrs of Morning, Dew-drops, which the Sun
       Impearls on every leaf and every flouer.
748.   Regions they pass'd, the mightie Regencies
       Of Seraphim and Potentates and Thrones
       In thir triple Degrees, Regions to which
       All thy Dominion, Adam, is no more
       Then what this Garden is to all the Earth,
       And all the Sea, from one entire globose
       Stretcht into Longitude; which having pass'd
755.   At length into the limits of the North
756.   They came, and Satan to his Royal seat
       High on a Hill, far blazing, as a Mount
       Rais'd on a Mount, with Pyramids and Towrs
       From Diamond Quarries hew'n, and Rocks of Gold,
760.   The Palace of great Lucifer, (so call
       That Structure in the Dialect of men
       Interpreted) which not long after, he
763.   Affecting all equality with God,
       In imitation of that Mount whereon
       Messiah was declar'd in sight of Heav'n,
       The Mountain of the Congregation call'd;
767.   For thither he assembl'd all his Train,
       Pretending so commanded to consult
       About the great reception of thir King,
       Thither to come, and with calumnious Art
       Of counterfeted truth thus held thir ears.
772.   Thrones, Dominations, Princedoms, Vertues, Powers,
       If these magnific Titles yet remain
       Not meerly titular, since by Decree
       Another now hath to himself ingross't
       All Power, and us eclipst under the name
777.   Of King anointed, for whom all this haste

729.   *We better prepare for battle."*

733.   The Son calmly answered, "*Father, I know you're laughing at their stupid plan. They may hate me, but we both know they'll only end up giving me that much more glory when I defeat them for you."*

743.   Meanwhile, Satan and his huge host of angels, like a galaxy of stars, were on their way.

748.   They passed over many regions governed by other archangels. The distance they traveled was many times farther than if the Earth's globe was stretched out flat.

755.   Finally they reached the northernmost place in Heaven.
756.   Satan took his place on his throne, the highest point on a high hill, surrounded with diamond pyramids and golden towers.

760.   You can think of it as a palace. His name was Lucifer back then.

763.   He was playing God now, about to speak to his followers the way God had spoken from his holy mountain yesterday.

767.   When they had all assembled, he began to spew his malicious-ness and deception.

772.   "*Thrones, Dominations, Princedoms, Virtues, Powers, and so forth—tell me, do those titles of yours mean anything any-more?—since we just learned that we have a new king who has been given all the power.*

777.   *I got you here in a hurry so we could decide how to handle him when he comes here expecting us to kneel to him. Haven't we had enough of that disgusting custom with one? Do we have to do twice as much bowing and scraping now?*

Of midnight march, and hurried meeting here,
This onely to consult how we may best
With what may be devis'd of honours new
Receive him coming to receive from us
Knee-tribute yet unpaid, prostration vile,
Too much to one, but double how endur'd,
To one and to his image now proclaim'd?

785. But what if better counsels might erect
Our minds and teach us to cast off this Yoke?

787. Will ye submit your necks, and chuse to bend

788. The supple knee? ye will not, if I trust
To know ye right, or if ye know your selves

790. Natives and Sons of Heav'n possest before
By none, and if not equal all, yet free,
Equally free; for Orders and Degrees
Jarr not with liberty, but well consist.

794. Who can in reason then or right assume
Monarchie over such as live by right
His equals, if in power and splendor less,
In freedome equal? or can introduce
Law and Edict on us, who without law

799. Erre not, much less for this to be our Lord,
And look for adoration to th' abuse
Of those Imperial Titles which assert
Our being ordain'd to govern, not to serve?

803. 　　Thus farr his bold discourse without controule
Had audience, when among the Seraphim
Abdiel, then whom none with more zeale ador'd
The Deitie, and divine commands obeid,
Stood up, and in a flame of zeale severe
The current of his fury thus oppos'd.

809. 　　O argument blasphemous, false and proud!
Words which no eare ever to hear in Heav'n
Expected, least of all from thee, ingrate
In place thy self so high above thy Peeres.
Canst thou with impious obloquie condemne
The just Decree of God, pronounc't and sworn,
That to his only Son by right endu'd
With Regal Scepter, every Soule in Heav'n
Shall bend the knee, and in that honour due

818. Confess him rightful King? unjust thou saist
Flatly unjust, to binde with Laws the free,
And equal over equals to let Reigne,
One over all with unsucceeded power.

822. Shalt thou give Law to God, shalt thou dispute
With him the points of libertie, who made
Thee what thou art, and formd the Pow'rs of Heav'n
Such as he pleasd, and circumscrib'd thir being?

826. Yet by experience taught we know how good,

785.   *Shouldn't we say the hell with this, we've had enough!*

787.   *Or would you rather get down on your knees again?*
788.   *Not if I know you like I think I do, or if you know yourselves.*

790.   *You were never owned by anybody. You may not be equal in rank, but you have always been equally free.*

794.   *Who is he to have power over us who are his equals? Who is he to give us laws? We've done okay without them up to now.*

799.   *Most of all, who is he to be our God, and expect us to worship him? We're leaders, not servants!"*

803.   Suddenly, Abdiel stood up in the audience. Nobody was more faithful to God than this angel.

809.   *"Lies and blasphemy!"* he cried. *"Nobody ever expected to hear such ungrateful, disloyal words in Heaven. Least of all from you, who are in such a highly respected position.*

818.   *You say it's unjust to impose laws on free angels, and we should just let everybody rule equally.*

822.   *Are you going to tell God what to do? Are you going to teach him about liberty—the one who created you, and gave each of us our powers, and decided what their limits should be?*

826.   *We know from experience how good he is, and how he knows what's best for us.*

And of our good, and of our dignitie

828. How provident he is, how farr from thought
To make us less, bent rather to exalt
Our happie state under one Head more neer
United. But to grant it thee unjust,

832. That equal over equals Monarch Reigne:

833. Thy self though great and glorious dost thou count,
Or all Angelic Nature joind in one,
Equal to him begotten Son, by whom

836. As by his Word the mighty Father made
All things, ev'n thee, and all the Spirits of Heav'n
By him created in thir bright degrees,
Crownd them with Glory, and to thir Glory nam'd
Thrones, Dominations, Princedoms, Vertues, Powers,

841. Essential Powers, nor by his Reign obscur'd,
But more illustrious made, since he the Head
One of our number thus reduc't becomes,
His Laws our Laws, all honour to him done

845. Returns our own. Cease then this impious rage,
And tempt not these; but hast'n to appease
Th' incensed Father, and th' incensed Son,
While Pardon may be found in time besought.

849.   So spake the fervent Angel, but his zeale
None seconded, as out of season judg'd,
Or singular and rash, whereat rejoic'd
Th' Apostat, and more haughty thus repli'd.

853.   That we were formd then saist thou? and the work
Of secondarie hands, by task transferd
From Father to his Son? strange point and new!
Doctrin which we would know whence learnt: who saw

857. When this creation was? rememberst thou
Thy making, while the Maker gave thee being?
We know no time when we were not as now;
Know none before us, self-begot, self-rais'd
By our own quick'ning power, when fatal course
Had circl'd his full Orbe, the birth mature
Of this our native Heav'n, Ethereal Sons.

864. Our puissance is our own, our own right hand
Shall teach us highest deeds, by proof to try
Who is our equal: then thou shalt behold
Whether by supplication we intend
Address, and to begirt th' Almighty Throne

869. Beseeching or besieging. This report,
These tidings carrie to th' anointed King;
And fly, ere evil intercept thy flight.

872.   He said, and as the sound of waters deep
Hoarce murmur echo'd to his words applause
Through the infinite Host, nor less for that
The flaming Seraph fearless, though alone

828. *He's not trying to make us less, but to make us happier and more united.*

832. *You're right that it wouldn't be fair for an equal to act as a king over his equals.*
833. *But do you—great and powerful as you may be—do you really consider yourself equal to the Son of God?*
836. *God created all things through his Son—even you. He created all the angels in all their glory, and gave them their various ranks.*

841. *Placing him at our head doesn't lessen our state. It makes him one of us, his laws become our laws, and his glory is shared by all of us.*

845. *So please take back your angry words before you go too far."*

849.   Satan was pleased that nobody was showing Abdiel any support.

853.   *"Well, it's news to me that we were created by the Son of God. Where did you hear that?*

857. *Do you remember being made? We don't. We remember always being here. We are part of Heaven, self-created, self-taught. We make our own power.*

864. *He'll find out who's equal or not equal when he finds out if we circle his almighty throne as beggars or as warriors!*

869. *Take that message back to your new king. Now you better get out of here while you still can."*

872.   The crowd murmured their approval and some applauded, but Abdiel was not afraid.

        Encompass'd round with foes, thus answerd bold.

877.   O alienate from God, O spirit accurst,
        Forsak'n of all good; I see thy fall
        Determind, and thy hapless crew involv'd
        In this perfidious fraud, contagion spred

881.   Both of thy crime and punishment: henceforth
        No more be troubl'd how to quit the yoke
        Of Gods Messiah; those indulgent Laws
        Will not now be voutsaft, other Decrees
        Against thee are gon forth without recall;
        That Golden Scepter which thou didst reject
        Is now an Iron Rod to bruise and breake

888.   Thy disobedience. Well thou didst advise,
        Yet not for thy advise or threats I fly
        These wicked Tents devoted, least the wrauth
        Impendent, raging into sudden flame
        Distinguish not: for soon expect to feel
        His Thunder on thy head, devouring fire.
        Then who created thee lamenting learne,
        When who can uncreate thee thou shalt know.

896.   So spake the Seraph Abdiel faithful found,
        Among the faithless, faithful only hee;
        Among innumerable false, unmov'd,
        Unshak'n, unseduc'd, unterrifi'd
        His Loyaltie he kept, his Love, his Zeale;
        Nor number, nor example with him wrought
        To swerve from truth, or change his constant mind

903.   Though single. From amidst them forth he passd,
        Long way through hostile scorn, which he susteind
        Superior, nor of violence fear'd aught;

906.   And with retorted scorn his back he turn'd
        On those proud Towrs to swift destruction doom'd.

877.   Abdiel said, "*You are accursed, and you're spreading your crime and your punishment to all your poor followers like a disease.*

881. *Don't worry about Messiah's gentle laws. They're not for you. Some not-so-gentle new ones have already gone out, just for you.*

888. *I'll go quickly alright, but not because of your threats. I just don't want to be here when God sets this whole place on fire, with you all in it. He created you and he can uncreate you as well, as you'll all soon find out."*

896.   Abdiel was the only faithful angel of all of them. They couldn't shake his loyalty to God.

903. It was a long walk out of there, among all those hostile faces, but he was not afraid.

906. He sent their dirty looks right back at them and moved on. He turned his back on Satan's doomed empire forever.

Book VI

PARADISE LOST

1.   All night the dreadless Angel unpursu'd
Through Heav'ns wide Champain held his way, till Morn,
Wak't by the circling Hours, with rosie hand
4.   Unbarr'd the gates of Light. There is a Cave
Within the Mount of God, fast by his Throne,
Where light and darkness in perpetual round
Lodge and dislodge by turns, which makes through Heav'n
Grateful vicissitude, like Day and Night;
Light issues forth, and at the other dore
Obsequious darkness enters, till her houre
11. To veile the Heav'n, though darkness there might well
12. Seem twilight here; and now went forth the Morn
Such as in highest Heav'n, arrayd in Gold
Empyreal, from before her vanisht Night,
Shot through with orient Beams: when all the Plain
Coverd with thick embatteld Squadrons bright,
Chariots and flaming Armes, and fierie Steeds
Reflecting blaze on blaze, first met his view:
19. Warr he perceav'd, warr in procinct, and found
Already known what he for news had thought
21. To have reported: gladly then he mixt
Among those friendly Powers who him receav'd
With joy and acclamations loud, that one
That of so many Myriads fall'n, yet one
25. Returnd not lost: On to the sacred hill
They led him high applauded, and present
Before the seat supream; from whence a voice
28. From midst a Golden Cloud thus milde was heard.
      Servant of God, well done, well hast thou fought
The better fight, who single hast maintaind
Against revolted multitudes the Cause
32. Of Truth, in word mightier then they in Armes;
33. And for the testimonie of Truth hast born
Universal reproach, far worse to beare
Then violence: for this was all thy care
To stand approv'd in sight of God, though Worlds
37. Judg'd thee perverse: the easier conquest now
Remains thee, aided by this host of friends,
Back on thy foes more glorious to return
40. Then scornd thou didst depart, and to subdue
By force, who reason for thir Law refuse,
Right reason for thir Law, and for thir King

Chapter 6

IN PLAIN ENGLISH

1.   The brave angel traveled all night, till morning. Nobody chased after him.

4. In Heaven, there's a cave near God's throne. Light and darkness take turns coming out of it and travel through Heaven, like day and night.

11. Night there is like twilight on Earth.

12. Abdiel saw the whole plain covered with squadrons of chariots, reflecting the morning light.

19. He could see God's army was ready for war. Apparently they already knew what he was coming to report.

21. He was happy to be home. They all greeted him and praised him for being the only one of all of Satan's followers who wouldn't rebel against God.

25. They brought him before God's throne.

28.   God's gentle voice said, "*Well done, Abdiel. You held your own against the pack.*

32. *The truth made you stronger than them, with all their weapons.*

33. *In return you were mocked, and had to face all their contempt. That can be tougher to take than violence. But you only cared about getting my approval.*

37. *Your next victory will be much easier. You'll go back and fight them, backed up by my whole army. You left there being ridiculed, but you'll return in glory.*

40. *We'll have to use force against those who reject their rightful King Messiah and his laws.*

Messiah, who by right of merit Reigns.

44. Go Michael of Celestial Armies Prince,
     And thou in Military prowess next

46. Gabriel, lead forth to Battel these my Sons
     Invincible, lead forth my armed Saints
     By Thousands and by Millions rang'd for fight;
     Equal in number to that Godless crew

50. Rebellious, them with Fire and hostile Arms

51. Fearless assault, and to the brow of Heav'n
     Pursuing drive them out from God and bliss,
     Into thir place of punishment, the Gulf
     Of Tartarus, which ready opens wide
     His fiery Chaos to receave thir fall.

56.   So spake the Sovran voice, and Clouds began
     To darken all the Hill, and smoak to rowl
     In duskie wreathes, reluctant flames, the signe

59. Of wrauth awak't: nor with less dread the loud
     Ethereal Trumpet from on high gan blow:

61. At which command the Powers Militant,
     That stood for Heav'n, in mighty Quadrate joyn'd
     Of Union irresistible, mov'd on
     In silence thir bright Legions, to the sound
     Of instrumental Harmonie that breath'd
     Heroic Ardor to advent'rous deeds
     Under thir God-like Leaders, in the Cause

68. Of God and his Messiah. On they move
     Indissolubly firm; nor obvious Hill
     Nor streit'ning Vale, nor Wood, nor Stream divides
     Thir perfet ranks; for high above the ground
     Thir march was, and the passive Air upbore

73. Thir nimble tread, as when the total kind
     Of Birds in orderly array on wing
     Came summond over Eden to receive

76. Thir names of thee; so over many a tract
     Of Heav'n they march'd, and many a Province wide
     Tenfold the length of this terrene: at last

79. Farr in th' Horizon to the North appeer'd
     From skirt to skirt a fierie Region, stretcht
     In battailous aspect, and neerer view
     Bristl'd with upright beams innumerable
     Of rigid Spears, and Helmets throng'd, and Shields
     Various, with boastful Argument portraid,
     The banded Powers of Satan hasting on

86. With furious expedition; for they weend
     That self same day by fight, or by surprize
     To win the Mount of God, and on his Throne
     To set the envier of his State, the proud
     Aspirer, but thir thoughts prov'd fond and vain

91. In the mid way: though strange to us it seemd

44. *Michael, you are my highest military leader.*

46. *And Gabriel, next in rank, both of you go lead my army in battle against the rebels. Take as many thousands as you need to equal theirs.*

50. *Use whatever weapons you need.*
51. *Drive them right out of Heaven into their place of punishment. Hell is wide open and ready for them to fall into it."*

56.   Heaven got dark and fiery. It was a sign of God's anger.

59. Equally scary was the trumpet that blew.

61. All of God's powerful army came out when they heard it. It motivated them to go fight.

68. On they went. Hills and woods were no obstacle. They just flew over them.

73. It was like when all the different kinds of birds came to get their names from you, Adam, all perfectly lined up.

76. They traveled a very long distance.

79. Finally they could begin to see shields and spears, spread all across the horizon. It was Satan's army, speedily advancing.

86. Satan's forces had planned to take God by surprise and take over his throne, but they could see that wasn't going to work.

91. We may find it hard to imagine gentle creatures like angels fighting a war, but that's exactly what happened next.

At first, that Angel should with Angel warr,
And in fierce hosting meet, who wont to meet
So oft in Festivals of joy and love
Unanimous, as sons of one great Sire
Hymning th' Eternal Father: but the shout
Of Battel now began, and rushing sound
Of onset ended soon each milder thought.

99. High in the midst exalted as a God
Th' Apostate in his Sun-bright Chariot sate
Idol of Majesty Divine, enclos'd
With Flaming Cherubim, and golden Shields;

103. Then lighted from his gorgeous Throne, for now

104. 'Twixt Host and Host but narrow space was left,
A dreadful intervall, and Front to Front
Presented stood in terrible array
Of hideous length: before the cloudie Van,
On the rough edge of battel ere it joyn'd,

109. Satan with vast and haughtie strides advanc't,
Came towring, armd in Adamant and Gold;

111. Abdiel that sight endur'd not, where he stood
Among the mightiest, bent on highest deeds,
And thus his own undaunted heart explores.
    O Heav'n! that such resemblance of the Highest
Should yet remain, where faith and realtie

116. Remain not; wherefore should not strength and might
There fail where Vertue fails, or weakest prove
Where boldest; though to sight unconquerable?
His puissance, trusting in th' Almightie's aide,
I mean to try, whose Reason I have tri'd
Unsound and false; nor is it aught but just,
That he who in debate of Truth hath won,
Should win in Arms, in both disputes alike
Victor; though brutish that contest and foule,
When Reason hath to deal with force, yet so
Most reason is that Reason overcome.

127.   So pondering, and from his armed Peers
Forth stepping opposite, half way he met
His daring foe, at this prevention more
Incens't, and thus securely him defi'd.

131.   Proud, art thou met? thy hope was to have reacht
The highth of thy aspiring unoppos'd,
The Throne of God unguarded, and his side
Abandond at the terror of thy Power

135. Or potent tongue; fool, not to think how vain
Against th' Omnipotent to rise in Arms;
Who out of smallest things could without end
Have rais'd incessant Armies to defeat
Thy folly; or with solitarie hand
Reaching beyond all limit at one blow

99. In the middle of the crowd sat Satan in a fancy chariot, like a god, surrounded with bright angels with golden shields.

103. He got down off his throne.
104. The two armies were in very long lines, face to face , with just a little space between them.

109. Satan stepped forward, full of pride and defiance.

111. Abdiel, who was just across from him, couldn't stand the sight of Satan looking so majestic.

116.   "*Let's see if his power is as phony as his words,*" Abdiel said to himself. "*I beat him in a battle of words and I can do it with weapons as well, although I hate violence. God will help me.*"

127.   He stepped forward in front of Satan, who got really annoyed at this.

131.   Abdiel said, "*I guess you expected to find us all hiding, afraid of your great power.*

135. *How stupid you are. Don't you know God could create endless armies to defeat you, or simply crush you all single handedly.*

      Unaided could have finisht thee, and whelmd

142.   Thy Legions under darkness; but thou seest
      All are not of thy Train; there be who Faith
      Prefer, and Pietie to God, though then
      To thee not visible, when I alone
      Seemd in thy World erroneous to dissent
      From all: my Sect thou seest, now learn too late
      How few somtimes may know, when thousands err.

149.   Whom the grand foe with scornful eye askance
      Thus answerd. Ill for thee, but in wisht houre
      Of my revenge, first sought for thou returnst
      From flight, seditious Angel, to receave
      Thy merited reward, the first assay
      Of this right hand provok't, since first that tongue
      Inspir'd with contradiction durst oppose
      A third part of the Gods, in Synod met

157.   Thir Deities to assert, who while they feel
      Vigour Divine within them, can allow

159.   Omnipotence to none. But well thou comst
      Before thy fellows, ambitious to win
      From me som Plume, that thy success may show

162.   Destruction to the rest: this pause between
      (Unanswerd least thou boast) to let thee know;

164.   At first I thought that Libertie and Heav'n
      To heav'nly Soules had bin all one; but now
      I see that most through sloth had rather serve,
      Ministring Spirits, traind up in Feast and Song;

168.   Such hast thou arm'd, the Minstrelsie of Heav'n,
      Servilitie with freedom to contend,
      As both thir deeds compar'd this day shall prove.

171.   To whom in brief thus Abdiel stern repli'd.
      Apostat, still thou errst, nor end wilt find
      Of erring, from the path of truth remote:
      Unjustly thou deprav'st it with the name
      Of Servitude to serve whom God ordains,
      Or Nature; God and Nature bid the same,
      When he who rules is worthiest, and excells

178.   Them whom he governs. This is servitude,
      To serve th' unwise, or him who hath rebelld
      Against his worthier, as thine now serve thee,
      Thy self not free, but to thy self enthrall'd;
      Yet leudly dar'st our ministring upbraid.
      Reign thou in Hell thy Kingdom, let mee serve

184.   In Heav'n God ever blest, and his Divine
      Behests obey, worthiest to be obey'd,

186.   Yet Chains in Hell, not Realms expect: mean while
      From mee returnd, as erst thou saidst, from flight,
      This greeting on thy impious Crest receive.

189.   So saying, a noble stroke he lifted high,

142. *Look around. It seems everybody doesn't think like you after all. Maybe now you can see I'm not the only one who's faithful to God."*

149.   *"Well, look who's back from his hasty retreat, looking for glory,"* said Satan, *"the little smart mouth who thought he knew better than a third of Heaven's host, and now wants to see how strong we are.*

157. *We're strong all right, but nobody is going to be allowed to be Almighty.*

159. *Come on, step forward and show off in front of your friends. Let them watch me destroy you.*

162. *But first let me take a minute to straighten you out. I wouldn't want you to claim I was afraid to answer you.*

164. *You know, I used to think Heaven was all about freedom. But now I see how most of you would rather grovel like slaves. All you can do is fill your bellies and sing hymns.*

168. *What a joke! An army made up of folk singers and choirboys. Well, let's see what wins today—slavery or freedom!"*

171.   Abdiel said, *"There's no end to your stupidity. You call it slavery to serve God's Son. There couldn't be anybody more worthy to rule over us.*

178. *The only slavery around here is the way your men serve you— a clueless rebel. You're a slave to your own self. And you ridicule us?*

184. *You go be a king in Hell. I'll stay here and be a servant to God and his divine rule. But don't expect much of a kingdom down there when you're bound in chains.*

186. *Meanwhile, this 'little smart mouth' back from his 'hasty retreat' brings you this greeting!"*

189.   With that, Abdiel let fly a blow to Satan's head so sudden that Satan couldn't raise his shield fast enough.

Which hung not, but so swift with tempest fell
On the proud Crest of Satan, that no sight,
Nor motion of swift thought, less could his Shield
193. Such ruin intercept: ten paces huge
He back recoild; the tenth on bended knee
195. His massie Spear upstaid; as if on Earth
Winds under ground or waters forcing way
Sidelong, had push't a Mountain from his seat
198. Half sunk with all his Pines. Amazement seis'd
The Rebel Thrones, but greater rage to see
Thus foil'd thir mightiest, ours joy filld, and shout,
Presage of Victorie and fierce desire
202. Of Battel: whereat Michael bid sound
Th' Arch-Angel trumpet; through the vast of Heaven
It sounded, and the faithful Armies rung
205. Hosanna to the Highest: nor stood at gaze
The adverse Legions, nor less hideous joyn'd
207. The horrid shock: now storming furie rose,
And clamour such as heard in Heav'n till now
209. Was never, Arms on Armour clashing bray'd
Horrible discord, and the madding Wheeles
Of brazen Chariots rag'd; dire was the noise
Of conflict; over head the dismal hiss
Of fiery Darts in flaming volies flew,
And flying vaulted either Host with fire.
215. So under fierie Cope together rush'd
Both Battels maine, with ruinous assault
And inextinguishable rage; all Heav'n
218. Resounded, and had Earth bin then, all Earth
219. Had to her Center shook. What wonder? when
Millions of fierce encountring Angels fought
On either side, the least of whom could weild
These Elements, and arm him with the force
223. Of all thir Regions: how much more of Power
Armie against Armie numberless to raise
Dreadful combustion warring, and disturb,
Though not destroy, thir happie Native seat;
Had not th' Eternal King Omnipotent
From his strong hold of Heav'n high over-rul'd
229. And limited thir might; though numberd such
As each divided Legion might have seemd
A numerous Host, in strength each armed hand
A Legion; led in fight, yet Leader seemd
Each Warriour single as in Chief, expert
When to advance, or stand, or turn the sway
Of Battel, open when, and when to close
236. The ridges of grim Warr; no thought of flight,
None of retreat, no unbecoming deed
That argu'd fear; each on himself reli'd,

193. He stumbled backwards and went down on one knee, supporting himself with his spear.

195. He was like a mountain moved by an earthquake.

198. The rebel angels were stunned and enraged, while our side shouted for joy.

202. Michael made them sound the trumpets, and they all shouted praise to God.

205. Then the battle began.

207. Nobody ever heard such violence in Heaven before.

209. Swords banged against shields, chariots roared, and burning arrows shot back and forth through the air.

215. The fighting was intense.

218. If Earth existed back then, the whole planet would have shaken to its core.

219. But what do you expect, when millions of godlike angels fight? The weakest of them was like Superman.

223. Their violent fighting would have destroyed Heaven, except that God had made sure to limit their power to do that.

229. Each legion seemed like a whole army, each angel seemed like a legion, and every warrior seemed like a leader and an expert in every military maneuver.

236. Nobody thought about retreat. There was no fear. Each one acted like the whole outcome of victory or defeat depended on him. Their bravery was infinite.

As onely in his arm the moment lay
Of victorie; deeds of eternal fame
Were don, but infinite: for wide was spred

242. That Warr and various; somtimes on firm ground
A standing fight, then soaring on main wing
Tormented all the Air; all Air seemd then

245. Conflicting Fire: long time in eeven scale

246. The Battel hung; till Satan, who that day
Prodigious power had shewn, and met in Armes
No equal, raunging through the dire attack
Of fighting Seraphim confus'd, at length
Saw where the Sword of Michael smote, and fell'd
Squadrons at once, with huge two-handed sway
Brandisht aloft the horrid edge came down

253. Wide wasting; such destruction to withstand
He hasted, and oppos'd the rockie Orb
Of tenfold Adamant, his ample Shield

256. A vast circumference: At his approach
The great Arch-Angel from his warlike toile
Surceas'd, and glad as hoping here to end
Intestine War in Heav'n, the arch foe subdu'd
Or Captive drag'd in Chains, with hostile frown
And visage all enflam'd first thus began.

262.   Author of evil, unknown till thy revolt,
Unnam'd in Heav'n, now plenteous, as thou seest
These Acts of hateful strife, hateful to all,
Though heaviest by just measure on thy self
And thy adherents: how hast thou disturb'd
Heav'ns blessed peace, and into Nature brought
Miserie, uncreated till the crime
Of thy Rebellion? how hast thou instill'd

270. Thy malice into thousands, once upright

271. And faithful, now prov'd false. But think not here
To trouble Holy Rest; Heav'n casts thee out
From all her Confines. Heav'n the seat of bliss
Brooks not the works of violence and Warr.

275. Hence then, and evil go with thee along
Thy ofspring, to the place of evil, Hell,
Thou and thy wicked crew; there mingle broiles,
Ere this avenging Sword begin thy doome,
Or som more sudden vengeance wing'd from God
Precipitate thee with augmented paine.

281.   So spake the Prince of Angels; to whom thus
The Adversarie. Nor think thou with wind
Of airie threats to aw whom yet with deeds

284. Thou canst not. Hast thou turnd the least of these
To flight, or if to fall, but that they rise

286. Unvanquisht, easier to transact with mee
That thou shouldst hope, imperious, and with threats

242. Sometimes they fought on the ground and sometimes they fought in the air.

245. For a long time they seemed evenly matched.

246. Satan was beating everybody he fought with. And on our side, he noticed Michael was defeating whole squadrons.

253. Satan headed straight for him.

256. Michael paused when he saw Satan coming. He welcomed the chance to end the battle then and there by defeating him. He was very angry.

262.   He said, "*You brought evil into Heaven! You're causing all this misery, but the worst of it will fall back on you.*

270. *You corrupted thousands of angels.*

271. *Don't think you can continue to disrupt Heaven like this.*

275. *Get out now! Go to Hell, you and your gang and your violence, before I finish you off with my sword, or God sends something more painful to deal with you!"*

281.   Satan said, "*You don't really think your empty threats are going to scare me when your actions don't.*

284. *Have you made a single one of my men run away? Or if they were knocked down, didn't they get right back up again?*

286. *Do you think you'll have it easier with me?—just threaten me and I'll run?*

288. To chase me hence? erre not that so shall end
      The strife which thou call'st evil, but wee style
      The strife of Glorie: which we mean to win,
      Or turn this Heav'n it self into the Hell
      Thou fablest, here however to dwell free,

293. If not to reign: mean while thy utmost force,
      And join him nam'd Almighty to thy aid,
      I flie not, but have sought thee farr and nigh.

296.   They ended parle, and both addresst for fight
      Unspeakable; for who, though with the tongue
      Of Angels, can relate, or to what things
      Liken on Earth conspicuous, that may lift
      Human imagination to such highth

301. Of Godlike Power: for likest Gods they seemd,
      Stood they or mov'd, in stature, motion, arms
      Fit to decide the Empire of great Heav'n.

304. Now wav'd thir fierie Swords, and in the Aire
      Made horrid Circles; two broad Suns thir Shields
      Blaz'd opposite, while expectation stood

307. In horror; from each hand with speed retir'd
      Where erst was thickest fight, th' Angelic throng,
      And left large field, unsafe within the wind

310. Of such commotion, such as to set forth
      Great things by small, If Natures concord broke,
      Among the Constellations warr were sprung,
      Two Planets rushing from aspect maligne
      Of fiercest opposition in mid Skie,
      Should combat, and thir jarring Sphears confound.

316. Together both with next to Almightie Arme,
      Uplifted imminent one stroke they aim'd
      That might determine, and not need repeate,

319. As not of power, at once; nor odds appeerd
      In might or swift prevention; but the sword
      Of Michael from the Armorie of God
      Was giv'n him temperd so, that neither keen

323. Nor solid might resist that edge: it met
      The sword of Satan with steep force to smite
      Descending, and in half cut sheere, nor staid,
      But with swift wheele reverse, deep entring shar'd

327. All his right side; then Satan first knew pain,
      And writh' d him to and fro convolv'd; so sore
      The griding sword with discontinuous wound

330. Passd through him, but th' Ethereal substance clos'd
      Not long divisible, and from the gash
      A stream of Nectarous humor issuing flow'd
      Sanguin, such as Celestial Spirits may bleed,
      And all his Armour staind ere while so bright.

335. Forthwith on all sides to his aide was run
      By Angels many and strong, who interpos'd

288. *Make no mistake, what you call evil we call glory. And we will win if we have to turn this Heaven itself into your so called Hell, and live here free at least, if not as kings.*

293. *Don't expect me to run away from your worst attack, even if you get help from the one you call Almighty. I've been after you for a long time."*

296.   The argument ended, and they began a fight I can hardly describe, even with the power God has given me. There's just nothing on Earth to compare it to. You would need to have the imagination of a god.

301. They were like gods, the way they moved and fought, like they alone would decide Heaven's fate.

304. They waved their swords in fiery circles. Their shields blazed like two suns.

307. Where they were there had been many angels fighting, but now they all moved out of the way for their own safety.

310. It's a weak comparison, but imagine war taking place among the stars, and you see two planets shooting through the sky about to collide.

316. The two angels simultaneously lifted their arms, each one trying for one mighty stroke that would finish his opponent.

319. Neither one seemed more powerful or skilled in attack or defense, but Michael's sword came from God's arsenal, and nothing could resist its edge.

323. It came down hard and cut Satan's sword in half. And swinging it back up again, Michael cut open Satan's right side.

327. It was the first time Satan felt pain, and it was terrible. The wound was deep, causing him to roll back and forth in anguish.

330. Red fluid poured out all over his armor, the kind angels bleed. But the wound quickly closed by itself, because his body was spirit, not solid.

335. His angels all ran to help him. Some ran defense while others carried him back to his chariot on their shields.

      Defence, while others bore him on thir Shields
      Back to his Chariot; where it stood retir'd

339. From off the files of warr; there they him laid
      Gnashing for anguish and despite and shame
      To find himself not matchless, and his pride
      Humbl'd by such rebuke, so farr beneath
      His confidence to equal God in power.

344. Yet soon he heal'd; for Spirits that live throughout
      Vital in every part, not as frail man
      In Entrailes, Heart or Head, Liver or Reines;

347. Cannot but by annihilating die;
      Nor in thir liquid texture mortal wound
      Receive, no more then can the fluid Aire:

350. All Heart they live, all Head, all Eye, all Eare,
      All Intellect, all Sense, and as they please,
      They Limb themselves, and colour, shape or size
      Assume, as likes them best, condense or rare.

354.   Mean while in other parts like deeds deservd
355. Memorial, where the might of Gabriel fought,
      And with fierce Ensignes pierc'd the deep array
      Of Moloc furious King, who him defi'd
      And at his Chariot wheeles to drag him bound
      Threatn'd, nor from the Holie One of Heav'n

360. Refrein'd his tongue blasphemous; but anon
      Down clov'n to the waste, with shatterd Armes
      And uncouth paine fled bellowing. On each wing

363. Uriel and Raphael his vaunting foe,
      Though huge, and in a Rock of Diamond Armd,
      Vanquish'd Adramelec, and Asmadai,
      Two potent Thrones, that to be less then Gods
      Disdain'd, but meaner thoughts learnd in thir flight,
      Mangl'd with gastly wounds through Plate and Maile,

369. Nor stood unmindful Abdiel to annoy
      The Atheist crew, but with redoubl'd blow
      Ariel and Arioc, and the violence
      Of Ramiel scorcht and blasted overthrew.

373. I might relate of thousands, and thir names
      Eternize here on Earth; but those elect
      Angels contented with thir fame in Heav'n

376. Seek not the praise of men: the other sort
      In might though wondrous and in Acts of Warr,
      Nor of Renown less eager, yet by doome
      Canceld from Heav'n and sacred memorie,
      Nameless in dark oblivion let them dwell.

381. For strength from Truth divided and from Just,
      Illaudable, naught merits but dispraise
      And ignominie, yet to glorie aspires
      Vain glorious, and through infamie seeks fame:
      Therfore Eternal silence be thir doome.

339. They laid him there, grumbling and moaning in pain and anger and shame. His pride and his idea of equaling God's power were crushed.

344. He healed quickly, though, because angels are all spirit and don't have entrails or organs like men.

347. To kill an angel you would have to totally destroy him. You can't kill us by wounding us any more than you could kill the air.

350. Our bodies are all head, all eye, all ear, all mind, and we can change our shape and size, or become more solid or more spirit, however we want.

354.   Meanwhile on the battlefield, I should mention some of the other heroic action.

355. Gabriel was faced with fierce Moloch, who cursed and swore and threatened to tie him up and drag him behind his chariot.

360. But he ran away howling when Gabriel cut him open down to the waist.

363. Uriel and I took care of Adramelech and Asmodeus, two giant rebels with weapons as tough as diamond. They wanted to be like gods, but felt differently as they fled with ugly wounds under their crumpled armor.

369. Abdiel continued to irritate the rebels. He took on two at a time with Ariel and Arioch, and brought down the violent Ramiel.

373. I could tell you about thousands more, but those heroes don't look for fame on Earth.

376. As for the other side, they were mighty, and would have welcomed a legacy in Heaven, but they are forgotten there.

381. For strength does not equal truth or righteousness. And evil does not bring fame, only silence forever.

386.   And now thir Mightiest quelld, the battel swerv'd,
           With many an inrode gor'd; deformed rout
388.   Enter'd, and foul disorder; all the ground
           With shiverd armour strow'n, and on a heap
           Chariot and Charioter lay overturnd
           And fierie foaming Steeds; what stood, recoyld
392.   Orewearied, through the faint Satanic Host
           Defensive scarse, or with pale fear surpris'd,
           Then first with fear surpris'd and sense of paine
           Fled ignominious, to such evil brought
           By sin of disobedience, till that hour
           Not liable to fear or flight or paine.
398.   Far otherwise th' inviolable Saints
           In Cubic Phalanx firm advanc't entire,
400.   Invulnerable, impenitrably arm'd:
           Such high advantages thir innocence
           Gave them above thir foes, not to have sinnd,
           Not to have disobei'd; in fight they stood
           Unwearied, unobnoxious to be pain'd
           By wound, though from thir place by violence mov'd.
406.   Now Night her course began, and over Heav'n
           Inducing darkness, grateful truce impos'd,
           And silence on the odious dinn of Warr:
           Under her Cloudie covert both retir'd,
           Victor and Vanquisht: on the foughten field
           Michael and his Angels prevalent
           Encamping, plac'd in Guard thir Watches round,
           Cherubic waving fires: on th' other part
414.   Satan with his rebellious disappeerd,
           Far in the dark dislodg'd, and void of rest,
           His Potentates to Councel call'd by night;
           And in the midst thus undismai'd began.
418.   O now in danger tri'd, now known in Armes
           Not to be overpowerd, Companions deare,
           Found worthy not of Libertie alone,
           Too mean pretense, but what we more affect,
423.   Honour, Dominion, Glorie, and renowne,
           Who have sustaind one day in doubtful fight
           (And if one day, why not Eternal dayes?)
           What Heavens Lord had powerfullest to send
           Against us from about his Throne, and judg'd
           Sufficient to subdue us to his will,
428.   But proves not so: then fallible, it seems,
           Of future we may deem him, though till now
430.   Omniscient thought. True is, less firmly arm'd,
           Some disadvantage we endur'd and paine,
           Till now not known, but known as soon contemnd,
           Since now we find this our Empyreal form
           Incapable of mortal injurie

386.   And now Satan's side was losing.

388.   The ground was littered with broken armor and turned over chariots and worn out horses that shied away.

392.   The rebels retreated. They were experiencing fear and pain they never knew before, brought on by their sin.

398.   On the other hand, God's army of angels marched on in proud formation.

400.   They didn't like violence, but they withstood the pain and the attacks easily. Their innocence gave them the advantage over their enemies.

406.   When night came, the fighting stopped for a while and both sides set up camp.

414.   Satan's side couldn't sleep because they were losing, so they had a meeting.

418.   But Satan put a good spin on it: "*We withstood one day's battle, and we can withstand as many more as we have to.*

423.   *God sent all the forces against us that he thought it would take to defeat us, but they failed.*

428.   *Maybe he's not the all-powerful God we thought he was.*

430.   *True, we may have experienced some pain, something we never felt before, but we now know one thing for sure: we can't die. Our wounds just heal themselves.*

Imperishable, and though pierc'd with wound,
Soon closing, and by native vigour heal'd.
Of evil then so small as easie think

438. The remedie; perhaps more valid Armes,
Weapons more violent, when next we meet,
May serve to better us, and worse our foes,
Or equal what between us made the odds,
In Nature none: if other hidden cause
Left them Superiour, while we can preserve
Unhurt our mindes, and understanding sound,
Due search and consultation will disclose.

446.   He sat; and in th' assembly next upstood
Nisroc, of Principalities the prime;
As one he stood escap't from cruel fight,
Sore toild, his riv'n Armes to havoc hewn,
And cloudie in aspect thus answering spake.

451. Deliverer from new Lords, leader to free
Enjoyment of our right as Gods; yet hard
For Gods, and too unequal work we find
Against unequal arms to fight in paine,
Against unpaind, impassive; from which evil

456. Ruin must needs ensue; for what availes
Valour or strength, though matchless, quelld with pain
Which all subdues, and makes remiss the hands

459. Of Mightiest. Sense of pleasure we may well
Spare out of life perhaps, and not repine,
But live content, which is the calmest life:
But pain is perfet miserie, the worst
Of evils, and excessive, overturnes

464. All patience. He who therefore can invent
With what more forcible we may offend
Our yet unwounded Enemies, or arme
Our selves with like defence, to me deserves
No less then for deliverance what we owe.

469.   Whereto with look compos'd Satan repli'd.
Not uninvented that, which thou aright
Believst so main to our success, I bring;

472. Which of us who beholds the bright surface
Of this Ethereous mould whereon we stand,
This continent of spacious Heav'n, adornd
With Plant, Fruit, Flour Ambrosial, Gemms & Gold,

476. Whose Eye so superficially surveyes
These things, as not to mind from whence they grow
Deep under ground, materials dark and crude,
Of spiritous and fierie spume, till toucht
With Heav'ns ray, and temperd they shoot forth
So beauteous, op'ning to the ambient light.

482. These in thir dark Nativitie the Deep
Shall yield us pregnant with infernal flame,

438. *I think all we need are more violent weapons to level the playing field. If not that, then whatever we need to win, we'll figure out, as long as we have functioning brains."*

446.   He sat down and Nisroch, leader of the order of Principalities, stood up next. He had a rough time in the fight. His shield and weapons were all bent and broken.

451. *"I don't know, Satan, this pain thing really hurts!*

456. *It's too hard to fight when you hurt like that. It's killing us. And they don't seem to be feeling any pain at all. They must have some kind of protection.*

459. *It's one thing to give up pleasure. I don't mind if I have to live a calm life, without much joy, but this pain is just too much.*

464. *We'd owe everything to somebody who could invent some way to give back to them what they're dishing out to us. Maybe then we'd have a chance of winning."*

469.   Satan said, *"Maybe the answer is right under our feet.*

472. *Look at all these beautiful plants and flowers, and all the precious gems and gold.*

476. *You'd never think they came from sulfur and such crude black materials as are deep in the ground.*

482. *We'll dig up this material and stuff it into long hollow engines. We'll light the other end with fire.*

Which into hallow Engins long and round
Thick-rammd, at th' other bore with touch of fire
486. Dilated and infuriate shall send forth
From far with thundring noise among our foes
Such implements of mischief as shall dash
To pieces, and orewhelm whatever stands
Adverse, that they shall fear we have disarmd
The Thunderer of his only dreaded bolt.
492. Nor long shall be our labour, yet ere dawne,
Effect shall end our wish. Mean while revive;
Abandon fear; to strength and counsel joind
Think nothing hard, much less to be despaird.
496. He ended, and his words thir drooping chere
Enlightn'd, and thir languisht hope reviv'd.
Th' invention all admir'd, and each, how hee
To be th' inventor miss'd, so easie it seemd
Once found, which yet unfound most would have thought
Impossible: yet haply of thy Race
502. In future dayes, if Malice should abound,
Some one intent on mischief, or inspir'd
With dev'lish machination might devise
Like instrument to plague the Sons of men
For sin, on warr and mutual slaughter bent.
507. Forthwith from Councel to the work they flew,
None arguing stood, innumerable hands
509. Were ready, in a moment up they turnd
Wide the Celestial soile, and saw beneath
Th' originals of Nature in thir crude
Conception; Sulphurous and Nitrous Foame
They found, they mingl'd, and with suttle Art,
Concocted and adusted they reduc'd
To blackest grain, and into store convey'd:
516. Part hidd'n veins diggd up (nor hath this Earth
Entrails unlike) of Mineral and Stone,
Whereof to found thir Engins and thir Balls
Of missive ruin; part incentive reed
Provide, pernicious with one touch to fire.
521. So all ere day-spring, under conscious Night
Secret they finish'd, and in order set,
With silent circumspection unespi'd.
524. Now when fair Morn Orient in Heav'n appeerd
Up rose the Victor Angels, and to Arms
The matin Trumpet Sung: in Arms they stood
Of Golden Panoplie, refulgent Host,
528. Soon banded; others from the dawning Hills
Lookd round, and Scouts each Coast light-armed scoure,
Each quarter, to descrie the distant foe,
Where lodg'd, or whither fled, or if for fight,
532. In motion or in alt: him soon they met

486. *The explosion will send some serious damage on our enemies'*
      heads. They'll think we stole God's worst weapon for our own
      use.

492. *These weapons won't be hard to build. We'll have them ready*
      by morning. So cheer up and get busy."

496. At this, they felt hopeful again, and really admired Satan's bril-
      liance. It seemed so simple. Why didn't I think of that, they all
      said.

502. If evil spreads among you humans, don't be surprised if some-
      day somebody invents something very similar, that will cause
      you people misery, with endless wars and endless killing.

507. They went straight to work.

509. They dug up sulfur and potassium nitrate from under the soil
      and baked it into gunpowder.

516. They dug up minerals and stone, just like you have on Earth,
      and made cannons and cannon balls that could be fired by
      lighting with a reed.

521. They worked under cover of night and were done by daybreak.

524. In the morning the good angels woke up and the trumpets
      called them to arms.

528. Scouts went up the hills to see if the enemy was around.

532. They saw them approaching slowly. The cherub, Zophiel, hurried
      back and cried out from mid air:

Under spred Ensignes moving nigh, in slow
But firm Battalion; back with speediest Sail
Zophiel, of Cherubim the swiftest wing,
Came flying, and in mid Aire aloud thus cri'd.

537.   Arme, Warriours, Arme for fight, the foe at hand,
Whom fled we thought, will save us long pursuit
This day, fear not his flight; so thick a Cloud
He comes, and settl'd in his face I see
Sad resolution and secure: let each
His Adamantine coat gird well, and each
Fit well his Helme, gripe fast his orbed Shield,
Born eevn or high, for this day will pour down,
If I conjecture aught, no drizling showr,
But ratling storm of Arrows barbd with fire.

547. So warnd he them aware themselves, and soon
In order, quit of all impediment;
Instant without disturb they took Allarm,

550. And onward move Embattelld; when behold
Not distant far with heavie pace the Foe
Approaching gross and huge; in hollow Cube

553. Training his devilish Enginrie, impal'd
On every side with shaddowing Squadrons Deep,

555. To hide the fraud. At interview both stood
A while, but suddenly at head appeerd
Satan: And thus was heard Commanding loud.

558.   Vanguard, to Right and Left the Front unfould;

559. That all may see who hate us, how we seek
Peace and composure, and with open brest
Stand readie to receive them, if they like
Our overture, and turn not back perverse;
But that I doubt, however witness Heaven,
Heav'n witness thou anon, while we discharge
Freely our part; yee who appointed stand
Do as you have in charge, and briefly touch
What we propound, and loud that all may hear.

568.   So scoffing in ambiguous words he scarce

569. Had ended; when to Right and Left the Front
Divided, and to either Flank retir'd.
Which to our eyes discoverd new and strange,
A triple mounted row of Pillars laid
On Wheels (for like to Pillars most they seem'd
Or hollow'd bodies made of Oak or Firr
With branches lopt, in Wood or Mountain fell'd)

576. Brass, Iron, Stonie mould, had not thir mouthes
With hideous orifice gap't on us wide,

578. Portending hollow truce; at each behind
A Seraph stood, and in his hand a Reed

580. Stood waving tipt with fire; while we suspense,
Collected stood within our thoughts amus'd,

537.   *"To arms men! We won't have to go looking for the rebels. They didn't run away after all. They're on their way here, well armed it looks like. Better get your armor on."*

547. So they got going.

550. They saw the enemy coming on in huge square formation.

553. Inside, hidden on all four sides by the squadrons, were the weapons they had made.

555. Soon they were face to face. They stood staring at each other for a while. Then Satan shouted orders.

558.   He ordered his men in front to move left and right to reveal what was hidden. He said he wanted to make a gesture of peace, like a soldier removing his protective armor.

559. *"After all, we mean no harm. I kind of doubt they'll believe us. Nevertheless, let's show all Heaven how sincere we are. Let's send our message of peace, and let's make it loud, so everybody can hear us!"*

568.   (He was being sarcastic.)

569. The angels in front moved, and we saw this strange arrangement of three rows of what looked like hollowed out trees or columns on wheels.

576. In front were openings like wide open mouths.

578. Behind each one a Seraph stood holding a reed that was like a big lit match.

580. We stood waiting to see what would happen.

582.   Not long, for sudden all at once thir Reeds
Put forth, and to a narrow vent appli'd
With nicest touch. Immediate in a flame,
But soon obscur'd with smoak, all Heav'n appeerd,
From those deep throated Engins belcht, whose roar
Emboweld with outragious noise the Air,
And all her entrails tore, disgorging foule

589.   Thir devilish glut, chaind Thunderbolts and Hail
Of Iron Globes, which on the Victor Host
Level'd, with such impetuous furie smote,
That whom they hit, none on thir feet might stand,
Though standing else as Rocks, but down they fell
By thousands, Angel on Arch-Angel rowl'd;

595.   The sooner for thir Arms, unarm'd they might
Have easily as Spirits evaded swift
By quick contraction or remove; but now

598.   Foule dissipation follow'd and forc't rout;
Nor serv'd it to relax thir serried files.
What should they do? if on they rusht, repulse
Repeated, and indecent overthrow
Doubl'd, would render them yet more despis'd,
And to thir foes a laughter; for in view
Stood rankt of Seraphim another row
In posture to displode thir second tire
Of Thunder: back defeated to return

607.   They worse abhorr'd. Satan beheld thir plight,
And to his Mates thus in derision call'd.

609.   O Friends, why come not on these Victors proud?
Ere while they fierce were coming, and when wee,
To entertain them fair with open Front
And Brest, (what could we more?) propounded terms
Of composition, strait they chang'd thir minds,
Flew off, and into strange vagaries fell,
As they would dance, yet for a dance they seemd
Somwhat extravagant and wilde, perhaps

617.   For joy of offerd peace: but I suppose
If our proposals once again were heard
We should compel them to a quick result.

620.   To whom thus Belial in like gamesom mood,

621.   Leader, the terms we sent were terms of weight,
Of hard contents, and full of force urg'd home,

623.   Such as we might perceive amus'd them all,

624.   And stumbl'd many, who receives them right,
Had need from head to foot well understand;
Not understood, this gift they have besides,
They shew us when our foes walk not upright.

628.   So they among themselves in pleasant veine
Stood scoffing, highthn'd in thir thoughts beyond

630.   All doubt of victorie, eternal might

582. Suddenly they all lit the cannons. There was a roar, and flames, and a lot of smoke.

589. A shower of iron balls fell on God's army. Thousands of angels who usually stand like rocks were knocked down on top of each other.

595. Their heavy armor made it hard for them to dodge the cannon balls.

598. They didn't know what to do. They didn't want to retreat, but ahead of them they could see their enemies getting ready to light a second row of cannons.

607. Satan made fun of them to his men:

609.   *"My friends, will you look at this! When we offered our terms of peace, those proud angels who were about to fight us started this crazy dance for joy.*

617. *Maybe if they hear our proposals again they'll give us a more proper response."*

620.   Belial continued the wise cracks:

621. *"Leader, the terms we sent were heavy and had hard contents, and we urged them forcefully.*

623. *Yet they seemed bewildered, and stumbled in their response.*

624. *Crawling around on all fours, they seemed to be telling us they didn't understand our generous offer."*

628.   So they continued mocking their enemies, certain they were winning.

630. They were confident their cannons were more powerful than God's might.

To match with thir inventions they presum'd
So easie, and of his Thunder made a scorn,
633. And all his Host derided, while they stood
A while in trouble; but they stood not long,
Rage prompted them at length, and found them arms
Against such hellish mischief fit to oppose.
637. Forthwith (behold the excellence, the power
Which God hath in his mighty Angels plac'd)
Thir Arms away they threw, and to the Hills
(For Earth hath this variety from Heav'n
Of pleasure situate in Hill and Dale)
Light as the Lightning glimps they ran, they flew,
From thir foundations loosning to and fro
They pluckt the seated Hills with all thir load,
Rocks, Waters, Woods, and by the shaggie tops
646. Up lifting bore them in thir hands: Amaze,
Be sure, and terrour seis'd the rebel Host,
When coming towards them so dread they saw
The bottom of the Mountains upward turn'd,
650. Till on those cursed Engins triple-row
They saw them whelm'd, and all thir confidence
Under the weight of Mountains buried deep,
653. Themselves invaded next, and on thir heads
Main Promontories flung, which in the Air
Came shadowing, and opprest whole Legions arm'd,
656. Thir armor help'd thir harm, crush't in and bruis'd
Into thir substance pent, which wrought them pain
Implacable, and many a dolorous groan,
659. Long strugling underneath, ere they could wind
Out of such prison, though Spirits of purest light,
Purest at first, now gross by sinning grown.
662. The rest in imitation to like Armes
Betook them, and the neighbouring Hills uptore;
664. So Hills amid the Air encounterd Hills
Hurl'd to and fro with jaculation dire,
That under ground, they fought in dismal shade;
667. Infernal noise; Warr seem'd a civil Game
To this uproar; horrid confusion heapt
669. Upon confusion rose: and now all Heav'n
Had gone to wrack, with ruin overspred,
Had not th' Almightie Father where he sits
Shrin'd in his Sanctuarie of Heav'n secure,
Consulting on the sum of things, foreseen
This tumult, and permitted all, advis'd:
That his great purpose he might so fulfill,
To honour his Anointed Son aveng'd
Upon his enemies, and to declare
All power on him transferr'd: whence to his Son
Th' Assessor of his Throne he thus began.

633. But the good angels suddenly got really mad.

637. They threw away their weapons and (wait till you hear the power God gives his angels!) they ran to the hills (the hills on Earth are copies of what is in Heaven) and after some tugging back and forth, pulled whole hills out of the ground with all their rocks, water and woods in one big load, lifting them with their bare hands.

646. You can be sure the rebel army were stunned when they saw the bottoms of upside-down mountains coming at them.

650. Down they came burying all their damned cannons, and all their confidence as well.

653. And they were the next targets, as mountains cast shadows over whole legions, and came down on their heads.

656. Their armor made matters worse, as it was crushed and pushed into their bodies, causing great pain.

659. It took a lot of struggling to get out of that mess.

662. The rest of Satan's army decided to copy what the other side was doing. They took off for the nearby hills.

664. Now hills were crashing into other hills in mid-air, while on the ground the angels were fighting in their shadow.

667. What a racket they made! The war up to now seemed like a game compared to this terrible chaos.

669. They would have destroyed Heaven, if it wasn't for the fact that God predicted all this, and permitted it to go on in order to give his son the chance to use the power he had given him.

680.   Effulgence of my Glorie, Son belov'd,
          Son in whose face invisible is beheld
          Visibly, what by Deitie I am,
          And in whose hand what by Decree I doe,
          Second Omnipotence, two dayes are past,
685.   Two dayes, as we compute the dayes of Heav'n,
          Since Michael and his Powers went forth to tame
687.   These disobedient; sore hath been thir fight,
          As likeliest was, when two such Foes met arm'd;
          For to themselves I left them, and thou knowst,
          Equal in thir Creation they were form'd,
691.   Save what sin hath impaird, which yet hath wrought
          Insensibly, for I suspend thir doom;
693.   Whence in perpetual fight they needs must last
          Endless, and no solution will be found:
          Warr wearied hath perform'd what Warr can do,
          And to disorder'd rage let loose the reines,
          With Mountains as with Weapons arm'd, which makes
          Wild work in Heav'n, and dangerous to the maine.
699.   Two dayes are therefore past, the third is thine;
700.   For thee I have ordain'd it, and thus farr
          Have sufferd, that the Glorie may be thine
          Of ending this great Warr, since none but Thou
703.   Can end it. Into thee such Vertue and Grace
          Immense I have transfus'd, that all may know
          In Heav'n and Hell thy Power above compare,
          And this perverse Commotion governd thus,
          To manifest thee worthiest to be Heir
          Of all things, to be Heir and to be King
          By Sacred Unction, thy deserved right.
710.   Go then thou Mightiest in thy Fathers might,
          Ascend my Chariot, guide the rapid Wheeles
          That shake Heav'ns basis, bring forth all my Warr,
          My Bow and Thunder, my Almightie Arms
          Gird on, and Sword upon thy puissant Thigh;
715.   Pursue these sons of Darkness, drive them out
          From all Heav'ns bounds into the utter Deep:
717.   There let them learn, as likes them, to despise
          God and Messiah his anointed King.
719.   He said, and on his Son with Rayes direct
          Shon full, he all his Father full exprest
          Ineffably into his face receiv'd,
          And thus the filial Godhead answering spake.
723.   O Father, O Supream of heav'nly Thrones,
          First, Highest, Holiest, Best, thou alwayes seekst
          To glorifie thy Son, I alwayes thee,
726.   As is most just; this I my Glorie account,
          My exaltation, and my whole delight,
          That thou in me well pleas'd, declarst thy will

680.   *"My beloved Son," he said, "Your face makes my invisible presence seen, and your hands fulfill my decree.*

685.   *It's been two days since Michael led my army into battle against Satan's forces.*

687.   *Their fight was extreme, as you would expect, since I left them on their own, and both sides were created with equal power.*

691.   *Sin will eventually weaken Satan's side, but they don't know it yet.*

693.   *But this war could go on forever, throwing mountains around, turning all Heaven into ruins.*

699.   *They've been at it for two days, the third one is yours.*

700.   *I put up with all this nonsense just so you could be the one to end it, like I planned.*

703.   *I put enough power in you to win the war single-handedly, to show everybody that you are worthy and have the right to be king.*

710.   *So go with all my power. Take my chariot and use my full force.*

715.   *Chase these bastards and drive them out of Heaven straight into Hell.*

717.   *Let them sit there and hate us to their hearts content."*

719.   There was more that God expressed which we wouldn't understand. He expressed it by shining rays onto his Son's face.

723.   The Son said, *"Father, you're always glorifying me, and I feel the same about you.*

726.   *All I want to do is please you.*

Fulfill'd, which to fulfil is all my bliss.

730. Scepter and Power, thy giving, I assume,
731. And gladlier shall resign, when in the end
Thou shalt be All in All, and I in thee
For ever, and in mee all whom thou lov'st:
734. But whom thou hat'st, I hate, and can put on
Thy terrors, as I put thy mildness on,
736. Image of thee in all things; and shall soon,
Armd with thy might, rid heav'n of these rebell'd,
738. To thir prepar'd ill Mansion driven down
To chains of darkness, and th' undying Worm,
That from thy just obedience could revolt,
Whom to obey is happiness entire.
742. Then shall thy Saints unmixt, and from th' impure
Farr separate, circling thy holy Mount
Unfeigned Halleluiahs to thee sing,
Hymns of high praise, and I among them chief.
746. So said, he o're his Scepter bowing, rose
From the right hand of Glorie where he sate,
748. And the third sacred Morn began to shine
Dawning through Heav'n: forth rush'd with whirl-wind sound
The Chariot of Paternal Deitie,
751. Flashing thick flames, Wheele within Wheele, undrawn,
It self instinct with Spirit, but convoyd
753. By four Cherubic shapes, four Faces each
Had wondrous, as with Starrs thir bodies all
And Wings were set with Eyes, with Eyes the wheels
Of Beril, and careering Fires between;
757. Over thir heads a chrystal Firmament,
Whereon a Saphir Throne, inlaid with pure
Amber, and colours of the showrie Arch.
760. Hee in Celestial Panoplie all armd
Of radiant Urim, work divinely wrought,
762. Ascended, at his right hand Victorie
763. Sate Eagle-wing'd, beside him hung his Bow
And Quiver with three-bolted Thunder stor'd,
765. And from about him fierce Effusion rowld
Of smoak and bickering flame, and sparkles dire;
Attended with ten thousand thousand Saints,
He onward came, farr off his coming shon,
And twentie thousand (I thir number heard)
Chariots of God, half on each hand were seen:
771. Hee on the wings of Cherub rode sublime
On the Chrystallin Skie, in Saphir Thron'd.
773. Illustrious farr and wide, but by his own
774. First seen, them unexpected joy surpriz'd,
When the great Ensign of Messiah blaz'd
Aloft by Angels born, his Sign in Heav'n:
777. Under whose Conduct Michael soon reduc'd

730. *I will take on all the power you give me.*
731. *Someday you and I and everybody you love will be all one.*

734. *But whoever you hate, I hate. And I can be as tough as I can be loving.*
736. *I'll rid Heaven of these insurgents.*

738. *Hell is ready and waiting for them.*

742. *Then you can be sure that all the angels who surround you singing praises, including me, are all pure and faithful. All the impure ones will have been eliminated."*

746. The Son got up from his throne on the right hand of God, and bowed.
748. On the third morning, the chariot of God the Father came roaring out, sending out flames.
751. There was nothing pulling it. It was living spirit.
753. It was guided by four cherubs. Each one had four faces with many eyes all over their faces and bodies, like stars. The wheels were made of emeralds and had eyes also. The speeding wheels shot out fire.
757. Above them was a crystal carriage, with a sapphire throne, inlaid with amber, with all the colors of the rainbow.
760. The Son climbed into the chariot. He wore radiant armor made of divine material.

762. On his right hand sat winged Victory.
763. He had a bow and a supply of arrows by his side. Each one was a triple thunderbolt.
765. There were sparks and flames and smoke all around him as he advanced, and thousands and thousands of angels, in twenty thousand chariots—half on each side of him.

771. He was a magnificent sight.

773. Among the battling angels, our side was the first to see the Messiah coming.
774. They were overjoyed.
777. Michael turned his army and his authority over to the Messiah, and they became one with him.

His Armie, circumfus'd on either Wing,
Under thir Head imbodied all in one.
Before him Power Divine his way prepar'd;
781. At his command the uprooted Hills retir'd
Each to his place, they heard his voice and went
Obsequious, Heav'n his wonted face renewd,
And with fresh Flourets Hill and Valley smil'd.
785. This saw his hapless Foes but stood obdur'd,
And to rebellious fight rallied thir Powers
787. Insensate, hope conceiving from despair.
788. In heav'nly Spirits could such perverseness dwell?
But to convince the proud what Signs availe,
Or Wonders move th' obdurate to relent?
They hard'nd more by what might most reclame,
Grieving to see his Glorie, at the sight
Took envie, and aspiring to his highth,
Stood reimbattell'd fierce, by force or fraud
795. Weening to prosper, and at length prevaile
Against God and Messiah, or to fall
In universal ruin last, and now
798. To final Battel drew, disdaining flight,
Or faint retreat; when the great Son of God
To all his Host on either hand thus spake.
801.   Stand still in bright array ye Saints, here stand
Ye Angels arm'd, this day from Battel rest;
Faithful hath been your warfare, and of God
Accepted, fearless in his righteous Cause,
And as ye have receivd, so have ye don
806. Invincibly; but of this cursed crew
The punishment to other hand belongs,
Vengeance is his, or whose he sole appoints;
Number to this dayes work is not ordain'd
Nor multitude, stand onely and behold
Gods indignation on these Godless pourd
812. By mee, not you but mee they have despis'd,
Yet envied; against mee is all thir rage,
Because the Father, t' whom in Heav'n supream
Kingdom and Power and Glorie appertains,
Hath honourd me according to his will.
Therefore to mee thir doom he hath assig'n'd;
818. That they may have thir wish, to trie with mee
In Battel which the stronger proves, they all,
Or I alone against them, since by strength
821. They measure all, of other excellence
Not emulous, nor care who them excells;
Nor other strife with them do I voutsafe.
824.   So spake the Son, and into terrour chang'd
His count'nance too severe to be beheld
And full of wrauth bent on his Enemies.

781. He told the hills to go back where they were, and they did, with all the flowers and everything back in place.

785. The enemy was not impressed.

787. They were desperate, and didn't have any sense or reason.

788. It's hard to believe angels could be that stupid, but they were so proud and stubborn that what should have moved them to relent only made them more envious.

795. They actually believed they could win against God.

798. So they were about to go at it with him, when the Son of God spoke:

801.   *"Those of you who have been faithful to God, you fought well against the rebels, but you can rest now.*

806. *God has appointed me alone to handle their punishment.*

812. *I'm the one they hate and envy because God gave me rule over them. So now he sent me to take care of them.*

818. *Now they'll get their wish. It's me against them, and we'll see who's stronger.*

821. *Since all they care about is power, I'll show them power. I wouldn't stoop to try to explain right and wrong to them."*

824.   Then on his face came a look of terrible rage.

827. At once the Four spred out thir Starrie wings
828. With dreadful shade contiguous, and the Orbes
     Of his fierce Chariot rowld, as with the sound
     Of torrent Floods, or of a numerous Host.
831. Hee on his impious Foes right onward drove,
     Gloomie as Night; under his burning Wheeles
     The stedfast Empyrean shook throughout,
     All but the Throne it self of God. Full soon
835. Among them he arriv'd; in his right hand
     Grasping ten thousand Thunders, which he sent
     Before him, such as in thir Soules infix'd
838. Plagues; they astonisht all resistance lost,
839. All courage; down thir idle weapons drop'd;
840. O're Shields and Helmes, and helmed heads he rode
841. Of Thrones and mighty Seraphim prostrate,
     That wisht the Mountains now might be again
     Thrown on them as a shelter from his ire.
844. Nor less on either side tempestuous fell
     His arrows, from the fourfold-visag'd Foure,
     Distinct with eyes, and from the living Wheels,
     Distinct alike with multitude of eyes,
848. One Spirit in them rul'd, and every eye
     Glar'd lightning, and shot forth pernicious fire
     Among th' accurst, that witherd all thir strength,
     And of thir wonted vigour left them draind,
     Exhausted, spiritless, afflicted, fall'n.
853. Yet half his strength he put not forth, but check'd
854. His Thunder in mid Volie, for he meant
     Not to destroy, but root them out of Heav'n:
856. The overthrown he rais'd, and as a Heard
     Of Goats or timerous flock together throngd
     Drove them before him Thunder-struck, pursu'd
     With terrors and with furies to the bounds
860. And Chrystal wall of Heav'n, which op'ning wide,
     Rowld inward, and a spacious Gap disclos'd
862. Into the wastful Deep; the monstrous sight
     Strook them with horror backward, but far worse
864. Urg'd them behind; headlong themselves they threw
     Down from the verge of Heav'n, Eternal wrauth
     Burnt after them to the bottomless pit.
867.   Hell heard th' unsufferable noise, Hell saw
     Heav'n ruining from Heav'n and would have fled
     Affrighted; but strict Fate had cast too deep
     Her dark foundations, and too fast had bound.
871. Nine dayes they fell; confounded Chaos roard,
     And felt tenfold confusion in thir fall
     Through his wilde Anarchie, so huge a rout
874. Incumberd him with ruin: Hell at last
     Yawning receavd them whole, and on them clos'd,

827. The living chariot spread out its starry wings, creating a big shadow.
828. The rolling wheels sounded like a flood, or a charging army.
831. His roaring chariot shook all Heaven, except where God sat on his throne.

835. When he got close to the enemy he grabbed ten thousand thunder-arrows and shot them, fixing them inside their souls.

838. They lost all their nerve.
839. They dropped their weapons.
840. He rode over their shields and helmets, some with their heads still in them.
841. They were lying all over the ground, wishing the mountains would be thrown on them again to protect them from his anger.

844. The four-faced, four cherub shapes shot arrows too.

848. The shapes were all made of one single spirit. All the eyes shot deadly fire which drained all the strength from the enemy, both physical and mental.

853. Messiah had not even used half his power.
854. He stopped his attack because he didn't want to kill them, just cast them out of Heaven.
856. He made them get up and chased them like a herd of frightened goats to the wall at the edge of Heaven.

860. The wall opened like a wide gate rolling inside and leaving a big opening where you could see down into blackness.
862. The rebel angels were horrified. But they were even more afraid of who was chasing them.
864. They jumped off the edge head first into the bottomless blackness.
867. Hell heard the racket and saw a bunch of angels falling. Hell would have run away frightened, but it couldn't because Fate had planted its foundation too deep and firm.

871. Their fall was so catastrophic, even Chaos was confused. They continued to fall for nine days.
874. At last Hell opened wide and they all fell in. Then Hell closed on them.

876. Hell thir fit habitation fraught with fire
     Unquenchable, the house of woe and paine.
878. Disburdnd Heav'n rejoic'd, and soon repaird
     Her mural breach, returning whence it rowld.
880. Sole Victor from th' expulsion of his Foes
     Messiah his triumphal Chariot turnd:
882. To meet him all his Saints, who silent stood
     Eye witnesses of his Almightie Acts,
     With Jubilie advanc'd; and as they went,
     Shaded with branching Palme, each order bright,
     Sung Triumph, and him sung Victorious King,
     Son, Heir, and Lord, to him Dominion giv'n,
888. Worthiest to Reign: he celebrated rode
     Triumphant through mid Heav'n, into the Courts
     And Temple of his mightie Father Thron'd
     On high: who into Glorie him receav'd,
892. Where now he sits at the right hand of bliss.
893.   Thus measuring things in Heav'n by things on Earth
     At thy request, and that thou maist beware
     By what is past, to thee I have reveal'd
896. What might have else to human Race bin hid;
     The discord which befel, and Warr in Heav'n
     Among th' Angelic Powers, and the deep fall
     Of those too high aspiring, who rebelld
900. With Satan, hee who envies now thy state,
     Who now is plotting how he may seduce
     Thee also from obedience, that with him
903. Bereavd of happiness thou maist partake
     His punishment, Eternal miserie;
905. Which would be all his solace and revenge,
     As a despite don against the most High,
     Thee once to gaine Companion of his woe.
908. But list'n not to his Temptations, warne
909. Thy weaker; let it profit thee to have heard
     By terrible Example the reward
     Of disobedience; firm they might have stood,
     Yet fell; remember, and fear to transgress.

876. Hell was where they belonged—a place full of fire that never went out—a place of misery and pain.

878. Heaven was happy to be rid of them. It closed its gates.

880. Messiah had single-handedly expelled the enemy and won the war. He turned his chariot around.

882. All the angels who had stood watching came to meet him. They carried palms and sang his praises. They sang that he deserved to be the victorious king and Lord and to inherit all his Father's kingdom.

888. He rode into the temple of his Father, who received him into glory.

892. Since then he sits at his Father's right hand.

893. That's the end of my story. I told it to you by describing heavenly events as if they were earthly events, so you could understand them.

896. Otherwise humans would never know about the war and about Satan's fall.

900. Now Satan envies you and all your happiness, and he's planning to get you to disobey God like he did.

903. He wants you to be as miserable as he is.

905. That would be his revenge against God. It's the only thing that would make him happy now.

908. But don't listen to him, and warn your wife too.

909. Learn your lesson well from the story I just told you, and don't forget what happens when you disobey God.

Book VII

1.   Descend from Heav'n Urania, by that name
If rightly thou art call'd, whose Voice divine
Following, above th' Olympian Hill I soare,
Above the flight of Pegasean wing.

5. The meaning, not the Name I call: for thou
Nor of the Muses nine, nor on the top
Of old Olympus dwell'st, but Heav'nlie borne,

8. Before the Hills appeerd, or Fountain flow'd,
Thou with Eternal Wisdom didst converse,
Wisdom thy Sister, and with her didst play
In presence of th' Almightie Father, pleas'd

12. With thy Celestial Song. Up led by thee
Into the Heav'n of Heav'ns I have presum'd,
An Earthlie Guest, and drawn Empyreal Aire,

15. Thy tempring; with like safetie guided down
Return me to my Native Element:
Least from this flying Steed unrein'd, (as once
Bellerophon, though from a lower Clime)
Dismounted, on th' Aleian Field I fall
Erroneous there to wander and forlorne.

21. Half yet remaines unsung, but narrower bound
Within the visible Diurnal Spheare;

23. Standing on Earth, not rapt above the Pole,
More safe I Sing with mortal voice, unchang'd
To hoarce or mute, though fall'n on evil dayes,
On evil dayes though fall'n, and evil tongues;

27. In darkness, and with dangers compast round,

28. And solitude; yet not alone, while thou
Visit'st my slumbers Nightly, or when Morn
Purples the East: still govern thou my Song,

31. Urania, and fit audience find, though few.

32. But drive farr off the barbarous dissonance

33. Of Bacchus and his Revellers, the Race
Of that wilde Rout that tore the Thracian Bard
In Rhodope, where Woods and Rocks had Eares
To rapture, till the savage clamor dround
Both Harp and Voice; nor could the Muse defend

38. Her Son. So fail not thou, who thee implores:
For thou art Heav'nlie, shee an empty dreame.

40.   Say Goddess, what ensu'd when Raphael,
The affable Arch-Angel, had forewarn'd
Adam by dire example to beware
Apostasie, by what befell in Heaven

Chapter 7

IN PLAIN ENGLISH

1.   Come down from Heaven, Urania. (That's the best name I can think of for you.) Listening to you I get higher than Mount Olympus, even higher than Pegasus, the winged horse, can fly.

5. I'll call you that even though you're not one of the nine Muses or one of the Olympian gods. You were born in Heaven.

8. Before the world was created, you were already there. You made God happy as you talked and played and made poetry with your sister, Wisdom.

12. With your guidance I dared to go up into Heaven.

15. Now you better guide me safely back down to Earth where I belong, before I fall, like Bellerophon, who fell off Pegasus and ended up lost and wandering aimlessly.

21. I've told only half of my story now. The rest of it takes place here on Earth.

23. As a poet, I feel more confident writing about earthly rather than heavenly things. Although here is where I have many personal problems and dangers.

27. I'm blind, surrounded by darkness and solitude, but I am not alone.

28. You come to me in my dreams and inspire me to tell this story.

31. Not many people will read it though, only the really smart ones.

32. Keep the stupid, noisy ones away from us.

33. The Muse, Calliope, couldn't save her son, Orpheus. His music charmed even the trees and rocks till the drunken mob killed him.

38. But that won't happen to us because you really are from Heaven, not just a Greek myth, right?

40.   So, what happened after Raphael warned Adam that the same thing that happened to the bad angels could happen to him if he touched the forbidden tree?

To those Apostates, least the like befall
In Paradise to Adam or his Race,
Charg'd not to touch the interdicted Tree,
If they transgress, and slight that sole command,
So easily obeyd amid the choice
Of all tastes else to please thir appetite,

50. Though wandring. He with his consorted Eve
The storie heard attentive, and was fill'd
With admiration, and deep Muse to heare
Of things so high and strange, things to thir thought
So unimaginable as hate in Heav'n,
And Warr so neer the Peace of God in bliss
With such confusion: but the evil soon
Driv'n back redounded as a flood on those
From whom it sprung, impossible to mix

59. With Blessedness. Whence Adam soon repeal'd
The doubts that in his heart arose: and now
Led on, yet sinless, with desire to know
What neerer might concern him, how this World
Of Heav'n and Earth conspicious first began,
When, and whereof created, for what cause,
What within Eden or without was done
Before his memorie, as one whose drouth
Yet scarce allay'd still eyes the current streame,
Whose liquid murmur heard new thirst excites,

69. Proceeded thus to ask his Heav'nly Guest.
70.   Great things, and full of wonder in our eares,
71. Farr differing from this World, thou hast reveal'd
Divine interpreter, by favour sent
Down from the Empyrean to forewarne
Us timely of what might else have bin our loss,
Unknown, which human knowledg could not reach:
For which to the infinitly Good we owe

77. Immortal thanks, and his admonishment
Receave with solemne purpose to observe
Immutably his sovran will, the end

80. Of what we are. But since thou hast voutsaft
Gently for our instruction to impart
Things above Earthly thought, which yet concernd
Our knowing, as to highest wisdom seemd,
Deign to descend now lower, and relate
What may no less perhaps availe us known,

86. How first began this Heav'n which we behold
Distant so high, with moving Fires adornd
Innumerable, and this which yeelds or fills
All space, the ambient Aire, wide interfus'd

90. Imbracing round this florid Earth, what cause
Mov'd the Creator in his holy Rest
Through all Eternitie so late to build
In Chaos, and the work begun, how soon

50. He and his wife had listened carefully and were fascinated, hearing about things they could never have imagined, like the war in Heaven.

59. Adam was so impressed with Raphael's story that he became thirsty to hear more—like how and why the world was created, and what all happened before he was born.

69. So Adam said to Raphael:
70.   *"That was quite a story, sir!*
71. *We thank God for sending you to us. You warned us about things we wouldn't have known anything about otherwise, which could have been disastrous for us.*

77. *Now we're more determined than ever to obey his will forever.*

80. *And since you have been kind enough to teach us these wonderful high things, I was just wondering if maybe you might also be willing to tell us some more about some other things that it might be good for us to know about?*

86. *Like, for example, how did the sky with all the stars come to be? And the air that flows over all the plants and trees?*

90. *And what prompted the Creator in the first place, at this point in all eternity, to decide to create this world out of nothing? And how long did it take him to do it?*

94. Absolv'd, if unforbid thou maist unfould
What wee, not to explore the secrets aske
Of his Eternal Empire, but the more
To magnifie his works, the more we know.

98. And the great Light of Day yet wants to run
Much of his Race though steep, suspens in Heav'n
Held by thy voice, thy potent voice he heares,
And longer will delay to heare thee tell
His Generation, and the rising Birth
Of Nature from the unapparent Deep:

104. Or if the Starr of Eevning and the Moon
Haste to thy audience, Night with her will bring

106. Silence, and Sleep listning to thee will watch,
Or we can bid his absence, till thy Song
End, and dismiss thee ere the Morning shine.
      Thus Adam his illustrious Guest besought:

110.   And thus the Godlike Angel answerd milde.
This also thy request with caution askt
Obtaine: though to recount Almightie works
What words or tongue of Seraph can suffice,
Or heart of man suffice to comprehend?

115. Yet what thou canst attain, which best may serve
To glorifie the Maker, and inferr
Thee also happier, shall not be withheld
Thy hearing, such Commission from above
I have receav'd, to answer thy desire

120. Of knowledge within bounds; beyond abstain
To ask, nor let thine own inventions hope
Things not reveal'd, which th' invisible King,
Onely Omniscient hath supprest in Night,
To none communicable in Earth or Heaven:
Anough is left besides to search and know.

126. But Knowledge is as food, and needs no less
Her Temperance over Appetite, to know
In measure what the mind may well contain,
Oppresses else with Surfet, and soon turns
Wisdom to Folly, as Nourishment to Winde.

131.   Know then, that after Lucifer from Heav'n
(So call him, brighter once amidst the Host
Of Angels, then that Starr the Starrs among)
Fell with his flaming Legions through the Deep
Into his place, and the great Son returnd
Victorious with his Saints, th' Omnipotent
Eternal Father from his Throne beheld
Thir multitude, and to his Son thus spake.

139.   At least our envious Foe hath fail'd, who thought
All like himself rebellious, by whose aid
This inaccessible high strength, the seat
Of Deitie supream, us dispossest,

143. He trusted to have seis'd, and into fraud

94. *If it's not forbidden for you to reveal these things to us, we want to know them, not to be nosey about God's secrets, but because the more we know about his creation, the more we will admire him.*

98. *I'll bet Daylight will slow down just to hear you tell about how it was created, and how Nature was born.*

104. *And if the Evening Star and the Moon come out to hear your story, Night will make everything quiet so they can hear.*

106. *And Sleep will wait and listen too, or we'll tell him to go away until you finish your story."*

110.   The angel answered, "*I'll grant your request, though it's hard to put into words that you can understand what great things God can do.*

115. *But God told me to answer whatever questions you may have in ways you can understand, to make you happy and better able to glorify him.*

120. *But some things are none of your business, and those things you shouldn't ask about or even try to imagine.*

126. *Knowledge is like food, and when you seek too much, it turns into nonsense, the way too much food turns into gas.*

131.   *Okay, so after Lucifer and his legions fell into Hell, (He was called Lucifer at that time because he was brighter than the brightest star.) and the Son returned victorious, with all the angels, God looked at them from his throne and said. . .*

139.   "*Satan thought everybody would agree with him and help him take over our kingdom, but he failed.*

143. *Many of them believed his lies, and they're gone from here forever.*

Drew many, whom thir place knows here no more;
145. Yet farr the greater part have kept, I see,
     Thir station, Heav'n yet populous retaines
     Number sufficient to possess her Realmes
     Though wide, and this high Temple to frequent
     With Ministeries due and solemn Rites:
150. But least his heart exalt him in the harme
     Already done, to have dispeopl'd Heav'n
     My damage fondly deem'd, I can repaire
153. That detriment, if such it be to lose
154. Self-lost, and in a moment will create
     Another World, out of one man a Race
156. Of men innumerable, there to dwell,
     Not here, till by degrees of merit rais'd
     They open to themselves at length the way
     Up hither, under long obedience tri'd,
160. And Earth be chang'd to Heav'n, & Heav'n to Earth,
     One Kingdom, Joy and Union without end.
162. Mean while inhabit laxe, ye Powers of Heav'n,
163. And by my Word, begotten Son, by thee
164. This I perform, speak thou, and be it don:
165. My overshadowing Spirit and might with thee
166. I send along, ride forth, and bid the Deep
     Within appointed bounds be Heav'n and Earth,
168. Boundless the Deep, because I am who fill
     Infinitude, nor vacuous the space.
     Though I uncircumscrib'd my self retire,
171. And put not forth my goodness, which is free
     To act or not, Necessitie and Chance
     Approach not mee, and what I will is Fate.
174.   So spake th' Almightie, and to what he spake
     His Word, the Filial Godhead, gave effect.
176. Immediate are the Acts of God, more swift
     Then time or motion, but to human ears
     Cannot without process of speech be told,
     So told as earthly notion can receave.
180. Great triumph and rejoycing was in Heav'n
     When such was heard declar'd the Almightie's will;
182. Glorie they sung to the most High, good will
     To future men, and in thir dwellings peace:
     Glorie to him whose just avenging ire
     Had driven out th' ungodly from his sight
     And th' habitations of the just; to him
     Glorie and praise, whose wisdom had ordain'd
     Good out of evil to create, in stead
     Of Spirits maligne a better Race to bring
     Into thir vacant room, and thence diffuse
     His good to Worlds and Ages infinite.
192. So sang the Hierarchies: Mean while the Son
     On his great Expedition now appeer'd,

145. *But many more are still here—enough to fill Heaven's wide realm and perform their holy duties in my temple.*

150. *But I don't want him to think he's succeeded in harming us by depopulating Heaven.*

153. *I can easily fix that. (Though it's hardly a loss to lose those who are already lost by their own actions.)*
154. *It will only take me a moment to create another world, where a whole new race will come from one man.*
156. *They'll live there until they eventually prove themselves worthy to come up here.*
160. *Then Heaven and Earth will join into one happy kingdom forever.*

162. *In the meantime you can all spread out and make yourselves at home in all the empty space left by the fallen angels.*
163. *My Son, through you I will perform this creation.*
164. *You just say the words and it will happen.*
165. *My spirit and might will go with you.*
166. *Go tell Chaos where to make the new world.*
168. *Chaos is not empty space. It is filled by my presence, though I can withdraw my presence and my goodness if I choose to.*
171. *I don't create this world because I have to, nor do I leave anything to chance. I do this of my own free will. And my will determines all that happens."*
174. Those were God's words, and his Son was called his Word, because he put the words into action.
176. God's actions are faster than time, but to tell them to you humans I need to use the process of speech and put them in terms you can understand.
180. The angels were very happy to hear about God's plan, and they celebrated and sang his praises.
182. They wished good will and peace to future men, and praised God for turning something evil into something good by replacing the bad angels with a better race and spreading his goodness to other worlds and endless ages.

192. Meanwhile, the Son appeared in all his glory, ready for his great expedition.

Girt with Omnipotence, with Radiance crown'd
Of Majestie Divine, Sapience and Love
Immense, and all his Father in him shon.

197. About his Chariot numberless were pour'd
Cherub and Seraph, Potentates and Thrones,

199. And Vertues, winged Spirits, and Chariots wing'd,
From the Armoury of God, where stand of old
Myriads between two brazen Mountains lodg'd
Against a solemn day, harnest at hand,

203. Celestial Equipage; and now came forth
Spontaneous, for within them Spirit livd,

205. Attendant on thir Lord: Heav'n op'nd wide
Her ever during Gates, Harmonious sound
On golden Hinges moving, to let forth
The King of Glorie in his powerful Word
And Spirit coming to create new Worlds.

210. On heav'nly ground they stood, and from the shore
They view'd the vast immeasurable Abyss

212. Outrageous as a Sea, dark, wasteful, wilde,
Up from the bottom turn'd by furious windes
And surging waves, as Mountains to assault
Heav'ns highth, and with the Center mix the Pole.

216.   Silence, ye troubl'd waves, and thou Deep, peace,
Said then th' Omnific Word, your discord end:

218.   Nor staid, but on the Wings of Cherubim
Uplifted, in Paternal Glorie rode
Farr into Chaos, and the World unborn;

221. For Chaos heard his voice: him all his Traine
Follow'd in bright procession to behold
Creation, and the wonders of his might.

224. Then staid the fervid Wheeles, and in his hand
He took the golden Compasses, prepar'd
In Gods Eternal store, to circumscribe
This Universe, and all created things:

228. One foot he center'd, and the other turn'd
Round through the vast profunditie obscure,

230. And said, thus farr extend, thus farr thy bounds,
This be thy just Circumference, O World.

232. Thus God the Heav'n created, thus the Earth,
Matter unform'd and void: Darkness profound
Cover'd th' Abyss: but on the watrie calme

235. His brooding wings the Spirit of God outspred,
And vital vertue infus'd, and vital warmth

237. Throughout the fluid Mass, but downward purg'd
The black tartareous cold Infernal dregs

239. Adverse to life: then founded, then conglob'd
Like things to like, the rest to several place
Disparted, and between spun out the Air,

242. And Earth self ballanc't on her Center hung.

243.   Let ther be Light, said God, and forthwith Light

197. Multitudes of angels surrounded his chariot.

199. Also many winged chariots came out that had been stored between two mountains for eons, waiting for just such a solemn day as this.

203. They came out by themselves. Living spirits were in them.

205. Heaven's gates opened.

210. Everybody looked down into the dark, wild abyss.

212. It was like a sea in a really bad storm.

216.   God (through his Son) told everything to be quiet.

218.   Chaos got quiet, and he rode far out into it in his chariot carried by angels.

221. A procession of angels followed him. They wanted to watch him create the world.

224. The chariot's wheels came to a halt. He took out a golden compass he got from God's storehouse.

228. He centered one point and turned the other one around through the deep darkness.

230. He said, "*This will be the limit of the new universe.*"

232. So the heavens and the Earth were created, but they were still just an unformed mass.

235. He spread his wings like a giant incubator, providing life-giving warmth to the watery mass.

237. He got rid of the dirty stuff he couldn't use.

239. The rest he mixed together and sorted out into the elements and separated them with the air.

242. The Earth was in the middle of everything. It hung freely. It didn't need any support.

243.   He said, "*Let there be light,*" and light sprung up in a bright cloud that floated through the darkness. The sun was temporarily held in a sacred mist. It wasn't lit yet.

Ethereal, first of things, quintessence pure
Sprung from the Deep, and from her Native East
To journie through the airie gloom began,
Sphear'd in a radiant Cloud, for yet the Sun
Was not; shee in a cloudie Tabernacle
249. Sojourn'd the while. God saw the Light was good;
250. And light from darkness by the Hemisphere
Divided: Light the Day, and Darkness Night
252. He nam'd. Thus was the first Day Eev'n and Morn:
253. Nor past uncelebrated, nor unsung
By the Celestial Quires, when Orient Light
Exhaling first from Darkness they beheld;
Birth-day of Heav'n and Earth; with joy and shout
The hollow Universal Orb they fill'd,
And touch'd thir Golden Harps, and hymning prais'd
God and his works, Creatour him they sung,
Both when first Eevning was, and when first Morn.
261.   Again, God said, let ther be Firmament
Amid the Waters, and let it divide
263. The Waters from the Waters: and God made
The Firmament, expanse of liquid, pure,
Transparent, Elemental Air, diffus'd
In circuit to the uttermost convex
Of this great Round: partition firm and sure,
The Waters underneath from those above
Dividing: for as Earth, so he the World
Built on circumfluous Waters calme, in wide
Crystallin Ocean, and the loud misrule
Of Chaos farr remov'd, least fierce extreames
Contiguous might distemper the whole frame:
274. And Heav'n he nam'd the Firmament: So Eev'n
275. And Morning Chorus sung the second Day.
276.   The Earth was form'd, but in the Womb as yet
Of Waters, Embryon immature involv'd,
278. Appeer'd not: over all the face of Earth
Main Ocean flow'd, not idle, but with warme
Prolific humour soft'ning all her Globe,
Fermented the great Mother to conceave,
282. Satiate with genial moisture, when God said
Be gather'd now ye Waters under Heav'n
Into one place, and let dry Land appeer.
285. Immediately the Mountains huge appeer
Emergent, and thir broad bare backs upheave
Into the Clouds, thir tops ascend the Skie:
So high as heav'd the tumid Hills, so low
Down sunk a hollow bottom broad and deep,
290. Capacious bed of Waters: thither they
Hasted with glad precipitance, uprowld
As drops on dust conglobing from the drie;
Part rise in crystal Wall, or ridge direct,

249. God was pleased with the light.
250. He called it Day, and separated it from the darkness, which he called Night.
252. That was the first day.
253. That evening, having seen all this, the angels broke into song, praising God. They sang again when the first morning came.

261.   God said, "*Let there be sky.*"

263. And God made the great calm blue sky that separated Earth from wild Chaos beyond.

274. He called it Heaven.
275. And the angels sang in the evening of the second day, and again in the morning.
276.   Earth was created, but there was no life on Earth yet.
278. The Earth was covered with water, which would prepare the soil to grow living things later.

282. God said, "*Let the water form into oceans and let dry land appear.*"

285. Immediately big mountains grew up towards the sky and deep valleys formed to hold all the water.

290. First the water was lifted up high by the mountains.

294.   For haste; such flight the great command impress'd
       On the swift flouds: as Armies at the call
       Of Trumpet (for of Armies thou hast heard)

297.   Troop to thir Standard, so the watrie throng,
       Wave rowling after Wave, where way they found,
       If steep, with torrent rapture, if through Plaine,
       Soft-ebbing; nor withstood them Rock or Hill,

301.   But they, or under ground, or circuit wide
       With Serpent errour wandring, found thir way,

303.   And on the washie Oose deep Channels wore;

304.   Easie, e're God had bid the ground be drie,
       All but within those banks, where Rivers now
       Stream, and perpetual draw thir humid traine.
       The dry Land, Earth, and the great receptacle
       Of congregated Waters he call'd Seas:

309.   And saw that it was good, and said, Let th' Earth
       Put forth the verdant Grass, Herb yielding Seed,
       And Fruit Tree yielding Fruit after her kind;
       Whose Seed is in her self upon the Earth.

313.   He scarce had said, when the bare Earth, till then
       Desert and bare, unsightly, unadorn'd,
       Brought forth the tender Grass, whose verdure clad
       Her Universal Face with pleasant green,
       Then Herbs of every leaf, that sudden flour'd
       Op'ning thir various colours, and made gay
       Her bosom smelling sweet: and these scarce blown,

320.   Forth flourish't thick the clustring Vine, forth crept
       The smelling Gourd, up stood the cornie Reed
       Embattell'd in her field: and the humble Shrub,
       And Bush with frizl'd hair implicit: last

324.   Rose as in Dance the stately Trees, and spred
       Thir branches hung with copious Fruit; or gemm'd

326.   Thir blossoms: with high woods the hills were crownd,
       With tufts the vallies and each fountain side,
       With borders long the Rivers. That Earth now

329.   Seemd like to Heav'n, a seat where Gods might dwell,
       Or wander with delight, and love to haunt

331.   Her sacred shades: though God had yet not rain'd
       Upon the Earth, and man to till the ground
       None was, but from the Earth a dewie Mist
       Went up and waterd all the ground, and each
       Plant of the field, which e're it was in the Earth
       God made, and every Herb, before it grew

337.   On the green stemm; God saw that it was good.
       So Eev'n and Morn recorded the Third Day.

339.   Again th' Almightie spake: Let there be Lights
       High in th' expanse of Heaven to divide
       The Day from Night; and let them be for Signes,
       For Seasons, and for Dayes, and circling Years,
       And let them be for Lights as I ordaine

294. Everything happened so fast. The water ran down the slopes like an army responding to God's command.

297. The water went wherever it could. Some went like rapids and cascaded down steep hills, some filled the plains slowly.

301. Some went underground, some wandered like a snake.

303. Some of it created deep channels that became rivers.
304. He called the dry land earth and the large bodies of water seas.

309. He was satisfied. He said, "*Let there be grass and herbs and fruit trees, and let them all keep spreading their seeds to keep growing more of them.*"

313. He hardly finished saying it, when the grass grew all over, and herbs and flowers blossomed and spread their perfume.

320. And thick vines grew, and bamboo shoots, and all kinds of bushes.

324. Lastly, trees rose up and spread their branches like they were dancing. They were full of fruit and blossoms.
326. The hills were full of woods, and there were plants in the valleys and along the lakes and rivers.
329. The Earth was now as beautiful as Heaven.

331. God hadn't invented rain yet, and there was nobody around to take care of the land, so he made a mist rise out of the ground and come down like rain to water everything.

337. God was very satisfied, and that was the end of the third day.

339.   Then God said, "*Let there be lights in the sky that will shine on the Earth and create days and nights and seasons.*"

Thir Office in the Firmament of Heav'n
345. To give Light on the Earth; and it was so.
346. And God made two great Lights, great for thir use
To Man, the greater to have rule by Day,
The less by Night alterne: and made the Starrs,
And set them in the Firmament of Heav'n
To illuminate the Earth, and rule the Day
In thir vicissitude, and rule the Night,
And Light from Darkness to divide. God saw,
353. Surveying his great Work, that it was good:
354. For of Celestial Bodies first the Sun
A mightie Spheare he fram'd, unlightsom first,
Though of Ethereal Mould: then form'd the Moon
Globose, and every magnitude of Starrs,
358. And sowd with Starrs the Heav'n thick as a field:
359. Of Light by farr the greater part he took,
Transplanted from her cloudie Shrine, and plac'd
In the Suns Orb, made porous to receive
And drink the liquid Light, firm to retaine
Her gather'd beams, great Palace now of Light.
364. Hither as to thir Fountain other Starrs
Repairing, in thir gold'n Urns draw Light,
366. And hence the Morning Planet guilds her horns;
By tincture or reflection they augment
Thir small peculiar, though from human sight
So farr remote, with diminution seen.
370. First in his East the glorious Lamp was seen,
Regent of Day, and all th' Horizon round
Invested with bright Rayes, jocond to run
His Longitude through Heav'n's high rode: the gray
Dawn, and the Pleiades before him danc'd
375. Shedding sweet influence: less bright the Moon,
But opposite in leveld West was set
His mirror, with full face borrowing her Light
From him, for other light she needed none
In that aspect, and still that distance keepes
380. Till night, then in the East her turn she shines,
Revolvd on Heav'ns great Axle, and her Reign
With thousand lesser Lights dividual holds,
With thousand thousand Starres, that then appeer'd
Spangling the Hemisphere: then first adornd
With thir bright Luminaries that Set and Rose,
386. Glad Eevning and glad Morn crownd the fourth day.
387.   And God said, let the Waters generate
Reptil with Spawn abundant, living Soule:
And let Fowle flie above the Earth, with wings
Displayd on the op'n Firmament of Heav'n.
391. And God created the great Whales, and each
Soul living, each that crept, which plenteously
The waters generated by thir kindes,

345. And that's what happened.
346. God made daylight and night-light and stars.

353. He decided it looked good.
354. He made the sun and the moon, but they weren't lit up yet.

358. He made a whole lot of stars in all sizes and spread them all over the sky.
359. He put most of the light into the sun.

364. The stars would come to refill themselves with light from the sun, like it was a fountain.
366. The planets would just reflect the sun's light, making them look bigger, but still pretty small as seen from Earth.

370. So the sun appeared in the east for the first time, and moved across the heavens.

375. The moon was less bright because it just reflected the sun's light.

380. It would shine at night with all the many stars.

386. And that was the fourth day.
387.   And then God said, "*Let reptiles come out of the water and let birds be flying in the air.*"

391. He created whales and reptiles and all kinds of birds.

And every Bird of wing after his kinde;
395. And saw that it was good, and bless'd them, saying,
Be fruitful, multiply, and in the Seas
And Lakes and running Streams the waters fill;
And let the Fowle be multiply'd on the Earth.
399. Forthwith the Sounds and Seas, each Creek and Bay
With Frie innumerable swarme, and Shoales
Of Fish that with thir Finns and shining Scales
Glide under the green Wave, in Sculles that oft
Bank the mid Sea: part single or with mate
Graze the Sea weed thir pasture, and through Groves
Of Coral stray, or sporting with quick glance
Show to the Sun thir wav'd coats dropt with Gold,
407. Or in thir Pearlie shells at ease, attend
Moist nutriment, or under Rocks thir food
In jointed Armour watch: on smooth the Seale,
And bended Dolphins play: part huge of bulk
Wallowing unweildie, enormous in thir Gate
412. Tempest the Ocean: there Leviathan
Hugest of living Creatures, on the Deep
Stretcht like a Promontorie sleeps or swimmes,
And seems a moving Land, and at his Gilles
Draws in, and at his Trunck spouts out a Sea.
417. Mean while the tepid Caves, and Fens and shoares
Thir Brood as numerous hatch, from the Egg that soon
Bursting with kindly rupture forth disclos'd
Thir callow young, but featherd soon and fledge
They summ'd thir Penns, and soaring th' air sublime
With clang despis'd the ground, under a cloud
423. In prospect; there the Eagle and the Stork
On Cliffs and Cedar tops thir Eyries build:
425. Part loosly wing the Region, part more wise
In common, rang'd in figure wedge thir way,
Intelligent of seasons, and set forth
Thir Aierie Caravan high over Sea's
Flying, and over Lands with mutual wing
Easing thir flight; so stears the prudent Crane
Her annual Voiage, born on Windes; the Aire,
Floats, as they pass, fann'd with unnumber'd plumes:
433. From Branch to Branch the smaller Birds with song
Solac'd the Woods, and spred thir painted wings
Till Ev'n, nor then the solemn Nightingal
Ceas'd warbling, but all night tun'd her soft layes:
437. Others on Silver Lakes and Rivers Bath'd
Thir downie Brest; the Swan with Arched neck
Between her white wings mantling proudly, Rowes
Her state with Oarie feet: yet oft they quit
The Dank, and rising on stiff Pennons, towre
442. The mid Aereal Skie: Others on ground
Walk'd firm; the crested Cock whose clarion sounds

395. He thought it was good, so he told them to multiply and fill all the seas and the sky.

399. Right away all the seas of the Earth became full of fish.

407. There were also clams and lobsters and seals and dolphins.

412. There were also whales. They were so big they looked like pieces of land floating.

417. Meanwhile, in caves and swamps and seashores birds were hatching from eggs.

423. Eagles and storks were building their nests on cliffs and in the tops of trees.
425. Some would just fly all over the place, but some, like cranes, would fly in flocks and migrate with the seasons.

433. The smaller birds were colorful and sang all day, except the nightingale which sang all night.

437. Some swam on water as well as flew, like the swans.

442. Some preferred to walk, like the peacock, which had big fancy-colored tail feathers.

The silent hours, and th' other whose gay Traine
Adorns him, colour'd with the Florid hue
446. Of Rainbows and Starrie Eyes. The Waters thus
With Fish replenisht, and the Aire, with Fowle,
Ev'ning and Morn solemniz'd the Fift day.
449.   The Sixt, and of Creation last arose
450. With Eevning Harps and Mattin, when God said,
Let th' Earth bring forth Soul living in her kinde,
Cattel and Creeping things, and Beast of the Earth,
453. Each in their kinde. The Earth obey'd, and strait
op'ning her fertile Woomb teem'd at a Birth
Innumerous living Creatures, perfet formes,
456. Limb'd and full grown: out of the ground up rose
As from his Laire the wilde Beast where he wonns
In Forrest wilde, in Thicket, Brake, or Den;
Among the Trees in Pairs they rose, they walk'd:
460. The Cattel in the Fields and Meddowes green:
Those rare and solitarie, these in flocks
Pasturing at once, and in broad Herds upsprung.
463. The grassie Clods now Calv'd, now half appeer'd
The Tawnie Lion, pawing to get free
His hinder parts, then springs as broke from Bonds,
466. And Rampant shakes his Brinded main; the Ounce,
The Libbard, and the Tyger, as the Moale
Rising, the crumbl'd Earth above them threw
469. In Hillocks; the swift Stag from under ground
470. Bore up his branching head: scarse from his mould
Behemoth biggest born of Earth upheav'd
472. His vastness: Fleec't the Flocks and bleating rose,
As Plants: ambiguous between Sea and Land
The River Horse and scalie Crocodile.
475. At once came forth whatever creeps the ground,
476. Insect or Worme; those wav'd thir limber fans
For wings, and smallest Lineaments exact
In all the Liveries dect of Summers pride
With spots of Gold and Purple, azure and green:
480. These as a line thir long dimension drew,
Streaking the ground with sinuous trace; not all
482. Minims of Nature; some of Serpent kinde
Wondrous in length and corpulence involv'd
Thir Snakie foulds, and added wings. First crept
485. The Parsimonious Emmet, provident
Of future, in small room large heart enclos'd,
Pattern of just equalitie perhaps
Hereafter, join'd in her popular Tribes
489. Of Commonaltie: swarming next appeer'd
The Female Bee that feeds her Husband Drone
Deliciously, and builds her waxen Cells
492. With Honey stor'd: the rest are numberless,
And thou thir Natures know'st, & gav'st them Names,

446. So, with the waters full of fish and the skies full of birds, the fifth holy day ended.

449.   After some more evening and morning music, the sixth and last day began.

450. God said, "*Let the Earth produce cattle and insects and beasts of all kinds.*"

453. The Earth obeyed and many living things were born. They were all already fully grown.

456. They came up out of the ground in pairs and walked out of the forests.

460. Some of them came out alone and some were in big herds. It was like the pastures were giving birth.

463. A lion's front half appeared. He struggled to dig his rear end out of the ground, then he jumped out and shook the dirt off his mane.

466. Panthers and leopards and tigers dug themselves out like moles, making piles of dirt.

469. Deer's antlers were coming up out of the ground.

470. The biggest animals coming up were the elephants.

472. And there were goats and sheep and hippopotamuses and croco-diles.

475. Then everything that crawls on the ground came out—all the insects and worms.

476. Some of the insects had colorful, delicate little wings.

480. Some of them followed each other along the ground in long wavy lines.

482. They weren't all so small. Some of them were very long like snakes, or big and fat.

485. Among the first were the ants, who were tiny but very efficient workers. Their cooperation would be a good example for future men.

489. Then there were the bees. The females stored honey and fed the males.

492. There were so many more, but you know all about them, Adam. You named them all.

494. Needless to thee repeated; nor unknown
       The Serpent suttl'st Beast of all the field,
       Of huge extent somtimes, with brazen Eyes
       And hairie Main terrific, though to thee
       Not noxious, but obedient at thy call.

499. Now Heav'n in all her Glorie shon, and rowld
       Her motions, as the great first-Movers hand
       First wheeld thir course; Earth in her rich attire
       Consummate lovly smil'd; Aire,, Water, Earth,
       By Fowl, Fish, Beast, was flown, was swum, was walkt

504. Frequent; and of the Sixt day yet remain'd;

505. There wanted yet the Master work, the end
       Of all yet don; a Creature who not prone
       And Brute as other Creatures, but endu'd
       With Sanctitie of Reason, might erect
       His Stature, and upright with Front serene

510. Govern the rest, self-knowing, and from thence
       Magnanimous to correspond with Heav'n,
       But grateful to acknowledge whence his good
       Descends, thither with heart and voice and eyes
       Directed in Devotion, to adore
       And worship God Supream, who made him chief

516. Of all his works: therefore the Omnipotent
       Eternal Father (For where is not hee
       Present) thus to his Son audibly spake.

519.   Let us make now Man in our image, Man
       In our similitude, and let them rule
       Over the Fish and Fowle of Sea and Aire,,
       Beast of the Field, and over all the Earth,
       And every creeping thing that creeps the ground.

524. This said, he formd thee, Adam, thee O Man
       Dust of the ground, and in thy nostrils breath'd
       The breath of Life; in his own Image hee
       Created thee, in the Image of God
       Express, and thou becam'st a living Soul.

529. Male he created thee, but thy consort

530. Female for Race; then bless'd Mankinde, and said,
       Be fruitful, multiplie, and fill the Earth,
       Subdue it, and throughout Dominion hold
       Over Fish of the Sea, and Fowle of the Aire,,
       And every living thing that moves on the Earth.
       Wherever thus created, for no place

536. Is yet distinct by name, thence, as thou know'st
       He brought thee into this delicious Grove,
       This Garden, planted with the Trees of God,
       Delectable both to behold and taste;

540. And freely all thir pleasant fruit for food
       Gave thee, all sorts are here that all th' Earth yields,
       Varietie without end; but of the Tree
       Which tasted works knowledge of Good and Evil,

494. You know the snakes too. They could be very long, and have something mysterious in their eyes, though to you they may seem friendly.

499. So now the sun and stars moved across the sky, and the Earth was beautiful and had all these wonderful creatures.

504. But the sixth day wasn't over yet.
505. Now it was time to create the creature who could think and would walk upright and rule over the animals.

510. He would be able to talk to God and worship him.

516. So God (who is always everywhere) spoke to his Son:

519.   *"Now let's make the human beings. Let's make them more like us than the other creatures, and more powerful than them."*

524. That's when he made you, Adam. He made you out of dust.

529. And he made Eve, so you would have company, and so the two of you could have children.
530. Then he blessed the whole future human race and said it should fill the whole world and rule the world and all its creatures.

536. Then, as you know, he brought you to this beautiful garden, with its endless variety of delicious fruit.

540. He told you you could eat whatever you wanted except for the fruit from the Tree of Knowledge of Good and Evil.

544. Thou mai'st not; in the day thou eat'st, thou di'st;
      Death is the penaltie impos'd, beware,
      And govern well thy appetite, least sin
      Surprise thee, and her black attendant Death.

548. Here finish'd hee, and all that he had made
      View'd, and behold all was entirely good;
      So Ev'n and Morn accomplish't the Sixt day:
      Yet not till the Creator from his work

552. Desisting, though unwearied, up returnd
      Up to the Heav'n of Heav'ns his high abode,
      Thence to behold this new created World
      Th' addition of his Empire, how it shew'd
      In prospect from his Throne, how good, how faire,

557. Answering his great Idea. Up he rode
      Followd with acclamation and the sound
      Symphonious of ten thousand Harpes that tun'd
      Angelic harmonies: the Earth, the Aire,
      Resounded, (thou remember'st for thou heardst)
      The Heav'ns and all the Constellations rung,
      The Planets in thir stations list'ning stood,
      While the bright Pomp ascended jubilant.

566. Open, ye everlasting Gates, they sung,
      Open, ye Heav'ns, your living dores; let in
      The great Creator from his work returnd
      Magnificent, his Six days work, a World;
      Open, and henceforth oft; for God will deigne
      To visit oft the dwellings of just Men
      Delighted, and with frequent intercourse
      Thither will send his winged Messengers
      On errands of supernal Grace. So sung

574. The glorious Train ascending: He through Heav'n,
      That open'd wide her blazing Portals, led
      To Gods Eternal house direct the way,

577. A broad and ample rode, whose dust is Gold
      And pavement Starrs, as Starrs to thee appeer,
      Seen in the Galaxie, that Milkie way
      Which nightly as a circling Zone thou seest

581. Pouderd with Starrs. And now on Earth the Seventh
      Eev'ning arose in Eden, for the Sun
      Was set, and twilight from the East came on,
      Forerunning Night; when at the holy mount
      Of Heav'ns high-seated top, th' Impereal Throne
      Of Godhead, fixt for ever firm and sure,
      The Filial Power arriv'd, and sate him down
      With his great Father (for he also went
      Invisible, yet staid, such priviledge
      Hath Omnipresence) and the work ordain'd,
      Author and end of all things, and from work

592. Now resting, bless'd and hallowd the Seav'nth day,
      As resting on that day from all his work,

544. He said the day you ate that fruit you would die.

548. And that completed his job of creating everything. He decided it was a good job. And that ended the sixth day.

552. He went back up to Heaven where he could look down and get a better view of his work

557. There was a lot of singing and celebrating by all the angels as he went.

566. They sang for Heaven's gates to open and let him back in, and sang about how they would be opening often now because God would be wanting to visit the Earth often, and send angels too.

574. He went in through the gates and went straight to his Father's house.

577. The road was covered with gold dust. The pavement had stars. It would look like the milky way to you.

581. Night was coming on Earth when in Heaven the Son went and sat next to his Father (who had been with him the whole time anyway, although he was invisible).

592. He took a rest from all his work, and made that day, the seventh day, a holy day.

594. But not in silence holy kept; the Harp
     Had work and rested not, the solemn Pipe,
     And Dulcimer, all Organs of sweet stop,
     All sounds on Fret by String or Golden Wire
     Temper'd soft Tunings, intermixt with Voice
     Choral or Unison; of incense Clouds
     Fuming from Golden Censers hid the Mount.

601. Creation and the Six dayes acts they sung,
     Great are thy works, Jehovah, infinite
     Thy power; what thought can measure thee or tongue

604. Relate thee; greater now in thy return
     Then from the Giant Angels; thee that day
     Thy Thunders magnifi'd; but to create
     Is greater then created to destroy.

608. Who can impair thee, mighty King, or bound
     Thy Empire? easily the proud attempt
     Of Spirits apostat and thir Counsels vaine
     Thou hast repeld, while impiously they thought
     Thee to diminish, and from thee withdraw

613. The number of thy worshippers. Who seekes
     To lessen thee, against his purpose serves
     To manifest the more thy might: his evil
     Thou usest, and from thence creat'st more good.

617. Witness this new-made World, another Heav'n
     From Heaven Gate not farr, founded in view
     On the cleer Hyaline, the Glassie Sea;

620. Of amplitude almost immense, with Starr's
     Numerous, and every Starr perhaps a World
     Of destind habitation; but thou know'st

623. Thir seasons: among these the seat of men,
     Earth with her nether Ocean circumfus'd,
     Thir pleasant dwelling place. Thrice happie men,
     And sons of men, whom God hath thus advanc't,
     Created in his Image, there to dwell
     And worship him, and in reward to rule
     Over his Works, on Earth, in Sea, or Air,
     And multiply a Race of Worshippers
     Holy and just: thrice happie if they know
     Thir happiness, and persevere upright.

633.   So sung they, and the Empyrean rung,
634. With Halleluiahs: Thus was Sabbath kept.
635. And thy request think now fulfill'd, that ask'd
     How first this World and face of things began,
     And what before thy memorie was don
     From the beginning, that posteritie

639. Informd by thee might know; if else thou seek'st
     Aught, not surpassing human measure, say.

594. But it wasn't a quiet day. There was lots of music and singing.

601. They sang about the creation and how great God was.

604. They sang that this was an even greater accomplishment than winning the war against the bad angels, because it was creating rather than destroying.

608. Nobody can put any boundaries on your empire, they sang. The bad angels tried and failed.

613. Anybody who tries to weaken you ends up making you stronger, they sang. You just use their evil to make more good.

617. For example, just look at this new world. It's like another Heaven, they sang.

620. They sang about how there were so many stars and maybe each one might one day have people or creatures living there.

623. And they sang about the Earth and the humans and how happy they would all be if they just remembered to obey God.

633.   They added lots of halleluiahs.
634. That's how they spent the first Sunday.
635. And I think that about sums up the answer to your question about how the world began.

639. If there's anything else you'd like to know, tell me—but lets try to make it something humans would be capable of understanding.

Book VIII

PARADISE LOST

1.   The Angel ended, and in Adams Eare
So Charming left his voice, that he a while
Thought him still speaking, still stood fixt to hear;
4.   Then as new wak't thus gratefully repli'd.
5.   What thanks sufficient, or what recompence
Equal have I to render thee, Divine
Hystorian, who thus largely hast allayd
The thirst I had of knowledge, and voutsaf't
This friendly condescention to relate
Things else by me unsearchable, now heard
11.   With wonder, but delight, and, as is due,
With glorie attributed to the high
13.   Creator; something yet of doubt remaines,
Which onely thy solution can resolve.
15.   When I behold this goodly Frame, this World
Of Heav'n and Earth consisting, and compute,
Thir magnitudes, this Earth a spot, a graine,
An Atom, with the Firmament compar'd
And all her numberd Starrs, that seem to rowle
Spaces incomprehensible (for such
Thir distance argues and thir swift return
Diurnal) meerly to officiate light
Round this opacous Earth, this punctual spot,
One day and night; in all thir vast survey
25.   Useless besides, reasoning I oft admire,
How Nature wise and frugal could commit
Such disproportions, with superfluous hand
So many nobler Bodies to create,
Greater so manifold to this one use,
For aught appeers, and on thir Orbs impose
Such restless revolution day by day
Repeated, while the sedentarie Earth,
That better might with farr less compass move,
Serv'd by more noble then her self, attaines
Her end without least motion, and receaves,
As Tribute such a sumless journey brought
Of incorporeal speed, her warmth and light;
Speed, to describe whose swiftness Number failes.
39.   So spake our Sire, and by his count'nance seemd
Entring on studious thoughts abstruse, which Eve
Perceaving where she sat retir'd in sight,
42.   With lowliness Majestic from her seat,

Chapter 8

IN PLAIN ENGLISH

1.   Adam was so charmed listening to the angel that he was in a kind of daze.

4. He snapped out of it and said:

5. *"How can I ever thank you for telling me this amazing story, and teaching me things I would never find out otherwise.*

11. *It shows how glorious God is too.*

13. *But there's one more thing I'm curious about—something only you could answer.*

15. *When I think about how tiny the Earth is compared to the sky and all the many stars, and the immense distances they must have to travel every day around this Earth just to give us some light here at night, and how that's their only purpose—*

25. *I have to wonder why Nature would waste all that energy, when it would be so much easier for the Earth to move the little bit it would need to move, instead of the stars, to get the same result."*

39.   When Eve saw that Adam was getting so heady with his thoughts, she decided to leave.

42. (If anybody was paying attention, they would have asked her to stay, she was so beautiful.)

      And Grace that won who saw to wish her stay,
44.   Rose, and went forth among her Fruits and Flours,
      To visit how they prosper'd, bud and bloom,
      Her Nurserie; they at her coming sprung
      And toucht by her fair tendance gladlier grew.
48.   Yet went she not, as not with such discourse
      Delighted, or not capable her eare
50.   Of what was high: such pleasure she reserv'd,
      Adam relating, she sole Auditress;
52.   Her Husband the Relater she preferr'd
      Before the Angel, and of him to ask
      Chose rather: hee, she knew would intermix
      Grateful digressions, and solve high dispute
      With conjugal Caresses, from his Lip
57.   Not Words alone pleas'd her. O when meet now
      Such pairs, in Love and mutual Honour joyn'd?
59.   With Goddess-like demeanour forth she went;
      Not unattended, for on her as Queen
      A pomp of winning Graces waited still,
62.   And from about her shot Darts of desire
      Into all Eyes to wish her still in sight.
64.   And Raphael now to Adam's doubt propos'd
      Benevolent and facil thus repli'd.
66.   To ask or search I blame thee not, for Heav'n
      Is as the Book of God before thee set,
      Wherein to read his wondrous Works, and learne
69.   His Seasons, Hours, or Dayes, or Months, or Yeares:
70.   This to attain, whether Heav'n move or Earth,
      Imports not, if thou reck'n right, the rest
72.   From Man or Angel the great Architect
      Did wisely to conceal, and not divulge
      His secrets to be scann'd by them who ought
75.   Rather admire; or if they list to try
      Conjecture, he his Fabric of the Heav'ns
      Hath left to thir disputes, perhaps to move
      His laughter at thir quaint Opinions wide
      Hereafter, when they come to model Heav'n
      And calculate the Starrs, how they will weild
      The mightie frame, how build, unbuild, contrive
      To save appeerances, how gird the Sphear
      With Centric and Eccentric scribl'd o're,
      Cycle and Epicycle, Orb in Orb:
85.   Alreadie by thy reasoning this I guess,
86.   Who art to lead thy ofspring, and supposest
      That bodies bright and greater should not serve
      The less not bright, nor Heav'n such journies run,
      Earth sitting still, when she alone receaves
90.   The benefit: consider first, that Great
91.   Or Bright inferrs not Excellence: the Earth

44. She went out into the garden, and all the fruits and flowers seemed to perk up as soon as she walked by or touched them.

48. It wasn't that she wasn't interested in the subject Adam brought up, or that she didn't feel smart enough to understand it.

50. It was that she knew what a pleasure it would be to hear all about it from Adam later, when they were alone.

52. She actually preferred Adam's story telling skills to the angel's, because she knew he would make love to her while he was talking. She'd get a lot more than words from his lips.

57. You don't find couples like that these days.

59. She walked away looking like a goddess.

62. Any eye that caught sight of her did not want her to pass out of sight.

64. Raphael answered Adam:

66.   *"I can't blame you for being curious. The sky is like a book God placed there for you to learn from.*

69. *It's like a calendar for you to measure seasons, years, months, days and hours.*

70. *You don't need to know whether it's the sky or the Earth that moves to figure that out.*

72. *God decided not to reveal those secrets.*

75. *Maybe he just wanted to entertain himself, laughing at all the crazy theories men would come up with about how the universe works.*

85. *You're an example of that already.*

86. *You assume that bigger, brighter heavenly bodies shouldn't be serving smaller ones, and shouldn't have to go such long journeys, when Earth just sits still and gets all the benefit.*

90. *But being bigger or brighter doesn't necessarily mean something's better.*

91. *The Earth may be smaller, and maybe it doesn't produce light, but it's full of life. The sun is barren. It's own light doesn't do itself any good.*

Though, in comparison of Heav'n, so small,
Nor glistering, may of solid good containe
More plenty then the Sun that barren shines,
Whose vertue on it self workes no effect,
96. But in the fruitful Earth; there first receavd
His beams, unactive else, thir vigour find.
98. Yet not to Earth are those bright Luminaries
Officious, but to thee Earths habitant.
100. And for the Heav'ns wide Circuit, let it speak
The Makers high magnificence, who built
So spacious, and his Line stretcht out so farr;
That Man may know he dwells not in his own;
An Edifice too large for him to fill,
Lodg'd in a small partition, and the rest
Ordain'd for uses to his Lord best known.
107. The swiftness of those Circles attribute,
Though numberless, to his Omnipotence,
That to corporeal substances could adde
110. Speed almost Spiritual; mee thou thinkst not slow,
Who since the Morning hour set out from Heav'n
Where God resides, and ere mid-day arriv'd
In Eden, distance inexpressible
114. By Numbers that have name. But this I urge,
Admitting Motion in the Heav'ns, to shew
Invalid that which thee to doubt it mov'd;
Not that I so affirm, though so it seem
To thee who hast thy dwelling here on Earth.
119. God to remove his wayes from human sense,
Plac'd Heav'n from Earth so farr, that earthly sight,
If it presume, might erre in things too high,
122. And no advantage gaine. What if the Sun
Be Centre to the World, and other Starrs
By his attractive vertue and their own
Incited, dance about him various rounds?
Thir wandring course now high, now low, then hid,
Progressive, retrograde, or standing still,
128. In six thou seest, and what if sev'nth to these
The Planet Earth, so stedfast though she seem,
Insensibly three different Motions move?
131. Which else to several Spheres thou must ascribe,
Mov'd contrarie with thwart obliquities,
133. Or save the Sun his labour, and that swift
Nocturnal and Diurnal rhomb suppos'd,
Invisible else above all Starrs, the Wheele
Of Day and Night; which needs not thy beleefe,
If Earth industrious of her self fetch Day
Travelling East, and with her part averse
From the Suns beam meet Night, her other part
140. Still luminous by his ray. What if that light

96. *It's only when the sun's rays reach the Earth that they have any value.*

98. *And that value isn't to the Earth, but to you who live here.*

100. *As for the great distance of outer space, so magnificent, it's a space humans could never fill. What plans God may have for it are for him alone to know.*

107. *And as for the amazing speed those heavenly bodies travel in their orbits, God is able to give them such speed that it's almost spiritual.*

110. *Take me for example. I left Heaven early this morning and arrived here before noon, and you couldn't begin to understand how far that is.*

114. *But I'm not saying the stars move the way it may seem they do to you, watching them from Earth.*

119. *God placed the sky so far from the Earth that you could easily be wrong in what you think you are seeing. And guessing how it all works doesn't do you any good.*

122. *What if the stars and planets, including the Earth, are pulled by gravity and actually orbit the Sun instead of the Earth?*

128. *You see six planets above, moving in all different ways. What if Earth is the seventh one, and although it seems still to you, it's actually moving with them?*

131. *You'll find the motions of the stars and planets a lot less complicated when you look at it that way.*

133. *How much simpler it would be if the Earth turned eastward toward the Sun and then away from it creating day and night, rather than some gigantic daylight force that covers the whole universe moving overhead across the sky.*

140. *Maybe the Earth shines on the moon the same way the moon shines on the Earth.*

      Sent from her through the wide transpicuous aire,
      To the terrestrial Moon be as a Starr
      Enlightning her by Day, as she by Night
144. This Earth? reciprocal, if Land be there,
      Fields and Inhabitants: Her spots thou seest
      As Clouds, and Clouds may rain, and Rain produce
      Fruits in her soft'nd Soile, for some to eate
148. Allotted there; and other Suns perhaps
      With thir attendant Moons thou wilt descrie
      Communicating Male and Femal Light,
      Which two great Sexes animate the World,
      Stor'd in each Orb perhaps with some that live.
153. For such vast room in Nature unpossest
      By living Soule, desert and desolate,
      Onely to shine, yet scarce to contribute
      Each Orb a glimps of Light, conveyd so farr
      Down to this habitable, which returnes
      Light back to them, is obvious to dispute.
159. But whether thus these things, or whether not,
      Whether the Sun predominant in Heav'n
      Rise on the Earth, or Earth rise on the Sun,
      Hee from the East his flaming rode begin,
      Or Shee from West her silent course advance
      With inoffensive pace that spinning sleeps
      On her soft Axle, while she paces Eev'n,
      And beares thee soft with the smooth Air along,
      Sollicit not thy thoughts with matters hid,
168. Leave them to God above, him serve and feare;
169. Of other Creatures, as him pleases best,
170. Wherever plac't, let him dispose: joy thou
      In what he gives to thee, this Paradise
172. And thy faire Eve; Heav'n is for thee too high
      To know what passes there; be lowlie wise:
      Think onely what concernes thee and thy being;
      Dream not of other Worlds, what Creatures there
      Live, in what state, condition or degree,
177. Contented that thus farr hath been reveal'd
      Not of Earth onely but of highest Heav'n.
179.   To whom thus Adam cleerd of doubt, repli'd.
      How fully hast thou satisfi'd me, pure
      Intelligence of Heav'n, Angel serene,
      And freed from intricacies, taught to live
      The easiest way, nor with perplexing thoughts
      To interrupt the sweet of Life, from which
      God hath bid dwell farr off all anxious cares,
      And not molest us, unless we our selves
      Seek them with wandring thoughts, and notions vain.
188. But apt the Mind or Fancy is to roave
      Uncheckt, and of her roaving is no end;

144. *Who knows? Maybe the moon has land and people, and the dark patches you see on it are clouds that produce the rain that waters their crops.*

148. *There are many suns and moons above. Maybe there's life there too.*

153. *You might wonder why there'd be such a big universe with nobody living there, only stars that are so far away they hardly give any light down here.*

159. *But don't waste your time wondering whether all this is true or not—whether the sun rises on the Earth, or the Earth rises on the sun, or if the Earth is perhaps turning on its axle, so gently that you can't even feel it.*

168. *Leave these matters to God. Just serve him and obey him.*
169. *If he makes other creatures and where and what he does with them is not your business.*
170. *Just be happy with what he gave you—this Paradise and your beautiful wife.*
172. *You can't understand God's business. Don't waste your time wondering about other creatures in other worlds. Pay attention to the matters that concern you.*
177. *Be satisfied with what I have already taught you about things beyond this Earth."*
179.   *"I think I get what you mean, angel,"* said Adam, *"—not to let confusing thoughts get in the way of enjoying the simple life God planned for me.*

188. *You can go crazy thinking about all these crazy things. We should save our minds for what we need to know.*

Till warn'd, or by experience taught, she learne,
That not to know at large of things remote
From use, obscure and suttle, but to know
That which before us lies in daily life,
Is the prime Wisdom, what is more, is fume,
Or emptiness, or fond impertinence,
And renders us in things that most concerne
Unpractis'd, unprepar'd, and still to seek.

198.   Therefore from this high pitch let us descend
A lower flight, and speak of things at hand
Useful, whence haply mention may arise
Of somthing not unseasonable to ask
By sufferance, and thy wonted favour deign'd.

203.   Thee I have heard relating what was don
Ere my remembrance: now hear mee relate
My Storie, which perhaps thou hast not heard;

206.   And Day is yet not spent; till then thou seest
How suttly to detaine thee I devise,

208.   Inviting thee to hear while I relate,
Fond, were it not in hope of thy reply:
For while I sit with thee, I seem in Heav'n,

211.   And sweeter thy discourse is to my eare
Then Fruits of Palm-tree pleasantest to thirst
And hunger both, from labour, at the houre

214.   Of sweet repast; they satiate, and soon fill,
Though pleasant, but thy words with Grace Divine
Imbu'd, bring to thir sweetness no satietie.

217.   To whom thus Raphael answer'd heav'nly meek.
Nor are thy lips ungraceful, Sire of men,
Nor tongue ineloquent; for God on thee
Abundantly his gifts hath also pour'd
Inward and outward both, his image faire:
Speaking or mute all comliness and grace
Attends thee, and each word, each motion formes

224.   Nor less think wee in Heav'n of thee on Earth
Then of our fellow servant, and inquire
Gladly into the wayes of God with Man:
For God we see hath honour'd thee, and set

228.   On Man his Equal Love: say therefore on;
For I that Day was absent, as befell,
Bound on a voyage uncouth and obscure,
Farr on excursion toward the Gates of Hell;
Squar'd in full Legion (such command we had)
To see that none thence issu'd forth a spie,
Or enemie, while God was in his work,

235.   Least hee incenst at such eruption bold,
Destruction with Creation might have mixt.
Not that they durst without his leave attempt,
But us he sends upon his high behests

198.   *Let's talk about useful things, and maybe later I could ask you and you could tell me some interesting things it would be okay for me to know.*

203.   *You told me about what happened before I was born; now let me tell you my story, which you may not have heard.*

206.   *It's still early.*

208.   *I'm talking hoping to keep you here talking with me. Sitting here with you is like being in Heaven.*

211.   *Listening to you is like eating the sweetest fruit from the palm trees.*

214.   *They satisfy my hunger, but listening to you I only keep wanting to hear more."*

217.   Raphael politely answered, "*When God made you in his image, that included having a very pleasing voice, Adam.*

224.   *We angels in Heaven are just as interested in learning about you as you are us. We know God honors you with the same love he has for us.*

228.   *So please go ahead with your story. I was not around when you were created. I was a long way off, sent by God with my legion to check the gates of Hell and make sure the devils didn't send out a spy or try to interfere with God's work.*

235.   *God would have had to interrupt his creating to do some angry destroying instead.*

For state, as Sovran King, and to enure
240. Our prompt obedience. Fast we found, fast shut
The dismal Gates, and barricado'd strong;
But long ere our approaching heard within
243. Noise, other then the sound of Dance or Song,
Torment, and loud lament, and furious rage.
245. Glad we return'd up to the coasts of Light
Ere Sabbath Eev'ning: so we had in charge.
247. But thy relation now; for I attend,
Pleas'd with thy words no less then thou with mine.
249.   So spake the Godlike Power, and thus our Sire.
250. For Man to tell how human Life began
Is hard; for who himself beginning knew?
Desire with thee still longer to converse
253. Induc'd me. As new wak't from soundest sleep
Soft on the flourie herb I found me laid
In Balmie Sweat, which with his Beames the Sun
Soon dri'd, and on the reaking moisture fed.
257. Strait toward Heav'n my wondring Eyes I turnd,
258. And gaz'd a while the ample Skie, till rais'd
By quick instinctive motion up I sprung,
As thitherward endevoring, and upright
261. Stood on my feet; about me round I saw
Hill, Dale, and shadie Woods, and sunnie Plaines,
And liquid Lapse of murmuring Streams; by these,
264. Creatures that livd, and movd, and walk'd, or flew,
265. Birds on the branches warbling; all things smil'd,
With fragrance and with joy my heart oreflow'd.
267. My self I then perus'd, and Limb by Limb
Survey'd, and sometimes went, and sometimes ran
With supple joints, as lively vigour led:
270. But who I was, or where, or from what cause,
271. Knew not; to speak I tri'd, and forthwith spake,
My Tongue obey'd and readily could name
273. What e're I saw. Thou Sun, said I, faire Light,
And thou enlight'nd Earth, so fresh and gay,
Ye Hills and Dales, ye Rivers, Woods, and Plaines,
And ye that live and move, fair Creatures, tell,
Tell, if ye saw, how came I thus, how here?
278. Not of my self; by some great Maker then,
In goodness and in power præeminent;
Tell me, how may I know him, how adore,
From whom I have that thus I move and live,
And feel that I am happier then I know.
283. While thus I call'd, and stray'd I knew not whither,
From where I first drew Aire, and first beheld
This happie Light, when answer none return'd,
286. On a green shadie Bank profuse of Flours
Pensive I sate me down; there gentle sleep

240. *But we found Hell's gates securely locked.*

243. *There were terrible sounds coming from in there—sounds of suffering and sounds of anger.*

245. *We were glad to get back to Heaven for the evening of the Sabbath.*

247. *But now tell me your story. I enjoy listening to you as much as you do me."*

249.   So Adam began:

250. *"It's hard to say how human life began. We don't really see our own beginning. But I'll try, because I want our conversation to continue.*

253. . . . I first woke up like from a deep sleep. I was lying on a soft bed of flowery plants. I was covered with sweat. The sun dried it.

257. I lay there and gazed at the big blue sky for awhile.

258. Instinctively I jumped up.

261. I stood on my feet and saw the hills and woods and plains and streams all around.

264. There were creatures that walked and flew.

265. Birds sat on branches and sang, and everything smelled so good. My heart was overflowing with joy.

267. I examined my body and my arms and legs. I walked and ran a little. I felt energetic.

270. But I didn't know who or what I was.

271. I tried to talk and found that I instinctively knew the names of everything.

273. *"You, sun,"* I said, *"and you hills and dales and rivers, woods and plains, and all you creatures moving around, tell me if you saw how I got here.*

278. *Was it by some great Maker? Where can I find this good and powerful being who made me so happy?"*

283. I wandered around but I got no answer.

284. I sat down on a green shady bank full of flowers and got very sleepy.

First found me, and with soft oppression seis'd
My droused sense, untroubl'd, though I thought
290. I then was passing to my former state
Insensible, and forthwith to dissolve:
292. When suddenly stood at my Head a dream,
Whose inward apparition gently mov'd
My Fancy to believe I yet had being,
And livd: One came, methought, of shape Divine,
296. And said, thy Mansion wants thee, Adam, rise,
First Man, of Men innumerable ordain'd
First Father, call'd by thee I come thy Guide
To the Garden of bliss, thy seat prepar'd.
300. So saying, by the hand he took me rais'd,
And over Fields and Waters, as in Aire
Smooth sliding without step, last led me up
303. A woodie Mountain; whose high top was plaine,
A Circuit wide, enclos'd, with goodliest Trees
305. Planted, with Walks, and Bowers, that what I saw
Of Earth before scarce pleasant seemd. Each Tree
307. Load'n with fairest Fruit, that hung to the Eye
Tempting, stirr'd in me sudden appetite
309. To pluck and eate; whereat I wak'd, and found
Before mine Eyes all real, as the dream
311. Had lively shadowd: Here had new begun
My wandring, had not hee who was my Guide
Up hither, from among the Trees appeer'd,
314. Presence Divine. Rejoycing, but with aw,
In adoration at his feet I fell
316. Submiss: he rear'd me, and Whom thou soughtst I am,
Said mildely, Author of all this thou seest
Above, or round about thee or beneath.
319. This Paradise I give thee, count it thine
To Till and keep, and of the Fruit to eate:
321. Of every Tree that in the Garden growes
Eate freely with glad heart; fear here no dearth:
But of the Tree whose operation brings
Knowledg of good and ill, which I have set
The Pledge of thy Obedience and thy Faith,
Amid the Garden by the Tree of Life,
327. Remember what I warne thee, shun to taste,
And shun the bitter consequence: for know,
The day thou eat'st thereof, my sole command
Transgrest, inevitably thou shalt dye;
331. From that day mortal, and this happie State
Shalt loose, expell'd from hence into a World
Of woe and sorrow. Sternly he pronounc'd
334. The rigid interdiction, which resounds
Yet dreadful in mine eare, though in my choice
Not to incur; but soon his cleer aspect

290. I thought I was going back into the unconscious state I came from and would just disappear.

292. Then a vision came to me, as in a dream—a divine shape.

296. It said, "*Come with me, Adam. You are the first man, the first father of countless more men. I have prepared a place for you in the garden of Paradise.*"

300. I imagined he took me by the hand and we glided across the fields and lakes and landed on a wooded mountain.

303. The top was a wide plain surrounded with beautiful trees. It was designed with walks and shelters.

305. What I had seen on Earth so far was nothing compared to this.

307. Every tree was full of delicious looking fruit.

309. Now I was fully awake and I could see what seemed like a dream was all real.

311. I would have begun exploring this new place, but suddenly the Divine Presence appeared from between the trees.

314. I was in awe. I felt joyful. I knelt down before him.

316. He lifted me up and said, "*I am the one you were asking about. I created everything here.*

319. *I'm giving you this Paradise. You can consider everything in it yours. Take care of it and enjoy it.*

321. *You may eat all the fruit here except for what grows on the Tree which brings Knowledge of Good and Evil. That one's here to test your obedience and faith. It's right next to the Tree of Life.*

327. *Remember this warning. The day you eat from that tree you will have broken my only commandment and you will die.*

331. *You will become mortal and you will be expelled from here into a world full of pain and sadness.*"

334. That strict commandment that he gave still echoes in my ear. But then he continued more gently:

Return'd and gracious purpose thus renew'd.
338. Not onely these fair bounds, but all the Earth
To thee and to thy Race I give; as Lords
Possess it, and all things that therein live,
Or live in Sea, or Aire, Beast, Fish, and Fowle.
342. In signe whereof each Bird and Beast behold
After thir kindes; I bring them to receave
From thee thir Names, and pay thee fealtie
With low subjection; understand the same
346. Of Fish within thir watry residence,
Not hither summon'd, since they cannot change
Thir Element to draw the thinner Aire.
349. As thus he spake, each Bird and Beast behold
Approaching two and two, These cowring low
With blandishment, each Bird stoop'd on his wing.
352. I nam'd them, as they pass'd, and understood
Thir Nature, with such knowledg God endu'd
My sudden apprehension: but in these
355. I found not what me thought I wanted still;
And to the Heav'nly vision thus presum'd.
357.   O by what Name, for thou above all these,
Above mankinde, or aught then mankinde higher,
359. Surpassest farr my naming, how may I
Adore thee, Author of this Universe,
And all this good to man, for whose well being
So amply, and with hands so liberal
363. Thou hast provided all things: but with mee
I see not who partakes. In solitude
What happiness, who can enjoy alone,
Or all enjoying, what contentment find?
367. Thus I presumptuous; and the vision bright,
As with a smile more bright'nd, thus repli'd.
369.   What call'st thou solitude, is not the Earth
With various living creatures, and the Aire
Replenisht, and all these at thy command
To come and play before thee; know'st thou not
Thir language and thir wayes? They also know,
And reason not contemptibly; with these
Find pastime, and beare rule; thy Realm is large.
So spake the Universal Lord, and seem'd
So ordering. I with leave of speech implor'd,
And humble deprecation thus repli'd.
379.   Let not my words offend thee, Heav'nly Power,
My Maker, be propitious while I speak.
Hast thou not made me here thy substitute,
And these inferiour farr beneath me set?
Among unequals what societie
Can sort, what harmonie or true delight?
Which must be mutual, in proportion due

338. *"I'm not only giving you this garden, but the whole world. You and your entire race will be lords over the whole Earth and every living thing on it.*

342. *Now I'm going to send each bird and animal to you two by two for you to name. They will all show you that they understand that you are their master.*

346. *Of course the fish won't be able to make it, but the same goes for them anyway."*

349. As he spoke they all started to come two by two and bowed before me. The birds would lean forward on their wings.

352. I named them as they passed. I instinctively understood their ways.

355. But something was missing—I can't explain.

357. Then I said to him, *"But what should I call you? You are way too high above all these creatures and above mankind for me to name.*

359. *How should I pray to you, so I can thank you for all these wonderful things you have given?*

363. *It's all great, but how can I enjoy all this, all alone here?"*

367. I was being a little bold, but he just smiled.

369. *"How can you say you're alone? Didn't I give you all these creatures around you to rule over? They will entertain you all day if you want."*

379. *"Sir, please forgive me and be patient with me. But you have made these creatures so inferior to me that we can't really socialize that much. It would be fun if we could exchange and understand intellectual thoughts and ideas.*

Giv'n and receiv'd; but in disparitie
The one intense, the other still remiss
388. Cannot well suite with either, but soon prove
Tedious alike: Of fellowship I speak
Such as I seek, fit to participate
All rational delight, wherein the brute
Cannot be human consort; they rejoyce
393. Each with thir kinde, Lion with Lioness;
So fitly them in pairs thou hast combin'd;
Much less can Bird with Beast, or Fish with Fowle
So well converse, nor with the Ox the Ape;
Wors then can Man with Beast, and least of all.
398.   Whereto th' Almighty answer'd, not displeas'd.
A nice and suttle happiness I see
Thou to thyself proposest, in the choice
Of thy Associates, Adam, and wilt taste
No pleasure, though in pleasure, solitarie.
403. What think'st thou then of mee, and this my State,
Seem I to thee sufficiently possest
Of happiness, or not? who am alone
From all Eternitie, for none I know
Second to mee or like, equal much less.
408. How have I then with whom to hold converse
Save with the Creatures which I made, and those
To me inferiour, infinite descents
Beneath what other Creatures are to thee?
412.   He ceas'd, I lowly answer'd. To attaine
The highth and depth of thy Eternal wayes
All human thoughts come short, Supream of things;
Thou in thy self art perfet, and in thee
Is no deficience found; not so is Man,
417. But in degree, the cause of his desire
By conversation with his like to help,
419. Or solace his defects. No need that thou
Shouldst propagat, already infinite;
And through all numbers absolute, though One;
422. But Man by number is to manifest
His single imperfection, and beget
Like of his like, his Image multipli'd,
In unitie defective, which requires
Collateral love, and deerest amitie.
427. Thou in thy secresie although alone,
Best with thy self accompanied, seek'st not
Social communication, yet so pleas'd,
Canst raise thy Creature to what highth thou wilt
Of Union or Communion, deifi'd;
432. I by conversing cannot these erect
From prone, nor in thir wayes complacence find.
Thus I embold'nd spake, and freedom us'd

388.   *Otherwise it could get boring.*

393.   *You meant for these creatures to live in pairs, like lions with lionesses, but birds can't talk to mammals, or fish to birds, or an ox with a monkey, much less a man with an animal."*

398.   Patiently, God answered, *"Well, it seems you have decided that you cannot be happy here without having company like yourself.*

403.   *But what about me, Adam? Don't I seem happy to you? And I'm alone in all eternity. There's nobody second to me, much less equal to me.*

408.   *Who do I have to talk to except the creatures I make that are infinitely more inferior to me then these creatures are to you?"*

412.   *"You're perfect,"* I said, *"but man isn't.*

417.   *So he needs to get help and support by talking to others like himself.*

419.   *You are all things wrapped up in one.*

422.   *Man needs to come together with others in friendship so we can see our individual faults and overcome them.*

427.   *You are complete even when you are alone. And if you want to, you can make any creature you want able to communicate with you.*

432.   *But I can't make these creatures stand up and talk to me."*

435.   Permissive, and acceptance found, which gain'd
         This answer from the gratious voice Divine.
437.   Thus farr to try thee, Adam, I was pleas'd,
438.   And finde thee knowing not of Beasts alone,
         Which thou hast rightly nam'd, but of thy self,
         Expressing well the spirit within thee free,
441.   My Image, not imparted to the Brute,
         Whose fellowship therefore unmeet for thee
         Good reason was thou freely shouldst dislike,
444.   And be so minded still; I, ere thou spak'st,
         Knew it not good for Man to be alone,
         And no such companie as then thou saw'st
         Intended thee, for trial onely brought,
         To see how thou could'st judge of fit and meet:
449.   What next I bring shall please thee, be assur'd,
         Thy likeness, thy fit help, thy other self,
         Thy wish, exactly to thy hearts desire.
452.   Hee ended, or I heard no more, for now
         My earthly by his Heav'nly overpowerd,
         Which it had long stood under, streind to the highth
         In that celestial Colloquie sublime,
         As with an object that excels the sense,
         Dazl'd and spent, sunk down, and sought repair
         Of sleep, which instantly fell on me, call'd
         By Nature as in aide, and clos'd mine eyes.
460.   Mine eyes he clos'd, but op'n left the Cell
         Of Fancie my internal sight, by which
         Abstract as in a transe methought I saw,
         Though sleeping, where I lay, and saw the shape
         Still glorious before whom awake I stood;
465.   Who stooping op'nd my left side, and took
         From thence a Rib, with cordial spirits warme,
467.   And Life-blood streaming fresh; wide was the wound,
         But suddenly with flesh fill'd up and heal'd:
469.   The Rib he formd and fashond with his hands;
         Under his forming hands a Creature grew,
471.   Manlike, but different sex, so lovly faire,
472.   That what seemd fair in all the World, seemd now
473.   Mean, or in her summ'd up, in her containd
474.   And in her looks, which from that time infus'd
         Sweetness into my heart, unfelt before,
         And into all things from her Aire inspir'd
         The spirit of love and amorous delight.
478.   Shee disappeerd, and left me dark, I wak'd
479.   To find her, or for ever to deplore
         Her loss, and other pleasures all abjure:
481.   When out of hope, behold her, not farr off,
         Such as I saw her in my dream, adornd
         With what all Earth or Heaven could bestow

435. I spoke freely, and that was okay with God.

437.   He said, "*So far I'm impressed with you, Adam.*
438. *You not only understand the nature of animals, but you express your own free spirit very well.*

441. *I didn't create the animals in my image, so they are not suitable for intimate companionship with you.*

444. *I never meant for you to be alone. I was just testing you.*

449. *Now I'm going to give you your wish, exactly as your heart desires."*

452.   I don't know if he said anything more because I was so emotionally exhausted from talking to God that I just fell down and went to sleep.

460. My eyes were closed but God had put me in a kind of dream state where I could still see what was going on.

465. He stooped down and opened up my left side and took out a rib.
467. It was a wide cut with lots of bleeding, but he made it all heal up fast.
469. With his hands he formed the rib into a creature.
471. It was like a man but a different sex.
472. Everything beautiful I had ever seen in the world was nothing compared to her.
473. She was everything beautiful combined in one.
474. I felt the sweetness of romantic love for the first time.

478. Suddenly everything went black and she was gone.
479. I woke up, feeling that without her I could never be happy again.

481. But there she was! Every bit as beautiful as in my dream.

484. To make her amiable: On she came,
     Led by her Heav'nly Maker, though unseen,
486. And guided by his voice, nor uninformd
     Of nuptial Sanctitie and marriage Rites:
488. Grace was in all her steps, Heav'n in her Eye,
     In every gesture dignitie and love.
490. I overjoyd could not forbear aloud.
491.   This turn hath made amends; thou hast fulfill'd
     Thy words, Creator bounteous and benigne,
493. Giver of all things faire, but fairest this
     Of all thy gifts, nor enviest. I now see
495. Bone of my Bone, Flesh of my Flesh, my Self
     Before me; Woman is her Name, of Man
     Extracted; for this cause he shall forgoe
     Father and Mother, and to his Wife adhere;
     And they shall be one Flesh, one Heart, one Soule.
500.   She heard me thus, and though divinely brought,
     Yet Innocence and Virgin Modestie,
     Her vertue and the conscience of her worth,
     That would be woo'd, and not unsought be won,
     Not obvious, not obtrusive, but retir'd,
505. The more desirable, or to say all,
     Nature her self, though pure of sinful thought,
507. Wrought in her so, that seeing me, she turn'd;
     I follow'd her, she what was Honour knew,
     And with obsequious Majestie approv'd
510. My pleaded reason. To the Nuptial Bowre
     I led her blushing like the Morn: all Heav'n,
512. And happie Constellations on that houre
     Shed thir selectest influence; the Earth
     Gave sign of gratulation, and each Hill;
     Joyous the Birds; fresh Gales and gentle Aires
     Whisper'd it to the Woods, and from thir wings
     Flung Rose, flung Odours from the spicie Shrub,
     Disporting, till the amorous Bird of Night
     Sung Spousal, and bid haste the Eevning Starr
     On his Hill top, to light the bridal Lamp.
     Thus I have told thee all my State, and brought
     My Storie to the sum of earthly bliss
523. Which I enjoy, and must confess to find
     In all things else delight indeed, but such
     As us'd or not, works in the mind no change,
     Nor vehement desire, these delicacies
     I mean of Taste, Sight, Smell, Herbs, Fruits and Flours,
     Walks, and the melodie of Birds; but here
529. Farr otherwise, transported I behold,
     Transported touch; here passion first I felt,
     Commotion strange, in all enjoyments else
     Superiour and unmov'd, here onely weake

484. She came towards me, invisibly led by God, and guided by his voice.

486. She was completely ready to become my wife.

488. She moved with such grace. Heaven was in her eyes.

490. I was so overjoyed I couldn't keep quiet:
491.   *"You kept your word, God, and how!*

493. *You give me everything beautiful, but this is the best!*

495. *This is what a woman is. She was made out of me. Men will leave their parents and unite with women and the two of them will become like one person."*

500.   She heard me and even though God led her to me, she had enough modesty that she turned and was about to run away. This woman wasn't about to be had so easily.

505. It just made her all the more desirable to me.

507. I quickly went after her and spoke to her gently and I won her over.

510. I led her to my shelter. She was blushing.

512. What a night that was! Birds were singing and the breeze blew a sweet smell. The nightingale sang as the stars began to appear, and . . . *well, that's my story.*

523. *But I must tell you, everything I enjoy here—of taste, sight, smell, the fruits, the flowers, birds—none of it creates in me any intense desire, but with her . . .*

529. *She makes me weak with desire and passion.*

Against the charm of Beauties powerful glance.

Or Nature faild in mee, and left some part

535. Not proof enough such Object to sustain,

Or from my side subducting, took perhaps

537. More then enough; at least on her bestow'd

Too much of Ornament, in outward shew

Elaborate, of inward less exact.

For well I understand in the prime end

Of Nature her th' inferiour, in the mind

And inward Faculties, which most excell,

In outward also her resembling less

544. His Image who made both, and less expressing

The character of that Dominion giv'n

546. O're other Creatures; yet when I approach

Her loveliness, so absolute she seems

And in her self compleat, so well to know

Her own, that what she wills to do or say,

Seems wisest, vertuousest, discreetest, best;

All higher knowledge in her presence falls

Degraded, Wisdom in discourse with her

Looses discount'nanc't, and like folly shewes;

Authority and Reason on her waite,

As one intended first, not after made

Occasionally; and to consummate all,

Greatness of mind and nobleness thir seat

Build in her loveliest, and create an awe

About her, as a guard Angelic plac't.

560. To whom the Angel with contracted brow.

561.   Accuse not Nature, she hath don her part;

Do thou but thine, and be not diffident

563. Of Wisdom, she deserts thee not, if thou

Dismiss not her, when most thou needst her nigh,

565. By attributing overmuch to things

Less excellent, as thou thy self perceav'st.

For what admir'st thou, what transports thee so,

568. An outside? fair no doubt, and worthy well

Thy cherishing, thy honouring, and thy love,

Not thy subjection: weigh with her thy self;

571. Then value: Oft times nothing profits more

Then self esteem, grounded on just and right

Well manag'd; of that skill the more thou know'st,

The more she will acknowledge thee her Head,

And to realities yield all her shows:

Made so adorn for thy delight the more,

577. So awful, that with honour thou maist love

Thy mate, who sees when thou art seen least wise.

But if the sense of touch whereby mankind

Is propagated seem such dear delight

Beyond all other, think the same voutsaft

535. *It's like nature left something missing in me, or maybe took too much out of my side.*

537. *I know she's supposed to be inferior to me in intellect, but maybe nature tried to make up for that by giving her more outward beauty—almost more than I can stand.*

544. *You can tell by looking at her that she doesn't have that look of domination over other creatures like I have.*

546. *But when I'm with her, her beauty is so awesome and she seems so sure of herself that I can't deny her anything. She seems always right. My arguments fall flat. It's like she was created first instead of me."*

560. Raphael gently scolded him:

561. *"Don't blame nature. She did her part, now you do yours. Don't be such a sissy.*

563. *You've got a brain. Use it. Don't shut it down when you need it most.*

565. *Are you going to toss out all the excellence God placed in you? For what—the way she looks?*

568. *She's beautiful, no doubt, and well worth cherishing, but not for you to submit yourself to her domination.*

571. *Compare the two of you. You know, sometimes showing self-esteem, when it's justified, is the best way to gain someone's respect. She can see when you're acting stupid.*

577. *You should enjoy her beauty and love her honorably. And if sex seems like such great pleasure over everything else, just remember cows do it too.*

To Cattel and each Beast; which would not be
583. To them made common and divulg'd, if aught
Therein enjoy'd were worthy to subdue
The Soule of Man, or passion in him move.
586. What higher in her societie thou findst
Attractive, human, rational, love still;
In loving thou dost well, in passion not,
589. Wherein true Love consists not; love refines
The thoughts, and heart enlarges, hath his seat
In Reason, and is judicious, is the scale
By which to heav'nly Love thou maist ascend,
593. Not sunk in carnal pleasure, for which cause
Among the Beasts no Mate for thee was found.
595.   To whom thus half abash't Adam repli'd.
596. Neither her out-side formd so fair, nor aught
In procreation common to all kindes
(Though higher of the genial Bed by far,
And with mysterious reverence I deem)
So much delights me as those graceful acts,
Those thousand decencies that daily flow
From all her words and actions mixt with Love
And sweet compliance, which declare unfeign'd
Union of Mind, or in us both one Soule;
Harmonie to behold in wedded pair
606. More grateful then harmonious sound to the eare.
Yet these subject not; I to thee disclose
What inward thence I feel, not therefore foild,
Who meet with various objects, from the sense
Variously representing; yet still free
Approve the best, and follow what I approve.
612. To Love thou blam'st me not, for love thou saist
Leads up to Heav'n, is both the way and guide;
614. Bear with me then, if lawful what I ask;
Love not the heav'nly Spirits, and how thir Love
Express they, by looks onely, or do they mix
Irradiance, virtual or immediate touch?
618.   To whom the Angel with a smile that glow'd
Celestial rosie red, Loves proper hue,
620. Answer'd. Let it suffice thee that thou know'st
Us happie, and without Love no happiness.
622. Whatever pure thou in the body enjoy'st
(And pure thou wert created) we enjoy
In eminence, and obstacle find none
Of membrane, joynt, or limb, exclusive barrs:
626. Easier then Air with Air, if Spirits embrace,
Total they mix, Union of Pure with Pure
Desiring; nor restrain'd conveyance need
As Flesh to mix with Flesh, or Soul with Soul.
630. But I can now no more; the parting Sun

583. *God wouldn't have given it to them if it was something worthy to overcome man's very soul or overwhelm him with passion.*

586. *Love the things you find in her worth loving. Passion isn't love. It will only bring you trouble.*

589. *True love makes you wiser and your heart bigger, and leads to heavenly love.*

593. *Sex without love keeps you low. That's why no animal could ever be a mate for you."*

595.   Adam felt a little embarrassed.

596. *"But it isn't just her beauty or the sex (although I think our sex is more blessed than the animals')—but it's more than that. It's all the little things she does and says, so sweet and loving, that it makes it seem like we are in such nice wedded harmony, almost like one soul.*

606. *I'm just telling you all the things I feel inside. But that doesn't mean I'm going to let them overcome me. I'm still free to judge and choose the best thing to do.*

612. *You can't blame me for loving her, though. You said love is what leads us to Heaven.*

614. *But tell me something, do angels fall in love? And, if you don't mind my asking, do you angels have sex or anything like that?"*

618.   Raphael gave him a big rosy-faced grin.

620. *"Let's just say we're a happy bunch, and you can't have happiness without love.*

622. *What you enjoy in sex (and sex was given to you with God's full blessing) we enjoy in a different way. When we spirits embrace there are no arms or legs to get in the way.*

626. *It's like mixing air with air. It's total.*

630. *But I have to go now. It's getting late.*

Beyond the Earths green Cape and verdant Isles
Hesperean sets, my Signal to depart.

633. Be strong, live happie, and love, but first of all
Him whom to love is to obey, and keep

635. His great command; take heed lest Passion sway
Thy Judgment to do aught, which else free Will

637. Would not admit; thine and of all thy Sons
The weal or woe in thee is plac't; beware.

639. I in thy persevering shall rejoyce,

640. And all the Blest: stand fast; to stand or fall
Free in thine own Arbitrement it lies.
Perfet within, no outward aid require;

643. And all temptation to transgress repel.

644.   So saying, he arose; whom Adam thus

645. Follow'd with benediction. Since to part,
Go heavenly Guest, Ethereal Messenger,
Sent from whose sovran goodness I adore.

648. Gentle to me and affable hath been
Thy condescension, and shall be honour'd ever

650. With grateful Memorie: thou to mankind
Be good and friendly still, and oft return.

652.   So parted they, the Angel up to Heav'n
From the thick shade, and Adam to his Bowre.

633. *So you be strong, live happy, and love, but most of all love God, which means obey him.*

635. *Don't let passion sway your judgment.*

637. *Whether the future brings happiness or misery to you and all your descendants is all up to you.*

639. *With all our hearts, we in Heaven all want you to succeed.*

640. *But the choice is entirely yours. You have absolute free will. You don't need anything else.*

643. *Just don't give in to temptation."*

644.   He got up to leave and Adam wished him well.

645. "*Go if you must, messenger from God.*

648. *You've been so kind to me. I'll never forget this.*

650. *Stay a friend to mankind, and come again often."*

652.   The angel went up to Heaven and Adam went home to his shelter.

Book IX

PARADISE LOST

1.   No more of talk where God or Angel Guest
With Man, as with his Friend, familiar us'd
To sit indulgent, and with him partake
Rural repast, permitting him the while
5. Venial discourse unblam'd: I now must change
Those Notes to Tragic; foul distrust, and breach
Disloyal on the part of Man, revolt,
8. And disobedience: On the part of Heav'n
Now alienated, distance and distaste,
Anger and just rebuke, and judgement giv'n,
That brought into this World a world of woe,
Sinne and her shadow Death, and Miserie
12. Deaths Harbinger: Sad task, yet argument
Not less but more Heroic then the wrauth
14. Of stern Achilles on his Foe pursu'd
Thrice Fugitive about Troy Wall; or rage
Of Turnus for Lavinia disespous'd,
Or Neptun's ire or Juno's, that so long
Perplex'd the Greek and Cytherea's Son;
20. If answerable style I can obtaine
Of my Celestial Patroness, who deignes
Her nightly visitation unimplor'd,
And dictates to me slumb'ring, or inspires
Easie my unpremeditated Verse:
25. Since first this Subject for Heroic Song
Pleas'd me long choosing, and beginning late;
Not sedulous by Nature to indite
28. Warrs, hitherto the onely Argument
Heroic deem'd, chief maistrie to dissect
30. With long and tedious havoc fabl'd Knights
In Battels feign'd; the better fortitude
Of Patience and Heroic Martyrdom
33. Unsung; or to describe Races and Games,
Or tilting Furniture, emblazon'd Shields,
Impreses quaint, Caparisons and Steeds;
Bases and tinsel Trappings, gorgious Knights
At Joust and Torneament; then marshal'd Feast
Serv'd up in Hall with Sewers, and Seneshals;
The skill of Artifice or Office mean,
Not that which justly gives Heroic name
To Person or to Poem. Mee of these
42. Nor skilld nor studious, higher Argument

Chapter 9

IN PLAIN ENGLISH

1.   So much for the angel's friendly visit with Adam.

5. Now we're going to talk about sadder things—like when man lost faith and became disobedient to God.

8. And about how God got angry and passed judgment that brought suffering into the world.

12. And about Sin and Death, and about Misery, who tells us when Death is coming.

14. It's a sad story, but it's more impressive and inspiring than all those stories about anger and vengeance in the Iliad or the Aeneid or the Odyssey.

20. At least, it will be, if my heavenly muse keeps coming to me every night in my sleep and inspires me to write this poetry.

25. It took me a long time to get around to writing this epic.

28. It seemed like war was the only subject epics could ever be about.

30. All this tiresome stuff about brave knights in battles, while nobody talks about patience or sacrifice—things more worth admiring.

33. Or else they go on about these sports heroes and tournaments and their favorite teams and all the overblown celebrations. It's not my thing.

42. I prefer a different subject—one which is important enough to be truly called heroic.

Remaines, sufficient of it self to raise

44. That name, unless an age too late, or cold
Climat, or Years damp my intended wing
Deprest, and much they may, if all be mine,
Not Hers who brings it nightly to my Ear.

48.   The Sun was sunk, and after him the Starr
Of Hesperus, whose Office is to bring
Twilight upon the Earth, short Arbiter

51. Twixt Day and Night, and now from end to end
Nights Hemisphere had veild the Horizon round:

53. When Satan who late fled before the threats
Of Gabriel out of Eden, now improv'd

55. In meditated fraud and malice, bent
On mans destruction, maugre what might hap
Of heavier on himself, fearless return'd.

58. By Night he fled, and at Midnight return'd.
From compassing the Earth, cautious of day,
Since Uriel Regent of the Sun descri'd
His entrance, and forewarnd the Cherubim
That kept thir watch; thence full of anguish driv'n,

63. The space of seven continu'd Nights he rode
With darkness, thrice the Equinoctial Line
He circl'd, four times cross'd the Carr of Night
From Pole to Pole, traversing each Colure;

67. On the eighth return'd, and on the Coast averse
From entrance or Cherubic Watch, by stealth

69. Found unsuspected way. There was a place,
Now not, though Sin, not Time, first wraught the change,
Where Tigris at the foot of Paradise
Into a Gulf shot under ground, till part
Rose up a Fountain by the Tree of Life;

74. In with the River sunk, and with it rose
Satan involv'd in rising Mist, then sought

76. Where to lie hid; Sea he had searcht and Land

77. From Eden over Pontus, and the Poole
Mæotis, up beyond the River Ob;
Downward as farr Antartic; and in length
West from Orontes to the Ocean barr'd
At Darien, thence to the Land where flowes
Ganges and Indus: thus the Orb he roam'd

83. With narrow search; and with inspection deep
Consider'd every Creature, which of all
Most opportune might serve his Wiles, and found
The Serpent suttlest Beast of all the Field.
Him after long debate, irresolute
Of thoughts revolv'd, his final sentence chose
Fit Vessel, fittest Imp of fraud, in whom

90. To enter, and his dark suggestions hide
From sharpest sight: for in the wilie Snake,
Whatever sleights none would suspicious mark,

44. Maybe I'm too old to write in a way that does that subject justice, but Urania visits me each night and gives me the inspiration I need.

48.   The Sun had set and Venus, the twilight star, was gone also.

51. Night covered the entire horizon.

53. Gabriel had thrown Satan out of Eden, but he was coming back now.

55. He had worked out his plan for man's destruction and he was so determined he didn't care how risky it was.

58. He returned in the middle of the night, the same as he had fled, when Uriel had spotted him and alerted the angel guards.

63. He had circled the Earth for seven continuous nights, staying on the dark side of the Earth, and came down on the eighth.

67. He found a secret way into the garden.

69. There was a place (not there anymore, not because of time, but because sin destroyed it)—a place where the Tigris river went underground at the foot of the mountain and eventually came up as a stream in the garden, near the Tree of Life.

74. He swam through this tunnel and came up in the garden, surrounded by mist.

76. He had been searching for a good way to hide his presence here.

77. He had searched land and sea, from the Black Sea up as far as Siberia and down to Antarctica, then from Syria west to Panama and India.

83. He roamed the whole world and carefully studied every kind of creature and decided that the snake was the best one for him to sneak around in.

90. He figured that it was such a sneaky looking creature already that nobody would suspect anything unusual about his strange behavior once he was inside the snake.

As from his wit and native suttletie
Proceeding, which in other Beasts observ'd
Doubt might beget of Diabolic pow'r
Active within beyond the sense of brute.

SATAN REASONING

97. Thus he resolv'd, but first from inward griefe
His bursting passion into plaints thus pour'd:

99.   O Earth, how like to Heav'n, if not preferr'd
More justly, Seat worthier of Gods, as built

101. With' second thoughts, reforming what was old!
For what God after better worse would build?

103. Terrestrial Heav'n, danc't round by other Heav'ns
That shine, yet bear thir bright officious Lamps,
Light above Light, for thee alone, as seems,
In thee concentring all thir precious beams

107. Of sacred influence: As God in Heav'n
Is Center, yet extends to all, so thou
Centring receav'st from all those Orbs; in thee,

110. Not in themselves, all thir known vertue appeers
Productive in Herb, Plant, and nobler birth
Of Creatures animate with gradual life
Of Growth, Sense, Reason, all summ'd up in Man.

114. With what delight could I have walkt thee round,
If I could joy in aught, sweet interchange
Of Hill, and Vallie, Rivers, Woods and Plaines,
Now Land, now Sea, and Shores with Forrest crownd,

118. Rocks, Dens, and Caves; but I in none of these
119. Find place or refuge; and the more I see

INTERNAL CONFLICT

Pleasures about me, so much more I feel
Torment within me, as from the hateful siege
Of contraries; all good to me becomes
Bane, and in Heav'n much worse would be my state.

124. But neither here seek I, no nor in Heav'n
To dwell, unless by maistring Heav'ns Supreame;

126. Nor hope to be my self less miserable
By what I seek, but others to make such

128. As I, though thereby worse to me redound:
For onely in destroying I find ease

130. To my relentless thoughts; and him destroyd,
Or won to what may work his utter loss,

132. For whom all this was made, all this will soon
Follow, as to him linkt in weal or woe,
In wo then: that destruction wide may range:

135. To mee shall be the glorie sole among
The infernal Powers, in one day to have marr'd
What he Almightie styl'd, six Nights and Days

138. Continu'd making, and who knows how long
Before had bin contriving, though perhaps
Not longer then since I in one Night freed
From servitude inglorious welnigh half
Th' Angelic Name, and thinner left the throng

97. So that was decided. Now he paused a minute to do some venting of his frustrations.

99.   *"This Earth is like Heaven, if not better—even more suitable for angels.*

101. *God was more experienced when he created this world and did an even better job this time.*

103. *It's like an earthly Heaven surrounded by other Heavens in the sky that all shine just for here.*

107. *God is the center of Heaven, and this is the center of the universe.*

110. *All the magic of the stars comes to life, not up where they are, but down here where they shine, producing plants and animals and the highest animal, man.*

114. *What a time I could've had walking around these mountains and valleys, forests and seashores, that is, if I could enjoy anything anymore!*

118. *But there's no peace for me anywhere around here now.*

119. *The more I see of this beauty around me, the more it tortures me. And it would be even worse if I was still in Heaven.*

124. *But I'm not looking to settle here or in Heaven (unless I could overthrow God).*

126. *No, I'm not looking for any relief from my misery. I just want to make everybody else as miserable as I am.*

128. *I don't even care if it makes matters worse for me. The only relief I find is in destroying others.*

130. *I'll destroy man, or make him destroy himself.*

132. *This world will go too, since it was only made for him.*

135. *All my followers will cheer me that I could destroy in one day what it took God six days to make.*

138. *I doubt he could've been planning this creation for long. I think I surprised him by suddenly freeing nearly half of his slave-angels.*

Of his adorers: hee to be aveng'd,
And to repaire his numbers thus impair'd,
145. Whether such vertue spent of old now faild
More Angels to Create, if they at least
Are his Created, or to spite us more,
Determin'd to advance into our room
A Creature form'd of Earth, and him endow,
Exalted from so base original,
With Heav'nly spoils, our spoils: What he decreed
152. He effected; Man he made, and for him built
Magnificent this World, and Earth his seat,
Him Lord pronounc'd, and, O indignitie!
Subjected to his service Angel wings,
And flaming Ministers to watch and tend
157. Thir earthy Charge: Of these the vigilance
I dread, and to elude, thus wrapt in mist
Of midnight vapor glide obscure, and prie
In every Bush and Brake, where hap may finde
The Serpent sleeping, in whose mazie foulds
To hide me, and the dark intent I bring.
163. O foul descent! that I who erst contended
With Gods to sit the highest, am now constraind
Into a Beast, and mixt with bestial slime,
This essence to incarnate and imbrute,
That to the hight of Deitie aspir'd;
168. But what will not Ambition and Revenge
169. Descend to? who aspires must down as low
As high he soard, obnoxious first or last
To basest things. Revenge, at first though sweet,
Bitter ere long back on it self recoiles;
173. Let it; I reck not, so it light well aim'd,
Since higher I fall short, on him who next
Provokes my envie, this new Favorite
Of Heav'n, this Man of Clay, Son of despite,
Whom us the more to spite his Maker rais'd
From dust: spite then with spite is best repaid.
179.   So saying, through each Thicket Danck or Drie,
Like a black mist low creeping, he held on
His midnight search, where soonest he might finde
The Serpent: him fast sleeping soon he found
In Labyrinth of many a round self-rowld,
184. His head the midst, well stor'd with suttle wiles:
Not yet in horrid Shade or dismal Den,
Nor nocent yet, but on the grassie Herbe
187. Fearless unfeard he slept: in at his Mouth
The Devil enterd, and his brutal sense,
In heart or head, possessing soon inspir'd
With act intelligential; but his sleep
Disturbd not, waiting close th' approach of Morn.
192. Now when as sacred Light began to dawne

[handwritten annotation: EXTERNAL CONFLICT]

145. *I don't know whether he forgot how to create more angels or he created this man creature out of dirt and put him in our place just to spite us.*

152. *So he creates man and builds this magnificent world for him, and to add insult to injury, he reduces angels to nothing but man's servants.*

157. *And because of these flunkies guarding him I have to go sneak around looking for a snake to hide in.*

163. *Look what I've come to! Me, who battled angels for the throne of God—now I'll be slithering through slime, inside a snake!*
168. *This is what ambition and revenge get you.*

169. *The higher you aim, the harder you fall. Revenge is sweet at first, but it becomes bitter in the end.*

173. *So be it. I don't care anymore. As long as it lands squarely on man's head—this new favorite of God's—this man of clay— made just to spite us. It's payback time!"*

179.   So he searched through the night till he found a snake curled up asleep.

184. It was already a sneaky creature, but it was about to become something much worse.

187. Satan slipped in through its mouth while it was sleeping and possessed it. There he waited till morning.

192. When morning came Adam and Eve got up and said their morning prayers.

In Eden on the humid Flours, that breathd
Thir morning incense, when all things that breath,
From th' Earths great Altar send up silent praise
To the Creator, and his Nostrils fill
With grateful Smell, forth came the human pair
And joind thir vocal Worship to the Quire

199. Of Creatures wanting voice, that done, partake
The season, prime for sweetest Sents and Aires:
Then commune how that day they best may ply

202. Thir growing work: for much thir work outgrew
The hands dispatch of two Gardning so wide.
And Eve first to her Husband thus began.

205.   Adam, well may we labour still to dress
This Garden, still to tend Plant, Herb and Flour,
Our pleasant task enjoyn'd, but till more hands
Aid us, the work under our labour grows,
Luxurious by restraint; what we by day
Lop overgrown, or prune, or prop, or bind,
One night or two with wanton growth derides
Tending to wilde. Thou therefore now advise
Or hear what to my minde first thoughts present,

214. Let us divide our labours, thou where choice
Leads thee, or where most needs, whether to wind
The Woodbine round this Arbour, or direct
The clasping Ivie where to climb, while I
In yonder Spring of Roses intermixt
With Myrtle, find what to redress till Noon:

220. For while so near each other thus all day
Our taske we choose, what wonder if so near
Looks intervene and smiles, or object new
Casual discourse draw on, which intermits
Our dayes work brought to little, though begun
Early, and th' hour of Supper comes unearn'd.

226.   To whom mild answer Adam thus return'd.
Sole Eve, Associate sole, to me beyond
Compare above all living Creatures deare,
Well hast thou motion'd, well thy thoughts imployd
How we might best fulfill the work which here
God hath assign'd us, nor of me shalt pass
Unprais'd: for nothing lovelier can be found
In Woman, then to studie houshold good,
And good workes in her Husband to promote.

235. Yet not so strictly hath our Lord impos'd
Labour, as to debarr us when we need
Refreshment, whether food, or talk between,

238. Food of the mind, or this sweet intercourse
Of looks and smiles, for smiles from Reason flow,
To brute deni'd, and are of Love the food,
Love not the lowest end of human life.

242. For not to irksom toile, but to delight

199. They took a deep breath of the fresh morning air, then settled down to planning their gardening work.

202. There was an awful lot to do for only two people.

205.   "*Adam*," said Eve, "*We can work our heads off pruning and taking care of all these plants, but they grow so fast we can never keep up.*

214. *Why don't we go our separate ways until noontime. You go do what you do, guiding the vines or whatever, and I'll go over by the roses and see what I can do.*

220. *Because you know if we work together we're going to end up talking and fooling around and not get that much done."*

226.   Adam said, "*Eve, honey, you're so sweet when you show your domestic side, making sure everything runs smoothly.*

235. *But God never meant for us to work so hard that we don't get a break for refreshments or to enjoy each other's company.*

238. *Talk is like food. And loving smiles show we are thinking creatures, not like the animals.*

242. *He didn't make us to wear ourselves out working. He meant for us to enjoy it here.*

He made us, and delight to Reason joyn'd.

244. These paths & Bowers doubt not but our joynt hands
Will keep from Wilderness with ease, as wide
As we need walk, till younger hands ere long

247. Assist us: But if much converse perhaps
Thee satiate, to short absence I could yield.
For solitude somtimes is best societie,

250. And short retirement urges sweet returne.

251. But other doubt possesses me, least harm
Befall thee sever'd from me; for thou knowst

253. What hath bin warn'd us, what malicious Foe
Envying our happiness, and of his own
Despairing, seeks to work us woe and shame

256. By sly assault; and somwhere nigh at hand
Watches, no doubt, with greedy hope to find
His wish and best advantage, us asunder,
Hopeless to circumvent us joynd, where each
To other speedie aide might lend at need;
Whether his first design be to withdraw
Our fealtie from God, or to disturb
Conjugal Love, then which perhaps no bliss
Enjoy'd by us excites his envie more;

265. Or this, or worse, leave not the faithful side
That gave thee being, still shades thee and protects.
The Wife, where danger or dishonour lurks,
Safest and seemliest by her Husband staies,
Who guards her, or with her the worst endures.

270.   To whom the Virgin Majestie of Eve,
As one who loves, and some unkindness meets,
With sweet austeer composure thus reply'd,

273.   Ofspring of Heav'n and Earth, and all Earths Lord,
That such an Enemie we have, who seeks
Our ruin, both by thee informd I learne,
And from the parting Angel over-heard
As in a shadie nook I stood behind,
Just then returnd at shut of Evening Flours.

279. But that thou shouldst my firmness therfore doubt
To God or thee, because we have a foe
May tempt it, I expected not to hear.

282. His violence thou fear'st not, being such,
As wee, not capable of death or paine,
Can either not receave, or can repell.

285. His fraud is then thy fear, which plain inferrs
Thy equal fear that my firm Faith and Love
Can by his fraud be shak'n or seduc't;

288. Thoughts, which how found they harbour in thy brest
Adam, misthought of her to thee so dear?

290.   To whom with healing words Adam replyd.
Daughter of God and Man, immortal Eve,
For such thou art, from sin and blame entire:

244. *Don't worry, we'll be able to keep these shelters and walks clear enough until one day we have kids to help us.*

247. *Of course if you feel you had enough talk, I wouldn't mind separating for a while. Solitude can be good too sometimes.*

250. *Not to mention how good it would be when we got back together again.*

251. *The thing is, there's something else we have to worry about. You could get into trouble if you go off alone.*

253. *You remember what Raphael warned us about. The devil is jealous of us and is out to get us.*

256. *He's probably hiding, just waiting to find one of us alone. He wants to get us to disobey God, or come between us in some way, or who knows what.*

265. *We better stick together where it's safer. A wife belongs by her husbands side, where he can protect her."*

270.   Eve's feelings were hurt.

273.   *"You told me about Satan, and I also heard you and the angel talking about it.*

279. *But I never thought you would think I could ever be unfaithful to you or God, just because somebody out there might tempt me.*

282. *He can't hurt us by violence. We're protected from death or pain.*

285. *So you must be afraid he can trick me—and that I'm not strong enough to resist.*

288. *How can you think that about me, Adam?"*

290.   *"No, no, Eve,"* cried Adam. *"You're the immortal daughter of God and man. Nobody thinks you could ever sin. It's not that I have no confidence in you.*

Not diffident of thee do I dissuade
294. Thy absence from my sight, but to avoid
Th' attempt itself, intended by our Foe.
For hee who tempts, though in vain, at least asperses
The tempted with dishonour foul, suppos'd
Not incorruptible of Faith, not prooff
299. Against temptation: thou thy self with scorne
And anger wouldst resent the offer'd wrong,
301. Though ineffectual found: misdeem not then,
If such affront I labour to avert
303. From thee alone, which on us both at once
The Enemie, though bold, will hardly dare,
Or daring, first on mee th' assault shall light.
306. Nor thou his malice and false guile contemn;
Suttle he needs must be, who could seduce
Angels nor think superfluous others aid.
309. I from the influence of thy looks receave
Access in every Vertue, in thy sight
More wise, more watchful, stronger, if need were
Of outward strength; while shame, thou looking on,
Shame to be overcome or over-reacht
Would utmost vigor raise, and rais'd unite.
315. Why shouldst not thou like sense within thee feel
When I am present, and thy trial choose
With me, best witness of thy Vertue tri'd.
318.   So spake domestick Adam in his care
And Matrimonial Love; but Eve, who thought
Less attributed to her Faith sincere,
Thus her reply with accent sweet renewd.
322.   If this be our condition, thus to dwell
In narrow circuit strait'nd by a Foe,
Suttle or violent, we not endu'd
Single with like defence, wherever met,
How are we happie, still in fear of harm?
327. But harm precedes not sin: onely our Foe
328. Tempting affronts us with his foul esteem
Of our integritie: his foul esteeme
Sticks no dishonor on our Front, but turns
Foul on himself; then wherefore shund or feard
332. By us? who rather double honour gaine
From his surmise prov'd false, find peace within,
Favour from Heav'n, our witness from th' event.
And what is Faith, Love, Vertue unassaid
Alone, without exterior help sustaind?
337. Let us not then suspect our happie State
Left so imperfet by the Maker wise,
As not secure to single or combin'd.
Fraile is our happiness, if this be so,
And Eden were no Eden thus expos'd.
342.   To whom thus Adam fervently repli'd.

294. *It's just that, well, the attempt itself, even if he fails, would be an insult to you.*

299. *You, yourself, would resent the attempt.*

301. *And it's not just you. Staying together makes me stronger too.*

303. *First of all, he's too slick to try to get at us when we're together, but if he does, I'll be the one he has to confront first.*

306. *But don't underestimate this guy who was able to fool the angels.*

309. *With you here beside me I would be stronger and braver. A man doesn't want to look weak in front of his woman.*

315. *You should feel the same way about being with me."*

318. But Eve was convinced he didn't trust her.

322. *"If we have to live under these conditions, afraid to be apart for a minute, what kind of happiness is that?*

327. *But we can't be harmed if we just say no.*
328. *His trying to tempt us doesn't shame us, it shames him.*

332. *In fact, it's something to be proud of. After all, what's there to brag about if you never even have a chance to say no to evil.*

337. *I can't believe God really meant for us to live in fear in this Paradise."*

342. Adam said, *"Eve, God made everything perfect, including everything that protects us from harm.*

O Woman, best are all things as the will
Of God ordain'd them, his creating hand
Nothing imperfet or deficient left
Of all that he Created, much less Man,
Or aught that might his happie State secure,
348. Secure from outward force; within himself
The danger lies, yet lies within his power:
350. Against his will he can receave no harme.
But God left free the Will, for what obeyes
352. Reason, is free, and Reason he made right
353. But bid her well beware, and still erect,
Least by some faire appeering good surpris'd
She dictate false, and misinforme the Will
To do what God expresly hath forbid,
357. Not then mistrust, but tender love enjoynes,
That I should mind thee oft, and mind thou me.
Firm we subsist, yet possible to swerve,
Since Reason not impossibly may meet
Some specious object by the Foe subornd,
And fall into deception unaware,
Not keeping strictest watch, as she was warnd.
364. Seek not temptation then, which to avoide
Were better, and most likelie if from mee
Thou sever not: Trial will come unsought.
367. Wouldst thou approve thy constancie, approve
First thy obedience; th' other who can know,
Not seeing thee attempted, who attest?
370. But if thou think, trial unsought may finde
Us both securer then thus warnd thou seemst,
372. Go; for thy stay, not free, absents thee more;
373. Go in thy native innocence, relie
On what thou hast of vertue, summon all,
For God towards thee hath done his part, do thine.
376.   So spake the Patriarch of Mankinde, but Eve
Persisted, yet submiss, though last, repli'd.
378.   With thy permission then, and thus forewarnd
Chiefly by what thy own last reasoning words
Touchd onely, that our trial, when least sought,
May finde us both perhaps farr less prepar'd,
382. The willinger I goe, nor much expect
A Foe so proud will first the weaker seek,
So bent, the more shall shame him his repulse.
Thus saying, from her Husbands hand her hand
386. Soft she withdrew, and like a Wood-Nymph light
387. Oread or Dryad, or of Delia's Traine,
Betook her to the Groves, but Delia's self
In gate surpass'd and Goddess-like deport,
Though not as shee with Bow and Quiver armd,
But with such Gardning Tools as Art yet rude,
Guiltless of fire had formd, or Angels brought.

348. *But this danger is inside us. And it's up to us to control it.*

350. *Nothing can harm us against our will, but God gave us free will.*

352. *And to guide our free will God gave us the ability to develop reasonable thoughts.*

353. *But he warned that even thoughts can be fooled into mistaking evil for good.*

357. *So it's not mistrust, but love that makes me want to remind you often, as you should also remind me, that strong as we are, it's not impossible for us to fall into the devil's trap if we're not careful.*

364. *I think you should stay here with me. It's better to avoid temptation. Don't worry, we're sure to be tested without going looking for it.*

367. *You shouldn't be so anxious to prove your faithfulness. Prove your obedience first. Why try to show your faithfulness someplace where I won't be around to appreciate it?*

370. *But I know you believe it's better to face temptation head on, when you're prepared for it. Then, what can I say—go ahead.*

372. *What's the use of me trying to keep you here if it's only going to make you feel like you're in prison.*

373. *Go as you are, innocent, but wise and strong. God gave you everything you need."*

376. So, having won, Eve replied:

378. *"I'll go then, with your permission. It's true, facing temptation head on is better than letting it come to us when we're not expecting it.*

382. *Anyway, there's probably nothing to worry about. I can't believe somebody as proud as Satan would plan to attack the weaker sex first, knowing how striking out with me would shame him all the more."*

386. Then she gently pulled her hand away from her husband's.

387. She looked like Diana, goddess of hunting, as she disappeared into the woods, only instead of bow and arrows she carried gardening tools.

To Pales, or Pomona, thus adornd,
Likeliest she seemd, Pomona when she fled
Vertumnus, or to Ceres in her Prime,
Yet Virgin of Proserpina from Jove.

397. Her long with ardent look his Eye pursu'd
Delighted, but desiring more her stay.

399. Oft he to her his charge of quick returne
Repeated, shee to him as oft engag'd
To be returnd by Noon amid the Bowre,
And all things in best order to invite
Noontide repast, or Afternoons repose.

404. O much deceav'd, much failing, hapless Eve,
Of thy presum'd return! event perverse!
Thou never from that houre in Paradise
Foundst either sweet repast, or sound repose;

408. Such ambush hid among sweet Flours and Shades
Waited with hellish rancour imminent
To intercept thy way, or send thee back
Despoild of Innocence, of Faith, of Bliss.

412. For now, and since first break of dawne the Fiend,
Meer Serpent in appearance, forth was come,
And on his Quest, where likeliest he might finde
The onely two of Mankinde, but in them
The whole included Race, his purposd prey.

417. In Bowre and Field he sought, where any tuft
Of Grove or Garden-Plot more pleasant lay,
Thir tendance or Plantation for delight,
By Fountain or by shadie Rivulet

421. He sought them both, but wish'd his hap might find
Eve separate, he wish'd, but not with hope
Of what so seldom chanc'd, when to his wish,
Beyond his hope, Eve separate he spies,

425. Veild in a Cloud of Fragrance, where she stood,
Half spi'd, so thick the Roses bushing round
About her glowd, oft stooping to support

428. Each Flour of slender stalk, whose head though gay
Carnation, Purple, Azure, or spect with Gold,
Hung drooping unsustaind, them she upstaies

431. Gently with Mirtle band, mindless the while,
Her self, though fairest unsupported Flour,
From her best prop so farr, and storm so nigh.

434. Neerer he drew, and many a walk travers'd
Of stateliest Covert, Cedar, Pine, or Palme,
Then voluble and bold, now hid, now seen
Among thick-wov'n Arborets and Flours

438. Imborderd on each Bank, the hand of Eve:
Spot more delicious then those Gardens feign'd
Or of reviv'd Adonis, or renownd
Alcinous, host of old Laertes Son,
Or that, not Mystic, where the Sapient King

397. Adam watched her go, love struck, wishing she would stay.

399. Over and over he called to her to come back soon, and she kept calling back that she would be back in their shelter by noon and that they would enjoy lunch and a nap together.

404. Oh, Eve! Never in Paradise would either of you ever enjoy food or rest again!

408. Waiting for you among the flowers was an ambush that would send you back with your innocence and happiness lost forever!

412. Since dawn, Satan, now in the form of a snake, had been searching for the two people that represented the future of all mankind.

417. He searched all over, by shady streams or among flower beds or wherever it looked like they did their gardening.

421. He would've liked to find Eve alone, but he didn't think it was likely, when suddenly—there she was!

425. You could barely see her, there were so many roses around her.

428. She was lifting the multi-colored flowers that were hanging loose and tying them up with myrtle.

431. Eve was the one that could use some support now. But Adam was far away, and danger was very close.

434. The snake wound his way nearer, across open paths lined with tall trees, then disappeared among the thick bushes.

438. He moved through the sections Eve had lovingly tended— places more beautiful than the fictional garden where Adonis lived, or the real garden where Solomon made love.

Held dalliance with his fair Egyptian Spouse.

444. Much hee the Place admir'd, the Person more.

445. As one who long in populous City pent,
      Where Houses thick and Sewers annoy the Aire,
      Forth issuing on a Summers Morn to breathe
      Among the pleasant Villages and Farmes
      Adjoynd, from each thing met conceaves delight,
      The smell of Grain, or tedded Grass, or Kine,
      Or Dairie, each rural sight, each rural sound;
      If chance with Nymphlike step fair Virgin pass,
      What pleasing seemd, for her now pleases more,
      She most, and in her look summs all Delight.

455. Such Pleasure took the Serpent to behold
      This Flourie Plat, the sweet recess of Eve
      Thus earlie, thus alone; her Heav'nly forme
      Angelic, but more soft, and Feminine,

459. Her graceful Innocence, her every Aire
      Of gesture or lest action overawd
      His Malice, and with rapine sweet bereav'd
      His fierceness of the fierce intent it brought:
      That space the Evil one abstracted stood
      From his own evil, and for the time remaind
      Stupidly good, of enmitie disarm'd,
      Of guile, of hate, of envie, of revenge;

467. But the hot Hell that alwayes in him burnes,
      Though in mid Heav'n, soon ended his delight,

469. And tortures him now more, the more he sees
      Of pleasure not for him ordain'd: then soon

471. Fierce hate he recollects, and all his thoughts
      Of mischief, gratulating, thus excites.

473.   Thoughts, whither have ye led me, with what sweet
      Compulsion thus transported to forget
      What hither brought us, hate, not love, nor hope

476. Of Paradise for Hell, hope here to taste
      Of pleasure, but all pleasure to destroy,
      Save what is in destroying, other joy

479. To me is lost. Then let me not let pass
      Occasion which now smiles, behold alone
      The Woman, opportune to all attempts,

482. Her Husband, for I view far round, not nigh,
      Whose higher intellectual more I shun,
      And strength, of courage hautie, and of limb
      Heroic built, though of terrestrial mould,
      Foe not informidable, exempt from wound,
      I not; so much hath Hell debas'd, and paine
      Infeebl'd me, to what I was in Heav'n.

489. Shee fair, divinely fair, fit Love for Gods,
      Not terrible, though terrour be in Love
      And beautie, not approacht by stronger hate,

492. Hate stronger, under shew of Love well feign'd,

444. Satan admired the place, but he admired Eve even more.

445. He was like somebody who lived in a dirty slum, who takes a walk in the beautiful countryside among villages and farms, and enjoys the pleasant smells and sounds, and then a beautiful young girl walks by and everything seems even more beautiful, and her most of all.

455. Satan was so impressed with this wonderful place, and Eve. She looked like an angel, only softer.

459. Her grace and innocence overcame his hate and for a while Satan actually forgot his evil plans.

467. But the hot hell that always burns in his soul wherever he is, even in Paradise, soon woke him up from his trance.

469. He felt the torture of witnessing pleasures he could never have.

471. Intense hatred came back, and he returned to evil thoughts:

473.   *"Am I losing my mind? Am I forgetting what I'm here for—hate, not love!*

476. *I'm not here for pleasure. I'm here to destroy it—except for the pleasure I get in destroying. What else have I got?*

479. *I'm not going to pass up this chance now that I've got the woman alone.*

482. *I don't see her husband anywhere. He's more shrewd and stronger, while I'm weaker than I used to be.*

489. *She's a heavenly beauty. She's not scary—though love and beauty are a little scary.*

492. *But hate is stronger than love. I'll ruin her by disguising my hate as love."*

The way which to her ruin now I tend.

494.　　　So spake the Enemie of Mankind, enclos'd
　　　In Serpent, Inmate bad, and toward Eve
496.　Address'd his way, not with indented wave,
　　　Prone on the ground, as since, but on his reare,
　　　Circular base of rising foulds, that tour'd
　　　Fould above fould a surging Maze, his Head
500.　Crested aloft, and Carbuncle his Eyes;
　　　With burnisht Neck of verdant Gold, erect
　　　Amidst his circling Spires, that on the grass
503.　Floted redundant: pleasing was his shape,
　　　And lovely, never since of Serpent kind
　　　Lovelier, not those that in Illyria chang'd
　　　Hermione and Cadmus, or the God
　　　In Epidaurus; nor to which transformd
　　　Ammonian Jove, or Capitoline was seen,
　　　Hee with Olympias, this with her who bore
510.　Scipio the highth of Rome . With tract oblique
　　　At first, as one who sought access, but feard
　　　To interrupt, side-long he works his way.
513.　As when a Ship by skilful Stearsman wrought
　　　Nigh Rivers mouth or Foreland, where the Wind
　　　Veres oft, as oft so steers, and shifts her Saile;
516.　So varied hee, and of his tortuous Traine
　　　Curld many a wanton wreath in sight of Eve,
518.　To lure her Eye; shee busied heard the sound
　　　Of rusling Leaves, but minded not, as us'd
　　　To such disport before her through the Field,
521.　From every Beast, more duteous at her call,
　　　Then at Circean call the Herd disguis'd.
523.　Hee boulder now, uncall'd before her stood;
　　　But as in gaze admiring: Oft he bowd
　　　His turret Crest, and sleek enamel'd Neck,
　　　Fawning, and lick'd the ground whereon she trod.
527.　His gentle dumb expression turnd at length
　　　The Eye of Eve to mark his play; he glad
　　　Of her attention gaind, with Serpent Tongue
　　　Organic, or impulse of vocal Air,
　　　His fraudulent temptation thus began.
532.　　　Wonder not, sovran Mistress, if perhaps
　　　Thou canst, who art sole Wonder, much less arm
534.　Thy looks, the Heav'n of mildness, with disdain,
　　　Displeas'd that I approach thee thus, and gaze
　　　Insatiate, I thus single, nor have feard
　　　Thy awful brow, more awful thus retir'd.
538.　Fairest resemblance of thy Maker faire,
　　　Thee all things living gaze on, all things thine
　　　By gift, and thy Celestial Beautie adore
　　　With ravishment beheld, there best beheld
　　　Where universally admir'd; but here

494.   And the snake, possessed by the devil, headed towards Eve.

496. He wasn't flat on the ground like snakes move now. His body rose in a series of arcs with his head held high.

500. His eyes were like jewels and his tall neck was greenish gold.

503. He was more beautiful than the snakes described by Ovid and in Roman fables, or any other snake ever.

510. He edged up to Eve from the side, as if he was a little shy.

513. He was like a ship weaving its way along the coastline.

516. He coiled and uncoiled his body in various ways, trying to get Eve's attention.

518. She heard leaves rustling but paid no attention because she was used to having animals playing nearby.

521. The animals always came to her when she called. They obeyed her better than the beasts obeyed Circe.

523. But the snake came without being called. He came up to her and bowed a few times and licked the ground.

527. Finally he caught her eye, and he began his act:

532.   *"Don't be amazed, miss. You are the amazing one.*

534. *Don't be mad at me for not being afraid to come up to you like this and for staring at you.*

538. *You're so beautiful. Your beauty comes from Heaven. But here around all these animals, who can really appreciate your beauty besides one man.*

In this enclosure wild, these Beasts among,
Beholders rude, and shallow to discerne
Half what in thee is fair, one man except,

546. Who sees thee? (and what is one?) who shouldst be seen
A Goddess among Gods, ador'd and serv'd
By Angels numberless, thy daily Train.

549.   So gloz'd the Tempter, and his Proem tun'd;
Into the Heart of Eve his words made way,
Though at the voice much marveling; at length
Not unamaz'd she thus in answer spake.

553.   What may this mean? Language of Man pronounc't
By Tongue of Brute, and human sense exprest?

555. The first at lest of these I thought deni'd
To Beasts, whom God on thir Creation-Day
Created mute to all articulat sound;

558. The latter I demurre, for in thir looks
Much reason, and in thir actions oft appeers.

560. Thee, Serpent, suttlest beast of all the field
I knew, but not with human voice endu'd;

562. Redouble then this miracle, and say,
How cam'st thou speakable of mute, and how
To me so friendly grown above the rest
Of brutal kind, that daily are in sight?
Say, for such wonder claims attention due.

567.   To whom the guileful Tempter thus reply'd.
Empress of this fair World, resplendent Eve,
Easie to mee it is to tell thee all
What thou commandst and right thou shouldst be obeyd:
I was at first as other Beasts that graze

572. The trodden Herb, of abject thoughts and low,
As was my food, nor aught but food discern'd
Or Sex, and apprehended nothing high:

575. Till on a day roaving the field, I chanc'd
A goodly Tree farr distant to behold
Loaden with fruit of fairest colours mixt,
Ruddie and Gold: I nearer drew to gaze;

579. When from the boughes a savorie odour blow'n,

580. Grateful to appetite, more pleas'd my sense,
Then smell of sweetest Fenel or the Teats
Of Ewe or Goat dropping with Milk at Eevn,
Unsuckt of Lamb or Kid, that tend thir play.

584. To satisfie the sharp desire I had
Of tasting those fair Apples, I resolv'd
Not to deferr; hunger and thirst at once,
Powerful perswaders, quick'nd at the scent
Of that alluring fruit, urg'd me so keene.
About the mossie Trunk I wound me soon,

590. For high from ground the branches would require
Thy utmost reach or Adams: Round the Tree

592. All other Beasts that saw, with like desire

546. *You're a goddess who should be seen and served by multi-tudes of angels."*

549. Eve was amazed, and a little flattered.

553. *"What's this? A talking snake?*

555. *I didn't think God made any animals that could talk.*

558. *I'll admit they show a lot of wisdom in their ways, though.*

560. *I knew you snakes were the slyest creatures, but this is too much.*
562. *How did you learn to talk?"*

567. *"Well, I'll tell you, Eve,"* said the snake, *"I used to be like all the other dumb animals.*

572. *All I thought about was food and sex.*

575. *Then one day while I was out roaming around I saw this tree with red and yellow fruit on it that looked so delicious I decided to go take a closer look.*

579. *When I got there a breeze blew such a sweet aroma that I got suddenly very hungry.*
580. *It smelled sweeter than sweet goat's milk.*

584. *I couldn't wait to have at it, so I wound my way up around the trunk.*

590. *It was a pretty big tree. You and Adam would have to stretch on your toes to reach the fruit.*
592. *All the other animals who couldn't reach the fruit were jealously watching me.*

Longing and envying stood, but could not reach.
594. Amid the Tree now got, where plenty hung
Tempting so nigh, to pluck and eat my fill
I spar'd not, for such pleasure till that hour
At Feed or Fountain never had I found.
598. Sated at length, ere long I might perceave
Strange alteration in me, to degree
600. Of Reason in my inward Powers, and Speech
Wanted not long, though to this shape retain'd.
Thenceforth to Speculations high or deep
I turnd my thoughts, and with capacious mind
604. Considerd all things visible in Heav'n,
Or Earth, or Middle, all things fair and good;
606. But all that fair and good in thy Divine
Semblance, and in thy Beauties heav'nly Ray
United I beheld; no Fair to thine
Equivalent or second, which compel'd
Mee thus, though importune perhaps, to come
And gaze, and worship thee of right declar'd
Sovran of Creatures, universal Dame.
613.   So talk'd the spirited sly Snake; and Eve
Yet more amaz'd unwarie thus reply'd.
615.   Serpent, thy overpraising leaves in doubt
The vertue of that Fruit, in thee first prov'd:
617. But say, where grows the Tree, from hence how far?
618. For many are the Trees of God that grow
In Paradise, and various, yet unknown
To us, in such abundance lies our choice,
As leaves a greater store of Fruit untoucht,
Still hanging incorruptible, till men
Grow up to thir provision, and more hands
Help to disburden Nature of her Bearth.
625.   To whom the wilie Adder, blithe and glad.
Empress, the way is readie, and not long,
Beyond a row of Myrtles, on a Flat,
Fast by a Fountain, one small Thicket past
Of blowing Myrrh and Balme; if thou accept
My conduct, I can bring thee thither soon.
631.   Lead then, said Eve. Hee leading swiftly rowld
In tangles, and made intricate seem strait,
633. To mischief swift. Hope elevates, and joy
Bright'ns his Crest, as when a wandring Fire
Compact of unctuous vapor, which the Night
Condenses, and the cold invirons round,
Kindl'd through agitation to a Flame,
Which oft, they say, some evil Spirit attends
Hovering and blazing with delusive Light,
Misleads th' amaz'd Night-wanderer from his way
To Boggs and Mires, and oft through Pond or Poole,
There swallow'd up and lost, from succour farr.

594. *I ate my fill, and I tell you, I never tasted anything so delicious in all my life.*

598. *When I was finished, I began to feel funny.*

600. *Suddenly I was able to think high thoughts, and even speak them.*

604. *I could appreciate the beauty all around me.*

606. *But nothing could compare to your beauty. I just had to come and get a closer look."*

613.   He was slick, and Eve was naïve.

615.   *"Snake,"* she said, *"with all this flattery you're pouring on me, I'm beginning to wonder just how much that fruit improved your brain.*
617. *Where did you find this tree, anyway?*
618. *There's a lot of different kinds of trees here waiting to provide for future men. We haven't even seen all of them yet."*

625.   *"It's not far. I can take you right to it,"* said the snake.

631.   Eve said okay and off they went.

633.   His head glowed with excitement as he led her on. They say sometimes a person is lost in the woods at night and they follow a light, but it's really an evil spirit that leads them into quicksand.

643. So glister'd the dire Snake, and into fraud
644. Led Eve our credulous Mother, to the Tree
     Of prohibition, root of all our woe;
     Which when she saw, thus to her guide she spake.
647.   Serpent, we might have spar'd our coming hither,
     Fruitless to mee, though Fruit be here to excess,
     The credit of whose vertue rest with thee,
     Wondrous indeed, if cause of such effects.
     But of this Tree we may not taste nor touch;
     God so commanded, and left that Command
     Sole Daughter of his voice; the rest, we live
     Law to our selves, our Reason is our Law.
655.   To whom the Tempter guilefully repli'd.
     Indeed? hath God then said that of the Fruit
     Of all these Garden Trees ye shall not eate,
     Yet Lords declar'd of all in Earth or Aire?
659.   To whom thus Eve yet sinless. Of the Fruit
     Of each Tree in the Garden we may eate,
     But of the Fruit of this fair Tree amidst
     The Garden, God hath said, Ye shall not eate
     Thereof, nor shall ye touch it, least ye die.
664.   She scarse had said, though brief, when now more bold
     The Tempter, but with shew of Zeale and Love
     To Man, and indignation at his wrong,
667. New part puts on, and as to passion mov'd,
     Fluctuats disturbd, yet comely and in act
     Rais'd, as of som great matter to begin.
     As when of old som Orator renound
     In Athens or free Rome, where Eloquence
     Flourishd, since mute, to som great cause addrest,
673. Stood in himself collected, while each part,
     Motion, each act won audience ere the tongue,
     Somtimes in highth began, as no delay
     Of Preface brooking through his Zeal of Right.
     So standing, moving, or to highth upgrown
     The Tempter all impassiond thus began.
679.   O Sacred, Wise, and Wisdom-giving Plant,
     Mother of Science, Now I feel thy Power
     Within me cleere, not onely to discerne
     Things in thir Causes, but to trace the wayes
     Of highest Agents, deemd however wise.
684. Queen of this Universe, doe not believe
     Those rigid threats of Death; ye shall not Die:
686. How should ye? by the Fruit? it gives you Life
687. To Knowledge, By the Threatner, look on mee,
     Mee who have touch'd and tasted, yet both live,
     And life more perfet have attaind then Fate
690. Meant mee, by ventring higher then my Lot.
     Shall that be shut to Man, which to the Beast
692. Is open? or will God incense his ire

643. This was like that.
644. When Eve realized where he was taking her, she said:

647.   *"Oh, snake, I could've saved you the trouble. I know this tree. It's fruit may have been good for you, but God said we're not allowed to have any. We can't even touch it. We can do anything we want here except that."*

655.   The scheming snake said, *"What? Are you kidding me? God made you lords of the whole Earth and you can't even eat all the fruit here?"*

659.   Eve innocently answered, *"We get to eat all the other fruit—it's just this tree. God said if we touch it we'll die."*

664.   Now Satan wound up for his big pitch. He acted like he was upset that man had been cheated.

667.   He raised himself up like some great speaker in Greece or Rome about to give a momentous speech.

673.   He used all the same tricks they used, like when they would get the audience's attention with a movement or a facial expression, before they even began to speak. And then with great emotion:

679.   *"Oh sacred, wise, and wisdom-giving, miracle tree, now I understand everything.*
684.   *Queen of the Universe, don't you believe it! You won't die!*
686.   *How could you? This fruit isn't poison. It gives you wisdom.*
687.   *God won't kill you. Look at me. I touched it and ate it, and not only am I still alive, but now I have a more perfect life than nature ever meant for me.*
690.   *Are you going to be denied what animals can have?*
692.   *Why would God be angry with you for such a little thing? He'd probably admire your guts that you weren't afraid of dying, and that you were determined to become an even better person, knowing all about good and evil.*

For such a petty Trespass, and not praise
Rather your dauntless vertue, whom the pain
Of Death denounc't, whatever thing Death be,
Deterrd not from atchieving what might leade
To happier life, knowledge of Good and Evil;

698. Of good, how just? of evil, if what is evil
Be real, why not known, since easier shunnd?

700. God therefore cannot hurt ye, and be just;
Not just, not God; not feard then, nor obeyd:

702. Your feare it self of Death removes the feare.

703. Why then was this forbid? Why but to awe,
Why but to keep ye low and ignorant,

705. His worshippers; he knows that in the day
Ye Eate thereof, your Eyes that seem so cleere,
Yet are but dim, shall perfetly be then
Op'nd and cleerd, and ye shall be as Gods,
Knowing both Good and Evil as they know.

710. That ye should be as Gods, since I as Man,
Internal Man, is but proportion meet,
I of brute human, yee of human Gods.

713. So ye shall die perhaps, by putting off
Human, to put on Gods, death to be wisht,
Though threat'nd, which no worse then this can bring.

716. And what are Gods that Man may not become
As they, participating God-like food?

718. The Gods are first, and that advantage use
On our belief, that all from them proceeds;

720. I question it, for this fair Earth I see,
Warm'd by the Sun, producing every kind,

722. Them nothing: If they all things, who enclos'd
Knowledge of Good and Evil in this Tree,
That whoso eats thereof, forthwith attains
Wisdom without their leave? and wherein lies

726. Th' offence, that Man should thus attain to know?

727. What can your knowledge hurt him, or this Tree
Impart against his will if all be his?

729. Or is it envie, and can envie dwell

730. In Heav'nly brests? these, these and many more
Causes import your need of this fair Fruit.
Goddess humane, reach then, and freely taste.

733.   He ended, and his words replete with guile
Into her heart too easie entrance won:

735. Fixt on the Fruit she gaz'd, which to behold

736. Might tempt alone, and in her ears the sound
Yet rung of his perswasive words, impregn'd
With Reason, to her seeming, and with Truth;

739. Mean while the hour of Noon drew on, and wak'd
An eager appetite, rais'd by the smell
So savorie of that Fruit, which with desire,
Inclinable now grown to touch or taste,

698. *Isn't it better to know all about what's good? And if there's such a thing as evil, isn't it better to know about it so you can avoid it?*

700. *God can't punish you for this and still be considered fair. And God can't be unfair.*

702. *It doesn't make sense to fear him then.*

703. *I think he just wants to keep you weak and ignorant.*

705. *He knows that if you eat the fruit you'll become wise, knowing as much about good and evil as he knows, and you'll be like a god.*

710. *Just like the fruit made me become like a man, it will make you become like a god.*

713. *Maybe you will die, but only to be reborn as a god.*

716. *Why shouldn't you become like a god?*

718. *They came first and they tell you everything comes from them. I'm not so sure about that.*

720. *Look around, how the Earth is warmed by the sun and produces all kinds of life. Where do they come in?*

722. *If they control everything, who put the knowledge in this tree that they don't want anybody to have?*

726. *And what's the big crime in wanting to have knowledge any-way?*

727. *How is that going to hurt him if he's so all powerful?*

729. *Or is it just a matter of selfishness?*

730. *There are a lot of questions you should be asking, Eve, and this tree's fruit may be just the thing to give you the answers. Go ahead, eat some and see."*

733.   Eve bought all his lies so easily.

735. She was staring at the fruit, which was tempting all by itself.

736. Added to that were his persuasive arguments that seemed to make sense.

739. It was getting near noontime. She was getting hungry. And the fruit did look good.

Sollicited her longing eye; yet first
Pausing a while, thus to her self she mus'd.
745.   Great are thy Vertues, doubtless, best of Fruits.
Though kept from Man, and worthy to be admir'd,
Whose taste, too long forborn, at first assay
748. Gave elocution to the mute, and taught
The Tongue not made for Speech to speak thy praise:
750. Thy praise hee also who forbids thy use,
Conceales not from us, naming thee the Tree
Of Knowledge, knowledge both of good and evil;
753. Forbids us then to taste, but his forbidding
Commends thee more, while it inferrs the good
755. By thee communicated, and our want:
For good unknown, sure is not had, or had
And yet unknown, is as not had at all.
758. In plain then, what forbids he but to know,
Forbids us good, forbids us to be wise?
Such prohibitions binde not. But if Death
761. Bind us with after-bands, what profits then
Our inward freedom? In the day we eate
Of this fair Fruit, our doom is, we shall die.
How dies the Serpent? hee hath eat'n and lives,
And knows, and speaks, and reasons, and discerns,
766. Irrational till then. For us alone
767. Was death invented? or to us deni'd
This intellectual food, for beasts reserv'd?
769. For Beasts it seems: yet that one Beast which first
Hath tasted, envies not, but brings with joy
The good befall'n him, Author unsuspect,
Friendly to man, farr from deceit or guile.
773. What fear I then, rather what know to feare
Under this ignorance of good and Evil,
Of God or Death, of Law or Penaltie?
776. Here grows the Cure of all, this Fruit Divine,
Fair to the Eye, inviting to the Taste,
778. Of vertue to make wise: what hinders then
To reach, and feed at once both Bodie and Mind?
780.   So saying, her rash hand in evil hour
Forth reaching to the Fruit, she pluck'd, she eat:
782. Earth felt the wound, and Nature from her seat
Sighing through all her Works gave signs of woe,
784. That all was lost. Back to the Thicket slunk
The guiltie Serpent, and well might, for Eve
786. Intent now wholly on her taste, naught else
Regarded, such delight till then, as seemd,
In Fruit she never tasted, whether true
789. Or fansied so, through expectation high
Of knowledg, nor was God-head from her thought.
Greedily she ingorg'd without restraint,
792. And knew not eating Death: Satiate at length,

745.   She thought to herself, "*Fruit, you look so good. You've been kept from us too long.*

748. *You taught the snake how to speak, and he talked about how good you are.*

750. *And God did too. He told us your tree is the Tree of Knowledge of Good and Evil.*

753. *Then he forbids us to taste you. And that just makes you seem all the more desirable.*

755. *It doesn't make sense. How can we ever enjoy what is good if we aren't allowed to have the knowledge of what is good?*

758. *In plain English then, by forbidding us this fruit he's forbidding us all the good in the world. Nobody should have to obey silly rules like that.*

761. *But if we really will die after eating it, what good is the knowledge we get?*

766. *Are we the only ones who can die?*

767. *Are we the only ones who can't have this miraculous fruit while animals can?*

769. *The one creature who did eat it seems friendly and like he sincerely wants to share his good fortune with us.*

773. *What's there to be afraid of then? Or rather, I should say, how am I supposed to know what to be afraid of if I'm supposed to stay ignorant of good and evil?—and God and Death, and laws and penalties?*

776. *Here's the answer to everything. This fruit—so delicious looking, and with the power to make me wise.*

778. *What's to stop me? I'll feed my body and my mind at once.*"

780.   She picked a piece of fruit from a branch and ate it.

782. Earth felt the wound. Nature sighed. All was lost.

784. The snake slipped back into the bushes.

786. Eve was busy gorging herself on the fruit.

789. Maybe it really was the most delicious fruit she ever tasted, or maybe she just imagined it because she expected it to be.

792. She didn't know she was eating death.

And hight'nd as with Wine, jocond and boon,

794.   Thus to her self she pleasingly began.

795.   O Sovran, vertuous, precious of all Trees
In Paradise, of operation blest
To Sapience, hitherto obscur'd, infam'd,
And thy fair Fruit let hang, as to no end

799.   Created; but henceforth my early care,
Not without Song, each Morning, and due praise
Shall tend thee, and the fertil burden ease
Of thy full branches offer'd free to all;

803.   Till dieted by thee I grow mature
In knowledge, as the Gods who all things know;

805.   Though others envie what they cannot give;
For had the gift bin theirs, it had not here

807.   Thus grown. Experience, next to thee I owe,
Best guide; not following thee, I had remaind
In ignorance, thou op'nst Wisdoms way,
And giv'st access, though secret she retire.

811.   And I perhaps am secret; Heav'n is high,

812.   High and remote to see from thence distinct

813.   Each thing on Earth; and other care perhaps
May have diverted from continual watch
Our great Forbidder, safe with all his Spies

816.   About him. But to Adam in what sort

817.   Shall I appeer? shall I to him make known
As yet my change, and give him to partake
Full happiness with mee, or rather not,

820.   But keep the odds of Knowledge in my power
Without Copartner? so to add what wants
In Femal Sex, the more to draw his Love,
And render me more equal, and perhaps,

824.   A thing not undesireable, somtime
Superior: for inferior who is free?

826.   This may be well: but what if God have seen
And Death ensue? then I shall be no more,

828.   And Adam wedded to another Eve,

829.   Shall live with her enjoying, I extinct;

830.   A death to think. Confirm'd then I resolve,
Adam shall share with me in bliss or woe:
So dear I love him, that with him all deaths
I could endure, without him live no life.

834.   So saying, from the Tree her step she turnd,
But first low Reverence don, as to the power
That dwelt within, whose presence had infus'd
Into the plant sciential sap, deriv'd

838.   From Nectar, drink of Gods. Adam the while
Waiting desirous her return, had wove
Of choicest Flours a Garland to adorne
Her Tresses, and her rural labours crown,
As Reapers oft are wont thir Harvest Queen.

794. Instead she felt high, as if she just drank wine.

795.   She thought to herself, "*Oh tree, you are so good! All your goodness was hidden and your beautiful fruit just hung here as if it had no purpose.*

799. *But no more. From now on I'll be here every morning to take care of you and lighten your load.*

803. *Then I'll grow smarter and smarter till I'm like a god who knows everything.*

805. *Certain other persons may be jealous of what they can't give, because if it really was theirs to give, they wouldn't even put it here.*

807. *I'm glad I had the nerve to go ahead and do this. You can only learn from experience. Otherwise everything remains secret.*

811. *Let's just hope what I did stays secret. After all, Heaven is a long way off.*

812. *It's got to be hard to see every detail of what goes on here on Earth.*

813. *I'm sure God's got other things to think about.*

816. *But I wonder how Adam's going to take this.*

817. *I wonder if I should tell him how the fruit changed me, and have him eat it too.*

820. *Or maybe not. Maybe I should keep the odds in my favor. It would make up for what's missing in the female sex and make us more equal. Then maybe he'd love me even more.*

824. *Maybe I could even be a little superior sometimes. Being inferior limits one's freedom.*

826. *That's all well and good, but what if God does see everything, and I end up dead for it?*

828. *And Adam ends up getting a new wife.*

829. *No way! Just thinking about him being happy with somebody else makes me feel like I'm dying.*

830. *That's it then. Adam goes where I go. I love him so much I'd rather die with him than live without him.*"

834.   Before she stepped away from the tree she bowed to the wisdom-giving power that she imagined lived in there.

838. Meanwhile, Adam had been weaving a garland of flowers for Eve's hair, the way farmers crown their harvest queen.

843. Great joy he promis'd to his thoughts, and new
     Solace in her return, so long delay'd;
     Yet oft his heart, divine of somthing ill,
     Misgave him; hee the faultring measure felt;

847. And forth to meet her went, the way she took
     That Morn when first they parted; by the Tree

849. Of Knowledge he must pass, there he her met,
     Scarse from the Tree returning; in her hand
     A bough of fairest fruit that downie smil'd,
     New gatherd, and ambrosial smell diffus'd.

853. To him she hasted, in her face excuse
     Came Prologue, and Apologie to prompt,
     Which with bland words at will she thus addrest.

856.   Hast thou not wonderd, Adam, at my stay?

857. Thee I have misst, and thought it long, depriv'd
     Thy presence, agonie of love till now
     Not felt, nor shall be twice, for never more
     Mean I to trie, what rash untri'd I sought,
     The pain of absence from thy sight. But strange

862. Hath bin the cause, and wonderful to heare:

863. This Tree is not as we are told, a Tree
     Of danger tasted, nor to evil unknown

865. Op'ning the way, but of Divine effect
     To open Eyes, and make them Gods who taste;

867. And hath bin tasted such: the Serpent wise,
     Or not restraind as wee, or not obeying,

869. Hath eat'n of the fruit, and is become,
     Not dead, as we are threatn'd, but thenceforth
     Endu'd with human voice and human sense,

872. Reasoning to admiration, and with mee
     Perswasively hath so prevaild, that I
     Have also tasted, and have also found
     Th' effects to correspond, opener mine Eyes
     Dimm erst, dilated Spirits, ampler Heart,
     And growing up to Godhead; which for thee

878. Chiefly I sought, without thee can despise.
     For bliss, as thou hast part, to me is bliss,
     Tedious, unshar'd with thee, and odious soon.

881. Thou therefore also taste, that equal Lot
     May joyne us, equal Joy, as equal Love;

883. Least thou not tasting, different degree
     Disjoyne us, and I then too late renounce
     Deitie for thee, when Fate will not permit.

886.   Thus Eve with Countnance blithe her storie told;
     But in her Cheek distemper flushing glowd.

888. On th' other side, Adam, soon as he heard
     The fatal Trespass don by Eve, amaz'd,

890. Astonied stood and Blank, while horror chill
     Ran through his veins, and all his joynts relax'd;

892. From his slack hand the Garland wreath'd for Eve

843. He was expecting a happy reunion when she returned, but she was taking a little too long and he was getting uneasy.

847. So he went out to find her. He headed in the direction she went, which would lead him by the Tree of Knowledge.
849. And there she was, holding a branch from the tree, full of fruit.

853. She ran to meet him. Her face showed she was searching for excuses and apologies, but this is what she said:

856.   *"Were you wondering what was taking me so long, Adam?*
857. *I've missed you so much. This is the first and last time we try separating like that.*

862. *But wait'll I tell you what happened!*
863. *This tree isn't dangerous and evil like they told us.*

865. *It's a tree that opens your eyes and makes you like a god.*

867. *There was this snake that ate the fruit, since nobody told him not to.*
869. *And he didn't die. Instead, it gave him human intelligence and he was able to talk!*
872. *And he convinced me to eat the fruit too, and I did, and my eyes were opened, and my spirit grew bigger so now I'm like a god!*

878. *I did it for you. And I want you to share in it too. It's no good without you.*

881. *If you eat the fruit too we'll be in the same situation, able to share equal joy and equal love.*
883. *Otherwise, we're going to be on different levels, unable to connect, and you'll make me regret tasting the fruit."*
886.   Eve tried to sound casual, but her cheeks were red with guilt.
888. Adam just stood there, stunned.

890. He was horrified. His body went weak.

892. He dropped the garland and it fell apart.

Down drop'd, and all the faded Roses shed:
894. Speechless he stood and pale, till thus at length
First to himself he inward silence broke.
896.   O fairest of Creation, last and best
Of all Gods works, Creature in whom excell'd
Whatever can to sight or thought be formd,
Holy, divine, good, amiable, or sweet!
How art thou lost, how on a sudden lost,
Defac't, deflourd, and now to Death devote?
902. Rather how hast thou yeelded to transgress
The strict forbiddance, how to violate
The sacred Fruit forbidd'n! som cursed fraud
905. Of Enemie hath beguil'd thee, yet unknown,
906. And mee with thee hath ruind, for with thee
Certain my resolution is to Die;
How can I live without thee, how forgoe
Thy sweet Converse and Love so dearly joyn'd,
To live again in these wilde Woods forlorn?
911. Should God create another Eve, and I
Another Rib afford, yet loss of thee
913. Would never from my heart; no no, I feel
The Link of Nature draw me: Flesh of Flesh,
Bone of my Bone thou art, and from thy State
Mine never shall be parted, bliss or woe.
917.   So having said, as one from sad dismay
Recomforted, and after thoughts disturbd
Submitting to what seemd remediless,
Thus in calm mood his Words to Eve he turnd.
921.   Bold deed thou hast presum'd, adventrous Eve
And peril great provok't, who thus hath dar'd
Had it been onely coveting to Eye
That sacred Fruit, sacred to abstinence,
925. Much more to taste it under banne to touch.
926. But past who can recall, or don undoe?
Not God Omnipotent, nor Fate, yet so
928. Perhaps thou shalt not Die, perhaps the Fact
Is not so hainous now, foretasted Fruit,
Profan'd first by the Serpent, by him first
Made common and unhallowd ere our taste;
932. Nor yet on him found deadly, he yet lives,
Lives, as thou saidst, and gaines to live as Man
934. Higher degree of Life, inducement strong
To us, as likely tasting to attaine
Proportional ascent, which cannot be
But to be Gods, or Angels Demi-gods.
938. Nor can I think that God, Creator wise,
Though threatning, will in earnest so destroy
Us his prime Creatures, dignifi'd so high,
941. Set over all his Works, which in our Fall,
For us created, needs with us must faile,

894. He was speechless. He stood for a while and these thoughts ran through his head:

896.   *"How can this happen? This beautiful creature, the last and best God created, so good, so sweet and loving, now suddenly ruined, lost, sentenced to death?*

902. *What made her do this?*

905. *Some evil thing got to her.*
906. *I'm doomed also. I won't be able to live without her.*

911. *Even if God created another Eve, I would never get over losing her.*
913. *No! You're part of me—we can never be parted. I don't care what happens!"*

917.   So he resigned himself to what couldn't be changed and spoke to Eve calmly.

921.   *"Well, you really did a bold and dangerous thing, didn't you, Eve.*

925. *We were told not to even touch the fruit, but you not only touched it, you ate it.*
926. *Well, nobody can undo that now, not even God.*
928. *But maybe you won't die. Maybe the fruit lost its sacredness when the snake ate it first.*

932. *He survived okay, and it even made him become like us.*

934. *That's a strong incentive for us to try it too. We would probably become like gods or angels.*

938. *I don't think God would really kill us—the highest of all his creatures.*

941. *Since he made the world just for us, he'd have to destroy that too.*

943. Dependent made; so God shall uncreate,
Be frustrate, do, undo, and labour loose,
Not well conceav'd of God, who though his Power

946. Creation could repeate, yet would be loath
Us to abolish, least the Adversary

948. Triumph and say; Fickle their State whom God
Most Favors, who can please him long; Mee first
He ruind, now Mankind; whom will he next?

951. Matter of scorne, not to be given the Foe,

952. However I with thee have fixt my Lot,

953. Certain to undergoe like doom, if Death
Consort with thee, Death is to mee as Life;

955. So forcible within my heart I feel
The Bond of Nature draw me to my owne,
My own in thee, for what thou art is mine;

958. Our State cannot be severd, we are one,
One Flesh; to loose thee were to loose my self.

960.   So Adam, and thus Eve to him repli'd.
O glorious trial of exceeding Love,
Illustrious evidence, example high!

963. Ingaging me to emulate, but short
Of thy perfection, how shall I attaine,

965. Adam, from whose deare side I boast me sprung,
And gladly of our Union heare thee speak,
One Heart, one Soul in both; whereof good prooff
This day affords, declaring thee resolvd,
Rather then Death or aught then Death more dread
Shall separate us, linkt in Love so deare,

971. To undergoe with mee one Guilt, one Crime,
If any be, of tasting this fair Fruit,

973. Whose vertue, for of good still good proceeds,
Direct, or by occasion hath presented
This happie trial of thy Love, which else
So eminently never had bin known.

977. Were it I thought Death menac't would ensue
This my attempt, I would sustain alone
The worst, and not perswade thee, rather die
Deserted, then oblige thee with a fact
Pernicious to thy Peace, chiefly assur'd
Remarkably so late of thy so true,
So faithful Love unequald; but I feel

984. Farr otherwise th' event, not Death, but Life
Augmented, op'nd Eyes, new Hopes, new Joyes,

986. Taste so Divine, that what of sweet before
Hath toucht my sense, flat seems to this, and harsh.

988. On my experience, Adam, freely taste,
And fear of Death deliver to the Windes.

990.   So saying, she embrac'd him, and for joy
Tenderly wept, much won that he his Love
Had so enobl'd, as of choice to incurr

943. *He wouldn't have created all this just to destroy it all. God plans things better than that.*

946. *Of course he could replace us, but it would be a win for Satan.*

948. *He would say, 'What a shaky state God's favorites are in. First he destroys me, then mankind—who's next?'*

951. *He wouldn't want Satan making fun of him like that.*

952. *But I've joined my life with yours, and I'm ready to share your fate.*

953. *If your fate is death, then death is life to me.*

955. *That's how strong our bond is.*

958. *We're like one person. I could no more lose you than I could lose myself."*

960.   *"Oh, Adam," she cried, "what love you express! I'm so overwhelmed!*

963. *I only wish I could express my love for you as well as you do it.*

965. *I'm so proud that I came our of your side, and so happy to hear you express how united we are, saying that even death can't separate us.*

971. *You're ready to share my guilt and my crime, if there's any crime in tasting this wonderful fruit.*

973. *But even more good comes from the fruit: this example of your great love, which I wouldn't have seen otherwise.*

977. *But if I thought I was really going to die, I would take my punishment alone and not pull you down with me, now that I know how faithful you would remain.*

984. *But none of that is going to happen. This fruit doesn't bring death, it brings life, and open eyes, and new hopes, new joys.*

986. *Its taste is so divine that anything I ever ate before seems flat by comparison.*

988. *Trust me, Adam. Go ahead and try it. Don't be afraid."*

990.   And she threw her arms around him and cried happy tears, that he loved her so much that he would risk God's anger or even death (a fitting reward for that kind of mad love).

Divine displeasure for her sake, or Death.
In recompence (for such compliance bad
Such recompence best merits) from the bough
996. She gave him of that fair enticing Fruit
997. With liberal hand: he scrupl'd not to eat
Against his better knowledge, not deceav'd,
But fondly overcome with Femal charm.
1000. Earth trembl'd from her entrails, as again
In pangs, and Nature gave a second groan,
Skie lowr'd, and muttering Thunder, som sad drops
Wept at compleating of the mortal Sin
1004. Original; while Adam took no thought,
1005. Eating his fill, nor Eve to iterate
Her former trespass fear'd, the more to soothe
Him with her lov'd societie, that now
1008. As with new Wine intoxicated both
They swim in mirth, and fansie that they feel
Divinitie within them breeding wings
1011. Wherewith to scorne the Earth: but that false Fruit
Farr other operation first displaid,
1013. Carnal desire enflaming, hee on Eve
Began to cast lascivious Eyes, she him
As wantonly repaid; in Lust they burne:
Till Adam thus 'gan Eve to dalliance move,
1017. Eve, now I see thou art exact of taste,
And elegant, of Sapience no small part,
Since to each meaning savour we apply,
1020. And Palate call judicious; I the praise
Yeild thee, so well this day thou hast purvey'd.
Much pleasure we have lost, while we abstain'd
From this delightful Fruit, nor known till now
True relish, tasting; if such pleasure be
1025. In things to us forbidden, it might be wish'd,
For this one Tree had bin forbidden ten.
1027. But come, so well refresh't, now let us play,
As meet is, after such delicious Fare;
1029. For never did thy Beautie since the day
I saw thee first and wedded thee, adorn'd
With all perfections, so enflame my sense
With ardor to enjoy thee, fairer now
Then ever, bountie of this vertuous Tree.
1034. So said he, and forbore not glance or toy
Of amorous intent, well understood
Of Eve, whose Eye darted contagious Fire.
1037. Her hand he seis'd, and to a shadie bank,
Thick overhead with verdant roof imbowr'd
1039. He led her nothing loath; Flours were the Couch,
Pansies, and Violets, and Asphodel,
And Hyacinth, Earths freshest softest lap.
1042. There they thir fill of Love and Loves disport

996. She took some fruit off the branch and gave it to him.

997. Something told him he shouldn't, but against his better judg-ment he let himself be overcome by her female charms.

1000. A mild quake rumbled the Earth. There was distant thunder, and the sky let a few teardrops fall as the second half of the world's first mortal sin was completed.

1004. But Adam didn't notice. He was too busy enjoying the fruit.

1005. Eve didn't hesitate to join him, and they both ate their fill.

1008. Now they both acted like they were drunk, and fantasized about sprouting wings and becoming like gods.

1011. But something very different happened.

1013. They both became sexually aroused.

1017.   *"I see you do have good taste,"* said Adam. *"And in more things than just fruit.*

1020. *I've got to hand it to you, Eve. Today you show what real plea-sure there could be in tasting. We've been missing out on a lot.*

1025. *If forbidden things give this much pleasure, we should wish for ten forbidden trees.*

1027. *Now that we've eaten, let's go play.*

1029. *You never looked as hot as you do right now."*

1034.   They exchanged fiery glances.

1037. He took her hand and led her to a shady bank.

1039. There were plenty of flowers that would make for a soft bed.

1042. There they had their fill of sex play. And their mutual guilt was sealed.

        Took largely, of thir mutual guilt the Seale,
        The solace of thir sin, till dewie sleep
1045. Oppress'd them, wearied with thir amorous play.
1046. Soon as the force of that fallacious Fruit,
        That with exhilerating vapour bland
        About thir spirits had plaid, and inmost powers
        Made erre, was now exhal'd, and grosser sleep
        Bred of unkindly fumes, with conscious dreams
        Encumberd, now had left them, up they rose
1052. As from unrest, and each the other viewing,
        Soon found thir Eyes how op'nd, and thir minds
1054. How dark'nd; innocence, that as a veile
        Had shadow'd them from knowing ill, was gon,
1056. Just confidence, and native righteousness
        And honour from about them, naked left
1058. To guiltie shame hee cover'd, but his Robe
        Uncover'd more, so rose the Danite strong
        Herculean Samson from the Harlot-lap
        Of Philistean Dalilah, and wak'd
        Shorn of his strength, They destitute and bare
        Of all thir vertue: silent, and in face
1064. Confounded long they sate, as struck'n mute,
        Till Adam, though not less then Eve abasht,
        At length gave utterance to these words constraind.
1067.   O Eve, in evil hour thou didst give eare
        To that false Worm, of whomsoever taught
        To counterfet Mans voice, true in our Fall,
1070. False in our promis'd Rising; since our Eyes
        Op'nd we find indeed, and find we know
1073. Both Good and Evil, Good lost, and Evil got,
        Bad Fruit of Knowledge, if this be to know,
        Which leaves us naked thus, of Honour void,
        Of Innocence, of Faith, of Puritie,
        Our wonted Ornaments now soild and staind,
1077. And in our Faces evident the signes
        Of foul concupiscence; whence evil store;
        Even shame, the last of evils; of the first
1080. Be sure then. How shall I behold the face
        Henceforth of God or Angel, earst with joy
1082. And rapture so oft beheld? those heav'nly shapes
        Will dazle now this earthly, with thir blaze
1084. Insufferably bright. O might I here
        In solitude live savage, in some glade
        Obscur'd, where highest Woods impenetrable
        To Starr or Sun-light, spread thir umbrage broad,
        And brown as Evening: Cover me ye Pines,
        Ye Cedars, with innumerable boughs
        Hide me, where I may never see them more.
1091. But let us now, as in bad plight, devise
        What best may for the present serve to hide

1045. Finally, they fell asleep.
1046. Soon the intoxicating effects of the fruit wore off. They had unpleasant dreams and woke up.

1052. They looked at each other and understood just how their eyes had been opened.
1054. Their innocence, which protected them from knowing evil, was gone.
1056. All self confidence was gone.
1058. The way Samson woke up with his strength gone after Delilah cut off his long hair—that's how they were left bare naked to guilty shame when all their natural grace and honor was gone.

1064. They sat for a long while in stunned silence. Finally Adam broke the tension:

1067.   *"Oh Eve, why did you listen to that lying snake that some-body taught to speak!*

1070. *Our eyes are opened to good and evil all right—good lost and evil got.*
1073. *This kind of knowledge is no good. It leaves us naked, without honor. Our innocence is ruined.*

1077. *The shame in our faces is the result of our dirty lust.*

1080. *How am I going to face God now, or the angels, who I was always so glad to see.*
1082. *Those heavenly beings will blind me now with their brightness.*
1084. *I wish I could go hide in some dark woods where I'd never have to see them again.*

1091. *Let's go get some big leaves to tie around our waists to hide these middle parts that make us feel ashamed and dirty."*

The Parts of each from other, that seem most
To shame obnoxious, and unseemliest seen,
Some Tree whose broad smooth Leaves together sowd,
And girded on our loyns, may cover round
Those middle parts, that this new commer, Shame,
There sit not, and reproach us as unclean.

1099.   So counsel'd hee, and both together went
Into the thickest Wood, there soon they chose
The Figtree, not that kind for Fruit renown'd,
But such as at this day to Indians known
In Malabar or Decan spreds her Armes
Braunching so broad and long, that in the ground
The bended Twigs take root, and Daughters grow
About the Mother Tree, a Pillard shade
High overarch't, and echoing Walks between;

1108. There oft the Indian Herdsman shunning heate
Shelters in coole, and tends his pasturing Herds

1110. At Loopholes cut through thickest shade: Those Leaves
They gatherd, broad as Amazonian Targe,
And with what skill they had, together sowd,
To gird thir waste, vain Covering if to hide

1114. Thir guilt and dreaded shame; O how unlike
To that first naked Glorie. Such of late

1116. Columbus found th' American so girt
With featherd Cincture, naked else and wilde
Among the Trees on Iles and woodie Shores.

1119. Thus fenc't, and as they thought, thir shame in part
Coverd, but not at rest or ease of Mind,

1121. They sate them down to weep, nor onely Teares

1122. Raind at thir Eyes, but high Winds worse within
Began to rise, high Passions, Anger, Hate,
Mistrust, Suspicion, Discord, and shook sore
Thir inward State of Mind, calm Region once
And full of Peace, now tost and turbulent:

1127. For Understanding rul'd not, and the Will
Heard not her lore, both in subjection now
To sensual Appetite, who from beneathe
Usurping over sovran Reason claimd
Superior sway: From thus distemperd brest,

1132. Adam, estrang'd in look and alterd stile,
Speech intermitted thus to Eve renewd.

1134.   Would thou hadst heark'nd to my words, and stai'd
With me, as I besought thee, when that strange
Desire of wandring this unhappie Morn,

1137. I know not whence possessd thee; we had then
Remaind still happie, not as now, despoild
Of all our good, sham'd, naked, miserable.

1140.   Let none henceforth seek needless cause to approve
The Faith they owe; when earnestly they seek
Such proof, conclude, they then begin to faile.

1099.   So they went into the woods and found a kind of fig tree that didn't have any fruit but its leaves were big. They were so big the branches would bend as they grew and touch the ground and take root.

1108. Shepherds in India would take shelter from the heat under these trees.
1110. They sewed these together as best they could and put them on in a feeble attempt to hide their shame.

1114. What a difference from when they were glorious in their nudity.

1116. More recently, Columbus found the first wild Americans covered in a similar way with feathers.

1119. So Adam and Eve felt their shame was somewhat covered, but they were not comforted.
1121. They sat down and cried.
1122. Where their minds were once always peaceful, suddenly new bad emotions were growing, like anger and mistrust.

1127. Their ability to reason was clouded with their new appetites.

1132. Adam didn't look or sound like himself when he spoke to Eve:

1134.   *"Why couldn't you just listen to me in the first place? I don't know where you got that crazy idea to go wandering off alone.*
1137. *We would still be happy. We wouldn't be in this miserable mess.*

1140.   *Why do people always want to prove how good they are? That's asking for trouble."*

1143.   To whom soon mov'd with touch of blame thus Eve.
1144. What words have past thy Lips, Adam severe,
1145. Imput'st thou that to my default, or will
        Of wandring, as thou call'st it, which who knows
1147. But might as ill have happ'nd thou being by,
        Or to thy self perhaps: hadst thou been there,
1149. Or here th' attempt, thou couldst not have discernd
        Fraud in the Serpent, speaking as he spake;
        No ground of enmitie between us known,
        Why hee should mean me ill, or seek to harme.
1153. Was I to have never parted from thy side?
        As good have grown there still a liveless Rib.
1155. Being as I am, why didst not thou the Head
        Command me absolutely not to go,
        Going into such danger as thou saidst?
1158. Too facil then thou didst not much gainsay,
        Nay, didst permit, approve, and fair dismiss.
1160. Hadst thou bin firm and fixt in thy dissent,
        Neither had I transgress'd, nor thou with mee.
1162.   To whom then first incenst Adam repli'd,
1163. Is this the Love, is this the recompence
        Of mine to thee, ingrateful Eve, exprest
1165. Immutable when thou wert lost, not I,
        Who might have liv'd and joyd immortal bliss,
1167. Yet willingly chose rather Death with thee:
1168. And am I now upbraided, as the cause
        Of thy transgressing? not enough severe,
1170. It seems, in thy restraint: what could I more?
1171. I warn'd thee, I admonish'd thee, foretold
        The danger, and the lurking Enemie
        That lay in wait; beyond this had bin force,
1174. And force upon free Will hath here no place.
1175. But confidence then bore thee on, secure
1176. Either to meet no danger, or to finde
        Matter of glorious trial; and perhaps
1178. I also err'd in overmuch admiring
1179. What seemd in thee so perfet, that I thought
        No evil durst attempt thee, but I rue
1181. That errour now, which is become my crime,
        And thou th' accuser. Thus it shall befall
1183. Him who to worth in Women overtrusting
1184. Lets her Will rule; restraint she will not brook,
        And left to her self, if evil thence ensue,
        Shee first his weak indulgence will accuse.
1187.   Thus they in mutual accusation spent
        The fruitless hours, but neither self-condemning,
        And of thir vain contest appeer'd no end.

1143.   Eve became defensive.

1144. *"What a thing to say!*

1145. *So it's all my fault? My crazy idea to go wandering?*

1147. *You don't know. The same thing could've happened if you were there too.*

1149. *You would've been fooled by him the same as me.*

1153. *Did you expect me to stay glued to your side forever? I may as well have stayed one of your ribs.*

1155. *If I'm so helpless, and it was so dangerous, why didn't you stop me from going?*

1158. *You didn't complain much then, you just sent me on my way.*

1160. *Maybe if you were stronger, I wouldn't've gone and none of this would've happened."*

1162.   At this, Adam became really angry.

1163. *"Is this the way you show your love for what I did, you ungrateful woman!*

1165. *I gave you all my love when you were already lost, not me.*

1167. *I willingly chose to die with you.*

1168. *And now you blame me for your sin?*

1170. *What did you expect me to do?*

1171. *I warned you of the danger. I told you not to go. Did you want me to restrain you by force?*

1174. *We don't do things like that here.*

1175. *But you were so sure of yourself.*

1176. *Or you were looking for some kind of glorious victory.*

1178. *Maybe I was wrong in admiring you so much.*

1179. *I thought you were so perfect no evil could ever touch you.*

1181. *That was my mistake—the crime you now accuse me of.*

1183. *That's what happens when you trust a woman and let her have her way.*

1184. *She won't be talked out of it, but if she messes things up, you'll be blamed for not trying hard enough to stop her."*

1187.   They went on fighting like this for hours.

Book X

PARADISE LOST

1.   Meanwhile the hainous and despightfull act
Of Satan done in Paradise, and how
Hee in the Serpent, had perverted Eve,
Her Husband shee, to taste the fatall fruit,

5. Was known in Heav'n; for what can scape the Eye
Of God All-seeing, or deceave his Heart
Omniscient, who in all things wise and just,

8. Hinder'd not Satan to attempt the minde
Of Man, with strength entire, and free will arm'd,
Complete to have discover'd and repulst
Whatever wiles of Foe or seeming Friend.
For still they knew, and ought to have still remember'd
The high Injunction not to taste that Fruit,

14. Whoever tempted; which they not obeying,
Incurr'd, what could they less, the penaltie,
And manifold in sin, deserv'd to fall.

17. Up into Heav'n from Paradise in haste
Th' Angelic Guards ascended, mute and sad

19. For Man, for of his state by this they knew,
Much wondring how the suttle Fiend had stoln

21. Entrance unseen. Soon as th' unwelcome news
From Earth arriv'd at Heaven Gate, displeas'd

23. All were who heard, dim sadness did not spare
That time Celestial visages, yet mixt
With pitie, violated not thir bliss.

26. About the new-arriv'd, in multitudes
Th' ethereal People ran, to hear and know
How all befell: they towards the Throne Supream
Accountable made haste to make appear
With righteous plea, thir utmost vigilance,

31. And easily approv'd; when the most High
Eternal Father from his secret Cloud,
Amidst in Thunder utter'd thus his voice.

34.   Assembl'd Angels, and ye Powers return'd
From unsuccessful charge, be not dismaid,
Nor troubl'd at these tidings from the Earth,

37. Which your sincerest care could not prevent,

38. Foretold so lately what would come to pass,
When first this Tempter cross'd the Gulf from Hell.
I told ye then he should prevail and speed
On his bad Errand, Man should be seduc't
And flatter'd out of all, believing lies

Chapter 10

IN PLAIN ENGLISH

1.   God knew all about how the snake got Eve to eat the forbidden fruit, and how she did the same to her husband.

5. He knows and sees everything.

8. He didn't try to stop Satan because the couple had free will, which was all they needed to defend themselves.

14. But they disobeyed God and now they had to pay the penalty.

17. The guardian angels flew up to Heaven.

19. They knew about man's fall and they were sad. They couldn't figure out how Satan had got past them.

21. Soon the news reached Heaven.

23. Those who heard it were sorry and full of pity (though angels can never really be sad).

26. They surrounded the ones who returned from Earth to hear all about it, but they were hurrying to God's throne to explain how they tried their best to keep Satan out.

31. God reassured them that he was not holding them responsible.

34.   "*Those of you who have just returned from Earth, don't feel bad.*

37. *Nothing you did could have prevented man's fall.*

38. *Back when Satan was headed for Earth, I told you this would happen.*

43. Against his Maker; no Decree of mine
    Concurring to necessitate his Fall,
    Or touch with lightest moment of impulse
    His free Will, to her own inclining left
47. In eevn scale. But fall'n he is, and now
    What rests but that the mortal Sentence pass
    On his transgression Death denounc't that day,
50. Which he presumes already vain and void,
    Because not yet inflicted, as he fear'd,
    By some immediate stroak; but soon shall find
    Forbearance no acquittance ere day end.
    Justice shall not return as bountie scorn'd.
55. But whom send I to judge them? whom but thee
56. Vicegerent Son, to thee I have transferr'd
    All Judgement whether in Heav'n, or Earth, or Hell.
58. Easie it might be seen that I intend
    Mercie collegue with Justice, sending thee
60. Mans Friend his Mediator, his design'd
    Both Ransom and Redeemer voluntarie,
    And destin'd Man himself to judge Man fall'n.
63.   So spake the Father, and unfoulding bright
    Toward the right hand his Glorie, on the Son
    Blaz'd forth unclouded Deitie; he full
    Resplendent all his Father manifest
    Express'd, and thus divinely answer'd milde.
68.   Father Eternal, thine is to decree,
    Mine both in Heav'n and Earth to do thy will
    Supream, that thou in mee thy Son belov'd
71. Mayst ever rest well pleas'd. I go to judge
    On Earth these thy transgressors, but thou knowst,
73. Whoever judg'd, the worst on mee must light,
    When time shall be, for so I undertook
75. Before thee; and not repenting, this obtaine
    Of right, that I may mitigate thir doom
77. On me deriv'd, yet I shall temper so
    Justice with Mercie, as may illustrate most
    Them fully satisfied, and thee appease.
80. Attendance none shall need, nor Train, where none
    Are to behold the Judgement, but the judg'd,
82. Those two; the third best absent is condemn'd,
    Convict by flight, and Rebel to all Law
84. Conviction to the Serpent none belongs.
85.   Thus saying, from his radiant Seat he rose
86. Of high collateral glorie: him Thrones and Powers,
    Princedoms, and Dominations ministrant
    Accompanied to Heaven Gate, from whence
    Eden and all the Coast in prospect lay.
90. Down he descended strait; the speed of Gods
    Time counts not, though with swiftest minutes wing'd.

43. *Nothing I did affected man's fall. I left him entirely to his own free will, without the slightest influence from me.*

47. *But he did fall, and now we have to pass sentence on him, which will be death.*

50. *He's trying to convince himself that it's not going to happen, since he didn't die immediately. He's wrong.*

55. *There's nobody else I would send to judge them but you, my son.*
56. *I gave over all jurisdiction to you in Heaven, Hell, and Earth.*
58. *It's not hard to see that by sending you I want to add mercy to justice.*
60. *You're man's friend. You volunteered to become man yourself one day and be his Savior."*
63.   The Son appeared on the right side of his father with the glory of his father's light shining on him.

68.   He said, "*Father, you just say it and I'll do whatever it takes to please you.*

71. *I'll go judge the sinners.*

73. *But you and I both know I'll be the one who gets the worst of the punishment sooner or later.*
75. *I promised it so they wouldn't have to die, and I have no regrets.*
77. *I'll judge them fairly but mercifully, just the way you want it.*

80. *Nobody needs to come with me to witness this, just those two.*

82. *Satan already convicted himself by running away.*

84. *The snake was just the innocent stooge."*
85.   So he got up and went.
86. Angels accompanied him to Heaven's gate, where you could look down and see Eden.

90. He got to Earth in no time, literally.

92. Now was the Sun in Western cadence low
    From Noon, and gentle Aires due at thir hour
    To fan the Earth now wak'd, and usher in
95. The Eevning coole, when he from wrauth more coole
96. Came the mild Judge and Intercessor both
97. To sentence Man: the voice of God they heard
    Now walking in the Garden, by soft windes
    Brought to thir Ears, while day declin'd, they heard,
    And from his presence hid themselves among
    The thickest Trees, both Man and Wife, till God
    Approaching, thus to Adam call'd aloud.
103.   Where art thou Adam, wont with joy to meet
    My coming seen far off? I miss thee here,
105. Not pleas'd, thus entertaind with solitude,
106. Where obvious dutie erewhile appear'd unsaught:
107. Or come I less conspicuous, or what change
108. Absents thee, or what chance detains? Come forth.
109. He came, and with him Eve, more loth, though first
    To offend, discount'nanc't both, and discompos'd;
111. Love was not in thir looks, either to God
112. Or to each other, but apparent guilt,
    And shame, and perturbation, and despaire,
    Anger, and obstinacie, and hate, and guile.
115. Whence Adam faultring long, thus answer'd brief.
116.   I heard thee in the Garden, and of thy voice
    Affraid, being naked, hid my self. To whom
118. The gracious Judge without revile repli'd.
119.   My voice thou oft hast heard, and hast not fear'd,
    But still rejoyc't, how is it now become
121. So dreadful to thee? that thou art naked, who
122. Hath told thee? hast thou eaten of the Tree
    Whereof I gave thee charge thou shouldst not eat?
124.   To whom thus Adam sore beset repli'd.
    O Heav'n! in evil strait this day I stand
    Before my Judge, either to undergoe
127. My self the total Crime, or to accuse
    My other self, the partner of my life;
    Whose failing, while her Faith to me remaines,
    I should conceal, and not expose to blame
131. By my complaint; but strict necessitie
    Subdues me, and calamitous constraint
    Least on my head both sin and punishment,
    However insupportable, be all
135. Devolv'd; though should I hold my peace, yet thou
    Wouldst easily detect what I conceale.
137. This Woman whom thou mad'st to be my help,
    And gav'st me as thy perfet gift, so good,
    So fit, so acceptable, so Divine,
    That from her hand I could suspect no ill,

92. The sun was setting and gentle breezes brought the cool of the evening.

95. But his temperament was even cooler.

96. In sentencing them, he would play judge and defender at the same time.

97. When they heard his voice they ran and hid.

103.   *"Where are you, Adam?"* he called. *"You're usually so glad to see me you come running.*

105. *I don't like not being greeted by anybody.*

106. *You always come without being called.*

107. *Don't you see me? Can't you hear me?*

108. *What's keeping you? Come out now."*

109. He came out, and Eve too. She was even more reluctant, though she was the first one to sin.

111. Love was not in their looks, either to God or to each other.

112. You could see guilt and shame and anger and despair in them, and how much they wanted a way out of all this.

115. Adam stuttered, and finally said:

116.   *"I heard you coming, and I was afraid—because I was naked."*

118. Without scolding him, God responded:

119.   *"You heard my voice many times before and weren't afraid. Why are you so afraid this time?*

121. *And who told you you're naked?*

122. *Did you eat the fruit I told you not to eat?"*

124.   *"Oh God!"* cried Adam, *"What can I say?*

127. *Should I take on all the blame myself, or accuse the person I love, who I should be protecting?*

131. *It's no use, I'm not strong enough to bear the whole sin and punishment.*

135. *It's no good anyway, trying to keep the truth from you.*

137. *This woman you made to be my wife, your perfect gift, who seemed to do everything right, so good, so heavenly, that I could never expect any harm to come from her—she gave me the fruit, and I ate it."*

And what she did, whatever in it self,
Her doing seem'd to justifie the deed;
Shee gave me of the Tree, and I did eate.

144.   To whom the sovran Presence thus repli'd.
Was shee thy God, that her thou didst obey
Before his voice, or was shee made thy guide,
Superior, or but equal, that to her
Thou did'st resigne thy Manhood, and the Place

149. Wherein God set thee above her made of thee,
And for thee, whose perfection farr excell'd

151. Hers in all real dignitie: Adornd
She was indeed, and lovely to attract
Thy Love, not thy Subjection, and her Gifts

154. Were such as under Government well seem'd,
Unseemly to beare rule, which was thy part

156. And person, hadst thou known thy self aright.

157.   So having said, he thus to Eve in few:
Say Woman, what is this which thou hast done?

159.   To whom sad Eve with shame nigh overwhelm'd,
Confessing soon, yet not before her Judge
Bold or loquacious, thus abasht repli'd.

162.   The Serpent me beguil'd and I did eate.

163.   Which when the Lord God heard, without delay
To Judgement he proceeded on th' accus'd

165. Serpent though brute, unable to transferre
The Guilt on him who made him instrument
Of mischief, and polluted from the end
Of his Creation; justly then accurst,

169. As vitiated in Nature: more to know
Concern'd not Man (since he no further knew)
Nor alter'd his offence; yet God at last

172. To Satan first in sin his doom apply'd
Though in mysterious terms, judg'd as then best:
And on the Serpent thus his curse let fall.

175.   Because thou hast done this, thou art accurst
Above all Cattle, each Beast of the Field;

177. Upon thy Belly groveling thou shalt goe,
And dust shalt eat all the dayes of thy Life.

179. Between Thee and the Woman I will put
Enmitie, and between thine and her Seed;

181. Her Seed shall bruise thy head, thou bruise his heel.

182.   So spake this Oracle, then verifi'd
When Jesus son of Mary second Eve,

184. Saw Satan fall like Lightning down from Heav'n,
Prince of the Aire; then rising from his Grave

186. Spoild Principalities and Powers, triumpht
In open shew, and with ascension bright

188. Captivity led captive through the Aire,
The Realm it self of Satan long usurpt,

144.   God said, "*So you decided to obey her instead of me? Was she your God? Or did you decide to give up your manhood and let her become your master?*

149.   *You're the one I made of higher nobility, to be her superior.*

151.   *I made her lovely to attract your love, not your obedience.*

154.   *She was suited to obey you, not to become your leader.*

156.   *You should've known that was your place.*
157.   *Eve, what did you do?"*

159.   His question was short, and so was her answer:

162.   "*The snake tricked me and I ate the fruit."*
163.   When God heard that, he placed a curse on the snake.

165.   It was only a dumb animal, but it was made unholy when Satan used it.

169.   Man wasn't meant to fully understand or be concerned about the snake at that time.

172.   Because when God judged Satan, he did it in mysterious terms, speaking to the snake:

175.   "*You are the cursed one of all the animals.*

177.   *You'll crawl on your belly and eat dirt.*

179.   *You'll be enemies with the woman and her son.*

181.   *You'll bruise his heel, and he'll bruise your head."*
182.   This was a prophecy that would come true with Jesus, Mary's son.

184.   Jesus would see a vision of when Satan fell from Heaven, and he would be resurrected from his death on the cross.

186.   Everyone would see how he had won against the bad angels.

188.   And the air would be free of Satan's rule.

Whom he shall tread at last under our feet;

191. Eevn hee who now foretold his fatal bruise,
192. And to the Woman thus his Sentence turn'd.
193.   Thy sorrow I will greatly multiplie
By thy Conception; Children thou shalt bring
195. In sorrow forth, and to thy Husbands will
Thine shall submit, hee over thee shall rule.
197.   On Adam last thus judgement he pronounc'd.
Because thou hast heark'nd to the voice of thy Wife,
And eaten of the Tree concerning which
I charg'd thee, saying: Thou shalt not eate thereof,
Curs'd is the ground for thy sake, thou in sorrow
202. Shalt eate thereof all the days of thy Life;
Thorns also and Thistles it shall bring thee forth
Unbid, and thou shalt eate th' Herb of th' Field,
In the sweat of thy Face shalt thou eat Bread,
206. Till thou return unto the ground, for thou
Out of the ground wast taken, know thy Birth,
208. For dust thou art, and shalt to dust returne.
209.   So judg'd he Man, both Judge and Saviour sent,
210. And th' instant stroke of Death denounc't that day
211. Remov'd farr off; then pittying how they stood
Before him naked to the aire, that now
213. Must suffer change, disdain'd not to begin
Thenceforth the form of servant to assume,
As when he wash'd his servants feet so now
As Father of his Familie he clad
Thir nakedness with Skins of Beasts, or slain,
218. Or as the Snake with youthful Coate repaid;
219. And thought not much to cloath his Enemies:
220. Nor hee thir outward onely with the Skins
Of Beasts, but inward nakedness, much more
Opprobrious, with his Robe of righteousness,
Araying cover'd from his Fathers sight.
224. To him with swift ascent he up returnd,
Into his blissful bosom reassum'd
In glory as of old, to him appeas'd
227. All, though all-knowing, what had past with Man
Recounted, mixing intercession sweet.
229. Meanwhile ere thus was sin'd and judg'd on Earth,
Within the Gates of Hell sate Sin and Death,
In counterview within the Gates, that now
Stood open wide, belching outrageous flame
Farr into Chaos, since the Fiend pass'd through,
Sin opening, who thus now to Death began.
235.   O Son, why sit we here each other viewing
236. Idlely, while Satan our great Author thrives
In other Worlds, and happier Seat provides
238. For us his ofspring deare? It cannot be

191. He was foretelling his own fatal injury on the cross. He was the very one telling this story.
192. Then he passed sentence on Eve.
193.   *"Your misery will be multiplied many times by all the children women bring into this hard life through painful childbirth.*

195. *And you'll all have to obey your husbands' rules."*
197.   Then he said to Adam, *"Since you listened to your wife and ate the fruit I told you not to eat, I curse the ground it grew out of.*
202. *You'll be miserable from now on, working till you sweat, trying to grow food out of it. But it will produce a lot of thorny weeds.*
206. *Then your body will return to the ground you came from.*
208. *You were made from dirt, and you'll return to dirt."*
209.   That was God's judgment.
210. And instead of letting man die immediately, he made it a long time before he would die.
211. He felt sorry for how they were naked, now that the weather was going to get worse.
213. He didn't mind acting like their servant (like when he washed the apostles' feet when he was Jesus). He made them some clothes out of animal skins, like a father taking care of his family.
218. Some of the animals he killed, but some he just let their coats grow back, like snakes do.
219. He didn't mind doing this for them even though they had turned against him.
220. But he didn't stop there. He covered the much worse nakedness of their sinful souls with his holiness, so his father wouldn't have to look at it.
224. Then he went back up to Heaven.
227. Even though the Father already knew everything that happened, he told him all about it anyway, adding kind words on behalf of the human couple.
229. Meanwhile, Sin and Death were sitting at the wide open gates of Hell.
235.   Sin was saying to her son, *"What are we doing sitting here staring at each other?*
236. *Your father went out there to find us a better world, and so far no news is good news.*
238. *Because if he ran into trouble, no doubt they'd have driven him back here by now, since no place else would suit their hate for us.*

But that success attends him; if mishap,
Ere this he had return'd, with fury driv'n
By his Avengers, since no place like this
Can fit his punishment, or their revenge.

243. Methinks I feel new strength within me rise,
Wings growing, and Dominion giv'n me large
Beyond this Deep; whatever drawes me on,
Or sympathie, or som connatural force
Powerful at greatest distance to unite
With secret amity things of like kinde

249. By secretest conveyance. Thou my Shade
Inseparable must with mee along:
For Death from Sin no power can separate.

252. But least the difficultie of passing back
Stay his return perhaps over this Gulfe

254. Impassable, Impervious, let us try

255. Adventrous work, yet to thy power and mine
Not unagreeable, to found a path
Over this Maine from Hell to that new World

258. Where Satan now prevailes, a Monument
Of merit high to all th' infernal Host,

260. Easing thir passage hence, for intercourse,
Or transmigration, as thir lot shall lead.

262. Nor can I miss the way, so strongly drawn
By this new felt attraction and instinct.

264.   Whom thus the meager Shadow answerd soon.
Goe whither Fate and inclination strong
Leads thee, I shall not lag behinde, nor erre

267. The way, thou leading, such a sent I draw
Of carnage, prey innumerable, and taste
The savour of Death from all things there that live:

270. Nor shall I to the work thou enterprisest
Be wanting, but afford thee equal aid,

272.   So saying, with delight he snuff'd the smell
Of mortal change on Earth. As when a flock

274. Of ravenous Fowl, though many a League remote,
Against the day of Battel, to a Field,
Where Armies lie encampt, come flying, lur'd
With sent of living Carcasses design'd
For death, the following day, in bloodie fight.
So sented the grim Feature, and upturn'd
His Nostril wide into the murkie Air,
Sagacious of his Quarry from so farr.

282. Then Both from out Hell Gates into the waste
Wide Anarchie of Chaos damp and dark
Flew divers, and with Power (thir Power was great)
Hovering upon the Waters; what they met
Solid or slimie, as in raging Sea

287. Tost up and down, together crowded drove

243. *And furthermore I'm feeling stronger. That tells my intuition he must be okay.*

249. *I'm going to go meet him, and you're coming with me.*

252. *Maybe the difficulty of traveling though chaos is slowing him down.*
254. *Let's try to build a bridge from Hell to Earth.*
255. *A big job, but we have the power to do it.*

258. *What a monument to evil that would be!*

260. *Devils could travel back and forth easily.*

262. *Come on, I feel such a strong attraction I can't miss the way."*

264.   Sin said, "*Let's go. I'll be right behind you.*

267. *I can smell and almost taste all the living things there just waiting for me.*

270. *Don't worry, I can handle the work you're planning."*

272.   He took another sniff.

274. He was like the vultures who can smell living soldiers from miles away, and instinctively know they'll be dead in battle the next day, and provide tomorrow's meal.

282. Then they both flew out into chaos and using their great powers, started to pull together the various wet and dry substances that were being tossed around.

287. From both sides they pushed it all up against the opening at the mouth of Hell to form a solid foundation.

From each side shoaling towards the mouth of Hell.
289. As when two Polar Winds blowing adverse
Upon the Cronian Sea, together drive
291. Mountains of Ice, that stop th' imagin'd way
Beyond Petsora Eastward, to the rich
293. Cathaian Coast. The aggregated Soyle
Death with his Mace petrific, cold and dry,
As with a Trident smote, and fix't as firm
296. As Delos floating once; the rest his look
Bound with Gorgonian rigor not to move,
298. And with Asphaltic slime; broad as the Gate,
299. Deep to the Roots of Hell the gather'd beach
They fasten'd, and the Mole immense wraught on
Over the foaming deep high Archt, a Bridge
Of length prodigious joyning to the Wall
Immovable of this now fenceless world
304. Forfeit to Death; from hence a passage broad,
305. Smooth, easie, inoffensive down to Hell.
306. So, if great things to small may be compar'd,
Xerxes, the Libertie of Greece to yoke,
From Susa his Memnonian Palace high
Came to the Sea, and over Hellespont
Bridging his way, Europe with Asia joyn'd,
And scourg'd with many a stroak th' indignant waves.
312. Now had they brought the work by wondrous Art
Pontifical, a ridge of pendent Rock
314. Over the vext Abyss, following the track
Of Satan, to the self same place where hee
First lighted from his Wing, and landed safe
From out of Chaos to the out side bare
318. Of this round World: with Pinns of Adamant
And Chains they made all fast, too fast they made
320. And durable; and now in little space
The confines met of Empyrean Heav'n
And of this World, and on the left hand Hell
323. With long reach interpos'd; three sev'ral wayes
In sight, to each of these three places led.
325. And now thir way to Earth they had descri'd,
To Paradise first tending, when behold
Satan in likeness of an Angel bright
Betwixt the Centaure and the Scorpion stearing
His Zenith, while the Sun in Aries rose:
330. Disguis'd he came, but those his Children dear
Thir Parent soon discern'd, though in disguise.
332. Hee after Eve seduc't, unminded slunk
Into the Wood fast by, and changing shape
To observe the sequel, saw his guileful act
By Eve, though all unweeting, seconded
336. Upon her Husband, saw thir shame that sought

289. It looked like mountains of ice in the Arctic Ocean being pushed together by winds blowing from opposite sides till they blocked the sea.

291. Hudson never found the Northeast Passage to the Orient, maybe because of just such a blockage.

293. Death struck it solid with his three-pronged staff, firmly anchoring it, the way Zeus attached the floating island of Delos to the sea floor.

296. Then he turned it all to stone just by looking at it—something like the power Medusa was supposed to have.

298. They laid the whole thing over with asphalt as wide as the gate.

299. From this foundation rooted in Hell, they built a great arched highway ending on the solid shell around our universe.

304. Our defenseless world was given over to Death.

305. Now there would forever be a smooth, easy passage from Earth to Hell.

306. It was like when the king of ancient Persia wanted to invade Greece and he made a bridge of boats that connected Europe to Asia across the Dardanelles strait.

312. Now the amazing work of architecture was complete—a big stone bridge suspended across chaos.

314. It followed the same route Satan took to get here, ending exactly where he landed on the shell of the universe.

318. They attached it firmly—too firmly for our good.

320. So now, in addition to Earth's short connection to Heaven, there was this long, left-handed connection to Hell.

323. Each of the three places was connected to the other two.

325. The pair were on their way to Earth when they saw Satan disguised as a good angel, flying between the constellations of Centaur and the Scorpion, while keeping out of the sunlight.

330. He was in disguise but his children knew him right away.

332. After he tempted Eve, he had snuck into the woods and changed back into his normal shape and watched Eve tempt Adam.

336. He saw how they were ashamed of being naked.

337. Vain covertures; but when he saw descend
 The Son of God to judge them terrifi'd
339. Hee fled, not hoping to escape, but shun
 The present, fearing guiltie what his wrauth
341. Might suddenly inflict; that past, return'd
 By Night, and listening where the hapless Paire
 Sate in thir sad discourse, and various plaint,
344. Thence gatherd his own doom, which understood
 Not instant, but of future time. With joy
346. And tidings fraught, to Hell he now return'd,
347. And at the brink of Chaos, neer the foot
 Of this new wondrous Pontifice, unhop't
 Met who to meet him came, his Ofspring dear.
350. Great joy was at thir meeting, and at sight
 Of that stupendious Bridge his joy encreas'd.
 Long hee admiring stood, till Sin, his faire
 Inchanting Daughter, thus the silence broke.
354.   O Parent, these are thy magnific deeds,
 Thy Trophies, which thou view'st as not thine own,
 Thou art thir Author and prime Architect:
357. For I no sooner in my Heart divin'd,
 My Heart, which by a secret harmonie
 Still moves with thine, join'd in connexion sweet,
 That thou on Earth hadst prosper'd, which thy looks
 Now also evidence, but straight I felt
362. Though distant from thee Worlds between, yet felt
 That I must after thee with this thy Son;
 Such fatal consequence unites us three:
365. Hell could no longer hold us in her bounds,
 Nor this unvoyageable Gulf obscure
 Detain from following thy illustrious track.
368. Thou hast atchiev'd our libertie, confin'd
 Within Hell Gates till now, thou us impow'rd
 To fortifie thus farr, and overlay
 With this portentous Bridge the dark Abyss.
372. Thine now is all this World, thy vertue hath won
373. What thy hands builded not, thy Wisdom gain'd
 With odds what Warr hath lost, and fully aveng'd
375. Our foile in Heav'n; here thou shalt Monarch reign,
376. There didst not; there let him still Victor sway,
 As Battel hath adjudg'd, from this new World
378. Retiring, by his own doom alienated,
 And henceforth Monarchie with thee divide
 Of all things parted by th' Empyreal bounds,
 His Quadrature, from thy Orbicular World,
 Or trie thee now more dang'rous to his Throne.
383.   Whom thus the Prince of Darkness answerd glad.
 Fair Daughter, and thou Son and Grandchild both,
 High proof ye now have giv'n to be the Race

337. But when he saw the Son of God come down to judge them he took off.
339. He was afraid of what God might do to him in a sudden fit of anger.
341. That night he came back and eavesdropped again and heard what God had said about him.
344. He didn't understand what God was talking about, with the bruise and all that, but he heard that his punishment would be way in the future.
346. He was glad about that.
347. Now at the foot of this great new bridge he met his children.
350. He was happy to see them. He just stood there admiring the bridge.

354. *"It's all your doing,"* said Sin to Satan, meaning the bridge.

357. *"I could feel in my heart that you were successful on Earth, and now I see I was right.*

362. *As far apart as we were, I knew I had to come to you with your son.*

365. *Hell couldn't hold us anymore, and chaos couldn't stop us.*

368. *You won our freedom for us, and you gave us the power to build this bridge.*

372. *Now the world is yours.*
373. *You really built this bridge. You won back what you lost in war.*

375. *You'll be king on Earth, if not in Heaven.*
376. *Let him be king up there. He's given up on this world anyway.*

378. *With him there and you here, he just may find you a lot more dangerous."*

383. Satan answered, *"My sweet daughter, and you, my son and grandson, you proved yourselves worthy to be my children.*

Of Satan (for I glorie in the name,
Antagonist of Heav'ns Almightie King)
Amply have merited of me, of all

389. Th' Infernal Empire, that so neer Heav'ns dore
Triumphal with triumphal act have met,

391. Mine with this glorious Work, and made one Realm
Hell and this World, one Realm, one Continent

393. Of easie thorough-fare. Therefore while I
Descend through Darkness, on your Rode with ease
To my associate Powers, them to acquaint
With these successes, and with them rejoyce,
You two this way, among these numerous Orbs
All yours, right down to Paradise descend;

399. There dwell and Reign in bliss, thence on the Earth
Dominion exercise and in the Aire,
Chiefly on Man, sole Lord of all declar'd,
Him first make sure your thrall, and lastly kill.
My Substitutes I send ye, and Create
Plenipotent on Earth, of matchless might

405. Issuing from mee: on your joynt vigor now
My hold of this new Kingdom all depends,
Through Sin to Death expos'd by my exploit.

408. If your joynt power prevailes, th' affaires of Hell
No detriment need feare, goe and be strong.

410.   So saying he dismiss'd them, they with speed
Thir course through thickest Constellations held
Spreading thir bane; the blasted Starrs lookt wan,
And Planets, Planet-strook, real Eclips

414. Then sufferd. Th' other way Satan went down
The Causey to Hell Gate; on either side

416. Disparted Chaos over built exclaimd,
And with rebounding surge the barrs assaild,
That scorn'd his indignation: through the Gate,

419. Wide open and unguarded, Satan pass'd,
And all about found desolate; for those
Appointed to sit there, had left thir charge,

422. Flown to the upper World; the rest were all
Farr to the inland retir'd, about the walls
Of Pandæmonium, Citie and proud seate
Of Lucifer, so by allusion calld,
Of that bright Starr to Satan paragond.

427. There kept thir Watch the Legions, while the Grand
In Council sate, sollicitous what chance
Might intercept thir Emperour sent, so hee
Departing gave command, and they observ'd.

431. As when the Tartar from his Russian Foe
By Astracan over the Snowie Plaines
Retires, or Bactrian Sophi from the hornes
Of Turkish Crescent, leaves all waste beyond

389. *Meeting me here like this, right under God's nose, with this terrific bridge!*

391. *You joined up Hell and this world almost like one place.*

393. *While I head back to Hell, you two go down to Earth. It's all yours now.*

399. *Take it over—and mainly, enslave man, and then kill him.*

405. *We've got them where we want them now. Everything depends on you.*

408. *As long as you stay strong, nothing can stop us."*

410.   They headed down into the universe. The stars dimmed as they passed.

414. Satan went the other way towards Hell.

416. On either side of the highway Chaos was making a lot of noise, as if complaining about the bridge.

419. When Satan got there the gate was wide open and nobody was around.

422. Everybody was deep inside around the Palace of Pandemonium.

427. Some were keeping watch outside while the grand council sat inside, as Satan had ordered. They were a little worried about him.

431. Like Tartars retreating across the snow from the Russians, or the Persians retreating from the Turks, these outcasts of Heaven had all retreated from the plains to their little city in the middle of Hell, expecting any minute he might show up.

The Realm of Aladule, in his retreate
To Tauris or Casbeen. So these the late
Heav'n-banisht Host, left desert utmost Hell
Many a dark League, reduc't in careful Watch
Round thir Metropolis, and now expecting
Each hour thir great adventurer from the search
441.   Of Forrein Worlds: he through the midst unmarkt,
In shew Plebeian Angel militant
Of lowest order, past; and from the dore
Of that Plutonian Hall, invisible
445.   Ascended his high Throne, which under state
Of richest texture spred, at th' upper end
447.   Was plac't in regal lustre. Down a while
He sate, and round about him saw unseen:
449.   At last as from a Cloud his fulgent head
And shape Starr bright appeer'd, or brighter, clad
With what permissive glory since his fall
452.   Was left him, or false glitter: All amaz'd
At that so sudden blaze the Stygian throng
Bent thir aspect, and whom they wish'd beheld,
Thir mighty Chief returnd: loud was th' acclaime:
456.   Forth rush'd in haste the great consulting Peers,
Rais'd from thir dark Divan, and with like joy
Congratulant approach'd him, who with hand
459.   Silence, and with these words attention won.
460.   Thrones, Dominations, Princedoms, Vertues, Powers,
For in possession such, not onely of right,
462.   I call ye and declare ye now, returnd
463.   Successful beyond hope, to lead ye forth
Triumphant out of this infernal Pit
Abominable, accurst, the house of woe,
And Dungeon of our Tyrant: Now possess,
As Lords, a spacious World, to our native Heaven
Little inferiour, by my adventure hard
469.   With peril great atchiev'd. Long were to tell
What I have don, what sufferd, with what paine
471.   Voyag'd th' unreal, vast, unbounded deep
Of horrible confusion, over which
473.   By Sin and Death a broad way now is pav'd
To expedite your glorious march; but I
475.   Toild out my uncouth passage, forc't to ride
Th' untractable Abysse, plung'd in the womb
Of unoriginal Night and Chaos wilde,
That jealous of thir secrets fiercely oppos'd
My journey strange, with clamorous uproare
480.   Protesting Fate supreame; thence how I found
The new created World, which fame in Heav'n
Long had foretold, a Fabrick wonderful
483.   Of absolute perfection, therein Man

441. He entered the great palace disguised as an ordinary low rank-
ing soldier angel.

445. He went up to his fancy throne. Nobody noticed him.

447. He sat there awhile.

449. Finally he showed his bright self. (whatever little brightness was
left)

452. They were all startled by the sudden bright light.

456. They ran up to him and cheered.

459. He raised his hand to silence them and began his speech.
460.   *"Thrones, Dominations, Princedoms—I'm calling you by your
old titles because you can consider them yours again.*
462. *I've been successful beyond anything we hoped for.*
463. *I'm going to lead you out of this damned pit up to a place
which is as beautiful as Heaven. And it's all ours.*

469. *It's a long story.*

471. *It was a long, hard journey across chaos.*

473. *Sin and Death built a highway to make the journey easier for you
now.*
475. *But I had to struggle through the wildness of chaos, full of ter-
rible storms and wild uproar.*

480. *Eventually I found the newly created world. What a place!
Beautiful. Perfect.*

483. *Man lives there, happily, thanks to our defeat.*

Plac't in a Paradise, by our exile
485. Made happie: Him by fraud I have seduc'd
486. rom his Creator, and the more to increase
Your wonder, with an Apple; he thereat
488. Offended, worth your laughter, hath giv'n up
Both his beloved Man and all his World,
To Sin and Death a prey, and so to us,
491. Without our hazard, labour, or allarme,
To range in, and to dwell, and over Man
To rule, as over all he should have rul'd.
494. True is, mee also he hath judg'd, or rather
Mee not, but the brute Serpent in whose shape
Man I deceav'd: that which to mee belongs,
497. Is enmity, which he will put between
Mee and Mankinde; I am to bruise his heel;
His Seed, when is not set, shall bruise my head:
A World who would not purchase with a bruise,
501. Or much more grievous pain? Ye have th' account
Of my performance: What remains, ye Gods,
But up and enter now into full bliss.
504.   So having said, a while he stood, expecting
Thir universal shout and high applause
506. To fill his eare, when contrary he hears
On all sides, from innumerable tongues
A dismal universal hiss, the sound
Of public scorn; he wonderd, but not long
510. Had leasure, wondring at himself now more;
His Visage drawn he felt to sharp and spare,
His Armes clung to his Ribs, his Leggs entwining
513. Each other, till supplanted down he fell
A monstrous Serpent on his Belly prone,
515. Reluctant, but in vaine: a greater power
Now rul'd him, punisht in the shape he sin'd,
517. According to his doom: he would have spoke,
But hiss for hiss returnd with forked tongue
To forked tongue, for now were all transform'd
Alike, to Serpents all as accessories
521. To his bold Riot: dreadful was the din
Of hissing through the Hall, thick swarming now
523. With complicated monsters head and taile,
Scorpion and Asp, and Amphisbæna dire,
Cerastes hornd, Hydrus, and Ellops drear,
526. And Dipsas (not so thick swarm'd once the Soil
Bedropt with blood of Gorgon, or the Isle
528. Ophiusa) but still greatest hee the midst,
Now Dragon grown, larger then whom the Sun
Ingenderd in the Pythian Vale on slime,
Huge Python, and his Power no less he seem'd
Above the rest still to retain; they all

485. *But I got him to turn away from his creator.*
486. *And I did it with, of all things, an apple!*

488. *And do you want to laugh? God was so offended by this that he gave up his precious man and all his world to Sin and Death, and to us.*
491. *We get to roam all over that world without fear of harm, and take over everything.*
494. *Of course he passed judgment on me too, or rather on the snake I used to trick man.*

497. *My punishment is that man will be my enemy. It was pre-dicted that I will bruise his heel and he'll bruise my head—a small price to pay for a whole world, don't you think?*

501. *Anyway, that's my story. What's left now but for us to celebrate?"*

504.   He stood up, expecting applause and cheers.

506. Instead he heard a lot of hissing.

510. The next thing he knew he felt his arms sticking to his sides and his legs wrapping around each other, and he fell down.

513. He had become a snake again.
515. God turned him back into the shape he was in when he sinned.

517. He tried to speak but all he could do was hiss like the rest of the crowd. They were all snakes. Because they all shared his guilt.

521. The sound of hissing was awful.

523. The place was a tangled mess of all kinds of snakes—vipers, asps, and some headed at both ends.

526. No tropical island ever had as many snakes. The Gorgon's blood never grew as many.
528. Satan was the biggest one, bigger than the giant python in Greek mythology. He was almost like a dragon.

533. Him follow'd issuing forth to th' open Field,
534. Where all yet left of that revolted Rout
        Heav'n-fall'n, in station stood or just array,
        Sublime with expectation when to see
        In Triumph issuing forth thir glorious Chief;
538. They saw, but other sight instead, a crowd
539. Of ugly Serpents; horror on them fell,
        And horrid sympathie; for what they saw,
        They felt themselvs now changing; down thir arms,
542. Down fell both Spear and Shield, down they as fast,
        And the dire hiss renew'd, and the dire form
        Catcht by Contagion, like in punishment,
        As in thir crime. Thus was th' applause they meant,
        Turn'd to exploding hiss, triumph to shame
        Cast on themselves from thir own mouths. There stood
548. A Grove hard by, sprung up with this thir change,
        His will who reigns above, to aggravate
        Thir penance, laden with Fruit like that
        Which grew in Paradise, the bait of Eve
        Us'd by the Tempter: on that prospect strange
        Thir earnest eyes they fix'd, imagining
        For one forbidden Tree a multitude
        Now ris'n, to work them furder woe or shame;
556. Yet parcht with scalding thurst and hunger fierce,
        Though to delude them sent, could not abstain,
558. But on they rould in heaps, and up the Trees
559. Climbing, sat thicker then the snakie locks
        That curld Megæra: greedily they pluck'd
561. The Frutage fair to sight, like that which grew
        Neer that bituminous Lake where Sodom flam'd;
563. This more delusive, not the touch, but taste
        Deceav'd; they fondly thinking to allay
        Thir appetite with gust, instead of Fruit
        Chewd bitter Ashes, which th' offended taste
567. With spattering noise rejected: oft they assayd,
568. Hunger and thirst constraining, drugd as oft,
        With hatefullest disrelish writh'd thir jaws
        With soot and cinders fill'd; so oft they fell
571. Into the same illusion, not as Man
572. Whom they triumph'd once lapst. Thus were they plagu'd
        And worn with Famin, long and ceasless hiss,
        Till thir lost shape, permitted, they resum'd,
575. Yearly enjoynd, some say, to undergo
        This annual humbling certain number'd days,
        To dash thir pride, and joy for Man seduc't.
578. However some tradition they dispers'd
        Among the Heathen of thir purchase got,
580. And Fabl'd how the Serpent, whom they calld
        Ophion with Eurynome, the wide-

533. They all followed him outside.
534. All the soldiers standing out there were expecting to see their king come out in all his glory.

538. Instead a swarm of ugly snakes came out.
539. They were in for a bigger shock, though, when they felt themselves turn into snakes too.

542. Spears and shields and soldiers were falling down all over the place, and there was more hissing.

548. Then God made a grove of fruit trees spring up, like the ones in Paradise. (He wasn't done torturing them yet.)

556. They all suddenly got very hungry and thirsty.
558. The fruit trees looked irresistible, so they crawled over to them and up the trunks.
559. They were hanging from the branches like the snakes that grew out of Medusa's head.
561. When God burned the sinful city of Sodom, there were some fruit trees left by the Dead Sea. And if you picked the fruit, it would turn to ashes in your hand.
563. This time, it was when they went to eat the fruit that they found their mouths full of bitter ashes.
567. They spit them out.
568. Then they'd get hungry again and couldn't resist eating the fruit again, and again it would turn into soot and ashes in their mouths.
571. Man fell into temptation once, but these devils were fooled over and over again.
572. This went on a long time until God permitted them to return to their normal shapes.
575. Some people believe God makes them suffer like this every year for a certain number of days, to cut their joy over man's fall.

578. Others think they came right down and started to spread out on Earth.
580. And they would tell all the pagans that the snake and Eve were the first gods of Olympus, who were thrown out by Saturn and his wife—all before Jupiter was born.

Encroaching Eve perhaps, had first the rule
Of high Olympus, thence by Saturn driv'n
And Ops, ere yet Dictæan Jove was born.

585. Mean while in Paradise the hellish pair
Too soon arriv'd, Sin there in power before,
Once actual, now in body, and to dwell
Habitual habitant; behind her Death

589. Close following pace for pace, not mounted yet
On his pale Horse: to whom Sin thus began.

591.   Second of Satan sprung, all conquering Death,
What thinkst thou of our Empire now, though earnd
With travail difficult, not better farr
Then stil at Hels dark threshold to have sate watch,
Unnam'd, undreaded, and thy self half starv'd?

596.   Whom thus the Sin-born Monster answerd soon.
To mee, who with eternal Famin pine,
Alike is Hell, or Paradise, or Heaven,
There best, where most with ravin I may meet;
Which here, though plenteous, all too little seems
To stuff this Maw, this vast unhide-bound Corps.

602.   To whom th' incestuous Mother thus repli'd.
Thou therefore on these Herbs, and Fruits, and Flours
Feed first, on each Beast next, and Fish, and Fowle,
No homely morsels, and whatever thing
The Sithe of Time mowes down, devour unspar'd,

607. Till I in Man residing through the Race,
His thoughts, his looks, words, actions all infect,
And season him thy last and sweetest prey.

610.   This said, they both betook them several wayes,
Both to destroy, or unimmortal make
All kinds, and for destruction to mature

613. Sooner or later; which th' Almightie seeing,
From his transcendent Seat the Saints among,
To those bright Orders utterd thus his voice.

616.   See with what heat these Dogs of Hell advance
To waste and havoc yonder World, which I
So fair and good created, and had still

619. Kept in that State, had not the folly of Man
Let in these wastful Furies, who impute
Folly to mee, so doth the Prince of Hell
And his Adherents, that with so much ease
I suffer them to enter and possess
A place so heav'nly, and conniving seem
To gratifie my scornful Enemies,

626. That laugh, as if transported with some fit
Of Passion, I to them had quitted all,
At random yielded up to their misrule;

629. And know not that I call'd and drew them thither
My Hell-hounds, to lick up the draff and filth

585. Meanwhile Sin and Death arrived in Paradise—sin already there in action, now in person.

589. Death wasn't riding his pale horse yet.

591. *"Well, how do you like your new home?"* Sin asked her son.

596. *"Paradise, Heaven, Hell—it's all the same to me,"* he answered. *"I'll go wherever I can find the most prey, which I see too little of around here to feed my hungry mouth."*

602. *"You can start with these fruits and flowers,"* said his mother. *"Then eat the animals and fish and birds that get old and weak. That ought to hold you for a while.*

607. *Man will be your last and sweetest meal when I get through with him."*

610. Then they went their separate ways to destroy life, or remove its immortality so everything would die sooner or later.

613. God was watching them and said:

616. *"Look at those dogs of Hell getting ready to lay waste and ruin everything in the world I made so beautiful.*

619. *They laugh at me like Satan does, that I would turn over the world to them so easily. But it's man's foolishness that caused this.*

626. *They think I just gave up on everything in some fit of anger.*

629. *They don't know that I sent them there to suck up all the filth that covers everything that is not pure anymore because of man's sin.*

Which mans polluting Sin with taint hath shed
On what was pure, till cramm'd and gorg'd, nigh burst
With suckt and glutted offal, at one sling

634. Of thy victorious Arm, well-pleasing Son,
Both Sin, and Death, and yawning Grave at last
Through Chaos hurld, obstruct the mouth of Hell
For ever, and seal up his ravenous Jawes.

638. Then Heav'n and Earth renewd shall be made pure
To sanctitie that shall receive no staine:
Till then the Curse pronounc't on both precedes.

641.   He ended, and the Heav'nly Audience loud
Sung Halleluia, as the sound of Seas,
Through multitude that sung: Just are thy ways,
Righteous are thy Decrees on all thy Works;
Who can extenuate thee? Next, to the Son,
Destin'd restorer of Mankind, by whom
New Heav'n and Earth shall to the Ages rise,
Or down from Heav'n descend. Such was thir song,

649. While the Creator calling forth by name
His mightie Angels gave them several charge,
As sorted best with present things. The Sun

652. Had first his precept so to move, so shine,
As might affect the Earth with cold and heat
Scarce tollerable, and from the North to call
Decrepit Winter, from the South to bring
Solstitial summers heat. To the blanc Moone

657. Her office they prescrib'd, to th' other five
Thir planetarie motions and aspects
In Sextile, Square, and Trine, and Opposite,
Of noxious efficacie, and when to joyne
In Synod unbenigne, and taught the fixt
Thir influence malignant when to showre,
Which of them rising with the Sun, or falling,

664. Should prove tempestuous: To the Winds they set
Thir corners, when with bluster to confound
Sea, Aire, and Shoar, the Thunder when to rowle
With terror through the dark Aereal Hall.

668. Some say he bid his Angels turne ascanse
The Poles of Earth twice ten degrees and more
From the Suns Axle; they with labour push'd
Oblique the Centric Globe: Som say the Sun

672. Was bid turn Reines from th' Equinoctial Rode
Like distant breadth to Taurus with the Seav'n
Atlantick Sisters, and the Spartan Twins
Up to the Tropic Crab; thence down amaine
By Leo and the Virgin and the Scales,
As deep as Capricorne, to bring in change

678. Of Seasons to each Clime; else had the Spring
Perpetual smil'd on Earth with vernant Flours,

634. *Someday when they're finished, you, my son, will toss them both back into Hell. Their over-stuffed bodies will seal up the entrance forever.*

638. *Then the whole Earth will be clean and pure again."*

641.   The angels cheered and sang about how nobody could undermine God's works for long, and that he and his son would restore everything to its original glory.

649. For now, though, God called together certain angels to go make certain necessary changes on Earth.

652. First, the way the sun shined on the Earth had to be changed so it would produce weather so cold in winter and so hot in summer it would be almost unbearable.

657. Then the moon and planets and stars were arranged to influence conditions on Earth.

664. The winds were set to create terrible storms and raise damaging seas.

668. Some people think this is when God had the angels tilt the axis of the Earth.

672. That's how the seasons would change. (Some used to believe he did it by changing the sun's movements around the Earth.)

678. Otherwise there would have been unending springtime all over the world, even at the south and north poles.

Equal in Days and Nights, except to those
Beyond the Polar Circles; to them Day
682. Had unbenighted shon, while the low Sun
To recompence his distance, in thir sight
Had rounded still th' Horizon, and not known
Or East or West, which had forbid the Snow
From cold Estotiland, and South as farr
Beneath Magellan. At that tasted Fruit
688. The Sun, as from Thyestean Banquet, turn'd
His course intended; else how had the World
Inhabited, though sinless, more then now,
Avoided pinching cold and scorching heate?
692. These changes in the Heav'ns, though slow, produc'd
Like change on Sea and Land, sideral blast,
Vapour, and Mist, and Exhalation hot,
Corrupt and Pestilent: Now from the North
696. Of Norumbega, and the Samoed shoar
Bursting thir brazen Dungeon, armd with ice
And snow and haile and stormie gust and flaw,
Boreas and Cæcias and Argestes loud
And Thrascias rend the Woods and Seas upturn;
With adverse blast up-turns them from the South
Notus and Afer black with thundrous Clouds
From Serraliona; thwart of these as fierce
Forth rush the Levant and the Ponent Windes
Eurus and Zephir with thir lateral noise,
706. Sirocco, and Libecchio. Thus began
707. Outrage from liveless things; but Discord first
Daughter of Sin, among th' irrational,
Death introduc'd through fierce antipathie:
Beast now with Beast gan war, and Fowle with Fowle,
And Fish with Fish; to graze the Herb all leaving,
712. Devourd each other; nor stood much in awe
713. Of Man, but fled him, or with count'nance grim
Glar'd on him passing: these were from without
715. The growing miseries, which Adam saw
Alreadie in part, though hid in gloomiest shade,
717. To sorrow abandond, but worse felt within,
And in a troubl'd Sea of passion tost,
Thus to disburd'n sought with sad complaint.
720.   O miserable of happie! is this the end
Of this new glorious World, and mee so late
The Glory of that Glory, who now becom
Accurst of blessed, hide me from the face
Of God, whom to behold was then my highth
725. Of happiness: yet well, if here would end
The miserie, I deserv'd it, and would beare
My own deservings; but this will not serve;
728. All that I eat or drink, or shall beget,

682. At the poles the sun would travel low across the horizon and shine continuously all day, with no night. So it never would get cold enough to snow.

688. But the sun turned away his face when man sinned, as it did in the Greek myth when Atreus murdered his brother's sons and served them to him at a feast.

692. These gradual changes in the sky caused all kinds of dangerous conditions on land and sea.

696. Blizzards came from the north, and from the south hurricanes and tornadoes.

706. This was the turmoil that happened among lifeless things.
707. But then Discord, Sin's first daughter, working together with Death, made the animals start to fight among themselves.

712. Instead of grazing in the fields, they started preying on each other.
713. They watched man suspiciously now, and ran away when he came close.
715. Adam noticed some of these bad changes around him, while he hid in the shadows.
717. But what he felt inside was much worse.
720.   *"Is this where happiness ends?"* he asked himself. *"Will I never get to see God again?*

725. *It would be okay if it ended there, since that's what I deserve, but it won't end there.*

728. *That happy blessing he once gave: 'Increase and multiply' is now a curse. What else can I multiply but curses on my own head?*

Is propagated curse. O voice once heard
Delightfully, Encrease and multiply,
Now death to hear! for what can I encrease
Or multiplie, but curses on my head?

733.   Who of all Ages to succeed, but feeling
The evil on him brought by me, will curse
My Head, Ill fare our Ancestor impure,
For this we may thank Adam; but his thanks
Shall be the execration; so besides
Mine own that bide upon me, all from mee
Shall with a fierce reflux on mee redound,
On mee as on thir natural center light

741.   Heavie, though in thir place. O fleeting joyes
Of Paradise, deare bought with lasting woes!

743.   Did I request thee, Maker, from my Clay
To mould me Man, did I sollicite thee

745.   From darkness to promote me, or here place
In this delicious Garden? as my Will

747.   Concurd not to my being, it were but right
And equal to reduce me to my dust,
Desirous to resigne, and render back
All I receav'd, unable to performe
Thy terms too hard, by which I was to hold
The good I sought not. To the loss of that,

753.   Sufficient penaltie, why hast thou added
The sense of endless woes? inexplicable

755.   Thy Justice seems; yet to say truth, too late,

756.   I thus contest; then should have been refusd
Those terms whatever, when they were propos'd:

758.   Thou didst accept them; wilt thou enjoy the good,
Then cavil the conditions? and though God

760.   Made thee without thy leave, what if thy Son
Prove disobedient, and reprov'd, retort,
Wherefore didst thou beget me? I sought it not

763.   Wouldst thou admit for his contempt of thee
That proud excuse? yet him not thy election,
But Natural necessity begot.

766.   God made thee of choice his own, and of his own
To serve him, thy reward was of his grace,
Thy punishment then justly is at his Will.
Be it so, for I submit, his doom is fair,

770.   That dust I am, and shall to dust returne:
O welcom hour whenever! why delayes
His hand to execute what his Decree
Fixd on this day? why do I overlive,

774.   Why am I mockt with death, and length'nd out
To deathless pain? how gladly would I meet
Mortalitie my sentence, and be Earth
Insensible, how glad would lay me down

733. *All my descendants will have me to thank for all their misery.*

741. *The short-lived joys of Paradise are exchanged for long-lasting misery.*

743. *But I didn't ask to be born.*

745. *You decided to make me, God, and put me in this Paradise.*

747. *The terms you set turned out to be too hard for me. So go ahead and turn me into dust again.*

753. *Isn't that enough? Why do you have to make endless misery for everybody?*

755. *What you're doing makes no sense to me.*

756. *But it's a little late for me to complain, I know. I should've refused the terms when they were offered.*

758. *But I accepted them. I enjoyed the goods, now I'm trying to argue the price.*

760. *What if I had a son who misbehaved, then used the lame excuse that he didn't ask to be born?*

763. *Would I accept that excuse? Not likely, even though in that case I didn't plan his birth.*

766. *But God chose to make me, and reward me when I was good. It's only fair he gets to punish me when I'm bad.*

770. *So let me be turned to dust. I welcome it. But what's taking so long?*

774. *Why do I have to go on suffering? How glad I would be to just lay down and die.*

778. As in my Mothers lap! There I should rest
     And sleep secure; his dreadful voice no more
     Would Thunder in my ears, no fear of worse
     To mee and to my ofspring would torment me
782. With cruel expectation. Yet one doubt
783. Pursues me still, least all I cannot die,
784. Least that pure breath of Life, the Spirit of Man
     Which God inspir'd, cannot together perish
786. With this corporeal Clod; then in the Grave,
     Or in some other dismal place who knows
     But I shall die a living Death? O thought
789. Horrid, if true! yet why? it was but breath
790. Of Life that sinn'd; what dies but what had life
     And sin? the Bodie properly hath neither.
792. All of me then shall die: let this appease
793. The doubt, since humane reach no further knows.
794. For though the Lord of all be infinite,
     Is his wrauth also? be it, man is not so,
     But mortal doom'd. How can he exercise
     Wrath without end on Man whom Death must end?
798. Can he make deathless Death? that were to make
     Strange contradiction, which to God himself
     Impossible is held, as Argument
801. Of weakness, not of Power. Will he, draw out,
     For angers sake, finite to infinite
     In punisht man, to satisfie his rigour
     Satisfi'd never; that were to extend
     His Sentence beyond dust and Natures Law,
     By which all Causes else according still
     To the reception of thir matter act,
     Not to th' extent of thir own Spheare. But say
809. That Death be not one stroak, as I suppos'd,
     Bereaving sense, but endless miserie
811. From this day onward, which I feel begun
     Both in me, and without me, and so last
813. To perpetuitie; Ay me, that fear
     Comes thundring back with dreadful revolution
     On my defensless head; both Death and I
     Am found Eternal, and incorporate both,
817. Nor I on my part single, in mee all
     Posteritie stands curst: Fair Patrimonie
819. That I must leave ye, Sons; O were I able
     To waste it all my self, and leave ye none!
821. So disinherited how would ye bless
822. Me now your curse! Ah, why should all mankind
     For one mans fault thus guiltless be condemn'd,
824. If guiltless? But from mee what can proceed,
     But all corrupt, both Mind and Will deprav'd,
     Not to do onely, but to will the same

778. *Not to have to hear his awful voice in my ear. Not to have to be afraid of what might come to me and my descendants.*

782. *But there's one thing that really scares me.*
783. *What if I can't die?*
784. *What if the spirit God placed in me can't be destroyed the way my body can?*
786. *Then I'll be trapped in my grave, or some other dark place, dead but still alive!*
789. *What a horrible nightmare that would be!*
790. *But it was my soul that sinned, not just my body.*

792. *Then all of me should die.*
793. *I can't see it any other way.*
794. *God is infinite. But man is not. Would God be eternally angry at man? But how could he punish man endlessly if death would end man?*
798. *Can he make death live forever? That makes no sense.*

801. *Would he extend man's punishment beyond death, disregarding the laws of nature that he made.*

809. *But maybe death is not a one time thing. Maybe it's just endless misery from that day forward.*
811. *Which feels like it's already begun, inside me and all around me.*

813. *Oh God, I'm back to that terrible thought, that death lives forever.*

817. *And not just for me. That curse will be with all my descendants.*

819. *Oh, sons, how I wish I could take it all myself, and leave none for you.*
821. *You'd bless me instead of curse me.*
822. *Why should all mankind suffer for one man's sin when they're all innocent?*
824. *But will they be innocent? What kind of sons will I have? They'll all inherit my sinful faults.*

With me? how can they then acquitted stand
828. In sight of God? Him after all Disputes
829. Forc't I absolve: all my evasions vain
And reasonings, though through Mazes, lead me still
But to my own conviction: first and last
On mee, mee onely, as the sourse and spring
Of all corruption, all the blame lights due;
834. So might the wrauth. Fond wish! couldst thou support
That burden heavier then the Earth to bear
Then all the World much heavier, though divided
837. With that bad Woman? Thus what thou desir'st,
And what thou fearst, alike destroyes all hope
839. Of refuge, and concludes thee miserable
Beyond all past example and future,
To Satan only like both crime and doom.
842. O Conscience, into what Abyss of fears
And horrors hast thou driv'n me; out of which
I find no way, from deep to deeper plung'd!
845.   Thus Adam to himself lamented loud
846. Through the still Night, not now, as ere man fell,
Wholsom and cool, and mild, but with black Air
Accompanied, with damps and dreadful gloom,
Which to his evil Conscience represented
850. All things with double terror: On the ground
Outstretcht he lay, on the cold ground, and oft
Curs'd his Creation, Death as oft accus'd
Of tardie execution, since denounc't
854. The day of his offence. Why comes not Death,
Said hee, with one thrice acceptable stroke
856. To end me? Shall Truth fail to keep her word,
Justice Divine not hast'n to be just?
858. But Death comes not at call, Justice Divine
Mends not her slowest pace for prayers or cries.
860. O Woods, O Fountains, Hillocks, Dales and Bowrs,
With other echo late I taught your Shades
To answer, and resound farr other Song.
863. Whom thus afflicted when sad Eve beheld,
Desolate where she sate, approaching nigh,
Soft words to his fierce passion she assay'd:
But her with stern regard he thus repell'd.
867.   Out of my sight, thou Serpent, that name best
868. Befits thee with him leagu'd, thy self as false
And hateful; nothing wants, but that thy shape,
Like his, and colour Serpentine may shew
871. Thy inward fraud, to warn all Creatures from thee
Henceforth; least that too heav'nly form, pretended
To hellish falshood, snare them. But for thee
874. I had persisted happie, had not thy pride
875. And wandring vanitie, when lest was safe,

828. *What good is it trying to argue against God's ways. He's always right in the end.*
829. *I go round in circles, and it always comes back to me. It's all my fault.*

834. *And here I am asking for all the punishment to fall on me—some joke! How could I bear that weight, heavier than the whole Earth, even if I do share it with that bad woman.*
837. *Everything is hopeless.*

839. *I'm more miserable than any past or future example you can name, except maybe Satan.*

842. *My conscience has sent me into a dark pit of fear, with no way out."*

845.   All through the night Adam was crying out these sad thoughts.
846. The night wasn't cool and mild like before man fell. It was black and damp and gloomy, and made his thoughts that much more terrifying.
850. He was lying stretched out on the cold ground.

854. *"Why don't I die!"* he cried.

856. *"Isn't Truth going to keep her word? What's Justice waiting for?*

858. *But death doesn't come when you want it to. And justice won't hurry up one bit for all your prayers or cries.*
860. *What a different song I used to sing to these hills and valleys, and what a different echo they sounded, not so long ago."*

863. Eve was sitting not far off. It broke her heart to see him like this. She went over to him and tried to comfort him with kind words.
867.   *"Get out of my sight, you snake!"* he shouted.
868. *"The only difference between you and him is your shape!*
871. *With you it's that too heavenly form that snares unsuspecting creatures.*

874. *If it wasn't for you I'd still be happy.*
875. *You wouldn't listen. You had to be in the spotlight, even if your only audience was the devil himself.*

Rejected my forewarning, and disdain'd
Not to be trusted, longing to be seen
Though by the Devil himself, him overweening
To over-reach, but with the Serpent meeting

880. Fool'd and beguil'd, by him thou, I by thee,
881. To trust thee from my side, imagin'd wise,
Constant, mature, proof against all assaults,
And understood not all was but a shew
Rather then solid vertu, all but a Rib
Crooked by nature, bent, as now appears,
More to the part sinister from me drawn,
Well if thrown out, as supernumerarie

888. To my just number found. O why did God,
Creator wise, that peopl'd highest Heav'n
With Spirits Masculine, create at last
This noveltie on Earth, this fair defect
Of Nature, and not fill the World at once
With Men as Angels without Feminine,

894. Or find some other way to generate
Mankind? this mischief had not then befall'n,
896. And more that shall befall, innumerable
897. Disturbances on Earth through Femal snares,
And straight conjunction with this Sex: for either
He never shall find out fit Mate, but such
As some misfortune brings him, or mistake,
Or whom he wishes most shall seldom gain
Through her perversness, but shall see her gaind
By a farr worse, or if she love, withheld
By Parents, or his happiest choice too late
Shall meet, alreadie linkt and Wedlock-bound
To a fell Adversarie, his hate or shame:

907. Which infinite calamitie shall cause
To Humane life, and houshold peace confound.
909. He added not, and from her turn'd, but Eve
910. Not so repulst, with Tears that ceas'd not flowing,
And tresses all disorderd, at his feet
912. Fell humble, and imbracing them, besaught
His peace, and thus proceeded in her plaint.
914. Forsake me not thus, Adam, witness Heav'n
What love sincere, and reverence in my heart
916. I beare thee, and unweeting have offended,
Unhappilie deceav'd; thy suppliant
918. I beg, and clasp thy knees; bereave me not,
Whereon I live, thy gentle looks, thy aid,
Thy counsel in this uttermost distress,
921. My onely strength and stay: forlorn of thee,
Whither shall I betake me, where subsist?
923. While yet we live, scarse one short hour perhaps,
Between us two let there be peace, both joyning,

880. *He fooled you, and you fooled me.*

881. *I trusted you, I thought you were smart, mature, but it was all a joke, a rib, a crooked one, one that should have been thrown out as useless.*

888. *Why did God have to create this novelty, this pretty but defective creature. Why not fill the Earth with masculine types only, like he did the angels?*

894. *He could've found some other way for people to reproduce.*

896. *That would have avoided a lot of trouble.*

897. *Just wait till men start getting involved with females, like when they end up marrying the ones who turn out to be no good, or desire the ones they can never get. A man will have to watch her give in to someone lower than he is, or if she loves him, her parents will come between them, or else he'll meet her too late, when she's already married.*

907. *It will be impossible to enjoy a peaceful life."*

909. He turned away, but Eve would not give up.

910. Her hair was all wild and tears were running down her face.

912. She got down and put her arms around his feet.

914. She was begging him, "*Don't turn away from me, Adam. Heaven knows how much I love you.*

916. *I never meant to hurt you.*

918. *You can't desert me at a time like this.*

921. *You're my strength. Without you where would I be?*

923. *While we're still alive—even if it's only for one short hour—let there be peace between us.*

925.   As joyn'd in injuries, one enmitie
       Against a Foe by doom express assign'd us,
       That cruel Serpent: On me exercise not
928.   Thy hatred for this miserie befall'n,
       On me alreadie lost, mee then thy self
930.   More miserable; both have sin'd, but thou
       Against God onely, I against God and thee,
932.   And to the place of judgment will return,
       There with my cries importune Heaven, that all
       The sentence from thy head remov'd may light
       On me, sole cause to thee of all this woe,
       Mee mee onely just object of his ire.
937.   She ended weeping, and her lowlie plight,
       Immovable till peace obtain'd from fault
       Acknowledg'd and deplor'd, in Adam wraught
       Commiseration; soon his heart relented
       Towards her, his life so late and sole delight,
       Now at his feet submissive in distress,
       Creature so faire his reconcilement seeking,
       His counsel whom she had displeas'd, his aide;
945.   As one disarm'd, his anger all he lost,
       And thus with peaceful words uprais'd her soon.
947.   Unwarie, and too desirous, as before,
       So now of what thou knowst not, who desir'st
949.   The punishment all on thy self; alas,
       Beare thine own first, ill able to sustaine
       His full wrauth whose thou feelst as yet lest part,
       And my displeasure bearst so ill. If Prayers
953.   Could alter high Decrees, I to that place
       Would speed before thee, and be louder heard,
       That on my head all might be visited,
       Thy frailtie and infirmer Sex forgiv'n,
       To me committed and by me expos'd.
958.   But rise, let us no more contend, nor blame
960.   Each other, blam'd enough elsewhere, but strive
       In offices of Love, how we may light'n
962.   Each others burden in our share of woe;
       Since this days Death denounc't, if ought I see,
       Will prove no sudden, but a slow-pac't evill,
       A long days dying to augment our paine,
       And to our Seed (O hapless Seed!) deriv'd.
966.   To whom thus Eve, recovering heart, repli'd.
       Adam, by sad experiment I know
       How little weight my words with thee can finde,
       Found so erroneous, thence by just event
       Found so unfortunate; nevertheless,
       Restor'd by thee, vile as I am, to place
       Of new acceptance, hopeful to regaine
973.   Thy Love, the sole contentment of my heart

925.   *We both have the same enemy—the snake.*

928.   *Don't hate me. I'm already more miserable than you.*

930.   *We both sinned, but you only did it against God, I did it against God and you.*

932.   *I'll go back where he judged us and beg him to excuse you and put all the punishment on me. I'm the only one to blame."*

937.   She broke down and cried. Adam was moved. He couldn't stand to see the woman he had loved so much in such a pitiful state.

945.   He lost all his anger. He gently lifted her to her feet.

947.   *"There you go again,"* He said, *"ready to head off straight into things you know nothing about.*

949.   *You want to take on all God's anger all by yourself, when you can hardly even stand me being mad at you.*

953.   *But if prayers could change anything, believe me, I'd be the first to go to him and take all the blame myself for not keeping you safe as I should have done.*

958.   *Come on, get up. Let's not fight anymore.*

960.   *We should be supporting each other through this trouble.*

962.   *It looks like death won't be coming anytime soon. I think we're in for a long, drawn-out punishment, not only for us but for all our unfortunate descendants."*

966.   Eve felt a little better. She said, *"Adam, I don't blame you if you don't want to listen to me anymore, but there's something I've got to say.*

973.   *I love you so much, and I want to end this misery for both of us.*

Living or dying, from thee I will not hide
What thoughts in my unquiet brest are ris'n,
Tending to some relief of our extremes,
Or end, though sharp and sad, yet tolerable,
As in our evils, and of easier choice.

979. If care of our descent perplex us most,
Which must be born to certain woe, devourd
By Death at last, and miserable it is
To be to others cause of misery,
Our own begotten, and of our Loines to bring
Into this cursed World a woful Race,
That after wretched Life must be at last
Food for so foule a Monster, in thy power

987. It lies, yet ere Conception to prevent
The Race unblest, to being yet unbegot.
Childless thou art, Childless remaine:
So Death shall be deceav'd his glut, and with us two
Be forc'd to satisfie his Rav'nous Maw.

992. But if thou judge it hard and difficult,
Conversing, looking, loving, to abstain
From Loves due Rites, Nuptial imbraces sweet,
And with desire to languish without hope,
Before the present object languishing
With like desire, which would be miserie
And torment less then none of what we dread,

999. Then both our selves and Seed at once to free
From what we fear for both, let us make short,

1001. Let us seek Death, or he not found, supply
With our own hands his Office on our selves;

1003. Why stand we longer shivering under feares,
That shew no end but Death, and have the power,

1005. Of many ways to die the shortest choosing,
Destruction with destruction to destroy.

1007.   She ended heer, or vehement despaire
Broke off the rest; so much of Death her thoughts

1009. Had entertaind, as di'd her Cheeks with pale.

1010. But Adam with such counsel nothing sway'd,
To better hopes his more attentive minde
Labouring had rais'd, and thus to Eve repli'd.

1013.   Eve, thy contempt of life and pleasure seems
To argue in thee somthing more sublime
And excellent then what thy minde contemnes;
But self-destruction therefore saught, refutes
That excellence thought in thee, and implies,
Not thy contempt, but anguish and regret
For loss of life and pleasure overlov'd.

1020. Or if thou covet death, as utmost end
Of miserie, so thinking to evade

1022. The penaltie pronounc't, doubt not but God

979. *And what's more, we don't want to bring a whole race of people into this world full of pain and sorrow.*

987. *We have the power to prevent this. We don't have to have any children.*

992. *And if we can't stand the thought of living together and never being able to make love again, then we can end it all right now.*

999. *We can set ourselves and all our descendants free.*

1001. *Let's go look for Death, and if we can't find him, we don't need him, we can kill ourselves.*

1003. *Why should we put up with so much suffering that's only going to end up in death anyway?*

1005. *There are lots of ways we could kill ourselves. We'll just pick the quickest way."*

1007. She was too upset to continue.

1009. Her cheeks were pale.

1010. But Adam was thinking more clearly now.

1013. *"Eve, it's wise of you to know that there are things more important than life, but when you talk about suicide, that shows the opposite—that you loved pleasure too much and can't stand to lose it.*

1020. *Or maybe you think death is a way to avoid the punishment God sentenced us to.*

1022. *But God is smarter than that. I'm afraid it would be even worse for us if we defy him like that. He'd make death a lasting thing we could never escape.*

      Hath wiselier arm'd his vengeful ire then so
      To be forestall'd; much more I fear least Death
      So snatcht will not exempt us from the paine
      We are by doom to pay; rather such acts
      Of contumacie will provoke the highest
      To make death in us live: Then let us seek
1029. Some safer resolution, which methinks
1030. I have in view, calling to minde with heed
      Part of our Sentence, that thy Seed shall bruise
1032. The Serpents head; piteous amends, unless
      Be meant, whom I conjecture, our grand Foe
      Satan, who in the Serpent hath contriv'd
1035. Against us this deceit: to crush his head
      Would be revenge indeed; which will be lost
1037. By death brought on our selves, or childless days
      Resolv'd, as thou proposest; so our Foe
      Shall scape his punishment ordain'd, and wee
1040. Instead shall double ours upon our heads.
1041. No more be mention'd then of violence
      Against our selves, and wilful barrenness,
      That cuts us off from hope, and savours onely
1044. Rancor and pride, impatience and despite,
      Reluctance against God and his just yoke
1046. Laid on our Necks. Remember with what mild
      And gracious temper he both heard and judg'd
1048. Without wrauth or reviling; wee expected
      Immediate dissolution, which we thought
      Was meant by Death that day, when lo, to thee
1051. Pains onely in Child-bearing were foretold,
1052. And bringing forth, soon recompenc't with joy,
1053. Fruit of thy Womb: On mee the Curse aslope
      Glanc'd on the ground, with labour I must earne
1055. My bread; what harm? Idleness had bin worse;
1056. My labour will sustain me; and least Cold
      Or Heat should injure us, his timely care
      Hath unbesaught provided, and his hands
1059. Cloath'd us unworthie, pitying while he judg'd;
1060. How much more, if we pray him, will his ear
1061. Be open, and his heart to pitie incline,
      And teach us further by what means to shun
      Th' inclement Seasons, Rain, Ice, Hail and Snow,
1064. Which now the Skie with various Face begins
      To shew us in this Mountain, while the Winds
      Blow moist and keen, shattering the graceful locks
      Of these fair spreading Trees; which bids us seek
1068. Som better shroud, som better warmth to cherish
      Our Limbs benumm'd, ere this diurnal Starr
1070. Leave cold the Night, how we his gather'd beams
      Reflected, may with matter sere foment,

1029. *We can find a better solution, and I think I know what it is.*
1030. *Do you remember that part of our sentence where he talked about your son bruising the snake's head?*
1032. *That didn't sound like much of a revenge—unless it meant Satan.*

1035. *Crushing his head would be sweet revenge.*

1037. *If we commit suicide, or never have children, we'll lose our chance to get even with that creep, and he'll escapes his punishment.*

1040. *And we'll just end up making things twice as bad for us.*
1041. *Let's drop those kinds of ideas.*

1044. *They only increase our bitterness. What good is it trying to resist God's power over us?*
1046. *Remember how gentle he was when he listened to us and passed his judgment?*
1048. *We expected him to kill us then and there.*

1051. *Instead, he told you only that you'd experience pains in child-birth.*
1052. *But then it would be replaced with great joy when the baby was born.*
1053. *For me, he said I would have to earn my living doing hard work.*

1055. *What's so bad about that? Doing nothing all day would be boring anyway.*
1056. *And so that we'd be protected from the cold, he gave us these clothes to wear.*
1059. *He was so kind to us while he judged us.*
1060. *I'm sure he'd listen to us if we prayed.*
1061. *He'll show pity on us even more now, and show us more how we can protect ourselves from the bad weather that's going to come.*
1064. *The sky is changing already, and the wind is picking up.*
1068. *We better find shelter now, to warm our hands and feet.*
1070. *Maybe there's a way to collect the sun's warmth to use at night.*

1072. Or by collision of two bodies grinde
       The Air attrite to Fire, as late the Clouds
1074. Justling or pusht with Winds rude in thir shock
       Tine the slant Lightning, whose thwart flame driv'n down
       Kindles the gummie bark of Firr or Pine,
       And sends a comfortable heat from farr,
1078. Which might supplie the Sun: such Fire to use,
1079. And what may else be remedie or cure
       To evils which our own misdeeds have wrought,
1081. Hee will instruct us praying, and of Grace
       Beseeching him, so as we need not fear
1083. To pass commodiously this life, sustain'd
       By him with many comforts, till we end
       In dust, our final rest and native home.
1086. What better can we do, then to the place
       Repairing where he judg'd us, prostrate fall
       Before him reverent, and there confess
       Humbly our faults, and pardon beg, with tears
       Watering the ground, and with our sighs the Air
1091. Frequenting, sent from hearts contrite, in sign
       Of sorrow unfeign'd, and humiliation meek.
       Undoubtedly he will relent and turn
       From his displeasure; in whose look serene,
       When angry most he seem'd and most severe,
       What else but favor, grace, and mercie shon?
1097.   So spake our Father penitent, nor Eve
       Felt less remorse: they forthwith to the place
       Repairing where he judg'd them prostrate fell
       Before him reverent, and both confess'd
       Humbly thir faults, and pardon beg'd, with tears
       Watering the ground, and with thir sighs the Air
       Frequenting, sent from hearts contrite, in sign
       Of sorrow unfeign'd, and humiliation meek.

1072.   *Or maybe he'll show us how to build a fire to keep warm.*

1074.   *I've seen how lightning strikes a tree and sets it on fire. You can feel the warmth even from a distance.*

1078.   *That could be a way to warm us when there's no sun.*
1079.   *I know he'll help us with this, and with whatever else we have to deal with, if we pray to him.*
1081.   *We'll pray for his grace to shine on us.*
1083.   *Then we won't be afraid to face this life, till we end in dust, where we came from.*

1086.   *The best thing we can do is go back where he judged us and kneel down and pray the best we know how.*

1091.   *If he was so kind to us when he was most angry, I'm sure he'll show us mercy now, if we are sincere and pray from our hearts."*

1097.   So they both went and knelt, and prayed, and cried.

Book XI

PARADISE LOST

1.   Thus they in lowliest plight repentant stood
   Praying, for from the Mercie-seat above
   Prevenient Grace descending had remov'd
   The stonie from thir hearts, & made new flesh
5. Regenerate grow instead, that sighs now breath'd
   Unutterable, which the Spirit of prayer
   Inspir'd, and wing'd for Heav'n with speedier flight
8. Then loudest Oratorie: yet thir port
   Not of mean suiters, nor important less
   Seem'd thir Petition, then when th' ancient Pair
   In Fables old, less ancient yet then these,
   Deucalion and chaste Pyrrha to restore
   The Race of Mankind drownd, before the Shrine
14. Of Themis stood devout. To Heav'n thir prayers
   Flew up, nor missd the way, by envious windes
   Blow'n vagabond or frustrate: in they passd
   Dimentionless through Heav'nly dores; then clad
   With incense, where the Golden Altar fum'd,
   By thir great Intercessor, came in sight
   Before the Fathers Throne: Them the glad Son
   Presenting, thus to intercede began.
22.   See Father, what first fruits on Earth are sprung
   From thy implanted Grace in Man, these Sighs
   And Prayers, which in this Golden Censer, mixt
   With Incense, I thy Priest before thee bring,
26. Fruits of more pleasing savour from thy seed
   Sow'n with contrition in his heart, then those
   Which his own hand manuring all the Trees
   Of Paradise could have produc't, ere fall'n
30. From innocence. Now therefore bend thine eare
   To supplication, heare his sighs though mute;
32. Unskilful with what words to pray, let mee
33. Interpret for him, mee his Advocate
   And propitiation, all his works on mee
   Good or not good ingraft, my Merit those
   Shall perfet, and for these my Death shall pay.
37. Accept me, and in mee from these receave
   The smell of peace toward Mankinde, let him live
   Before thee reconcil'd, at least his days
40. Numberd, though sad, till Death, his doom (which I
   To mitigate thus plead, not to reverse)
42. To better life shall yeeld him, where with mee

Chapter 11

IN PLAIN ENGLISH

1.   They prayed sincerely. God's grace had removed all the bad emotions from their hearts.

5. Their sad sighs told him more than any words they could have said.

8. The Greeks have a myth about Deucalion and his wife, who survived a world-wide flood, like Noah. They prayed that mankind could be restored—the same thing Adam and Eve were praying for now.

14. Their invisible prayers reached Heaven, where the Son of God covered them with incense and brought them to his father's throne.

22.   *"Father, let me show you the first results of the heavenly grace you placed on man,"* he said. *"As your priest, I bring you these sighs and prayers, mixed with incense, in this gold cup.*

26. *These are sweeter than all the delicious fruits he could have grown in Paradise before he fell.*

30. *Listen to his sighs.*

32. *He may not have the greatest skill in choosing the right words to pray with, so let me speak for him.*

33. *I'll be his advocate. I'll place my spirit in him. I'll help him perfect his good qualities, and I'll pay for his sins with my own death.*

37. *Let me bring peace to mankind for the limited time he has to live.*

40. *I only want to soften his punishment, not eliminate it. He must die, after all.*

42. *But a better life waits for him.*

43. All my redeemd may dwell in joy and bliss,
    Made one with me as I with thee am one.
45.   To whom the Father, without Cloud, serene.
    All thy request for Man, accepted Son,
47. Obtain, all thy request was my Decree:
48. But longer in that Paradise to dwell,
    The Law I gave to Nature him forbids:
50. Those pure immortal Elements that know
    No gross, no unharmoneous mixture foule,
    Eject him tainted now, and purge him off
    As a distemper, gross to aire as gross,
54. And mortal food, as may dispose him best
    For dissolution wrought by Sin, that first
    Distemperd all things, and of incorrupt
57. Corrupted. I at first with two fair gifts
    Created him endowd, with Happiness
59. And Immortalitie: that fondly lost,
    This other serv'd but to eternize woe;
61. Till I provided Death; so Death becomes
62. His final remedie, and after Life
    Tri'd in sharp tribulation, and refin'd
    By Faith and faithful works, to second Life,
    Wak't in the renovation of the just,
    Resignes him up with Heav'n and Earth renewd.
67. But let us call to Synod all the Blest
    Through Heav'ns wide bounds; from them I will not hide
    My judgments, how with Mankind I proceed,
70. As how with peccant Angels late they saw;
    And in thir state, though firm, stood more confirmd.
72.   He ended, and the Son gave signal high
    To the bright Minister that watchd, hee blew
74. His Trumpet, heard in Oreb since perhaps
    When God descended, and perhaps once more
    To sound at general Doom. Th' Angelic blast
77. Filld all the Regions: from thir blissful Bowrs
78. Of Amarantin Shade, Fountain or Spring,
    By the waters of Life, where ere they sate
80. In fellowships of joy: the Sons of Light
    Hasted, resorting to the Summons high,
    And took thir Seats; till from his Throne supream
    Th' Almighty thus pronouncd his sovran Will.
84.   O Sons, like one of us Man is become
    To know both Good and Evil, since his taste
86. Of that defended Fruit; but let him boast
    His knowledge of Good lost, and Evil got,
88. Happier, had suffic'd him to have known
    Good by it self, and Evil not at all.
90. He sorrows now, repents, and prayes contrite,
    My motions in him, longer then they move,

43. *Then everybody who is saved can live a new, happy life, joined with me, the way I am joined with you."*

45.   The Father answered, *"Of course I'll grant all your requests, Son.*

47. *We both want the same things.*

48. *But man can't stay in Paradise any longer.*

50. *That perfect place is too pure for him now. It can't accept his presence.*

54. *He'll have to go where he'll breath regular air and eat regular food—the kind that will make him mortal, and eventually die, because he sinned.*

57. *I created him with two gifts: happiness and immortality.*

59. *Now that he lost his happiness, the immortality would only make his unhappiness last forever.*

61. *Death is his only way out.*

62. *But after a long, hard life, if he remains faithful to me, he'll wake up in a second life where Heaven and Earth are new again.*

67. *Let's call all the angels together and let them know how I judged man.*

70. *They saw how I judged the bad angels, and I think it may have encouraged them to be good, though they are pretty good angels already."*

72.   When he finished speaking, the Son signaled the angel on watch to blow his trumpet.

74. It was probably the same trumpet that blew when God brought the Ten Commandments to Moses, and it might blow again at the end of the world.

77. The trumpet could be heard everywhere.

78. The angels all came out of their shelters, or from around the fountains, or wherever they were sitting enjoying each others company.

80. They hurried to God's throne and took their seats to hear him announce what he had decided.

84.   *"My sons,"* he said, *"man has tasted the forbidden fruit, and now, like us, he knows about good and evil.*

86. *Unfortunately, what he's finding out is that he lost what was good and got what is evil.*

88. *He would've been better off knowing good only and evil not at all.*

90. *Now he's sorry and begs forgiveness.*

92. His heart I know, how variable and vain
93. Self-left. Least therefore his now bolder hand
    Reach also of the Tree of Life, and eat,
    And live for ever, dream at least to live
    For ever, to remove him I decree,
97. And send him from the Garden forth to Till
    The Ground whence he was taken, fitter soile.
99.   Michael, this my behest have thou in charge,
    Take to thee from among the Cherubim
    Thy choice of flaming Warriours, least the Fiend
    Or in behalf of Man, or to invade
    Vacant possession som new trouble raise:
    Hast thee, and from the Paradise of God
    Without remorse drive out the sinful Pair,
    From hallowd ground th' unholie, and denounce
    To them and to thir Progenie from thence
108. Perpetual banishment. Yet least they faint
    At the sad Sentence rigorously urg'd,
    For I behold them softn'd and with tears
    Bewailing thir excess, all terror hide.
    If patiently thy bidding they obey,
113. Dismiss them not disconsolate; reveale
    To Adam what shall come in future dayes,
    As I shall thee enlighten, intermix
    My Cov'nant in the womans seed renewd;
117. So send them forth, though sorrowing, yet in peace:
118. And on the East side of the Garden place,
    Where entrance up from Eden easiest climbes,
120. Cherubic watch, and of a Sword the flame
    Wide waving, all approach farr off to fright,
    And guard all passage to the Tree of Life:
123. Least Paradise a receptacle prove
    To Spirits foule, and all my Trees thir prey,
    With whose stol'n Fruit Man once more to delude.
126.   He ceas'd; and th' Archangelic Power prepar'd
    For swift descent, with him the Cohort bright
128. Of watchful Cherubim; four faces each
    Had, like a double Janus, all thir shape
    Spangl'd with eyes more numerous then those
    Of Argus, and more wakeful then to drouze,
    Charm'd with Arcadian Pipe, the Pastoral Reed
    Of Hermes, or his opiate Rod. Mean while
134. To resalute the World with sacred Light
    Leucothea wak'd, and with fresh dews imbalmd
    The Earth, when Adam and first Matron Eve
    Had ended now thir Orisons, and found,
    Strength added from above, new hope to spring
    Out of despaire, joy, but with fear yet linkt;
    Which thus to Eve his welcome words renewd.

92. *But I know how undependable he can be.*

93. *So before he goes to eat from the Tree of Life, trying to live forever, we've got to get him out of there.*

97. *He's got to leave the Garden and go work in the ground he came from. That's where he belongs now.*

99.   *Michael, take some reinforcements with you, in case you run into Satan. Go and expel Adam and Eve out of Paradise, permanently.*

108. *Break it to them gently because they're going to take it hard.*

113. *Show Adam what the future will bring, including the coming of Christ. I'll explain it all to you.*

117. *Then send them off.*

118. *Post some cherubs as guards over on the east side of the garden where it's easiest to climb up and get in.*

120. *And place a burning sword waving back and forth in front of the Tree of Life, so it can be seen far off and frighten away any intruders.*

123. *Otherwise the place could become overrun with devils, stealing fruit and heading out to trick men all over again."*

126.   Michael got ready to go. He took a squadron of cherubs.

128. They each had four faces with glowing eyes all around, more than the mythological guardian Argos had, and more alert too. (Mercury played on his flute and got Argos's hundred eyes to go to sleep. Then he killed him.)

134. Meanwhile, Adam and Eve were feeling more hopeful after praying, but still a little afraid.

141.   Eve, easily may Faith admit, that all
        The good which we enjoy, from Heav'n descends;
143.   But that from us ought should ascend to Heav'n
        So prevalent as to concerne the mind
        Of God high-blest, or to incline his will,
146.   Hard to belief may seem; yet this will Prayer,
        Or one short sigh of humane breath, up-borne
148.   Ev'n to the Seat of God. For since I saught
        By Prayer th' offended Deitie to appease,
        Kneel'd and before him humbl'd all my heart,
        Methought I saw him placable and mild,
152.   Bending his eare; perswasion in me grew
        That I was heard with favour; peace returnd
        Home to my brest, and to my memorie
155.   His promise, that thy Seed shall bruise our Foe;
        Which then not minded in dismay, yet now
        Assures me that the bitterness of death
158.   Is past, and we shall live. Whence Haile to thee,
        Eve rightly call'd, Mother of all Mankind,
        Mother of all things living, since by thee
        Man is to live, and all things live for Man.
162.   To whom thus Eve with sad demeanour meek.
        Ill worthie I such title should belong
164.   To me transgressour, who for thee ordaind
        A help, became thy snare; to mee reproach
        Rather belongs, distrust and all dispraise:
167.   But infinite in pardon was my Judge,
        That I who first brought Death on all, am grac't
        The sourse of life; next favourable thou,
        Who highly thus to entitle me voutsaf'st,
        Farr other name deserving. But the Field
        To labour calls us now with sweat impos'd,
173.   Though after sleepless Night; for see the Morn,
        All unconcern'd with our unrest, begins
        Her rosie progress smiling; let us forth,
176.   I never from thy side henceforth to stray,
        Wherere our days work lies, though now enjoind
178.   Laborious, till day droop; while here we dwell,
        What can be toilsom in these pleasant Walkes?
        Here let us live, though in fall'n state, content.
181.   So spake, so wish'd much-humbl'd Eve, but Fate
182.   Subscrib'd not; Nature first gave Signs, imprest
        On Bird, Beast, Aire, Aire suddenly eclips'd
        After short blush of Morn; nigh in her sight
185.   The Bird of Jove, stoopt from his aerie tour,
        Two Birds of gayest plume before him drove:
187.   Down from a Hill the Beast that reigns in Woods,
        First hunter then, pursu'd a gentle brace,
        Goodliest of all the Forrest, Hart and Hinde;

141.   Adam said, "*Eve, we know that all the good things we got came from Heaven.*

143.   *But it's hard to believe anything we say could reach Heaven and get his attention, or change his mind.*

146.   *And yet, that's what prayer does, even if it's only a little sigh.*

148.   *Because when I kneeled and opened my heart to him, I imagined I saw him listening.*

152.   *I felt like he approved my prayers. I felt so peaceful.*

155.   *And then I remembered his promise, that your son would bruise our enemy. I was too upset to get it then.*

158.   *But now I see that means we're going to live. And it's thanks to you, Eve. You're going to be the Mother of Mankind."*

162.   Eve said, "*I'm not worthy of that title.*

164.   *I'm just a sinner. I was put here to be your help and instead I caused your downfall.*

167.   *But God is infinite in his mercy. Now I am called the Mother of Mankind. I deserve to be called something much worse.*

173.   *It's morning now, and everything looks as beautiful as if nothing bad ever happened.*

176.   *We may as well go back to work. I'll never leave your side again.*

178.   *Our work will be harder now, he told us. But how can we complain? We're sinners now, but at least we still get to live in this wonderful place."*

181.   But that was not to be the case.

182.   The bad signs began to come. First the sunny morning got darker.

185.   Adam saw an eagle going after two brightly colored birds.

187.   Then a lion chased a deer out of the woods.

190. Direct to th' Eastern Gate was bent thir flight.
Adam observ'd, and with his Eye the chase
Pursuing, not unmov'd to Eve thus spake.

193.   O Eve, some furder change awaits us nigh,
Which Heav'n by these mute signs in Nature shews

195. Forerunners of his purpose, or to warn

196. Us haply too secure of our discharge
From penaltie, because from death releast
Some days; how long, and what till then our life,
Who knows, or more then this, that we are dust,
And thither must return and be no more.

201. Why else this double object in our sight
Of flight pursu'd in th' Air and ore the ground
One way the self-same hour? why in the East

204. Darkness ere Dayes mid-course, and Morning light

205. More orient in yon Western Cloud that draws
O're the blew Firmament a radiant white,
And slow descends, with somthing heav'nly fraught.

208.   He err'd not, for by this the heav'nly Bands
Down from a Skie of Jasper lighted now
In Paradise, and on a Hill made alt,

211. A glorious Apparition, had not doubt
And carnal fear that day dimm'd Adams eye.
Not that more glorious, when the Angels met
Jacob in Mahanaim, where he saw
The field Pavilion'd with his Guardians bright;
Nor that which on the flaming Mount appeerd
In Dothan, cover'd with a Camp of Fire,
Against the Syrian King, who to surprize
One man, Assassin-like had levied Warr,

220. Warr unproclam'd. The Princely Hierarch
In thir bright stand, there left his Powers to seise
Possession of the Garden; hee alone,
To find where Adam shelterd, took his way,
Not unperceav'd of Adam, who to Eve,
While the great Visitant approachd, thus spake.

226.   Eve, now expect great tidings, which perhaps
Of us will soon determin, or impose
New Laws to be observ'd; for I descrie
From yonder blazing Cloud that veils the Hill
One of the heav'nly Host, and by his Gate
None of the meanest, some great Potentate
Or of the Thrones above, such Majestie
Invests him coming? yet not terrible,
That I should fear, nor sociably mild,
As Raphael, that I should much confide,

236. But solemn and sublime, whom not to offend,
With reverence I must meet, and thou retire.

238. He ended; and th' Arch-Angel soon drew nigh,

190. Adam watched them as they all headed for the east gate.

193.   *"Oh, this doesn't look good."* said Adam.

195. *"I think he's trying to tell us something.*
196. *We may have been too sure of ourselves about what the future has in store. He's reminding us that we're going to return to dust.*

201. *What else could it mean? Two predators chasing their prey, one in the air and one on the ground, both headed to the exact same place at the same time.*
204. *And why is it getting dark before noon?*
205. *And look over there in the west. A bright cloud is floating down. And it doesn't look like it comes from this universe."*

208.   He was right. A band of angels was landing on a high hill in Paradise.

211. Neither the angels Jacob saw, nor the ones that saved Elisha presented a more glorious spectacle. Ordinarily, Adam would've been thrilled at the a sight, but not now.

220. Michael told his angels to take control of the garden and headed down to see Adam.

226.   *"Eve, we're about to get some major news."* said Adam. *"This one is no low ranking angel. He's more serious looking than Raphael.*

236. *I better show respect and go meet him. You stay here."*

238. Michael wasn't in his heavenly shape. He was dressed as a soldier, like the heroes of olden days.

Not in his shape Celestial, but as Man
Clad to meet Man; over his lucid Armes
A militarie Vest of purple flowd
Livelier then Meliboean, or the graine
Of Sarra, worn by Kings and Hero's old
In time of Truce; Iris had dipt the wooff;

245. His starrie Helme unbuckl'd shew'd him prime
In Manhood where Youth ended; by his side

247. As in a glistering Zodiac hung the Sword,
Satans dire dread, and in his hand the Spear.

249. Adam bowd low, hee Kingly from his State
Inclin'd not, but his coming thus declar'd.

251.   Adam, Heav'ns high behest no Preface needs:

252. Sufficient that thy Prayers are heard, and Death,
Then due by sentence when thou didst transgress,
Defeated of his seisure many dayes
Giv'n thee of Grace, wherein thou may'st repent,
And one bad act with many deeds well done

257. Mayst cover: well may then thy Lord appeas'd
Redeem thee quite from Deaths rapacious claime;

259. But longer in this Paradise to dwell
Permits not; to remove thee I am come,
And send thee from the Garden forth to till
The ground whence thou wast tak'n, fitter Soile.

263.   He added not, for Adam at the newes
Heart-strook with chilling gripe of sorrow stood,
That all his senses bound; Eve, who unseen
Yet all had heard, with audible lament
Discover'd soon the place of her retire.

268.   O unexpected stroke, worse then of Death!

269. Must I thus leave thee Paradise? thus leave
Thee Native Soile, these happie Walks and Shades,
Fit haunt of Gods? where I had hope to spend,
Quiet though sad, the respit of that day
That must be mortal to us both. O flours,

274. That never will in other Climate grow,

275. My early visitation, and my last
At Eev'n, which I bred up with tender hand
From the first op'ning bud, and gave ye Names,

278. Who now shall reare ye to the Sun, or ranke
Your Tribes, and water from th' ambrosial Fount?

280. Thee lastly nuptial Bowre, by mee adornd
With what to sight or smell was sweet; from thee

282. How shall I part, and whither wander down
Into a lower World, to this obscure

284. And wilde, how shall we breath in other Aire
Less pure, accustomd to immortal Fruits?

286.   Whom thus the Angel interrupted milde.

287. Lament not Eve, but patiently resigne

245. From his unbuckled helmet you could see he looked about the age when a boy becomes a man.

247. The sword he used to wound Satan in the war was hanging by his side, and he had a spear in his hand.

249. Adam bowed when they met. The angel didn't.

251.   Michael called out as he was approaching, *"Adam, I'll get right to the point.*

252. *God heard your prayers. He postponed your death sentence and gave you a long grace period so you'll have a chance to make up for your sin with many good deeds.*

257. *Then maybe he'll forgive you and you'll escape death.*

259. *But you can't stay in Paradise any more. I have to expel you. You have to go live and work on the land you came out of. That's where you belong now."*

263.   Adam's heart sunk at the news. And Eve, who was hiding, heard everything and cried out:

268.   *"Oh, no! That's worse than death!*

269. *You're saying I have to leave Paradise?—my beautiful home where I planned to spend the rest of my life?*

274. *Leave all these beautiful flowers that could never grow anywhere else?*

275. *I took care of them from the minute they bloomed. I named them. I watered them and made sure they got enough sunlight. I visited them first thing every morning, and the last thing before I went to bed.*

278. *Who's going to take care of them now?*

280. *And my home, my shelter that I decorated with such loving care, our wedding home!*

282. *But where will we go? Just wander in the wilderness?*

284. *After you're used to the pureness of Paradise, the air everyplace else will stink by comparison."*

286.   The angel gently interrupted her:

287. *"Don't be sad, Eve. You have to face what you lost. You're not alone in this. You have your husband. You're bound to him. Wherever he goes, that will be your new home."*

What justly thou hast lost; nor set thy heart,
Thus over-fond, on that which is not thine;
Thy going is not lonely, with thee goes
Thy Husband, him to follow thou art bound;
Where he abides, think there thy native soile.

293.   Adam by this from the cold sudden damp
Recovering, and his scatterd spirits returnd,
To Michael thus his humble words addressd.

296.   Celestial, whether among the Thrones, or nam'd
Of them the Highest, for such of shape may seem

298. Prince above Princes, gently hast thou tould
Thy message, which might else in telling wound,

300. And in performing end us; what besides
Of sorrow and dejection and despair
Our frailtie can sustain, thy tidings bring,

303. Departure from this happy place, our sweet
Recess, and onely consolation left

305. Familiar to our eyes, all places else
Inhospitable appeer and desolate,
Nor knowing us nor known: and if by prayer

308. Incessant I could hope to change the will
Of him who all things can, I would not cease
To wearie him with my assiduous cries:

311. But prayer against his absolute Decree
No more availes then breath against the winde,
Blown stifling back on him that breaths it forth:
Therefore to his great bidding I submit.

315. This most afflicts me, that departing hence,
As from his face I shall be hid, deprivd

317. His blessed count'nance; here I could frequent,
With worship, place by place where he voutsaf'd
Presence Divine, and to my Sons relate;
On this Mount he appeerd, under this Tree
Stood visible, among these Pines his voice
I heard, here with him at this Fountain talk'd:
So many grateful Altars I would reare
Of grassie Terfe, and pile up every Stone
Of lustre from the brook, in memorie,
Or monument to Ages, and thereon
Offer sweet smelling Gumms and Fruits and Flours:

328. In yonder nether World where shall I seek
His bright appearances, or foot step-trace?

330. For though I fled him angrie, yet recall'd
To life prolongd and promisd Race, I now
Gladly behold though but his utmost skirts
Of glory, and farr off his steps adore.

334.   To whom thus Michael with regard benigne.
Adam, thou know'st Heav'n his, and all the Earth.

336. Not this Rock onely; his Omnipresence fills

293.   Recovering from his shock, Adam said:

296.   *"It's obvious you are one of the highest ranking angels.*

298.   *You gave us the bad news as gently as you could.*

300.   *But there's not much more we can take.*

303.   *This place was all we had left to comfort us.*

305.   *Out there, we'll feel unwelcome and lost.*

308.   *If I thought I could change God's mind, I'd never stop praying.*

311.   *But I know he's made up his mind absolutely this time.*

315.   *The worst of it is that I'll be leaving the place where he used to visit.*
317.   *Here, I could go to all the places he used to appear, and build shrines. And later, I could show them to my sons.*

328.   *Out in the wilderness there won't be any sign of him.*

330.   *I ran and hid from him when he was angry, but now I'd give anything for even the slightest glimpse of his glory."*

334.   *"Adam, you know all Heaven and Earth is his, not just this garden,"* said Michael.
336.   *"He's present in land, sea, and air, and in everything that lives.*

Land, Sea, and Aire, and every kinde that lives,
Fomented by his virtual power and warmd:

339. All th' Earth he gave thee to possess and rule,
No despicable gift; surmise not then
His presence to these narrow bounds confin'd

342. Of Paradise or Eden: this had been
Perhaps thy Capital Seate, from whence had spred
All generations, and had hither come
From all the ends of th' Earth, to celebrate
And reverence thee thir great Progenitor.

347. But this præeminence thou hast lost, brought down
To dwell on eeven ground now with thy Sons:

349. Yet doubt not but in Vallie and in Plaine
God is as here, and will be found alike
Present, and of his presence many a signe
Still following thee, still compassing thee round
With goodness and paternal Love, his Face
Express, and of his steps the track Divine.

355. Which that thou mayst beleeve, and be confirmd
Ere thou from hence depart, know I am sent
To shew thee what shall come in future dayes

358. To thee and to thy Ofspring; good with bad

359. Expect to hear, supernal Grace contending
With sinfulness of Men; thereby to learn

361. True patience, and to temper joy with fear
And pious sorrow, equally enur'd
By moderation either state to beare,
Prosperous or adverse: so shalt thou lead

365. Safest thy life, and best prepar'd endure
Thy mortal passage when it comes. Ascend

367. This Hill; let Eve (for I have drencht her eyes)

368. Here sleep below while thou to foresight wak'st,
As once thou slepst, while Shee to life was formd.

370.   To whom thus Adam gratefully repli'd.
Ascend, I follow thee, safe Guide, the path
Thou lead'st me, and to the hand of Heav'n submit,
However chast'ning, to the evil turne
My obvious breast, arming to overcom
By suffering, and earne rest from labour won,
If so I may attain. So both ascend

377. In the Visions of God: It was a Hill
Of Paradise the highest, from whose top
The Hemisphere of Earth in cleerest Ken
Stretcht out to amplest reach of prospect lay.

381. Not higher that Hill nor wider looking round,
Whereon for different cause the Tempter set
Our second Adam in the Wilderness,

384. To shew him all Earths Kingdomes and thir Glory.

385. His Eye might there command wherever stood

339. *He gave you the whole world. That's no small gift.*

342. *This might've been your capital seat, where all future generations would come to pay their respects to their great father.*

347. *You lost that. Now you're just another man, like everybody else.*

349. *But don't worry. You'll see signs of God's love still with you wherever you go.*

355. *Now I'm going to give you a look into the future, so you'll know what to expect for you and your descendants.*

358. *Some of it will be good, and some of it not so good.*

359. *It will be a constant struggle between God's good grace and man's sinful ways.*

361. *You'll learn to be patient and to be happy, but never to forget your fallen state and the dangers it brings.*

365. *That's the best way to live.*

367. *Now follow me up this hill. Let's let Eve sleep here awhile."*

368. Michael caused her to fall asleep the same way God did to Adam when Eve was created.

370.   Adam thanked him and they headed up the hill.

377. It was the highest hill in Paradise. The view was so clear you could see the whole horizon all around.

381. The hill Satan brought Jesus to when he tried to tempt him was no higher than this one.

384. Satan wanted to tempt Jesus by showing him all the richest kingdoms on Earth.

385. From where he stood Adam could see where all the great civilizations would be someday:

City of old or modern Fame, the Seat
Of mightiest Empire, from the destind Walls
388. Of Cambalu, seat of Cathaian Can
And Samarchand by Oxus, Temirs Throne,
To Paquin of Sinæan Kings, and thence
391. To Agra and Lahor of great Mogul
392. Down to the golden Chersonese, or where
393. The Persian in Ecbatan sate, or since
394. In Hispahan, or where the Russian Ksar
395. In Mosco, or the Sultan in Bizance,
Turchestan-born; nor could his eye not ken
397. Th' Empire of Negus to his utmost Port
Ercoco and the less Maritim Kings
399. Mombaza, and Quiloa, and Melind,
400. And Sofala thought Ophir, to the Realme
401. Of Congo, and Angola fardest South;
Or thence from Niger Flood to Atlas Mount
403. The Kingdoms of Almansor, Fez and Sus,
Marocco and Algiers, and Tremisen;
405. On Europe thence, and where Rome was to sway
The World: in Spirit perhaps he also saw
407. Rich Mexico the seat of Motezume,
408. And Cusco in Peru, the richer seat
Of Atabalipa, and yet unspoil'd
410. Guiana, whose great Citie Geryons Sons
Call El Dorado: but to nobler sights
412. Michael from Adams eyes the Filme remov'd
Which that false Fruit that promis'd clearer sight
Had bred; then purg'd with Euphrasie and Rue
The visual Nerve, for he had much to see;
And from the Well of Life three drops instill'd.
417. So deep the power of these Ingredients pierc'd,
Eevn to the inmost seat of mental sight,
That Adam now enforc't to close his eyes,
Sunk down and all his Spirits became intranst:
421. But him the gentle Angel by the hand
Soon rais'd, and his attention thus recall'd.
423.   Adam, now ope thine eyes, and first behold
Th' effects which thy original crime hath wrought
In some to spring from thee, who never touch'd
Th' excepted Tree, nor with the Snake conspir'd,
Nor sinn'd thy sin, yet from that sin derive
Corruption to bring forth more violent deeds.
429.   His eyes he op'nd, and beheld a field,
Part arable and tilth, whereon were Sheaves
New reapt, the other part sheep-walks and foulds;
432. Ith' midst an Altar as the Land-mark stood
Rustic, of grassie sord; thither anon
434. A sweatie Reaper from his Tillage brought

388.   - China

391.   - India
392.   - Siam (Thailand)
393.   - Persia (Iran)
394.   - Russia
395.   - Byzantium (Turkey)
397.   - Ethiopia

399.   - Kenya, Tanzania
400.   - Congo
401.   - Angola

403.   - Morocco, Algeria, Spain

405.   - Rome

407.   - Mexico
408.   - Peru

410.   - Guiana

412. Michael removed the clouded vision from Adam's eyes caused by the forbidden fruit and cleaned his eyes with herbs. Then he put in three magic drops from the Well of Life.

417. They were so powerful, Adam almost fainted.

421. Michael lifted him up.

423.   He said, "*Adam, open your eyes. Now you'll see how your sin will affect the behavior of your sons, even though they never touched the forbidden tree.*"

429.   Adam saw a field. Half of it was being farmed and the other half had sheep.

432. In between them a little table was built that served as a holy alter.

434. A sweaty farmer brought some ears of corn just as they were picked, without cleaning them.

First Fruits, the green Eare, and the yellow Sheaf,
436. Uncull'd, as came to hand; a Shepherd next
More meek came with the Firstlings of his Flock
Choicest and best; then sacrificing, laid
439. The Inwards and thir Fat, with Incense strew'd,
On the cleft Wood, and all due Rites perform'd.
441. His Offring soon propitious Fire from Heav'n
Consum'd with nimble glance, and grateful steame;
443. The others not, for his was not sincere;
444. Whereat hee inlie rag'd, and as they talk'd,
Smote him into the Midriff with a stone
That beat out life; he fell, and deadly pale
Groand out his Soul with gushing bloud effus'd.
448. Much at that sight was Adam in his heart
Dismai'd, and thus in haste to th' Angel cri'd.
450.   O Teacher, some great mischief hath befall'n
To that meek man, who well had sacrific'd;
Is Pietie thus and pure Devotion paid?
453.   T' whom Michael thus, hee also mov'd, repli'd.
These two are Brethren, Adam, and to come
Out of thy loyns; th' unjust the just hath slain,
For envie that his Brothers Offering found
From Heav'n acceptance; but the bloodie Fact
458. Will be aveng'd, and th' others Faith approv'd
Loose no reward, though here thou see him die,
Rowling in dust and gore. To which our Sire.
461.   Alas, both for the deed and for the cause!
462. But have I now seen Death? Is this the way
I must return to native dust? O sight
Of terrour, foul and ugly to behold,
Horrid to think, how horrible to feel!
466.   To whom thus Michael. Death thou hast seen
In his first shape on man; but many shapes
Of Death, and many are the wayes that lead
To his grim Cave, all dismal; yet to sense
470. More terrible at th' entrance then within.
471. Some, as thou saw'st, by violent stroke shall die,
By Fire, Flood, Famin, by Intemperance more
473. In Meats and Drinks, which on the Earth shall bring
474. Diseases dire, of which a monstrous crew
Before thee shall appear; that thou mayst know
What miserie th' inabstinence of Eve
Shall bring on men. Immediately a place
478. Before his eyes appeard, sad, noysom, dark,
A Lazar-house it seemd, wherein were laid
480. Numbers of all diseas'd, all maladies
Of gastly Spasm, or racking torture, qualmes
Of heart-sick Agonie, all feavorous kinds,
Convulsions, Epilepsies, fierce Catarrhs,

436. A gentle shepherd brought a slaughtered lamb. It was the best one he had.

439. He laid it on the alter and prayed.

441. The fire consumed it, showing that God accepted the sacrifice.

443. The farmer's offering wasn't accepted, though, because it wasn't sincere.

444. The two of them had an argument about it. Then the farmer picked up a stone and hit the shepherd in the chest with it and killed him.

448. Adam was horrified.

450.   *"What did he do to him! That man was making a holy sacrifice! How can this happen?"* he cried.

453.   Michael answered, *"They're brothers—your own future sons. The one killed the other out of jealousy, because God accepted the other's offering and not his own.*

458. *But the killer will be punished, and even though the other one is dead and covered in blood, his faith will be rewarded."*

461.   *"This is terrible,"* said Adam. *"Jealousy and violence!*

462. *Is this what death is like? Is this the way my life will end—this horrible sight?"*

466.   Michael said, *"This man was the first human being to die. But there are many other ways you can die.*

470. *They're all scary, but less scary once you're on the other side.*

471. *Some people will die violently, like you saw. And some by fire, or floods, or starvation.*

473. *But more people will die from terrible diseases caused by poor diets or drinking.*

474. *Brace yourself, because I'm going to show you some of them."*

478. Suddenly Adam was in a hospital.

480. Everywhere people were suffering from all kinds of diseases, both mental and physical.

Intestin Stone and Ulcer, Colic pangs,
Dæmoniac Phrenzie, moaping Melancholie
And Moon-struck madness, pining Atrophie
Marasmus and wide-wasting Pestilence,
Dropsies, and Asthma's, and Joint-racking Rheums.

489. Dire was the tossing, deep the groans, despair
Tended the sick busiest from Couch to Couch;
And over them triumphant Death his Dart
Shook, but delaid to strike, though oft invokt
With vows, as thir chief good, and final hope.

494. Sight so deform what heart of Rock could long
Drie-ey'd behold? Adam could not, but wept,
Though not of Woman born; compassion quell'd
His best of Man, and gave him up to tears
A space, till firmer thoughts restraind excess,
And scarce recovering words his plaint renew'd.

500.   O miserable Mankind, to what fall
Degraded, to what wretched state reserv'd!

502. Better end heer unborn. Why is life giv'n
To be thus wrested from us? rather why
Obtruded on us thus? who if we knew
What we receive, would either not accept
Life offer'd, or soon beg to lay it down,
Glad to be so dismist in peace. Can thus

508. Th' Image of God in man created once
So goodly and erect, though faultie since,
To such unsightly sufferings be debas't
Under inhuman pains? Why should not Man,
Retaining still Divine similitude
In part, from such deformities be free,
And for his Makers Image sake exempt?

515.   Thir Makers Image, answerd Michael, then
Forsook them, when themselves they villifi'd
To serve ungovern'd appetite, and took
His Image whom they serv'd, a brutish vice,
Inductive mainly to the sin of Eve.
Therefore so abject is thir punishment,
Disfiguring not Gods likeness, but thir own,
Or if his likeness, by themselves defac't
While they pervert pure Natures healthful rules
To loathsom sickness, worthily, since they
Gods Image did not reverence in themselves.

526.   I yield it just, said Adam, and submit.
But is there yet no other way, besides
These painful passages, how we may come
To Death, and mix with our connatural dust?

530.   There is, said Michael, if thou well observe
The rule of not too much, by temperance taught
In what thou eatst and drinkst, seeking from thence

489. The moaning and groaning was terrible. They were begging for death as their only relief.

494. Adam broke down and cried. When he finally pulled himself together, he said:

500.   *"I can't stand seeing these people so degraded.*

502. *Why is life given to us to be taken away so cruelly? If people knew this is what was in store for them, they'd wish they were never born.*

508. *Aren't we supposed to be made in God's image? How can they be so deformed by disease and pain?"*

515.   *"They didn't respect God's image in them,"* Michael answered. *"They chose to give in to unrestrained appetite (not so different from Eve). They disregarded nature's healthful rules, and ruined their own image, not God's."*

526.   *"Okay, but isn't there some other way to die that isn't so painful?"* Adam asked.

530.   *"Yes,"* said Michael, *"if you watch what you eat and drink, and don't overdo it.*

Due nourishment, not gluttonous delight,
534. Till many years over thy head return:
So maist thou live, till like ripe Fruit thou drop
Into thy Mothers lap, or be with ease
Gatherd, not harshly pluckt, for death mature:
538. This is old age; but then thou must outlive
Thy youth, thy strength, thy beauty, which will change
540. To witherd weak and gray; thy Senses then
Obtuse, all taste of pleasure must forgoe,
542. To what thou hast, and for the Aire of youth
Hopeful and cheerful, in thy blood will reigne
A melancholly damp of cold and dry
To weigh thy spirits down, and last consume
The Balme of Life. To whom our Ancestor.
547.   Henceforth I flie not Death, nor would prolong
Life much, bent rather how I may be quit
Fairest and easiest of this combrous charge,
Which I must keep till my appointed day
Of rendring up, and patiently attend
My dissolution. Michael repli'd,
553.   Nor love thy Life, nor hate; but what thou livst
Live well, how long or short permit to Heav'n:
555. And now prepare thee for another sight.
556.   He lookd and saw a spacious Plaine, whereon
Were Tents of various hue; by some were herds
558. Of Cattel grazing: others, whence the sound
Of Instruments that made melodious chime
Was heard, of Harp and Organ; and who moovd
Thir stops and chords was seen: his volant touch
Instinct through all proportions low and high
Fled and pursu'd transverse the resonant fugue.
564. In other part stood one who at the Forge
Labouring, two massie clods of Iron and Brass
Had melted (whether found where casual fire
Had wasted woods on Mountain or in Vale,
Down to the veins of Earth, thence gliding hot
To som Caves mouth, or whether washt by stream
From underground) the liquid Ore he dreind
Into fit moulds prepar'd; from which he formd
First his own Tooles; then, what might else be wrought
Fusil or grav'n in mettle. After these,
574. But on the hether side a different sort
From the high neighbouring Hills, which was thir Seat,
Down to the Plain descended: by thir guise
577. Just men they seemd, and all thir study bent
To worship God aright, and know his works
Not hid, nor those things last which might preserve
Freedom and Peace to men: they on the Plain
581. Long had not walkt, when from the Tents behold

534. *Then you can live a long life. Then when you get old you'll die a more peaceful death.*

538. *But before that happens you'll lose your youth and strength and beauty. You'll turn wrinkled and gray.*
540. *Your eyesight and hearing will get weak. You won't have much fun anymore.*
542. *You'll lose all your youthful enthusiasm for life and become melancholy."*

547.   "*So much for a long life,*" said Adam. "*I think from now on I'll plan on getting it over with as quick and painlessly as possible."*

553.   "*Don't hate your life—or love it too much,*" said Michael. "*Just live the best way you know how, whatever comes.*
555. *Now get ready for another vision."*
556.   Adam looked and saw a wide plain with different colored tents.
558. There were herds of cattle grazing, and some people were sitting around playing nice music.

564. In another part, a blacksmith was working, making tools and things.

574. Some men came down from the nearby hills, where they lived.

577. They seemed nice enough people.

581. When they got to the plain, a bunch of women came out of the tents wearing fancy dresses and jewelry.

        A Beavie of fair Women, richly gay

583.   In Gems and wanton dress; to the Harp they sung
        Soft amorous Ditties, and in dance came on:

585.   The Men though grave, ey'd them, and let thir eyes
        Rove without rein, till in the amorous Net

587.   Fast caught, they lik'd, and each his liking chose;
        And now of love they treat till th'Eevning Star

589.   Loves Harbinger appeerd; then all in heat
        They light the Nuptial Torch, and bid invoke
        Hymen, then first to marriage Rites invok't;
        With Feast and Musick all the Tents resound.

593.   Such happy interview and fair event
        Of love and youth not lost, Songs, Garlands, Flours,
        And charming Symphonies attach'd the heart
        Of Adam, soon enclin'd to admit delight,
        The bent of Nature; which he thus express'd.

598.   True opener of mine eyes, prime Angel blest,
        Much better seems this Vision, and more hope
        Of peaceful dayes portends, then those two past;
        Those were of hate and death, or pain much worse,
        Here Nature seems fulfilld in all her ends.

603.   To whom thus Michael. Judg not what is best
        By pleasure, though to Nature seeming meet,
        Created, as thou art, to nobler end
        Holie and pure, conformitie divine.

607.   Those Tents thou sawst so pleasant, were the Tents
        Of wickedness, wherein shall dwell his Race
        Who slew his Brother; studious they appere

610.   Of Arts that polish Life, Inventers rare,
        Unmindful of thir Maker, though his Spirit
        Taught them, but they his gifts acknowledg'd none.

613.   Yet they a beauteous ofspring shall beget;
        For that fair femal Troop thou sawst, that seemd
        Of Goddesses, so blithe, so smooth, so gay,
        Yet empty of all good wherein consists
        Womans domestic honour and chief praise;

618.   Bred onely and completed to the taste
        Of lustful appetence, to sing, to dance,
        To dress, and troule the Tongue, and roule the Eye.

621.   To these that sober Race of Men, whose lives
        Religious titl'd them the Sons of God,
        Shall yield up all thir vertue, all thir fame
        Ignobly, to the traines and to the smiles

625.   Of these fair Atheists, and now swim in joy,
        (Erelong to swim at large) and laugh; for which
        The world erelong a world of tears must weepe.

628.   To whom thus Adam of short joy bereft.
        O pittie and shame, that they who to live well
        Enterd so faire, should turn aside to tread

583. They sang and danced.

585. The men were turned on by the sight.

587. Each man chose the woman he liked and started making love to her. This went on all day.

589. That night they performed marriages and celebrated with a feast and music.

593. It was only natural that a young man like Adam would be charmed by all this.

598. *"This is more like it, Michael,"* he said. *"After all those scenes of pain and death. This is the way nature meant things to be."*

603. Michael said, *"Don't judge a book by its cover. This may all look very enjoyable to you, but you were given a brain to understand what really matters.*

607. *The people in those tents are descended from the one you saw kill his brother.*

610. *They're all artistic and skillful, but they don't even know their gifts come from God.*

613. *Their beautiful daughters put on a good show, but have no domestic skills.*

618. *All they know is how to entice men and stir up lust in them.*

621. *Those good men will give up their honor for alluring smiles.*

625. *They swim in joy now (Later they'll swim in a flood) but their laughter will lead to tears."*

628. Adam said, *"That's a shame. But there it is again—all man's trouble comes from women."*

Paths indirect, or in the mid way faint!
But still I see the tenor of Mans woe
Holds on the same, from Woman to begin.

634.   From Mans effeminate slackness it begins,
Said th' Angel, who should better hold his place
By wisdome, and superiour gifts receav'd.
But now prepare thee for another Scene.

638.   He lookd and saw wide Territorie spred
Before him, Towns, and rural works between,
Cities of Men with lofty Gates and Towrs,

641. Concours in Arms, fierce Faces threatning Warr,
Giants of mightie Bone, and bould emprise;
Part wield thir Arms, part courb the foaming Steed,
Single or in Array of Battel rang'd
Both Horse and Foot, nor idely mustring stood;

646. One way a Band select from forage drives
A herd of Beeves, faire Oxen and faire Kine
From a fat Meddow ground; or fleecy Flock,
Ewes and thir bleating Lambs over the Plaine,

650. Thir Bootie; scarce with Life the Shepherds flye,

651. But call in aide, which makes a bloody Fray;
With cruel Tournament the Squadrons joine;

653. Where Cattle pastur'd late, now scatterd lies
With Carcasses and Arms th'ensanguind Field

655. Deserted: Others to a Citie strong
Lay Seige, encampt; by Batterie, Scale, and Mine,

657. Assaulting; others from the Wall defend
With Dart and Jav'lin, Stones and sulfurous Fire;

659. On each hand slaughter and gigantic deeds.

660. In other part the scepter'd Haralds call
To Council in the Citie Gates: anon
Grey-headed men and grave, with Warriours mixt,
Assemble, and Harangues are heard, but soon
In factious opposition, till at last

665. Of middle Age one rising, eminent
In wise deport, spake much of Right and Wrong,
Of Justice, of Religion, Truth and Peace,
And Judgment from above: him old and young

669. Exploded, and had seiz'd with violent hands,
Had not a Cloud descending snatch'd him thence
Unseen amid the throng: so violence

672. Proceeded, and Oppression, and Sword-Law
Through all the Plain, and refuge none was found.

674. Adam was all in tears, and to his guide

675. Lamenting turnd full sad; O what are these,
Deaths Ministers, not Men, who thus deal Death
Inhumanly to men, and multiply

678. Ten thousandfould the sin of him who slew
His Brother; for of whom such massacher

634. Michael said, "*No, it comes from men acting like women, being weak and stupid. And now here's another scene.*"

638. Adam saw a wide view of towns and villages and tall cities.

641. Many warlike men, some on horseback, were charging into a meadow waving their weapons.

646. One band stole a herd of cattle, another a flock of sheep.

650. The shepherds barely escaped the attack with their lives.
651. But they came back and brought help with them. It turned into a bloody battle.
653. Where the cattle were grazing before, now there were dead bodies all over. The fields were all bloody.
655. In another place a city was under attack.

657. They defended themselves from inside the walls, shooting out stones and spears and fire.
659. It was very violent. There were many deaths on both sides.
660. They tried having a peace council, but there was too much hostility all around.

665. One man tried to bring the wisdom of God's word, but it just made them angrier.

669. They went to attack him, but he suddenly disappeared into a cloud.

672. So the violence continued everywhere.

674. Adam was crying.
675. He said, "*Are these men or inhuman monsters sent by Death to do his work?*

678. *This is ten thousand times worse than when the man killed his brother! Aren't we all brothers after all?*

Make they but of thir Brethren, men of men?
681. But who was that Just Man, whom had not Heav'n
Rescu'd, had in his Righteousness bin lost?
683.   To whom thus Michael. These are the product
Of those ill mated Marriages thou saw'st:
Where good with bad were matcht, who of themselves
Abhor to joyn; and by imprudence mixt,
Produce prodigious Births of bodie or mind.
Such were these Giants, men of high renown;
689. For in those dayes Might onely shall be admir'd,
And Valour and Heroic Vertu call'd;
To overcome in Battle, and subdue
692. Nations, and bring home spoils with infinite
Man-slaughter, shall be held the highest pitch
Of human Glorie, and for Glorie done
Of triumph, to be styl'd great Conquerours,
Patrons of Mankind, Gods, and Sons of Gods,
Destroyers rightlier call'd and Plagues of men.
698. Thus Fame shall be atchiev'd, renown on Earth,
And what most merits fame in silence hid.
700. But hee the seventh from thee, whom thou beheldst
701. The onely righteous in a World perverse,
702. And therefore hated, therefore so beset
With Foes for daring single to be just,
704. And utter odious Truth, that God would come
To judge them with his Saints: Him the most High
706. Rapt in a balmie Cloud with winged Steeds
Did, as thou sawst, receave, to walk with God
High in Salvation and the Climes of bliss,
Exempt from Death; to shew thee what reward
710. Awaits the good, the rest what punishment?
Which now direct thine eyes and soon behold.
712.   He look'd, and saw the face of things quite chang'd;
The brazen Throat of Warr had ceast to roar,
714. All now was turn'd to jollitie and game,
To luxurie and riot, feast and dance,
Marrying or prostituting, as befell,
Rape or Adulterie, where passing faire
Allurd them; thence from Cups to civil Broiles.
719. At length a Reverend Sire among them came,
And of thir doings great dislike declar'd,
And testifi'd against thir wayes; hee oft
Frequented thir Assemblies, whereso met,
Triumphs or Festivals, and to them preachd
Conversion and Repentance, as to Souls
In prison under Judgments imminent:
But all in vain: which when he saw, he ceas'd
727. Contending, and remov'd his Tents farr off;
728. Then from the Mountain hewing Timber tall,

681. *But who was that man who was rescued from the mob by some miracle?"*
683.   Michael said, "*These abnormally huge men come from those marriages you saw before, between the good men and the bad women.*

689. *They're all obsessed with fighting and conquering other nations.*

692. *The more killing there is and the more they steal, the more they are glorified and admired.*

698. *They're the so-called heroes of their time. Nobody cares about goodness or anything of real value any more.*
700. *The man you asked about is Enoch. He will come seven generations after you.*
701. *He was the only decent man left in the world.*
702. *So everybody hated him.*
704. *Nobody wanted to hear him talk about God coming to judge them.*
706. *You saw how God saved him from death when they attacked him. He got to go up to Heaven in a cloud with winged horses.*

710. *That's to show you how God rewards goodness. Now you'll see what happens to the bad ones."*
712.   Adam looked around and everything had changed.
714. Instead of war there were wild parties, with drinking and brawling, and a lot of loose sex, including prostitution and rape.

719. One day an evangelist came and went to all their parties and tried to preach repentance, but it was no use.

727. He gave up and moved away.
728. He began cutting down trees and building a huge covered boat with a door in the side.

Began to build a Vessel of huge bulk,
Measur'd by Cubit, length, and breadth, and highth,
Smeard round with Pitch, and in the side a dore
732. Contriv'd, and of provisions laid in large
733. For Man and Beast: when loe a wonder strange!
Of every Beast, and Bird, and Insect small
Came seavens, and pairs, and enterd in, as taught
736. Thir order; last the Sire, and his three Sons
737. With thir four Wives; and God made fast the dore.
738. Meanwhile the Southwind rose, and with black wings
Wide hovering, all the Clouds together drove
From under Heav'n; the Hills to their supplie
Vapour, and Exhalation dusk and moist,
742. Sent up amain; and now the thick'nd Skie
Like a dark Ceeling stood; down rush'd the Rain
Impetuous, and continu'd till the Earth
745. No more was seen; the floating Vessel swum
Uplifted; and secure with beaked prow
Rode tilting o're the Waves, all dwellings else
Flood overwhelmd, and them with all thir pomp
Deep under water rould; Sea cover'd Sea,
750. Sea without shoar; and in thir Palaces
Where luxurie late reign'd, Sea-monsters whelp'd
752. And stabl'd; of Mankind, so numerous late,
All left, in one small bottom swum imbark't.
754. How didst thou grieve then, Adam, to behold
The end of all thy Ofspring, end so sad,
Depopulation; thee another Floud,
Of tears and sorrow a Floud thee also drown'd,
And sunk thee as thy Sons; till gently reard
759. By th' Angel, on thy feet thou stoodst at last,
760. Though comfortless, as when a Father mourns
His Children, all in view destroyd at once;
And scarce to th' Angel utterdst thus thy plaint.
763.   O Visions ill foreseen! better had I
Liv'd ignorant of future, so had borne
My part of evil onely, each dayes lot
766. Anough to bear; those now, that were dispenst
The burd'n of many Ages, on me light
At once, by my foreknowledge gaining Birth
Abortive, to torment me ere thir being,
770. With thought that they must be. Let no man seek
Henceforth to be foretold what shall befall
Him or his Childern, evil he may be sure,
773. Which neither his foreknowing can prevent,
And hee the future evil shall no less
In apprehension then in substance feel
776. Grievous to bear: but that care now is past,
Man is not whom to warne: those few escapt

732. He filled it with food supplies.
733. Then, believe it or not, two of every kind of animal, bird, and insect in the world came marching in, in order.

736. Then he entered with his three sons and the four wives.
737. And God made the door shut tight.
738. The wind from the south was rising. Dark clouds were gathering moisture from the hills.

742. Then the rain poured down and continued until the whole Earth was underwater.

745. The boat was the only thing left floating. Everything else was covered by the flood.

750. Luxurious palaces were now full of fish.

752. The people in the boat were the only people left alive in the world.
754. Adam was grief stricken. He almost made another flood with his tears.

759. Michael lifted him to his feet but he couldn't be comforted.
760. He was like a father who just saw all his children killed before his eyes.

763.   *"These are terrible visions,"* he said. *"I would've been better off not knowing about the future. Didn't I have enough sadness to bear already?*
766. *Why do I have to be tortured by things that haven't even happened yet.*

770. *Nobody should try to see what the future holds for him or his children. You can bet it will be bad news.*

773. *You can't do anything to prevent it, and you have to experience the sorrow twice—before it happens and again when it really happens.*
776. *But who am I giving advice to? There's nobody left.*

778. Famin and anguish will at last consume
     Wandring that watrie Desert: I had hope
780. When violence was ceas't, and Warr on Earth,
     All would have then gon well, peace would have crownd
     With length of happy dayes the race of man;
     But I was farr deceav'd; for now I see
     Peace to corrupt no less then Warr to waste.
     How comes it thus? unfould, Celestial Guide,
786. And whether here the Race of man will end.
787.   To whom thus Michael. Those whom last thou sawst
     In triumph and luxurious wealth, are they
     First seen in acts of prowess eminent
     And great exploits, but of true vertu void;
     Who having spilt much blood, and don much waste
     Subduing Nations, and achievd thereby
     Fame in the World, high titles, and rich prey,
794. Shall change thir course to pleasure, ease, and sloth,
     Surfet, and lust, till wantonness and pride
     Raise out of friendship hostil deeds in Peace.
797. The conquerd also, and enslav'd by Warr
     Shall with thir freedom lost all vertu loose
     And fear of God, from whom thir pietie feign'd
     In sharp contest of Battel found no aide
     Against invaders; therefore coold in zeale
     Thenceforth shall practice how to live secure,
     Worldlie or dissolute, on what thir Lords
     Shall leave them to enjoy; for th' Earth shall bear
     More then anough, that temperance may be tri'd:
806. So all shall turn degenerate, all deprav'd,
     Justice and Temperance, Truth and Faith forgot;
     One Man except, the onely Son of light
     In a dark Age, against example good,
     Against allurement, custom, and a World
     Offended; fearless of reproach and scorn,
     Or violence, hee of wicked wayes
813. Shall them admonish, and before them set
     The paths of righteousness, how much more safe,
     And full of peace, denouncing wrauth to come
     On thir impenitence; and shall returne
     Of them derided, but of God observd
818. The one just Man alive; by his command
     Shall build a wondrous Ark, as thou beheldst,
     To save himself and houshold from amidst
     A World devote to universal rack.
822. No sooner hee with them of Man and Beast
     Select for life shall in the Ark be lodg'd,
     And shelterd round, but all the Cataracts
     Of Heav'n set open on the Earth shall powre
     Raine day and night, all fountains of the Deep

778. *Those few people that survive will probably die of starvation.*

780. *I was glad when I saw war and violence come to an end, but it seems peace corrupts people and leads to the same sad results.*

786. *Why must it come to this, Michael? Will this be the end of mankind?"*

787.   Michael answered, "*You saw how these people got fame and riches by conquering nations and spilling so much blood.*

794. *Then you saw them become corrupt and lazy.*

797. *And the ones they conquered and enslaved lost faith in God, and became lazy too, and dependant on their new masters.*

806. *So there was no justice, no faith anywhere, just a lot of selfishness and greed.*

813. *The path of righteousness was laid right before them all, but God found only one man who accepted it.*

818. *So God told him to build the boat you saw, to save him and his family, since the rest of the world had gone all to hell.*

822. *Then with him and all the animals inside, God made it rain until even the highest mountains were covered with the flood.*

Broke up, shall heave the Ocean to usurp
Beyond all bounds, till inundation rise
Above the highest Hills: then shall this Mount

830. Of Paradise by might of Waves be moovd
Out of his place, pushd by the horned floud,

832. With all his verdure spoil'd, and Trees adrift
Down the great River to the op'ning Gulf,

834. And there take root an Iland salt and bare,
The haunt of Seales and Orcs, and Sea-mews clang.

836. To teach thee that God attributes to place
No sanctitie, if none be thither brought
By Men who there frequent, or therein dwell.

839. And now what further shall ensue, behold.

840.   He lookd, and saw the Ark hull on the floud,
Which now abated, for the Clouds were fled,

842. Drivn by a keen North- winde, that blowing drie
Wrinkl'd the face of Deluge, as decai'd;
And the cleer Sun on his wide watrie Glass

845. Gaz'd hot, and of the fresh Wave largely drew,
As after thirst, which made thir flowing shrink
From standing lake to tripping ebbe, that stole
With soft foot towards the deep, who now had stopt
His Sluces, as the Heav'n his windows shut.

850. The Ark no more now flotes, but seems on ground
Fast on the top of som high mountain fixt.

852. And now the tops of Hills as Rocks appeer;

853. With clamor thence the rapid Currents drive
Towards the retreating Sea thir furious tyde.

855. Forthwith from out the Arke a Raven flies,
And after him, the surer messenger,
A Dove sent forth once and agen to spie
Green Tree or ground whereon his foot may light;

859. The second time returning, in his Bill
An Olive leafe he brings, pacific signe:

861. Anon drie ground appeers, and from his Arke
The ancient Sire descends with all his Train;
Then with uplifted hands, and eyes devout,
Grateful to Heav'n, over his head beholds

865. A dewie Cloud, and in the Cloud a Bow
Conspicuous with three listed colours gay,
Betok'ning peace from God, and Cov'nant new.

868. Whereat the heart of Adam erst so sad
Greatly rejoyc'd, and thus his joy broke forth.

870.   O thou that future things canst represent
As present, Heav'nly instructer, I revive
At this last sight, assur'd that Man shall live
With all the Creatures, and thir seed preserve.

874. Farr less I now lament for one whole World
Of wicked Sons destroyd, then I rejoyce

830. *When that happens even this hill of Paradise will be washed away.*

832. *All the trees will be torn up and everything here will be destroyed.*

834. *It will all end up as an island somewhere, all bare except for seals and seagulls.*

836. *God wants to show that if man doesn't respect the place he calls home, God won't either.*

839. *Now take a look at what happens next."*

840.   Adam saw the ark floating on the flood.

842. The rain had stopped and the sky was clearing.

845. The sun shined bright, and little by little the water began to lower.

850. Soon the boat seemed to touch bottom, probably on top of a mountain.

852. The tops of other hills and rocks began to appear.

853. Now the water was running down the sides of the hills like rapids.

855. A raven flew out of the boat. And then they sent out a dove to see if it landed anyplace.

859. It came back and they sent it out again. When it came back the second time, it had an olive leaf in its mouth (the symbol of peace).

861. Finally, there was dry land all around. The old man and his family came out. He raised his hands up and thanked God.

865. There was a rainbow in the sky. It was a sign from God—a sign of peace and of a new beginning.

868. The sight lifted Adam's spirits. He expressed his joy:

870.   *"Michael, this sight shows me that man and all the creatures will continue to live, after all.*

874. *This good person made God stop being angry and start a new generation from him. I feel more happiness over this one man than I feel sadness for all those who were lost.*

BOOK XI

For one Man found so perfet and so just,
That God voutsafes to raise another World
From him, and all his anger to forget.

879. But say, what mean those colourd streaks in Heavn,
880. Distended as the Brow of God appeas'd,
      Or serve they as a flourie verge to binde
      The fluid skirts of that same watrie Cloud,
      Least it again dissolve and showr the Earth?

884.   To whom th' Archangel. Dextrously thou aim'st;
885. So willingly doth God remit his Ire,
      Though late repenting him of Man deprav'd,
      Griev'd at his heart, when looking down he saw
      The whole Earth fill'd with violence, and all flesh
      Corrupting each thir way; yet those remoov'd,

890. Such grace shall one just Man find in his sight,
      That he relents, not to blot out mankind,
      And makes a Covenant never to destroy
      The Earth again by flood, nor let the Sea
      Surpass his bounds, nor Rain to drown the World
      With Man therein or Beast; but when he brings

896. Over the Earth a Cloud, will therein set
      His triple-colour'd Bow, whereon to look

898. And call to mind his Cov'nant: Day and Night,
      Seed time and Harvest, Heat and hoary Frost
      Shall hold thir course, till fire purge all things new,
      Both Heav'n and Earth, wherein the just shall dwell.

879. *But what are those pretty colored streaks in the sky?*
880. *They almost look like God's smooth forehead, showing that he's happy, or are they ribbons to tie up the clouds so they won't flood the Earth again?"*
884.   *"You're not so far off,"* said Michael.
885. *"God was full of anger and grief when he saw how violent and immoral men had become.*

890. *But he's so happy to find one good man that he swears never to destroy the Earth by flood again.*

896. *And from now on after it rains, he'll put up this colored bow to remind him and us of his promise.*
898. *So the world will go on, day and night, summer, winter, spring and fall, till this world ends and a new one begins for all good people."*

Book XII

PARADISE LOST

1.   As one who in his journey bates at Noone,
Though bent on speed, so heer the Archangel paus'd
Betwixt the world destroy'd and world restor'd,

4.   If Adam aught perhaps might interpose;
Then with transition sweet new Speech resumes.

6.   Thus thou hast seen one World begin and end;
And Man as from a second stock proceed.

8.   Much thou hast yet to see, but I perceave
Thy mortal sight to faile; objects divine
Must needs impaire and wearie human sense:

11.   Henceforth what is to com I will relate,
Thou therefore give due audience, and attend.

13.   This second sours of Men, while yet but few;
And while the dread of judgement past remains
Fresh in thir mindes, fearing the Deitie,
With some regard to what is just and right

17.   Shall lead thir lives and multiplie apace,
Labouring the soile, and reaping plenteous crop,
Corn wine and oyle; and from the herd or flock,
Oft sacrificing Bullock, Lamb, or Kid,
With large Wine-offerings pour'd, and sacred Feast,
Shal spend thir dayes in joy unblam'd, and dwell
Long time in peace by Families and Tribes

24.   Under paternal rule; till one shall rise
Of proud ambitious heart, who not content
With fair equalitie, fraternal state,
Will arrogate Dominion undeserv'd
Over his brethren, and quite dispossess

29.   Concord and law of Nature from the Earth,
Hunting (and Men not Beasts shall be his game)
With Warr and hostile snare such as refuse
Subjection to his Empire tyrannous:
A mightie Hunter thence he shall be styl'd
Before the Lord, as in despite of Heav'n,
Or from Heav'n claming second Sovrantie;
And from Rebellion shall derive his name,
Though of Rebellion others he accuse.

38.   Hee with a crew, whom like Ambition joyns
With him or under him to tyrannize,
Marching from Eden towards the West, shall finde
The Plain, wherein a black bituminous gurge
Boiles out from under ground, the mouth of Hell;

Chapter 12

1.   Like a traveler taking a break at noon, Michael paused in his story at the point where one world was destroyed and a new one was about to begin.

4. He thought Adam might want to say something, but he didn't. So Michael continued:

6.   *"So now you saw one world end and a new generation of men begin.*

8. *There's a lot more I wanted to show you, but I think the magic drops I put in your eyes are beginning to wear off.*

11. *So I'll just tell you the rest of the story.*

13. *This new generation, still just a small number of people, will behave themselves for a while. They'll remember only too well what God could do if they made him angry.*

17. *The population will quickly grow. They'll farm and raise live- stock, and they'll hold religious feasts and live in peaceful communes.*

24. *But there was a rebellious man, Nimrod, who wanted power over the others.*

29. *He ended the period of peace. He hunted men like they were animals. He killed anyone who refused to accept him as their ruler. He wanted to be like a god.*

38. *He got others to follow him. They went west from Eden, to a place where they could mine building materials.*

Of Brick, and of that stuff they cast to build
44. A Citie and Towre, whose top may reach to Heav'n;
And get themselves a name, least far disperst
In foraign Lands thir memorie be lost,
Regardless whether good or evil fame.
48. But God who oft descends to visit men
Unseen, and through thir habitations walks
50. To mark thir doings, them beholding soon,
Comes down to see thir Citie, ere the Tower
Obstruct Heav'n Towrs, and in derision sets
Upon thir Tongues a various Spirit to rase
Quite out thir Native Language, and instead
To sow a jangling noise of words unknown:
56. Forthwith a hideous gabble rises loud
Among the Builders; each to other calls
Not understood, till hoarse, and all in rage,
As mockt they storm; great laughter was in Heav'n
And looking down, to see the hubbub strange
And hear the din; thus was the building left
Ridiculous, and the work Confusion nam'd.
63.   Whereto thus Adam fatherly displeas'd.
O execrable Son so to aspire
Above his Brethren, to himself assuming
66. Authoritie usurpt, from God not giv'n:
He gave us onely over Beast, Fish, Fowl
Dominion absolute; that right we hold
By his donation; but Man over men
He made not Lord; such title to himself
Reserving, human left from human free.
72. But this Usurper his encroachment proud
Stayes not on Man; to God his Tower intends
74. Siege and defiance: Wretched man! what food
Will he convey up thither to sustain
Himself and his rash Armie, where thin Aire
Above the Clouds will pine his entrails gross,
And famish him of Breath, if not of Bread?
79.   To whom thus Michael. Justly thou abhorr'st
That Son, who on the quiet state of men
Such trouble brought, affecting to subdue
Rational Libertie; yet know withall,
83. Since thy original lapse, true Libertie
84. Is lost, which alwayes with right Reason dwells
Twinn'd, and from her hath no dividual being:
Reason in man obscur'd, or not obeyd,
Immediately inordinate desires
And upstart Passions catch the Government
From Reason, and to servitude reduce
90. Man till then free. Therefore since hee permits
Within himself unworthie Powers to reign

44. *They decided to build a tower tall enough to reach Heaven. They wanted to be famous world-wide. They didn't care if it was good fame or evil fame.*

48. *But sometimes God comes down and wanders around, invisible, to see what men are doing.*

50. *When he saw the tower they were trying to build, he cast a spell on them so that when they spoke to each other it seemed they were all speaking different languages and nobody could understand anybody.*

56. *There was loud babbling all over. All the builders were confused and angry and stormed off the job, leaving the building unfinished. The angels in Heaven were laughing."*

63.   "*What a stupid man,*" said Adam, "*to think he could make himself lord over his brothers.*

66. *God gave us authority over the animals only, not over people. He's the only one who can rule over us.*

72. *And to make matters worse he builds this tower to defy God.*

74. *How stupid! Where did he expect to get food to feed himself and his army up there?—that is, if he didn't run out of air to breath first,"*

79.   "*You're right about him,*" said Michael, "*but there's something else you have to understand.*

83. *Since you committed your original sin, there is really no true liberty anymore.*

84. *Liberty is linked to wisdom, so when a man is unwise or ignores what he should know, that's when unhealthy desires take over.*

90. *Then his mind becomes a slave to his desires.*

92. Over free Reason, God in Judgement just
    Subjects him from without to violent Lords;
    Who oft as undeservedly enthrall
    His outward freedom: Tyrannie must be,
96. Though to the Tyrant thereby no excuse.
97. Yet somtimes Nations will decline so low
    From vertue, which is reason, that no wrong,
    But Justice, and some fatal curse annext
    Deprives them of thir outward libertie,
101. Thir inward lost: Witness th' irreverent Son
    Of him who built the Ark, who for the shame
    Don to his Father, heard this heavie curse,
    Servant of Servants, on his vitious Race.
105. Thus will this latter, as the former World,
    Still tend from bad to worse, till God at last
    Wearied with their iniquities, withdraw
    His presence from among them, and avert
    His holy Eyes; resolving from thenceforth
    To leave them to thir own polluted wayes;
111. And one peculiar Nation to select
    From all the rest, of whom to be invok'd,
    A Nation from one faithful man to spring:
    Him on this side Euphrates yet residing,
    Bred up in Idol-worship; O that men
116. (Canst thou believe?) should be so stupid grown,
    While yet the Patriark liv'd, who scap'd the Flood,
    As to forsake the living God, and fall
    To worship thir own work in Wood and Stone
120. For Gods! yet him God the most High voutsafes
    To call by Vision from his Fathers house,
    His kindred and false Gods, into a Land
    Which he will shew him, and from him will raise
124. A mightie Nation, and upon him showre
    His benediction so, that in his Seed
    All Nations shall be blest; he straight obeys
    Not knowing to what Land, yet firm believes:
128. I see him, but thou canst not, with what Faith
129. He leaves his Gods, his Friends, and native Soile
    Ur of Chaldæa, passing now the Ford
    To Haran, after a cumbrous Train
    Of Herds and Flocks, and numerous servitude;
    Not wandring poor, but trusting all his wealth
    With God, who call'd him, in a land unknown.
135. Canaan he now attains, I see his Tents
136. Pitcht about Sechem, and the neighbouring Plaine
    Of Moreh; there by promise he receaves
    Gift to his Progenie of all that Land;
    From Hamath Northward to the Desert South
    (Things by thir names I call, though yet unnam'd)

92. *So God allows tyrants to come along and enslave his body as well.*

96. *Not that that excuses tyrants from blame.*
97. *Sometimes nations sink so low, that justice requires some deadly curse on them to set things straight.*

101. *Because of the bad behavior of Noah's son, Ham, Noah cursed his own grandson, that he should be enslaved.*

105. *So, you see, the next generation won't do any better than the last one, going from bad to worse, until God finally gets sick of their degenerate ways and totally turns his back on them.*

111. *But he would find one nation that would become his favorite. It would originate from one faithful man—a man who was brought up worshiping idols—can you believe it?*

116. *Men had actually become so stupid that, even while Noah was still alive, they turned their backs on God and build idols in wood and stone.*

120. *But God selected this one man and brought him to a new land where he would start a new nation.*

124. *He went forth with God's blessing, not knowing what was in store, but trusting in God.*

128. *I can see him now, but you can't.*
129. *He left his religion, his friends, his home, and wandered a long time, putting himself in God's hands.*

135. *Finally he arrived in Canaan. I can see where he put up his tents."*
136. Michael pointed out the boundaries of the land of Canaan that God promised to Abraham. He used their future names. The land included all of Palestine, from Syria on the north, to Arabia on the south, and from the Jordan River on the east to the Mediterranean Sea on the West.

From Hermon East to the great Western Sea,
Mount Hermon, yonder Sea, each place behold
In prospect, as I point them; on the shoare
Mount Carmel; here the double-founted stream
Jordan, true limit Eastward; but his Sons
Shall dwell to Senir, that long ridge of Hills.

147. This ponder, that all Nations of the Earth
Shall in his Seed be blessed; by that Seed
Is meant thy great deliverer, who shall bruise
The Serpents head; whereof to thee anon

151. Plainlier shall be reveald. This Patriarch blest,
Whom faithful Abraham due time shall call,

153. A Son, and of his Son a Grand-childe leaves,
Like him in faith, in wisdom, and renown;

155. The Grandchilde with twelve Sons increast, departs
From Canaan, to a land hereafter call'd
Egypt, divided by the River Nile;
See where it flows, disgorging at seaven mouthes
Into the Sea: to sojourn in that Land

160. He comes invited by a yonger Son
In time of dearth, a Son whose worthy deeds

162. Raise him to be the second in that Realme
Of Pharao: there he dies, and leaves his Race
Growing into a Nation, and now grown

165. Suspected to a sequent King, who seeks
To stop thir overgrowth, as inmate guests
Too numerous; whence of guests he makes them slaves
Inhospitably, and kills thir infant Males:

169. Till by two brethren (those two brethren call
Moses and Aaron) sent from God to claime
His people from enthralment, they return
With glory and spoile back to thir promis'd Land.

173. But first the lawless Tyrant, who denies
To know thir God, or message to regard,
Must be compelld by Signes and Judgements dire;

176. To blood unshed the Rivers must be turnd,
Frogs, Lice and Flies must all his Palace fill
With loath'd intrusion, and fill all the land;
His Cattel must of Rot and Murren die,
Botches and blaines must all his flesh imboss,
And all his people; Thunder mixt with Haile,
Haile mixt with fire must rend th' Egyptian Skie
And wheel on th' Earth, devouring where it rouls;
What it devours not, Herb, or Fruit, or Graine,
A darksom Cloud of Locusts swarming down
Must eat, and on the ground leave nothing green:
Darkness must overshadow all his bounds,
Palpable darkness, and blot out three dayes;
Last with one midnight stroke all the first-born

147. "*Think about this, Adam. All the nations on Earth will be blessed because of this man. The Great Deliverer will descend from him—that's the one who's going to bruise the serpent's head. But I'll explain that to you later.*
151. *This holy father was Abraham.*
153. *He had a son, Isaac, who had a son, Jacob, who had twelve sons.*
155. *Jacob and his sons went to what will be called Egypt, over there, where you can see the river Nile flowing into the sea from seven branches.*

160. *He was brought there by one of his youngest sons, Joseph.*

162. *Joseph had became second in rank to the Pharaoh. By the time he died, his people were becoming a new nation.*

165. *The Egyptian King didn't trust this growing population, so he made them slaves and he killed all the male infants.*

169. *Moses and Aaron rescued the Jews from slavery and brought them to their promised land.*

173. *But to accomplish that, God had to send terrible plagues on the Pharaoh and signs to convince him to let the people go.*

176. *Rivers turned to blood; there were frogs, lice, and flies; diseased cattle; fire from the sky; locusts killing crops; the sun disappeared for three days; and all the first-born children were killed.*

190. Of Egypt must lie dead. Thus with ten wounds
The River-dragon tam'd at length submits
To let his sojourners depart, and oft
193. Humbles his stubborn heart, but still as Ice
More hard'nd after thaw, till in his rage
Pursuing whom he late dismissd, the Sea
196. Swallows him with his Host, but them lets pass
As on drie land between two christal walls,
Aw'd by the rod of Moses so to stand
Divided, till his rescu'd gain thir shoar:
200. Such wondrous power God to his Saint will lend,
Though present in his Angel, who shall goe
Before them in a Cloud, and Pillar of Fire,
By day a Cloud, by night a Pillar of Fire,
To guide them in thir journey, and remove
205. Behinde them, while th' obdurat King pursues:
All night he will pursue, but his approach
Darkness defends between till morning Watch;
208. Then through the Firey Pillar and the Cloud
God looking forth will trouble all his Host
And craze thir Chariot wheels: when by command
Moses once more his potent Rod extends
211. Over the Sea; the Sea his Rod obeys;
On thir imbattelld ranks the Waves return,
And overwhelm thir Warr: the Race elect
215. Safe towards Canaan from the shoar advance
Through the wilde Desert, not the readiest way,
Least entring on the Canaanite allarmd
Warr terrifie them inexpert, and feare
Return them back to Egypt, choosing rather
Inglorious life with servitude; for life
To noble and ignoble is more sweet
Untraind in Armes, where rashness leads not on.
223. This also shall they gain by thir delay
In the wide Wilderness, there they shall found
Thir government, and thir great Senate choose
Through the twelve Tribes, to rule by Laws ordaind:
227. God from the Mount of Sinai, whose gray top
Shall tremble, he descending, will himself
In Thunder Lightning and loud Trumpets sound
Ordaine them Lawes; part such as appertaine
To civil Justice, part religious Rites
Of sacrifice, informing them, by types
And shadowes, of that destind Seed to bruise
The Serpent, by what meanes he shall achieve
235. Mankinds deliverance. But the voice of God
To mortal eare is dreadful; they beseech
That Moses might report to them his will,
And terror cease; he grants what they besaught

190. *Finally, Pharaoh gave in and let the Jews go.*

193. *But then he got angry and changed his mind again and led his army after them. But his army would drown in the sea.*

196. *God gave Moses the power to wave his staff and separate the sea so the Jews could pass on dry land between two walls of water.*

200. *God guided them with a cloud in the daytime and a column of fire at night.*

205. *Pharaoh chased them all night on the dry sea bottom, but he was slowed down by the darkness.*

208. *When morning came the cloud and the column of fire stopped the army.*

211. *Then Moses waved his staff again and the walls of water came down and drowned the army.*

215. *When the Jews got to the other side of the sea, they were afraid to continue on to Canaan through the desert, where they might have to fight the Canaanites. They were not very good at fighting.*

223. *So they settled in the desert and set up a government made up of twelve clans from the twelve brothers of Joseph.*

227. *Their religious laws and civil rights laws would follow the Ten Commandments sent down by God on Mount Sinai.*

235. *But they needed Moses to guide them about God's will.*

239. Instructed that to God is no access
Without Mediator, whose high Office now
Moses in figure beares, to introduce
One greater, of whose day he shall foretell,
And all the Prophets in thir Age the times
244. Of great Messiah shall sing. Thus Laws and Rites
Establisht, such delight hath God in Men
Obedient to his will, that he voutsafes
Among them to set up his Tabernacle,
The holy One with mortal Men to dwell:
249. By his prescript a Sanctuary is fram'd
Of Cedar, overlaid with Gold, therein
251. An Ark, and in the Ark his Testimony,
The Records of his Cov'nant, over these
253. A Mercie-seat of Gold between the wings
Of two bright Cherubim, before him burn
Seaven Lamps as in a Zodiac representing
256. The Heav'nly fires; over the Tent a Cloud
Shall rest by Day, a fiery gleame by Night,
258. Save when they journie, and at length they come,
Conducted by his Angel to the Land
Promisd to Abraham and his Seed: the rest
261. Were long to tell, how many Battels fought,
How many Kings destroyd, and Kingdoms won,
263. Or how the Sun shall in mid Heav'n stand still
A day entire, and Nights due course adjourne,
Mans voice commanding, Sun in Gibeon stand,
And thou Moon in the vale of Aialon,
267. Till Israel overcome; so call the third
From Abraham, Son of Isaac, and from him
His whole descent, who thus shall Canaan win.
270.   Here Adam interpos'd. O sent from Heav'n,
Enlightner of my darkness, gracious things
Thou hast reveald, those chiefly which concerne
Just Abraham and his Seed: now first I finde
Mine eyes true op'ning, and my heart much eas'd,
275. Erwhile perplext with thoughts what would becom
Of mee and all Mankind; but now I see
277. His day, in whom all Nations shall be blest,
Favour unmerited by me, who sought
Forbidd'n knowledge by forbidd'n means.
280. This yet I apprehend not, why to those
Among whom God will deigne to dwell on Earth
So many and so various Laws are giv'n;
283. So many Laws argue so many sins
284. Among them; how can God with such reside?
285.   To whom thus Michael. Doubt not but that sin
Will reign among them, as of thee begot;
287. And therefore was Law given them to evince

239. *Moses explained that another great leader, the Messiah, would come to take his place.*

244. *When God saw how well the people accepted his laws, he taught them to construct the Ark of the Covenant.*

249. *It was made of cedar and covered with gold.*

251. *Inside were two stone tablets with the Ten Commandments written on them.*

253. *On top was a golden seat between angel wings, representing God's throne. Seven torches represented the seven planets.*

256. *A cloud hid it in the daytime, and a fiery glow protected it at night, except when they carried it on their journey.*

258. *An angel guided them to the land promised to Abraham and his sons.*

261. *And then there's a lot more to the story: many battles, kings overthrown and kingdoms conquered.*

263. *One time Joshua made the sun and moon stand still until Israel was victorious.*

267. *Israel was the name given to Jacob, son of Isaac, grandson of Abraham, and also to the twelve clans and then to their whole kingdom."*

270.   Adam said, "*All these things you're telling me, about Abraham and his people, put me so much more at ease, Michael.*

275. *I was really worried about what would become of me and mankind.*

277. *But now I see how Abraham will gain God's blessing for his people (no thanks to me).*

280. *The only thing I don't get is why God makes so many rules.*

283. *You would think that the more rules there are, the more sinning there's going to be.*

284. *Why would God want that kind of a world?"*

285.   "*Oh, there'll be plenty of sin all right,*" said Michael,

287. "*The laws are there to show mankind how weak he is, and that sacrificing the blood of cattle and goats won't save him.*

Thir natural pravitie, by stirring up
Sin against Law to fight; that when they see
Law can discover sin, but not remove,
Save by those shadowie expiations weak,
The bloud of Bulls and Goats, they may conclude

293.   Some bloud more precious must be paid for Man,
294.   Just for unjust, that in such righteousness
To them by Faith imputed, they may finde
Justification towards God, and peace

297.   Of Conscience, which the Law by Ceremonies
Cannot appease, nor Man the moral part
Perform, and not performing cannot live.

300.   So Law appears imperfet, and but giv'n
With purpose to resign them in full time
Up to a better Cov'nant, disciplin'd
From shadowie Types to Truth, from Flesh to Spirit,
From imposition of strict Laws, to free
Acceptance of large Grace, from servil fear
To filial, works of Law to works of Faith.

307.   And therefore shall not Moses, though of God
Highly belov'd, being but the Minister
Of Law, his people into Canaan lead;
But Joshua whom the Gentiles Jesus call,
His Name and Office bearing, who shall quell
The adversarie Serpent, and bring back

313.   Through the worlds wilderness long wanderd man
Safe to eternal Paradise of rest.

315.   Meanwhile they in thir earthly Canaan plac't
316.   Long time shall dwell and prosper, but when sins
National interrupt thir public peace,

318.   Provoking God to raise them enemies:
From whom as oft he saves them penitent
By Judges first, then under Kings; of whom

321.   The second, both for pietie renownd
And puissant deeds, a promise shall receive
Irrevocable, that his Regal Throne
For ever shall endure; the like shall sing
All Prophecie, That of the Royal Stock
Of David (so I name this King) shall rise
A Son, the Womans Seed to thee foretold,
Foretold to Abraham, as in whom shall trust
All Nations, and to Kings foretold, of Kings

330.   The last, for of his Reign shall be no end.
331.   But first a long succession must ensue,
And his next Son for Wealth and Wisdom fam'd,
The clouded Ark of God till then in Tents
Wandring, shall in a glorious Temple enshrine.

335.   Such follow him, as shall be registerd
Part good, part bad, of bad the longer scrowle,

293. *It will take more precious blood than that.*
294. *The only way they're going to make it is to put their faith in God.*

297. *Performing ceremonies won't do it. And man will never become pure enough to undo all the sins on his soul.*

300. *So laws may seem too strict, but they show man that his survival can only come from God's grace.*

307. *Moses was the one chosen to present God's laws to his people, but Joshua would be the one to lead them into Canaan—just as Jesus (Who the Jews also called Joshua) would lead them into their Canaan in Heaven, by defeating their enemy, the snake.*

313. *After men wander for a long time, Jesus is the one who'll bring them safely home to Paradise.*

315. *In the meantime the Jews settled in their earthly Canaan.*

316. *They did well for a while, then sin reared its ugly head again.*

318. *Time after time, God would send enemies to punish them, they would repent, and God would save them.*

321. *King David, a powerful and good king, got a promise from God that the Savior I told you about would descend from his royal family.*

330. *The Savior will be the last king there ever will be, because he'll be king forever.*

331. *But before he comes there'll be a lot of other kings. After David there was Solomon, a wise and rich king. He'll build a temple for the ark.*

335. *After him there were a lot of kings, both good and bad—mostly bad. Some of the people worshiped idols.*

Whose foul Idolatries, and other faults

338. Heapt to the popular summe, will so incense
God, as to leave them, and expose thir Land,
Thir Citie, his Temple, and his holy Ark
With all his sacred things, a scorn and prey
To that proud Citie, whose high Walls thou saw'st
Left in confusion, Babylon thence call'd.
There in captivitie he lets them dwell

345. The space of seventie years, then brings them back,
Remembring mercie, and his Cov'nant sworn
To David, stablisht as the dayes of Heav'n.

348. Returnd from Babylon by leave of Kings
Thir Lords, whom God dispos'd, the house of God
They first re-edifie, and for a while
In mean estate live moderate, till grown

352. In wealth and multitude, factious they grow;
But first among the Priests dissension springs,
Men who attend the Altar, and should most

355. Endeavour Peace: thir strife pollution brings
Upon the Temple it self: at last they seise
The Scepter, and regard not Davids Sons,
Then loose it to a stranger, that the true

359. Anointed King Messiah might be born

360. Barr'd of his right; yet at his Birth a Starr
Unseen before in Heav'n proclaims him com,
And guides the Eastern Sages, who enquire

364. His place, to offer Incense, Myrrh, and Gold;
His place of birth a solemn Angel tells
To simple Shepherds, keeping watch by night;
They gladly thither haste, and by a Quire
Of squadrond Angels hear his Carol sung.

368. A Virgin is his Mother, but his Sire
The Power of the most High; he shall ascend

370. The Throne hereditarie, and bound his Reign
With earths wide bounds, his glory with the Heav'ns.

372.   He ceas'd, discerning Adam with such joy
Surcharg'd, as had like grief bin dew'd in tears,
Without the vent of words, which these he breathd.

375.   O Prophet of glad tidings, finisher
Of utmost hope! now clear I understand

377. What oft my steddiest thoughts have searcht in vain,
Why our great expectation should be call'd
The seed of Woman: Virgin Mother, Haile,

380. High in the love of Heav'n, yet from my Loynes
Thou shalt proceed, and from thy Womb the Son
Of God most High; So God with man unites.

383. Needs must the Serpent now his capital bruise

384. Expect with mortal paine: say where and when
Thir fight, what stroke shall bruise the Victors heel.

338. *Finally God got fed up with the lot of them and let them all be conquered by Babylon (the place where I told you about the confused languages).*

345. *They remained captive in Babylon for seventy years. Then God decided to release them.*

348. *When they got home they rebuilt their temple and lived a simple life for a while.*

352. *But when the priests began to accumulate wealth, they began fighting among themselves.*

355. *They even tried to take over the power of government, but the Romans put their own governor in place, who was the father of Herod.*

359. *The Messiah would not inherit David's royalty, after all.*

360. *But when he was born, a star appeared in the sky that nobody ever saw before. It guided three kings to him. They brought him precious gifts.*

364. *An angel told the shepherds about him. They went to see him. They heard a choir of angels singing.*

368. *His mother was a virgin. His father was the power of God.*

370. *He'll be king of the whole Earth, but his glory will fill the universe."*

372.   Even before Adam said anything, Michael could see that his sadness had turned into joy:

375.   *"At last some good news, and real hope!*

377. *Now I understand what had me so confused—why our best hope was in the woman's son—from a virgin mother.*

380. *And to think she will come from me, and the Son of God will come from her.*

383. *Now the snake will get what's coming to him.*

384. *Tell me about their fight, and how the snake is going to bruise the Savior's heel."*

386.   To whom thus Michael. Dream not of thir fight,
      As of a Duel, or the local wounds
      Of head or heel: not therefore joynes the Son
      Manhood to God-head, with more strength to foil
390.   Thy enemie; nor so is overcome
      Satan, whose fall from Heav'n, a deadlier bruise,
      Disabl'd not to give thee thy deaths wound:
      Which hee, who comes thy Saviour, shall recure,
394.   Not by destroying Satan, but his works
      In thee and in thy Seed: nor can this be,
396.   But by fulfilling that which thou didst want,
      Obedience to the Law of God, impos'd
      On penaltie of death, and suffering death,
      The penaltie to thy transgression due,
      And due to theirs which out of thine will grow:
401.   So onely can high Justice rest appaid.
402.   The Law of God exact he shall fulfill
      Both by obedience and by love, though love
404.   Alone fulfill the Law; thy punishment
405.   He shall endure by coming in the Flesh
      To a reproachful life and cursed death,
407.   Proclaiming Life to all who shall believe
      In his redemption, and that his obedience
      Imputed becomes theirs by Faith, his merits
      To save them, not thir own, though legal works.
411.   For this he shall live hated, be blasphem'd,
412.   Seis'd on by force, judg'd, and to death condemnd
413.   A shameful and accurst, naild to the Cross
      By his own Nation, slaine for bringing Life;
415.   But to the Cross he nailes thy Enemies,
416.   The Law that is against thee, and the sins
      Of all mankinde, with him there crucifi'd,
      Never to hurt them more who rightly trust
419.   In this his satisfaction; so he dies,
      But soon revives, Death over him no power
421.   Shall long usurp; ere the third dawning light
      Returne, the Starres of Morn shall see him rise
      Out of his grave, fresh as the dawning light,
424.   Thy ransom paid, which Man from death redeems,
      His death for Man, as many as offerd Life
      Neglect not, and the benefit imbrace
427.   By Faith not void of workes: this God-like act
      Annuls thy doom, the death thou shouldst have dy'd,
      In sin for ever lost from life; this act
430.   Shall bruise the head of Satan, crush his strength
431.   Defeating Sin and Death, his two maine armes,
432.   And fix farr deeper in his head thir stings
      Then temporal death shall bruise the Victors heel,
434.   Or theirs whom he redeems, a death like sleep,

386.   *"It won't be that kind of fight—not a physical duel,"* said Michael.

390. *"That's not how to handle Satan. He got a much worse bruise when he fell from Heaven, but that didn't stop him from giving you your death wound.*

394. *The fight will be won, not by destroying Satan, but by destroying his influence over you and your descendants.*

396. *And the only way that can be done is by fulfilling the penalty of death you were sentenced to—and as all men will be sentenced to.*

401. *It's the only way there can be justice.*

402. *And he will fulfill the law, by his obedience and by his love. Actually, all you need is love.*

404. *He'll take your place and suffer the punishment you should have suffered.*

405. *He'll be born human and live a hard life and die a terrible death, while he preaches hope and love to all.*

407. *He'll teach them that only he can save them, and only if they believe in him.*

411. *But some of them will hate him and curse him for that.*

412. *They'll arrest him and put him on trial and sentence him to death.*

413. *He'll be executed in a degrading way, being nailed to a cross by his own fellow Jews.*

415. *But by this sacrifice, he'll end all your troubles.*

416. *Your punishment and the sins of all mankind will be nailed to the cross with him, as long as they believe in him.*

419. *He'll die but he won't stay dead for long.*

421. *Before the third morning he'll rise from the grave, as alive and healthy as ever.*

424. *Your penalty will be paid.*

427. *His sacrifice will save you from the eternal death you were sentenced to.*

430. *This is what is meant by bruising the head of Satan.*

431. *It crushes his strength and defeats his two main assistants, Sin and Death.*

432. *This blow does him a lot more damage than the crucifixion does to bruise the Savior's heel.*

434. *As for all those who he saves, their deaths will become no more than a gentle floating away to eternal life.*

A gentle wafting to immortal Life.

436. Nor after resurrection shall he stay
Longer on Earth then certaine times to appeer
To his Disciples, Men who in his Life
Still follow'd him; to them shall leave in charge
To teach all nations what of him they learn'd
And his Salvation, them who shall beleeve
Baptizing in the profluent streame, the signe

443. Of washing them from guilt of sin to Life
Pure, and in mind prepar'd, if so befall,
For death, like that which the redeemer dy'd.

446. All Nations they shall teach; for from that day
Not onely to the Sons of Abrahams Loines
Salvation shall be Preacht, but to the Sons
Of Abrahams Faith wherever through the world;
So in his seed all Nations shall be blest.

451. Then to the Heav'n of Heav'ns he shall ascend
With victory, triumphing through the aire
Over his foes and thine; there shall surprise

454. The Serpent, Prince of aire, and drag in Chaines
Through all his Realme, and there confounded leave;

456. Then enter into glory, and resume
His Seat at Gods right hand, exalted high

458. Above all names in Heav'n; and thence shall come,
When this worlds dissolution shall be ripe,
With glory and power to judge both quick and dead
To judge th' unfaithful dead, but to reward
His faithful, and receave them into bliss,

463. Whether in Heav'n or Earth, for then the Earth
Shall all be Paradise, far happier place
Then this of Eden, and far happier daies.

466.   So spake th' Archangel Michael, then paus'd,
As at the Worlds great period; and our Sire
Replete with joy and wonder thus repli'd.

469.   O goodness infinite, goodness immense!
That all this good of evil shall produce,
And evil turn to good; more wonderful
Then that which by creation first brought forth

473. Light out of darkness! full of doubt I stand,
Whether I should repent me now of sin
By mee done and occasiond, or rejoyce
Much more, that much more good thereof shall spring,
To God more glory, more good will to Men
From God, and over wrauth grace shall abound.
But say, if our deliverer up to Heav'n

480. Must reascend, what will betide the few
His faithful, left among th' unfaithful herd,
The enemies of truth; who then shall guide
His people, who defend? will they not deale

436. *He'll stay on Earth just long enough to tell his followers to go teach everybody what they learned from him.*

443. *And he'll teach them to baptize all believers—a symbolic way of washing away their sins and preparing them for death.*

446. *And so his teaching and his blessing will spread throughout the world.*

451. *Jesus will go up to Heaven.*

454. *On his way there he'll surprise Satan, who is flying around, and chain him up and drag him down into Hell and dump him there, stunned and confused.*

456. *Then he'll go sit beside his father in Heaven.*

458. *And then when the end of the world comes, he'll come down again and judge everybody and reward all the faithful ones.*

463. *They could go to Heaven or stay on Earth, because Earth will become a Paradise again, even better than it was before."*

466.   Michael finished his story and Adam was so happy:

469.   *"Oh, this is great! To think that so much good could come out of so much evil!*

473. *I don't know anymore whether I should feel bad about my sin, or be glad that so much good will end up coming out of it.*

480. *But what about his followers? After he's gone, won't they be persecuted even worse than he was?"*

Wors with his followers then with him they dealt?

485.   Be sure they will, said th' Angel; but from Heav'n
Hee to his own a Comforter will send,
The promise of the Father, who shall dwell
His Spirit within them, and the Law of Faith
Working through love, upon thir hearts shall write,
To guide them in all truth, and also arme

491. With spiritual Armour, able to resist
Satans assaults, and quench his fierie darts,
What Man can do against them, not affraid,

494. Though to the death, against such cruelties
With inward consolations recompenc't,
And oft supported so as shall amaze
Thir proudest persecuters: for the Spirit

498. Powrd first on his Apostles, whom he sends
To evangelize the Nations, then on all
Baptiz'd, shall them with wondrous gifts endue
To speak all Tongues, and do all Miracles,
As did thir Lord before them. Thus they win

503. Great numbers of each Nation to receave
With joy the tidings brought from Heav'n: at length
Thir Ministry perform'd, and race well run,
Thir doctrine and thir story written left,

507. They die; but in thir room, as they forewarne,
Wolves shall succeed for teachers, grievous Wolves,
Who all the sacred mysteries of Heav'n
To thir own vile advantages shall turne
Of lucre and ambition, and the truth
With superstitions and traditions taint,
Left onely in those written Records pure,
Though not but by the Spirit understood.

515. Then shall they seek to avail themselves of names,
Places and titles, and with these to joine
Secular power, though feigning still to act
By spiritual, to themselves appropriating
The Spirit of God, promisd alike and giv'n
To all Beleevers; and from that pretense,

521. Spiritual Lawes by carnal power shall force
On every conscience; Laws which none shall finde
Left them inrould, or what the Spirit within
Shall on the heart engrave. What will they then
But force the Spirit of Grace it self, and binde
His consort Libertie; what, but unbuild
His living Temples, built by Faith to stand,
Thir own Faith not anothers: for on Earth
Who against Faith and Conscience can be heard
Infallible? yet many will presume:
Whence heavie persecution shall arise
On all who in the worship persevere

485.   "*They will,*" said Michael, "*but his spirit will stay with them to guide them and strengthen them.*

491. *They'll be fully protected from Satan, so they won't be afraid of anything men can do to them.*

494. *Their enemies will be amazed at how bravely they withstand cruelty and death.*

498. *His Apostles will teach others to go out and teach all over the world in all languages. They'll even perform miracles like he did.*

503. *Christianity will spread worldwide.*

507. *But later on, a lot of bad people will try to use religion for their own selfish gains.*

515. *They'll build churches and become priests, but their religions will all be phony.*

521. *But they'll force their laws on people, and use the law to persecute anybody who rejects them in favor of the real God.*

Of Spirit and Truth; the rest, farr greater part,
Well deem in outward Rites and specious formes

535. Religion satisfi'd; Truth shall retire
Bestuck with slandrous darts, and works of Faith
Rarely be found: so shall the World goe on,
To good malignant, to bad men benigne,

539. Under her own waight groaning till the day
Appeer of respiration to the just,
And vengeance to the wicked, at return
Of him so lately promiss'd to thy aid
The Womans seed, obscurely then foretold,
Now amplier known thy Saviour and thy Lord,
Last in the Clouds from Heav'n to be reveald

546. In glory of the Father, to dissolve
Satan with his perverted World, then raise

548. From the conflagrant mass, purg'd and refin'd,
New Heav'ns, new Earth, Ages of endless date
Founded in righteousness and peace and love
To bring forth fruits Joy and eternal Bliss.

552.   He ended; and thus Adam last reply'd.
How soon hath thy prediction, Seer blest,
Measur'd this transient World, the Race of time,
Till time stand fixt: beyond is all abyss,
Eternitie, whose end no eye can reach.

557. Greatly instructed I shall hence depart.
Greatly in peace of thought, and have my fill
Of knowledge, what this Vessel can containe;
Beyond which was my folly to aspire.

561. Henceforth I learne, that to obey is best,

562. And love with feare the onely God, to walk

563. As in his presence, ever to observe

564. His providence, and on him sole depend,
Merciful over all his works, with good
Still overcoming evil, and by small

567. Accomplishing great things, by things deemd weak
Subverting worldly strong, and worldly wise

569. By simply meek; that suffering for Truths sake
Is fortitude to highest victorie,

571. And to the faithful Death the Gate of Life;

572. Taught this by his example whom I now
Acknowledge my Redeemer ever blest.

574.   To whom thus also th' Angel last repli'd:
This having learnt, thou hast attained the summe
Of wisdom; hope no higher, though all the Starrs

577. Thou knewst by name, and all th' ethereal Powers,
All secrets of the deep, all Natures works,
Or works of God in Heav'n, Aire, Earth, or Sea,
And all the riches of this World enjoydst,
And all the rule, one Empire; onely add

535. *People will be afraid to speak the truth. It will seem like good people always suffer and bad people make out okay.*

539. *And so it will go until he comes down a second time—the one you now know as your Savior.*

546. *He'll destroy Satan and his world once and for all.*

548. *And he'll raise a new Earth based in goodness and full of peace and love and happiness forever."*

552. Adam said, "*In such a short time, you have told me so much about the world to come, from here to eternity.*

557. *When I leave now I'll have peace of mind, with your great teachings. You have given me everything I need to know.*

561. *I learned that you're better off obeying God.*
562. *And you should love him and fear him.*
563. *And you should act like he's always right there watching you.*
564. *And trust him to take care of everything.*

567. *And by just being nice, you can beat the big, strong ones.*

569. *And if you always tell the truth, you'll win in the end.*

571. *And that if your faithful, when you die you'll get a new life.*
572. *I learned all this from you by the example of hearing all about the one I now understand to be my Savior."*
574. Michael answered, "*Then you know everything you need to know.*
577. *If you knew the name of every star, and every angel, and all the secrets of nature and Heaven, and you were the richest man in the world, you would be no better off.*

582. Deeds to thy knowledge answerable, add Faith,
Add vertue, Patience, Temperance, add Love,
By name to come call'd Charitie, the soul
Of all the rest: then wilt thou not be loath
586. To leave this Paradise, but shalt possess
A Paradise within thee, happier farr.
588. Let us descend now therefore from this top
Of Speculation; for the hour precise
590. Exacts our parting hence; and see the Guards,
By mee encampt on yonder Hill, expect
Thir motion, at whose Front a flaming Sword,
In signal of remove, waves fiercely round;
594. We may no longer stay: go, waken Eve;
Her also I with gentle Dreams have calm'd
Portending good, and all her spirits compos'd
597. To meek submission: thou at season fit
Let her with thee partake what thou hast heard,
Chiefly what may concern her Faith to know,
The great deliverance by her Seed to come
(For by the Womans Seed) on all Mankind.
602. That ye may live, which will be many dayes,
Both in one Faith unanimous though sad,
With cause for evils past, yet much more cheer'd
With meditation on the happie end.
606.   He ended, and they both descend the Hill;
Descended, Adam to the Bowre where Eve
Lay sleeping ran before, but found her wak't;
And thus with words not sad she him receav'd.
610.   Whence thou returnst, and whither wentst, I know;
For God is also in sleep, and Dreams advise,
Which he hath sent propitious, some great good
Presaging, since with sorrow and hearts distress
614. Wearied I fell asleep: but now lead on;
In mee is no delay; with thee to goe,
Is to stay here; without thee here to stay,
Is to go hence unwilling; thou to mee
618. Art all things under Heav'n, all places thou,
619. Who for my wilful crime art banisht hence.
This further consolation yet secure
I carry hence; though all by mee is lost,
Such favour I unworthie am voutsaft,
By mee the Promis'd Seed shall all restore.
624.   So spake our Mother Eve, and Adam heard
Well pleas'd, but answer'd not; for now too nigh
Th' Archangel stood, and from the other Hill
627. To thir fixt Station, all in bright array
The Cherubim descended; on the ground
Gliding meteorous, as Ev'ning Mist
Ris'n from a River o're the marish glides,

582. *Now you just need to do good deeds, and be faithful, and patient, and not greedy, and be loving, which means be kind.*

586. *Then you won't mind leaving this Paradise because you'll have an even happier Paradise inside you.*
588. *Now it's time to go.*

590. *See the guards over there and that flaming sword. That's our signal.*

594. *Go wake up Eve. I sent her soothing dreams while we were away.*

597. *When the time is right, tell her everything, especially the part about the Savior coming from woman. She will like that.*

602. *Then you can live a long life together, both with the same faith. You'll always carry the sadness of the past with you, but now you'll be able to look forward to a happy ending."*

606. So they went down the hill and Adam went and found that Eve was already awake.

610. *"I don't know where you went,"* she said, *"but I was feeling so sad when I went to sleep and then God sent me dreams about some great good to come.*

614. *But I'm ready to go with you now. Wherever you are is where my Paradise is.*

618. *You're everything to me.*
619. *At least I can be happy about one thing. Although I caused us to lose everything, now I know through me the Savior will come and fix everything."*

624. Adam was glad to hear her say these things, but he didn't get a chance to respond because Michael was getting ready to perform his duty.
627. The cherubs floated down from the other hill like a glowing mist.

And gathers ground fast at the Labourers heel
632. Homeward returning. High in Front advanc't,
The brandisht Sword of God before them blaz'd
Fierce as a Comet; which with torrid heat,
635. And vapour as the Libyan Air adust,
Began to parch that temperate Clime; whereat
In either hand the hastning Angel caught
Our lingring Parents, and to th' Eastern Gate
Led them direct, and down the Cliff as fast
640. To the subjected Plaine; then disappeer'd.
They looking back, all th' Eastern side beheld
642. Of Paradise, so late thir happie seat,
Wav'd over by that flaming Brand, the Gate
644. With dreadful Faces throng'd and fierie Armes:
645. Som natural tears they drop'd, but wip'd them soon;
The World was all before them, where to choose
647. Thir place of rest, and Providence thir guide:
They hand in hand with wandring steps and slow,
Through Eden took thir solitarie way.

CHAPTER 12

632. In front of them they brought the burning sword. It heated the air all around.

635. Michael took Adam and Eve by their hands and brought them out through the east gate and quickly down the cliff. Then he disappeared.

640. Looking back, they could see the whole eastern side of Paradise.

642. They saw the cherubs' scary faces at the gate, and the big burning sword waving back and forth.
644. They cried a little.
645. They had the whole world in front of them, and guidance from above.
647. Holding hands, they slowly wandered down into Eden.

CPSIA information can be obtained at www.ICGtesting.com
Printed in the USA
LVOW10s0402230114

370558LV00009B/123/P